Len Small:

Governors And Gangsters

Governor Len Small in the 1920s, When Al Capone Owned the Top Officials in Illinois

And A Look At The Other Crooked Illinois Governor From Kankakee, George H. Ryan

Jim Ridings

Side Show Books, PO Box 464, Herscher, IL 60941

LEN SMALL: GOVERNORS AND GANGSTERS

First edition June 2009.

ISBN 978-0-9824080-0-1

Printed in China

Published by Side Show Books
PO Box 464
Herscher, IL 60941
USA

Chapters

Other Books By Jim Ridings

Jim Ridings has written and published 17 books on local Illinois history. A few of these include:

County West: A Sesquicentennial History of Western Kankakee County (2003)

County West Companion: A Further History of Western Kankakee County (2005)

Cardiff: Ghost Town On The Prairie (2006)

Cardiff 2: A Further History of The Ghost Town on the Prairie (2008)

Greetings From Kankakee (2005), *Kankakee Makes Good* (2007)
Vol. 1 & 2 of Picture Postcard Views Of Old Kankakee

Len Small: Governors And Gangsters (2009)

Wild Kankakee (coming in 2010)

County West won a book award from the Illinois State Historical Society in 2004. ***Cardiff: Ghost Town On the Prairie*** won a Studs Terkel Humanities Service Award from the Illinois Humanities Council in 2006, and a book award from the Illinois State Historical Society in 2007. **Cardiff 2** won a book award from the Illinois State Historical Society in 2009.

About the author: Jim Ridings was educated at Providence High School in New Lenox and Joliet Junior College before earning a Bachelor of Science degree in Journalism from Southern Illinois University at Carbondale in 1976. He was a reporter for *The Daily Times* in Ottawa and *The Beacon-News* in Aurora, and at both newspapers won awards for investigative reporting, from AP, UPI, Copley Press and other organizations. Jim and Janet Ridings live in Herscher, Illinois (Kankakee County) and have two beautiful daughters, Stephanie and Laura.

Cover photo, Kankakee County Courthouse in 2003, by Jim Ridings

Introduction

State Treasurer Len Small in 1906

Len Small's career may be one the most unrepresented and least documented of any American public figure in modern history -- and yet, one of the most interesting and one of the most outrageous.

He was governor of Illinois during most of the 1920s. Almost all of Al Capone's career in Chicago happened at the same time, and there definitely was a tie between the governor and the gangster. But Small's corruption started long before that.

Len Small's first important office was on the board of the state asylum in Kankakee. He built a political power base using the patronage and he made a fortune from the lucrative building and coal contracts. He shook down state employees, forcing them to contribute part of their paychecks to his political slush fund.

When his brother ran for local judge in 1905, Len promised the Illinois Central Railroad that he would have Judge Small "fix" their cases if they helped him get elected.

As early as 1907, Small was accused of using his influence to "pack" grand juries with his own choices so they would not investigate his actions.

Len Small was elected to a two-year term as state treasurer in 1904, where he kept $200,000 in interest earned on state funds. The state legislature passed tighter laws to prevent this from happening again.

In his second term as state treasurer from 1917 to 1919, Small embezzled more than a million dollars in a money-laundering scheme. He deposited half the state's funds in a phony bank, loaned it at 8 per cent and paid the state 2 per cent.

After Small's term ended in January 1919, he continued on the state payroll as examiner of securities so that he could continue having state money deposited in a bank that did not exist!

Small paid the state only $306,424 in interest during his term. When he decided to run for governor in 1920, he suddenly remembered he owed another $143,585 in interest he had been holding for a year and a half after leaving office.

Small held onto $10 million in state funds for two years after leaving office, continuing the money laundering scheme with his successor. All that time, he used the money to earn more interest for himself. He finally gave it up when a new treasurer took office in 1921 -- and even then Small tried to short the man by $100,000.

After becoming governor in 1921, Small was indicted for the embezzlement. He had his lawyers argue in court that as governor, he was above the law, citing the "divine right of kings." Their argument was, "The King can do no wrong."

Small ran from the sheriff to avoid arrest. As commander of the state's National Guard, he threatened to call out the militia to keep the sheriff away "at the point of a bayonet." He also threatened to put Springfield under martial law and to use his "commander" authority to have his local political rivals put before a military court-martial. It sounds like a bluff or a joke, but Governor Small was serious.

At his trial, Small's henchmen did all they could to find and select jurors favorable to the governor. To seal the deal, jurors were bribed and intimidated by Al Capone's gangsters. Small was acquitted. Most of the jurors soon got state jobs.

Small's people first tried to bribe a grand juror not to indict, and then successfully bribed the trial jurors to acquit.

Another grand jury looked into "jury tampering" charges. Two gangsters who had bribed the jurors were granted immunity but still refused to testify. They were jailed for contempt of court -- and Governor Small quickly pardoned them.

And even though a jury acquitted him in his criminal trial, a civil lawsuit brought by the state resulted in the Illinois Supreme Court forcing Governor Small to repay the state $650,000 of the money he stole.

Len Small did more than just help enable the Chicago Mob. He was an active participant in Organized Crime during the Capone era. Governor Small was a political partner of Chicago Mayor William Hale "Big Bill" Thompson, one of the most crooked politicians in the history of a city bulging with crooked politicians.

Mayor Thompson's policy of giving Capone and other mobsters a free hand was no secret. And there is no question that Al Capone ruled Chicago in the 1920s. Al Capone's famous quote, "I own the police," didn't go far enough. Capone also owned judges, the mayor, the governor and a lot of others.

Len Small sold thousands of pardons and paroles as governor, including pardons to gangsters, murderers, white slavers and even cop killers. Some were sold by Len Small and his emissaries to Al Capone and to other mobsters.

Small's administration operated a "pardon mill" where thousands of convicts could buy their way out of prison. Officials even solicited the convicts. Chapter 16 details a few of the more outrageous pardons.

What effects did some of these pardons have? Small's pardon of Spike O'Donnell put this mobster back in charge of his gang, and a violent and bloody beer war with Al Capone's gang was the result. Small's freeing of Bugs Moran put this killer back in action, and the St. Valentine's Day Massacre eventually followed. Psychopath Fur Sammons, back on the streets thanks to Small, enjoyed his new career as a machine gunner for the Capone Mob. Harry Guzik was able to continue his career in the prostitution and white slavery business after bribing the governor. With thousands of pardons and paroles traded for bribes, the list of murder and mayhem goes on and on. While the result may not always be direct, and the extent of culpability may be arguable, it does make one think.

When Small became governor, he wrecked the civil service system and brought back the spoils system, giving jobs based on politics rather than merit. He changed the utilities commission for the same political reasons. He tried to change the tax commission so that he could trades bribes for lower tax assessments.

Small surrounded himself with fellow crooks such as Frank L. Smith. Small appointed Smith head of the commerce commission, where Smith shook down the heads of the companies he was regulating. Smith used the money to run for the senate. The U.S. Senate refused to seat Smith because of this. Then, Governor Small tried to fill the vacant senate seat by appointing...Frank L. Smith!

There were several attempts to impeach Governor Small and he thwarted each attempt by questionable means. In one instance, he successfully had his Republican majority ram through a bill that exempted the present governor from the constitutional *quo warranto* provision for removal from office.

If that wasn't enough, Len Small was a favorite of the Ku Klux Klan, which endorsed his campaigns in 1924, 1928 and 1932.

Governor Small failed to send National Guard troops to prevent the Herrin Massacre in 1922 because he was too busy bribing his jury. When he left office in 1929, he stole the silverware and other valuables in the executive mansion.

Small's newspaper frequently indulged in the yellow journalism of the era, often disgracefully so, both in attacks against political opponents and in racial slurs.

And there is an interesting question: Was Len Small ever really legitimately elected governor? That question is explored in chapter 27.

Len Small's political philosophy consisted of a few basic tactics. First, he tried to ruin those who opposed him -- not just defeat them but ruin them. Second, he employed bribery whenever persuasion failed. Third, he lied and lied, about his enemies and about his own accomplishments, all the while claiming that everyone else was lying about him.

Len Small was one of the most corrupt public officials in American history. Yet there has been no biography of him, until now. Such a biography logically should have come out of his home town of Kankakee long ago but none has. Why not? Maybe because it is a story the local powers do not want to be told. Maybe it is because there is not enough positive information about the governor to fill a book, and no book could be written without telling the whole story, including the bad information -- and that would never come out of Kankakee, where the Small family owns the newspaper, the radio station and influences the local museum.

Any mention of Len Small in Kankakee today is brief and superficial. The local history books in Kankakee treat him like a hero, primarily citing his road building program. If you visit the Kankakee museum, you will see a shrine to a great man. You will see nothing of the nefarious deeds of Len Small that are mentioned in books about Al Capone and the other gangsters of the Roaring Twenties.

The research for this book settles some debate and corrects some myths which have been accepted since the 1920s. For example, it has been accepted that the attorney general obtained an indictment against Small as revenge because the governor cut his budget. This is false. In fact, the opposite is true. Small cut the attorney general's budget to cut off funds for an investigation that was under way. The questions and myths surrounding the phony "Grant Park Bank" and the "Good Roads Governor" are addressed. There is a lot of new material on Len Small previously not revealed, and it will be a surprise, especially to the people of Kankakee.

"Small has ruled Kankakee for many years and has been a dominant figure among the politicians who have corrupted Illinois until it has become the one state in the union which stands today boss-ridden and misrepresented by its government -- it has become a state for which its citizens blush in shame when its dark political deeds are recited," the *Kankakee Daily News* wrote. "If Small was the right man to lead the Republicans of Illinois, he would find united support at home instead of almost united opposition. Where he is best known, he finds his fewest friends."

This book is more than an isolated story about one corrupt governor. The corrupt history of Illinois politics continues to unfold up to this date and beyond.

While the career of Len Small is the primary focus of this book, I felt it necessary to add something about George Ryan, another crooked governor from Kankakee.

George Ryan's corruption was massive. Much of what has been written has hailed him as a hero for commuting the sentences of condemned prisoners. Chapter 28 gives the rest of the story, the facts of what these people did to earn a berth on Death Row.

Political corruption didn't start with Len Small and it didn't end with George Ryan or with Rod Blagojevich.

Illinois really is a great state but it is one of the most politically corrupt in the nation. Its great tragedy has been the kind of people who have grabbed power for their own benefit. I'm not sure what that says about us, the people who keep electing them.

Not all the gangsters of the 1920s were in Mob hideouts in Chicago. They also were in City Hall in Chicago and in the governor's mansion and in the Capitol building in Springfield. And you can still find them there today.

Dr. Abram Lennington Small

Chapter 1

Len Small's Early Years

Lennington Small was born June 16, 1862 on the family farm in Kankakee County, Illinois. Even though these were the early years of Kankakee County, his father, Dr. Abram Lennington Small, already was well known in the area.

Abram Lennington Small was born in Indiana on Sept. 5, 1830, to John and Mary (Lennington) Small. A generation earlier, Nathan Small had settled in Virginia. As a Quaker, Nathan was opposed to slavery, so he felt compelled to leave the slave state and move West. He settled on a farm in Wayne County, Indiana, where Nathan and his wife raised a family of four daughters and seven sons, including Abram's father, John.

Abram studied medicine at LaPorte Medical College in Indiana and practiced in Wilmington, Illinois, and in nearby Rockville Township in Kankakee County. He moved to Kankakee in 1855 when it was little more than a station on the Illinois Central Railroad line, buying land on the south side of the Kankakee River.

Abram graduated from Rush Medical College in Chicago and practiced medicine in Kankakee but his main love and skill was in horticulture. He started a nursery business and specialized in developing vegetables, particularly asparagus and rhubarb, as well as trees and shrubs. In later years, with his son and grandson, he advertised his business as "Small, Small & Small: The Largest Growers of the Largest Pie Plants in the World."

Abram Small married Calista Currier in 1853. They had six children: sons John and Len, Mary Small, Susanne Small, Calista Humrichouse and Mabel McKinstry.

Dr. Abram L. Small died in 1914. His wife Calista died in 1908.

Abram's oldest son, John Small (1858-1935), was admitted to the bar in 1883. He married Claribel Nichols in 1894. They had two children, both of whom died in infancy.

John Small practiced law in Kankakee, served as a county judge from 1894 to 1897 and then as a circuit court judge for six years before going back to practicing law. His own unfortunate experience in local politics is told in chapter 4.

Len Small was educated in local schools and at Valparaiso, Indiana. He worked in his father's nursery and gardening business. When he was 15, he got a couple of cows, milked them and peddled the milk from a wagon. He worked on a railroad grading crew during the summer to earn money for college. Len taught in a country school in Limestone Township for two years and then went into the family nursery business.

In 1883, when he was 21, Len Small was elected secretary of the State Horticultural Society and then was elected to the State Board of Agriculture. In 1890, he took the Kankakee Fair and made it prosperous for the next 40 years.

As a businessman, Small operated a 700-acre farm in Kankakee County. He was part of a group that organized the Illinois Orchard Co., with 1,000 acres downstate. His real estate group had some of its 300 acres developed into factory sites and it constructed several buildings in Kankakee.

Len Small was president of First National Bank of Kankakee, which became First Trust & Savings Bank after merging with Eastern Illinois Savings & Trust in May 1916.

Len Small bought one of the Kankakee newspapers in 1903. It has grown into a large newspaper chain today. He was a part owner of the Kankakee & Southwestern Electric Railroad, and the Kankakee Switch Line Railroad.

As a politician, Small got involved with the local Republican party and was elected Kankakee County clerk and recorder in 1896. The following year, he was appointed by Governor John Tanner to the board of trustees of the Eastern Illinois Hospital for the Insane in Kankakee, where he was named president of the board.

In 1900, Small was elected state senator for the 16th District. He served as hospital trustee and state senator until the end of 1904, when he was elected state treasurer.

Small made a strenuous run for the Republican nomination for governor in 1912. He lost. Small was elected to another term as state treasurer in 1916. He finally reached his goal of being elected governor of Illinois in 1920 and he was re-elected in 1924.

Len Small married Ida Moore on Nov. 21, 1883, and they had three children: Budd Small (1884-1940), Leslie Small (1887-1957) and Ida May Inglesh (1891-1946).

Budd worked in the family's agricultural businesses and was a director of the family's bank. Ida May's husband, Col. Arthur E. Inglesh (1888-1965), had several state jobs when Len Small was governor and was in the Illinois National Guard.

Leslie Small married Grace Burrell (1890-1981) in 1912. Her father once owned a foundry, Burrell Mfg. Co., in Bradley. Leslie worked as a teller in his father's bank until 1913 when he was named editor of his father's newspaper. He later became publisher and kept the job until he died. Leslie had important state jobs when his father was governor.

Leslie and Grace had two sons, Len Howard Small (1914-1980) and Burrell Leslie Small (1918-1981). Burrell Small joined the paper in 1940, became editor in 1942 and then publisher upon his father's death in 1957. Burrell married Reva Gray in 1938 and they had three children: Susanne Bergeron, Leslie H. Small and Stephen Burrell Small (Stephen figured in another sensational incident, see chapter 28). Reva Small (1919-2008) was a longtime benefactor of the Kankakee County Historical Society & Museum in Governor Small Memorial Park.

Len H. Small joined the newspaper as associate editor in 1955 after a 15-year career as a lawyer. He was killed in an automobile accident near Kankakee in 1980. His widow, Jean Alice Small, took over as publisher, holding the job until her death in 2002.

The name of the newspaper was changed to the *Kankakee Republican-News* in 1931 after it acquired the *Kankakee Daily News.* It became *The Kankakee Daily Journal* in 1945 and *The Daily Journal* in 1976.

Len and Burrell divided the company in 1969, with Len taking the newspapers and Burrell taking the broadcast operations. Radio station WKAN started in 1947 and about a dozen more broadcast properties were acquired over the years. The Kankakee Cable Co. started in 1965. The family sold most of its broadcast properties for $64 million in 1986.

Small Newspaper Group purchased *The Daily Times* in Ottawa in 1955, the *LaPorte* (Indiana) *Herald-Argus* in 1964, *The Daily Dispatch* in Moline in 1969, *The Rochester Post-Bulletin* (Minnesota) in 1977, *The Times-Press* in Streator in 1980, *The Palisadian Post* and *The Press-Tribune* (both in California) in 1981 and *The Argus* in Rock Island in 1986. The company's revenue was about $40 million in 1986. The sons of Len H. and Jean Alice Small -- Len Robert (Rob) Small and Thomas P. Small -- started to work for the company in 1971 at the Moline newspaper. Rob Small was named CEO of the company in 1983. Today (2009), Len R. Small is president of the company and editor and publisher, and Thomas P. Small is executive vice president and secretary.

The Small family has built its corporation into a sizable and a respectable newspaper chain. While not expressing embarrassment about their famous ancestor, the corporate website barely mentions Governor Small.

The Kankakee InterState Fair

One of the sources of Len Small's early power, and perhaps his greatest achievement in life, was his running of the annual Kankakee InterState Fair. It was a huge event in its day that rivaled the Illinois State Fair at Springfield. The Kankakee fair not only made a lot of money and gave Small prestige and influence, it also provided a platform for his political ambitions and those of his friends.

Kankakee County always has been an agricultural area. The first agricultural fair was held in 1856 in a grove south of town. A 15-acre parcel at the north end of town that had been used by Union troops as a camp ground during the Civil War became the site of the new fair after the war.

The fair remained a small event, primarily a "farmers' picnic" until 1890. That's when the farmers who preferred a more agricultural event split with the men who put on the horse racing. A larger effort was made at a different location for the races, but racing alone wasn't enough. A new group of men took control of the fair in 1890, with Len Small as the leader. Premiums for contestants were increased, better exhibits were arranged, and bigger and better acts were brought. From that point, the fair was a big success.

The fair had exhibits, amusements, good food, a fine grandstand and track for horse races, and a lot more.

A fire destroyed the huge grandstand in 1921 but it was rebuilt the following year.

Small was secretary of the Kankakee InterState Fair for decades. He said he had been an exhibitor at the Kankakee Fair since he was seven years old.

The financial problems of the Great Depression, and competition from the Chicago World's Fair, were factors in killing the Kankakee fair in 1933.

Len Small was named president of the Illinois State Fair in 1919 for a one-year term. In May 1920, he was elected president of the Kankakee County Soil & Crop Improvement Association.

Beside the local fair, one of the things Small was best known for in Kankakee County was rhubarb. Abram Small experimented with developing a superior strain of the plant. Len Small took it further, developing a commercial crop of superior quality. Len also developed a unique and complicated method of growing the plants indoors during the winter months.

Even today, the Kankakee Museum at Governor Small Memorial Park holds an annual rhubarb and strawberry festival.

"Up and down commissioner's row on South Water Street, Chicago, Len Small is better known as a grower of high class rhubarb than as the governor of the state," according to an Associated Press story in July 1923, the same week a jury was hearing testimony about Small's jury tampering.

The story crowned Len Small as the rhubarb king of the country.

These were genuine accomplishments. It can be argued that Len Small would have been a lot better off if he had stuck to agriculture instead of politics.

Horse racing at the Kankakee InterState Fair, early 1900s.

Chapter 2

Big Bill Thompson, William Lorimer and Fred Lundin

Big Bill Thompson

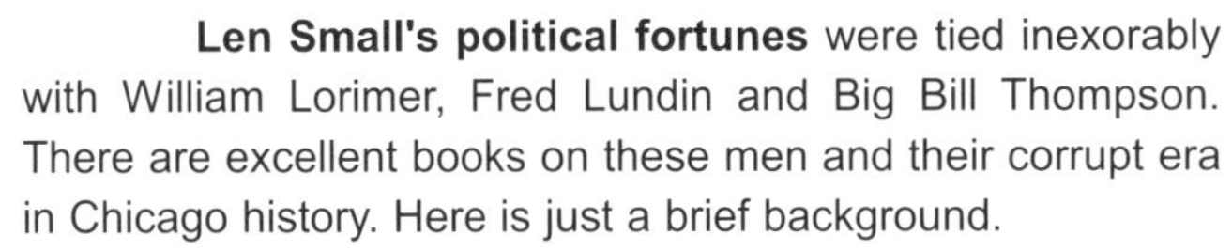

William Lorimer

Fred Lundin

Len Small's political fortunes were tied inexorably with William Lorimer, Fred Lundin and Big Bill Thompson. There are excellent books on these men and their corrupt era in Chicago history. Here is just a brief background.

William Hale Thompson, mayor of Chicago from 1915 to 1923 and from 1927 to 1931, was perhaps the most corrupt politician in Chicago history and that's saying a lot. Thompson's administration was marked with theft, corruption and wide open gangland violence. Gangsters ruled Chicago during Thompson's era. He was re-elected mayor with the support of Al Capone.

"Capone gangsters roamed the corridors of the City Hall, collaring aldermen with requests for favors and threatening those who refused to vote their way," wrote Lloyd Wendt and Herman Kogan in their 1953 book, *Big Bill of Chicago.*

On the office wall of the mayor of Chicago, Thompson had two portraits: Abraham Lincoln and Al Capone. And in his luxurious suite in the Lexington Hotel, Capone had three large portraits on his office wall: George Washington, Abraham Lincoln and Big Bill Thompson.

Thompson and his cohorts cheated Chicago out of $2.2 million in 1920 and 1921 in fake "expert fees" in a city real estate project. In 1928, they were convicted and ordered to pay $1.7 million, a decision their lawyers managed to get reversed on appeal.

Thompson and Lundin were involved in another big scandal where they were accused of stealing a million dollars in fake contracts for material for the Chicago schools. Lundin and 15 others went on trial in 1923 and beat the rap, largely due to false testimony from Big Bill.

When Thompson raised $140,000 for victims of the 1927 Mississippi flood, he was sued when he turned over just $18,000 to the American Red Cross.

As mayor, Thompson charged city drivers and inspectors $3 per month to raise money for a possible presidential campaign.

Thompson sued the *Chicago Tribune,* unsuccessfully, for $10 million in 1921, claiming that its stories about his mismanagement hurt the city's bond rating.

The scandals caused Thompson to decline to run for a third term in 1923. The people elected Judge William E. Dever, a reformer who was untouched by any hint of scandal. Dever did cause Johnny Torrio, Al Capone and other mobsters some trouble during his term, but Capone's empire was too vast to be handicapped.

Thompson again won the mayoral election in 1927, with a lot of cash and campaign help from Al Capone and other gangsters. A Thompson campaign promise was to re-open the thousand speakeasies closed by Mayor Dever's police raids "and open ten thousand more." Thompson made it clear he intended to continue the policy of his previous term -- a wide open town for bootleggers and gangsters.

The Chicago Crime Commission estimated that Capone donated more than a quarter million dollars to Thompson's 1927 campaign.

Mayor Thompson appointed a succession of crooked chiefs of police. Chief John Garrity was involved with pimps and bootleggers and was caught in a cover-up. Chief Charles Fitzmorris admitted that half his police force was involved in bootlegging, not just taking payoff but actually pushing it. Chief Mike Hughes went easy on gangsters and even attended the memorial service for slain Mob boss Dean O'Banion. Police Chief William Russell defended his position of not cracking down on gangsters: "Mayor Thompson was elected on an open-town platform. I assume the people knew what they wanted when they voted for him. I haven't any orders from downtown to interfere with the policy racket."

After winning re-election, Thompson promised to target reformers, who he said were the real criminals.

There was a lot of clown in Thompson. He was mayor during World War I, yet was pro-German and strongly anti-British. "Big Bill" became known as "Kaiser Bill." Thompson's rants went beyond being jingoistic. They were so extreme that many people considered him a traitor in wartime. It was a record that would follow him the rest of his career.

Thompson said America's biggest enemy was King George V. He promised to "punch the king of England in the snoot" if he ever showed up in Chicago.

Thompson was so anti-British that he ordered the Chicago Public Schools and the Chicago Public Library to rip out books that contained pro-British information, and he threatened to have a book-burning on the lakefront.

In Chicago, the gangsters were free from harassment from the city -- but the public libraries were not.

"While rival gangs in Chicago have signed an armistice and beer trucks pass unnoticed through the streets, Mayor Thompson rages against the British lion and orders the Mississippi to return to its natural bed," Dr. G. Sherwood Eddy, a YMCA worker told a Springfield luncheon assembly on March 13, 1928. "I have traveled in 30 countries and I do not know of a country or a state that can boast of such a combination as Governor Small, Col. Frank L. Smith, Mayor Thompson and Profiteer Insull."

During the 1927 election, Thompson held a debate between himself and two live rats, which he used to represent political enemies (Fred Lundin and John Dill Robertson at that time). In 1924, to keep public attention while out of office, Thompson got on a boat that he planned to sail down the Illinois & Michigan Canal, to the Illinois River, to the Mississippi River, to the Gulf of Mexico and on to the South Pacific on a "scientific" expedition to search for tree-climbing fish that lived on land. His boat didn't get past the I&M Canal.

Thompson harbored presidential ambitions almost from the day he took office as mayor. Every once in a while he would test the waters. When President Calvin Coolidge decided he would not seek re-election in 1928, Thompson started his own campaign. Len Small was there to support his bid. In a campaign stop in Louisiana, Governor Huey Long presented Thompson with a scroll designating him as "one of the greatest living Americans."

Thompson acted crazier than usual in his 1931 campaign. TIME magazine reported: "When his speeches grew so vicious that local papers refused to carry them, he screamed more insanely than ever against the Press." He called his opponent, Judge John Lyle, a "nutty judge" and a "dirty rat" among other things. Lyle is considered one of the few honest judges in Chicago during that era.

TIME said, "Judge Lyle focused his campaign on the charge that Mayor Thompson was in league with the underworld, that gangster Alphonse Capone had contributed $50,000 to the last Thompson campaign and was now ready to help the mayor steal the forthcoming primary election."

"The real issue is whether Al Capone is to be authorized to rule Chicago again through the medium of a dummy in the mayor's chair," Lyle said. At campaign appearances, Lyle displayed machine guns, shotguns and other weapons taken from gangsters. "Look at these," Lyle told crowds. "These are the fruits of William Hale Thompson's administration. I lay at the door of the Thompson administration every murder by gangsters in the last 12 years."

The honest 99 per cent of Chicago's population was held hostage by the mobsters, Lyle later wrote. One big reason, he said, was Thompson, who could have used his police to fight the gangs and his leadership to awaken the public's indignation. Instead, Thompson embraced the gangsters, took their money and let them have the town.

Thompson beat Lyle in the Republican primary in a crooked election. Not only did Thompson's men steal votes in the wards and beat up Lyle's people at the polls, Democrats took Republican ballots to vote for Thompson. Democrats did not need to vote in their own party's primary, since Anton Cermak was unopposed, so they voted for Thompson to give Cermak an easier opponent.

"Lyle tried to make me an issue and the public has given its answer," Capone told the press. The public had another answer in the general election when it overwhelmingly chose Cermak over Thompson.

After Thompson's defeat, the *Chicago Tribune* wrote, "For Chicago, Thompson has meant filth, corruption, obscenity, idiocy and bankruptcy. He has given the city an international reputation for moronic buffoonery, barbaric crime, triumphant hoodlumism, unchecked graft and a dejected citizenship. He nearly ruined the property and completely destroyed the pride of the city. He made Chicago a byword for the collapse of American civilization. In his attempt to continue this, he excelled himself as a liar and defamer of character."

Thompson's campaign speeches for Len Small in 1932 sank ever lower, in a continual and a vile racial denigration of Anton Cermak, a Bohemian, and Henry Horner, a Jewish probate court judge.

It may be no coincidence that Thompson was Chicago's last Republican mayor.

John Kobler, who wrote a biography of Al Capone, called Mayor Thompson "the hero of every pimp, whore, gambler, racketeer and bootlegger in Chicago."

It says a lot about a man who considered Al Capone a friend and Eliot Ness an enemy.

After Thompson's death, two safe deposit boxes in his name were found with about $2.1 million in cash.

That's a little about who Big Bill Thompson was.

William Lorimer was born in Manchester, England, in 1861. His family came to America in 1865, farming in Michigan and Ohio before moving to Chicago in 1870. Lorimer got involved in "politics" early, but not the kind of politics that was aimed towards public service. Politics then (and pretty much the same now) was a business where people did things for other people in exchange for what would be done for them, mostly for the acquisition of wealth and power. That might sound like a cynical description of what sometimes is called "public service" and it might be brutally harsh, but it is true. It was especially so in those early days, and it was not as disguised as it is today.

Lorimer, nicknamed "The Blond Boss," was very popular among Chicago's struggling immigrants in his early political career. They came to him for help and he gave it to them. They knew him as a good family man who kept his word. They, in turn, helped him with their votes. Lorimer was able to build his political machine this way. But the one thing Lorimer recognized very early was that political victory depended on organization, all the way down to the precinct level. And he built a Republican organization that brought in all the aspects of favors, patronage, benefits and rewards. That is how politics works. And it doesn't matter who you have to deal with to get your way. Lorimer saw his actions as something that helped the public, helped the party, and most importantly, helped Lorimer.

At the same time, Lorimer invested in a number of businesses, all of which benefited from his political connections by grabbing city contracts. That also is how politics works. He owned a delivery business, a brick company, a coal company, a construction company and more. His contractor company got a fair share of city business. And while the Thompson-Small political machine cried against the traction barons, Lorimer was negotiating 99-year franchises with Charles Yerkes and his streetcar companies.

As a kingmaker, Lorimer made Washburne, Swift and Busse mayor of Chicago. He made Tanner, Yates, Lowden and Small governor. He made Albert J. Hopkins senator. The list of lesser officials he made or destroyed is lengthy.

A legendary incident happened in 1910 when former President Theodore

Roosevelt was invited to speak at a banquet at the Hamilton Club in Chicago. Lorimer was one of the club's leading members. Roosevelt said he would not come if Lorimer was in attendance. Lorimer decided to skip the banquet.

Lorimer ran for Congress in 1894 and won. He was re-elected in 1896 and 1898 but lost in 1900. He regained his seat in 1902 and remained a congressman until he was elected to the U.S. Senate in 1909.

In those days, senators were chosen by the state legislature, not by the popular vote. It was proven that Lorimer bribed at least one state legislator to vote for him. The U.S. Senate held hearings and decided that Lorimer won his seat by "corrupt practices" and threw him out of the Senate on July 13, 1912.

Lorimer made his comeback into public life when Big Bill Thompson took office, and he helped build the Chicago Republican Machine bigger than ever.

The key to his comeback started in 1911, when the Senate was still debating on whether it would kick him out. It was then that Lorimer -- along with Thompson, Small, Lundin and a few others -- founded the Lincoln Protective League. It was a political organization for the benefit of its founders' interests, and that included opposition to direct election of senators and opposition to referendums and recalls. In other words, decisions should be made by the political leaders, not by the people.

The group's main activities were defending Lorimer against criminal charges and promoting Len Small's political chances. The press more accurately called it the Lorimer-Lincoln League because it really was an organization that was closer to Lorimer than to Lincoln.

It mostly was William Lorimer and Len Small who embraced the "anti-progressive" doctrine. Both men went across the state speaking against reform and against the move to take power from the hands of the bosses and put it in the hands of the people. And their speeches had appeal, as immigrants and downstate farmers saw reformers as those who were against their interests.

A Chicago taxi company sued Small and Lorimer in 1911 for non-payment of about $800 in taxi services during their campaigns.

Small's *Kankakee Daily Republican* supported Lorimer during all the Senate investigations in 1911 and 1912, constantly proclaiming his innocence.

Small invited Lorimer to be the special guest at the 1911 Kankakee Inter-State Fair and his newspaper played it up big. According to the articles, Lorimer spoke to 3,000 people with "round after round of applause." Not so coincidentally, the same newspaper edition reported on a "boom" for Len Small for governor. For months, stories in Small's newspaper reported on the growing "boom."

William Lorimer died Sept. 13, 1934, in a Chicago railway station.

Fred "Poor Swede" Lundin started out as a huckster with a patent medicine wagon. He would extol the benefits of his Juniper Ade drink while two black men with banjos provided the music to draw the crowds. He got into Chicago politics in the 1890s. He was elected in 1908 to one term in Congress, but his real talent was as a kingmaker and political boss. It was Lundin who picked playboy real estate developer William Hale Thompson and made him mayor.

Lundin sold Big Bill the same way he sold his snake oil medicine.

"He may not be too much on brains, but he gets through to the people," Lundin said of Thompson.

It was easy for the intelligent Lorimer and Lundin to control the not-very-bright Thompson. Even Al Capone was sharper than Thompson, which explains why the Mob boss operated so smoothly in the city of Chicago.

It was Lundin who was the "brains" of the Chicago political machine, whose job was making millions through shady deals, building a political army to turn out votes, and dispensing patronage jobs and favors. Thompson was the colorful candidate around whom Lorimer and Lundin could build a bigger political machine.

Between elections, it was Lundin's full time job to pass out political jobs to unqualified hacks and to see that employees kicked back part of their pay to the political machine, while robbing the city through bloated contracts.

Lundin and the Chicago school board went on trial in 1923, charged with stealing a million dollars in fraudulent contracts for the Chicago schools. Acclaimed lawyer Clarence Darrow won an acquittal.

Fred Lundin never was convicted in any of the scandals in which he was linked. A Chicago jury would not dare to do so.

Lundin's most famous quote, which sums up Chicago and Illinois politics, then and now, came from the school board scandal. The members of the school board were appointed by Mayor Thompson but they were picked by Fred Lundin. The goal was simple, as Lundin told school board member Hart Hanson -- "To hell with the public and our campaign promises. We're at the feedbox now."

Fred Lundin died in 1947 of a coronary thrombosis in Beverly Hills, Calif. TIME magazine noted his passing, calling him the "notorious GOP political boss of Chicago in its toughest, Al Capone-infested days...an old-time machine politician, Lundin was the power behind William Hale 'Big Bill' Thompson's 1915 election as mayor and Governor Len Small's infamous state administration."

Chicago Tribune publisher Col. Robert R. McCormick called the Cook County Republican Committee "a criminal organization conducted to the protection of crime for profit" when it was under the control of Thompson and Lundin.

This is the machine that Len Small was a big part of. And it was why Small was so disliked by so many people and so many newspapers, and it was why he got into so much trouble. But Len Small was no innocent victim. He made his Faustian pact with these people and this is how they, and he, operated.

Chapter 3

Edward C. Curtis

Edward C. Curtis of Grant Park was called "the brains of the Len Small Machine," both in a 1907 newspaper story in the *Kankakee Evening Democrat* and in a 1931 book by Carroll H. Wooddy.

He was the mentor of Len Small and was deeply revered by Small. Both men were partners in banking and in politics.

In politics, Curtis and Small were cohorts in a political machine that had taken control of Kankakee and had statewide influence beginning in the 1890s. Curtis was a director in Small's First Trust & Savings Bank in Kankakee. Curtis was an investor and a director in the *Kankakee Daily Republican.* Curtis also owned a half-interest in the *Momence Press-Reporter,* the paper that covered his northeast area of the county.

Small and Curtis consolidated banks to form the Ridgely National Bank of Springfield in November 1918 and both were directors. Curtis controlled the downstate Bank of Edwardsville and a number of other banks.

When Len Small became state treasurer in 1917, he deposited a lot of money in the Grant Park Bank. This got Len Small in a lot of trouble. Curtis escaped this trouble only by dying before the scandal broke.

Edward C. Curtis was one of four sons of Alonzo and Elizabeth Curtis. Alonzo came to Kankakee County in 1852, first to Momence and then to Grant Park in 1869. Alonzo was a grain dealer and a merchant.

Alonzo Curtis opened the Grant Park Bank in 1891 in his general store. It became the Grant Park National Bank in 1898.

But his biggest enterprise was the Alonzo Curtis Brick Co., which produced 225,000 bricks per day at its peak

Edward Curtis was born near Grant Park in 1865. Grant Park is a tiny village in Kankakee County (442 people in 1900, and 1,358 in 2000), not to be confused with the more famous Grant Park in downtown Chicago.

Edward worked in the family bank and was named cashier of the Grant Park National Bank in 1898. He was elected state representative in 1894 at the age of 29. His prominence in state politics was due in part to his connection with William Lorimer and Richard Yates, and he was named Speaker of the House in 1897.

Curtis was re-elected every two years until 1904 when he was elected to the state senate. He won re-election every four years through 1916. He held the position of chairman of the powerful Appropriations Committee.

His brother Vernon Curtis was born in 1878. He also worked in the family bank and brick works.

Edward Curtis was as disliked by a good part of the local Republican party as Len Small. The *Chicago Tribune* in December 1899 wrote, "The bitter feuds among the Kankakee Republicans and the revolts against the so-called 'ring' headed by Mr. Small have almost disrupted the party in that county. Mr. Small, in addition to boosting himself into the senate, will attempt to re-nominate Mr. Edward C. Curtis for the House. Two years ago, the 16th District was one of the battlegrounds of the state. The Republicans got into a quarrel and a determined fight against Curtis was made. Incidentally, it was waged as much against Small as Curtis."

He got a nickname "Gumboil Ed" in 1898 when he dodged his duties in the legislature, as a maneuver planned by himself and Governor Tanner, to avoid voting on the Allen bill, a piece of legislation to give Charles Yerkes a 50-year streetcar franchise. Curtis' excuse was a toothache that needed attention.

"Curtis promises everything to everybody," the *Chicago Tribune* wrote on Oct. 24, 1898. "He keeps no pledges but he always takes care of Curtis."

The "Small-Curtis Machine" already was a factor in February 1898, when fellow Republicans banded together to defeat what they saw as an unsavory group taking over their party. The leaders at that time were John Brayton, former Kankakee mayor, attorney William R. Hunter, Daniel Lee and former sheriff Arthur J. Byrns. The *Chicago Tribune* on Feb. 10 reported, "The anti-machine faction is strong in Kankakee, where it has begun to organize, but weak throughout the county. Len Small is an organizer of rare ability and has strengthened the machine by giving positions and patronage at the hospital to representative Republicans throughout the county."

He did win re-nomination the following month, after a very bitter battle. A *Chicago Tribune* report gave its assessment at that time, and it was incredibly insightful for that early era. It went into a few political maneuvers of Curtis, and then added, "Among other little items of patronage he got in Springfield was that incident at the Hospital for the Insane located here. It controls many appointees, to say nothing of minor matters, such as the income from dealing in supplies, etc., which goes to Curtis' friends. The boss of the deal is Len Small, who by the way is circuit clerk and the resident trustee of the asylum. Mr. Small was a horticulturist only a few years ago, selling fruit trees and currant and gooseberry bushes by sample. He's got a metaphorical orange grove in perpetual fruition now. Small and Curtis have made machine politics a study. Curtis is diplomatic and foxy...and if he can't gain a point in any other way, he will do the 'crying act.' Small fights square from the shoulder and never minces his words. So it is has come to be understood in Kankakee that all men who are on the payrolls of the asylum and all those selling supplies to the same and all those who handle the state's money must work for 'Gumboil' Curtis under pains, penalties, etc.

"And they must give of their coin beside! It is a matter of history in Springfield that for many months the state appointees have been compelled to stand assessments which are being collected for use in the early spring of 1900. The sum already collected is a whopper."

This was why, it added, that Governor Tanner put all his forces behind Curtis' campaign. Curtis was re-elected but could not hold on to his Speaker's job.

This is a little background on Edward Curtis. There will be a lot more about him in further chapters in this book.

There are more banking stories about Curtis and Grant Park. One involved William Lorimer, who got Curtis and Small into trouble before their infamous "Grant Park Bank" scandal.

Lorimer and partner Charles Munday founded several small Chicago banks, including the LaSalle Street National Bank (which later became the LaSalle Street Trust & Savings Co.) in 1909. Len Small was one of the bank's officers.

Although the banks did well for a short time, with taxpayer deposits, his banks got into trouble in 1912. There were many questionable practices including a $100,000 loan to Lorimer himself. When two of Lorimer's banks merged, Lorimer took a check for $1,250,000 to the Central Trust Co. and cashed it. Lorimer took the money to the LaSalle Street Trust & Savings so it would be on hand when the bank examiner visited. He then took the money back to Central Trust.

A state bank examiner closed the La Salle Street Trust & Savings Bank in June 1914. But three days before it was closed, $250,000 was withdrawn from the bank and deposited in the Grant Park Trust & Savings Bank owned by Edward Curtis. The Chicago depositors were ruined. Small and Curtis denied any wrongdoing. Lorimer, Munday and others were indicted for embezzlement.

Munday was convicted and went to jail.

Lorimer was acquitted in May 1916. He was nearly in tears -- possibly he was surprised at the verdict. Interestingly, the judge in the trial was William E. Dever, who became mayor of Chicago in 1923. And Lorimer's attorney was Albert Fink, who acted as a counsel for Len Small in 1921 and who was Al Capone's lawyer in his 1931 tax evasion trial.

The master in chancery looked into the bank's dealings in 1918. New information came to light. There was a $6,000 loan to Fred Lundin. There was a $7,500 note in November 1911 to Len Small's First Trust & Savings Bank in Kankakee, signed by Lorimer, Lundin, William Hale Thompson and David Franks. There were a number of other questionable financial transactions with other politicians who had voted for Lorimer in his fight to keep his senate seat. Lorimer's memory was poor about most of these dealings.

For such a small town, Grant Park had a lot of banks and a lot of banking troubles over the years. One was Farmers State & Savings Bank of Grant Park which was closed in April 1919 after a bank examiner found at least $208,000 in bad paper. A number of Grant Park businessmen and farmers put up their own money to save the bank and it reopened for a short time. The businessmen and farmers lost $160,000.

Charles Rayhorn, cashier of Farmer's Trust & Savings Bank, was indicted for having received deposits after the bank was insolvent but he was not brought to

Len Small and Edward C. Curtis in 1900

trial. A year before this, Rayhorn had been sued for defrauding 84-year-old Harriett Humiston of Pontiac of $195,000 in a Florida land fraud scheme. On May 30, 1927, Rayhorn went to Union Corners Cemetery at Grant Park and decorated his wife's grave. He returned to his Chicago home, turned on the gas and committed suicide.

The Grant Park State Bank was organized in 1924. The following year, it became the Home State Bank of Grant Park. Among the local people who started the bank were Norman Griffin, Ernest B. Griffin and Vernon Curtis. Home State Bank was dissolved on Jan. 10, 1928, by order of the state attorney general and state auditor of public accounts. A state bank examiner saw figures showing that the bank's assets equaled its liabilities, and he said this was fraudulent. He said the value of some notes was listed higher than they really were and some notes were worthless. Luther B. Bratton was appointed receiver, to convert some of the bank's assets to cash for its depositors.

Cass Hayden was a cashier at Grant Park Trust & Savings Bank, and his evasive answers during Small's corruption trial were a great help to the governor. Hayden later went to work for the nearby Momence Trust & Savings Bank. That bank closed its doors on Nov. 7, 1925 after its officers looted it. Hayden went on trial in June 1926 on charges he embezzled $15,000 from the bank. He pleaded guilty and was sentenced to 1-to-10 years. Governor Small pardoned him 11 months later.

Edward Curtis died in his Grant Park home on March 8, 1920. He was buried in Union Corners Cemetery, south of Grant Park. His timely death is what prevented him from being indicted with Small.

The Curtis name lives on today in Grant Park. There is the Bennett-Curtis House, rented for weddings and receptions. It is a beautiful 18-room mansion built in 1900 by George Bennett and purchased in 1919 by Edward Curtis.

Controversy continues in Grant Park to this day. Grant Park's police chief was arrested by FBI and IRS agents on June 4, 2008 on 10 counts of fraud, obstruction of justice and tax evasion. He was charged with running a large scale prostitution sting from the Grant Park Police Department and taking $400,000 in bribes to drop charges against men accused of soliciting prostitutes. He was suspended with pay and replaced by his brother. A Grant Park police lieutenant, fired after answering questions from the FBI and a grand jury, has sued the village.

Chapter 4

Ambition and Manipulation, 1897 - 1906

Scandal enveloped Len Small from the very beginning of his career.

Governor Small's scandal was not an isolated incident that just "happened" in 1921 through the "persecution" of a Chicago newspaper or a "vengeful" attorney general. Scandal became a way of life for Len Small from the time he started building his own political machine in Kankakee in the 1890s. His enemies then, and always, were fellow Republicans who did not like this unsavory character taking over and dirtying their political party.

Len Small's first big scandal happened when he became head of the board of trustees of the Kankakee asylum.

The Eastern Illinois Hospital For The Insane opened in Kankakee in 1879. There always had been scandals and corruption at the massive state hospital. But those that happened while Small was there found him right in the middle of it.

Small was put on the state hospital board in 1897 by Governor John Riley Tanner, elected the previous year through the efforts of the Chicago Republican Machine and William Lorimer. Small got his appointment through his political work for Tanner and his ties to Lorimer, along with help from State Rep. Edward C. Curtis.

The hospital was a big political position. It provided a great opportunity for theft and graft by those in charge. This was true of any large institution that was politically operated.

Tanner's predecessor, Governor John Peter Altgeld, was a Democrat. When Republican Tanner was elected, prize political plums changed hands.

While the governor technically was in charge of all state institutions, in reality each one was a private fiefdom for the local bosses who were put in control as a reward for political favors. And those in control on the local level got rich.

Len Small showed how this get-rich system worked. Small controlled hundred of patronage jobs there and his system doled out jobs based on favors and kickbacks. No one applied for a job at the state hospital without a letter from Len Small. No one got a job there without the approval of Small's political organization, based on party loyalty. And no one kept a job there without kicking back part of their salary to Len Small.

Small raised huge amounts of money by shaking down workers for "campaign" funds. Each employee was "assessed" five per cent of their pay for political purposes.

With four thousand patients, business contracts with local merchants for provisions were tools Small could use to reward or punish merchants and others in Kankakee.

And there were the bigger plums, such as the construction contracts and the coal contracts, from which Small grew rich (on a position that paid no set salary). It provided the riches by which Small was able to own a newspaper and a bank and a big farm and many other enterprises.

Among the suppliers growing rich from construction at the asylum, at prisons and at other state institutions was Murphy & Lorimer Brick Works of Chicago.

Len Small got rich off the coal contracts. A comparison among the state mental institutions shows a marked difference in what was paid for coal. At the state asylum at Anna, coal was bought for 50 cents a ton. It was $1.25 at the School For Feeble Minded Children at Lincoln. Kankakee's asylum was paying $2.35.

The actual cost of the coal, delivered, was $1 less than what the Kankakee asylum was paying. Kankakee's asylum was using 12,000 tons of coal a year.

That was a lot of profit in Len Small's pockets.

Kankakee's asylum bought its coal from O'Gara, King & Co. in Chicago. One of the owners of O'Gara, King & Co. was William Lorimer.

That was a lot of profit in Lorimer's pockets.

O'Gara, King & Co. got its contract with the Kankakee asylum in 1897, when John Tanner became governor and Len Small became head of the board.

When Charles Deneen -- yet another Republican who was anti-Small -- was running for re-election as governor in 1908, he came to Kankakee in July and asked the crowd why the bill for coal was $71,150 in 1905 when Small was running the place, and it was $40,886 in 1906, the year after Small left the board.

"Previous to their regime, Kankakee was one of the famous institutions of its kind in the world," Governor Deneen said. "Under those people, it became the most infamous."

The Kankakee asylum bought its goods from local merchants -- that is, merchants who were part of Len Small's political faction.

One local farmer named Hawkins sold milk to the asylum for 25 cents a gallon. His friend Hoekstra thought that was a good deal since he was getting just 10 cents for his milk. When Hoekstra went to the institution, he was told that because he had voted against the Small political organization his milk was not wanted at any price.

Grocer Charles Sadler, who also was not allied with Small's politics, stopped trying to do business with the institution. He had been rejected numerous times even though his bids were lower than the pro-Small merchants doing business at the asylum.

J.F. Jelly owned a hotel and restaurant outside the hospital grounds, a business that depended a lot on the employees and the visitors to the institution. He had to sell his business in 1902 after Len Small organized a boycott against him.

Jelly had voted for the independent ticket that year. Superintendent J.C. Corbus admitted he gave the order to employees to boycott the business.

W.S. Rowell, a salesman for a Bloomington grocer, said in 1902 that it was politics, not low prices that won contracts for his company. An angry Small responded that it was Rowell who insisted on no-bid contracts. Officials at a number of other state institutions denied Rowell's charges.

Flour was $1.54 per hundred pounds at Elgin and 18 cents more at Kankakee. The prices of other good also varied from institution to institution. Negotiating these deals proved very lucrative for Small.

There were other perks. In 1900, asylum workers laid the cement sidewalk in front of Small's house in Kankakee. They also put in his furnace and did some painting. When the annual Kankakee InterState Fair was in session, asylum attendants worked at the fair at the same time they were being paid to work at the state hospital. Small took dozens of benches and other property from the state hospital for use at the fair. Attendants in the hospital band played at the fair on company time. Small said this was his compensation for allowing a number of the patients into the fair for free.

It was "politics as usual" and it continues today in almost every aspect of Illinois government.

Dr. Clarke Gapen was the superintendent of the asylum under Governor Altgeld. He was replaced by Dr. William Stearns when Tanner became governor. A serious charge was made by Dr. Gapen as he left his job in April 1897. Gapen claimed that he was approached by an "emissary" of Tanner's administration and told that he could keep his job as superintendent if he paid $30,000.

Dr. Gapen told the *Chicago Times-Herald* he did not have that kind of money. He had not used his position to steal. And he would not submit to bribery to keep his job.

Who proposed the shakedown from Gapen and who would the money have benefited? Who was skilled in bribery? Lorimer, Small or someone else? The story in the pro-Republican *Kankakee Daily Gazette* did not name the man.

"These young men have undertaken to do the bidding of such old gangsters as Tanner and Van Cleave," Gapen said to the *Gazette* on Aug. 19, 1897. "Colonel" J.R.B. Van Cleave was a Chicago politician.

Small and fellow trustee, Col. George T. Buckingham, gave an interview to the *Chicago Inter-Ocean,* a newspaper that would be loyal to the Machine for decades. They blamed Gapen for poor management but they were not shy in talking about shaking down employees for campaign contributions.

Buckingham admitted that a "political assessment" was levied on the employees and officials at the asylum. In many instances, the pay of people was increased to reflect the amount they should contribute to the party. Those reluctant to pay were threatened with dismissal. He said Alexis Granger, the board treasurer, supervised the shakedown.

Gapen replied in the *Gazette,* saying conditions at the institution and the plunder done by the new administration in just a few months was terrible. "The political leech has been feeding steadily upon the breast of this great charity...politics and boodle has so handicapped the management that in three months' time, they find themselves with a deficit on hand." Gapen said salaries were withheld for two months so Small, Buckingham and John Magee could keep the money in the bank to draw more interest for themselves.

A *Chicago Tribune* story on Oct. 24, 1898 told of the "Small-Curtis Combine" using the state hospital for political purposes. "All the patronage of the insane asylum, all the contracts incident to that institution are being used for the sole purpose of the election of Edward C. Curtis. No man, unless he is a member of the Small combination, or a Democrat who promises to support Curtis, can get a grain of patronage or a contract from the Kankakee asylum. No farmer in Kankakee County can sell a can of milk to the asylum unless he promises to vote for Curtis."

The story cited the Kankakee Stone & Lime Co., a business owned by Democrats, which had been financially coerced into delivering the votes of its workers for Curtis. A Democrat clothier was given a contract for 175 suits of clothes for the asylum in exchange for votes. "Employees of the asylum have been bled by assessments until they are poverty stricken. One employee, W.H. Lanyon, said he presented vouchers for a $90 salary and was given a check for $60 in full payment, $30 being retained for the Curtis campaign fund.

"Small is working everything and everybody connected with the asylum in Curtis' interest. Every contract, every item of supply, every influence that can be used, is being exercised in Curtis' behalf. The Republicans get nothing out of that institution except they bow in obedience to Small and Curtis. If they whimper or murmur, if they even express disapproval of Small's methods, they are unmercifully skinned in Brother Dunlap's newspaper (*The Kankakee Times*)."

In November 1897, the big Horse Show in Chicago was marred by Small's very public and very vocal resignation from the State Board of Agriculture. John A. Logan, manager of the show, had a dispute with the board which ended with the board apologizing to him. That is, everyone on the board except Len Small. Small wrote an indignant letter, saying he did not go along with the apology and was quitting, and he had it published in a Chicago newspaper. The exact nature of the dispute is not known but Small's letter indicated it was about "the disposition of state funds" which was approved by the state board.

Kankakee County always has had a Democrat party, even though the county always has been Republican-dominated. In the Len Small era, the two major political parties were known as the Regular Republicans and the Anti Republicans. Len Small became the political boss of the county, and so he called his faction the Regular Republicans and he called his opposition the Anti Republicans.

His opposition should have been called the Real Republicans.

And Small's Republicans should have been called The Smalls.

Local politics always has been lively, but it never was more bitter and hateful as it was between Republican factions in the Len Small era.

In 1898, Small already has muscled his way into controlling a good part of the power in Kankakee County. His chairmanship of the state hospital board gave him patronage and money. He was county clerk and he used the patronage and influence that came with that job. He had powerful friends in Springfield.

When the county Republicans held their convention in 1898, Small was throwing his weight around, much to the irritation of others in the local Republican party. The convention was contentious, and one issue was the legitimacy of some of the delegates. Small was accused for the first time of something that he would be accused of many times in years to come -- that he was betraying his party to form a secret "combine" with Democrats -- Democrats desperate enough for power to also betray their party to join Small in scuttling Anti-Small Republicans.

Some of the Republican delegates, led by Levi Nutt and William R. Hunter, called for "fair play" and asked for a committee to check the credentials of the delegates. Hunter wanted to know how many of the delegates had been elected by Democrats who took Republican ballots in the primary. Small replied to conventioneers that Hunter's request was a "slick scheme by a paid attorney of one of the most dangerous corporations in the state of Illinois."

Small was referring to Hunter as an attorney for the Illinois Central Railroad. It was an extreme statement on Small's part and typical of the overkill and attempt to ruin the reputation of anyone in opposition. Such tactics became a cornerstone of Small's political playbook, as we will see again in this book.

Hunter did not back down. He told the convention that he represented the corporation that Small referred to in his sly manner, the corporation that gave Small free passes on its trains.

This election campaign made Hunter a political enemy of Small, and Hunter was never afraid to oppose Small and his tactics. So who was Hunter?

William R. Hunter (1858-1939) had been city attorney and state's attorney in Kankakee. When the Spanish-American War started in 1898, he recruited a company of volunteers and organized a committee to take care of their families. He did the same in 1916 when the Mexican border war started and in 1917 when America entered World War I. He organized the Red Cross chapter in Kankakee, helped organize the Kankakee YMCA, was chairman of the local Salvation Army and was one of three men who established Emergency Hospital (today Provena-St. Mary's Hospital) in 1897 in Kankakee -- all unselfish and unpaid efforts. Hunter was chosen to introduce President William McKinley on Oct. 15, 1898 -- the only incumbent president to visit Kankakee. Hunter was a circuit court judge from 1933 to 1939. He was a loyal Republican all his life. The residence he built in 1898 on South Chicago Avenue today remains one of Kankakee's premier historic houses.

This campaign in 1898 is interesting because it shows that even then, Len Small's political tactics were being questioned. Judge Orr told the conventioneers that their actions could end up in court. "Mr. Orr spoke against the dictation by any set of individuals," according to coverage in the March 17 *Kankakee Daily Gazette.* "A dozen individuals in the county have tried to thwart the will of the people, who have set the date of the convention six months in advance of the election. He understood that a difference of 80 votes in the primaries would have transferred the control of this convention from the hands of the individuals who are seeking to manipulate the politics of the county to the control of the people."

Orr and others were referring to Len Small's policy of bringing in questionable "workers" from the state hospital to vote.

Both Hunter and W.W. Huckins presented a minority report to the convention which stated that several districts around the county sent delegates who "were elected by Democratic votes and by money furnished by E.C. Curtis and Len Small to secure Democratic votes." The report added that minors were allowed to vote, that the committee on credentials would not affirm its findings and that carriages from the state hospital were used to take questionable voters to the polls.

"Mr. Hunter stated that the minority were stifled in the committee room and that every true American should resent this effort to prevent a large element of the party from obtaining a hearing," the *Gazette* continued. "The majority of the committee were afraid to permit the evidence which the minority was ready to produce to come before this convention."

Small replied that the statements in the minority report were "absolutely false." He said the minority's intentions were to have the convention continued another day to "spring surprises."

"Small denied that he had given Mr. Breen money...and that the minority element had voted Democrats and that the frauds were all on their side." Huckins said he "could prove that men had stated in the second district that they had been paid $10 apiece by Mr. Small and Mr. Curtis; that Mr. Leuth, who had handled the money of the machine in the Seventh District had told him that if he had used the dirty tactics which the machine asked him to use, he could have carried the Seventh District."

The election the following month also was tainted with charges of corruption. Even though Len Small was the one accused of election fraud, it was Small who filed a petition with the court to have the election of three candidates voided. Small wanted ballots from two precincts thrown out, which would have changed the results and given the election to his candidates.

Small's pretense was that there were technical irregularities in how those ballots were handled. But Small's charges were nothing compared to the accusations against him.

The *Gazette* reported what happened when election judge Joe Smith brought the Second Precinct votes into the town clerk's office. The report came from both Smith and a reporter who was there.

Smith said Small and other Republican leaders were waiting at the table and they started opening the envelopes of the tally sheets and poll books. "Mr. Small prepared a new sheet on which to make his figures," the newspaper reporter wrote. "Mr. Small was leaning on the envelopes from the other precincts containing the poll books and tally sheets. Mr. Lewis took these envelopes and opened them one by one and slid the tally sheets to Mr. Small, who unfolded the sheets and copied the official figures from them, commenting to Mr. Smith that the returns from the Second were not properly carried out in the 'total' column on the tally sheet. There was considerable inquiry about the returns from the First but Mr. Miller said he was sure his copy of the vote as recorded by the clerks at the First at the conclusion of the count was correct."

When Smith left the office and went to his store, where a group of people were awaiting the results, he told them the story of how the envelopes were opened. "And all at once, a general protest went up, and the rumor that the ballots were being tampered with spread upon the streets," the *Gazette* wrote.

Fred Ehrich defeated Ernest Radeke for county collector by one vote, out of more than 1,800 cast. Radeke filed a lawsuit, alleging that Len Small, Ed Jeffers and other Republicans opened the envelopes of the tally sheets and poll books "and unlawfully proceeded to canvass the returns and pretended to figure up the numbers of votes." The lawsuit charged that there were erasures and changes made on the tally sheets.

The lawsuit also accused Small of bringing insane patients to the polls, among other unqualified voters.

Small responded by calling it "a damned lie from beginning to end." Presumably, his lawsuit about opposition irregularities was the straight story.

No matter. Small's lawsuit was thrown out of court quickly. This "was generally expected, as it was considered a political move to counteract the sensation produced when the town election returns were opened before being canvassed by the town board," the June 21 *Gazette* said. Radeke won the lawsuit and election.

It would not be the last time Len Small was accused of dirty politics and stealing an election.

The same shenanigans went on a year later in the April 1899 election. The *Gazette* editorialized against state hospital workers being paid to campaign for Len Small's candidates rather than care for their patients. It wrote against "the business of the hospital used as a great lever to intimidate or bribe voters." And it decried how a promise of compromise by Small was a lie, and "when the board of supervisors met, the Anti members were placed on the poorest committees regardless of their qualifications or length of service, solely for the purpose of punishing those who had opposed Mr. Small's ambitious schemes and insatiable desire for political prestige."

In November 1899, a Kankakee County Republican Club was formed. It was an extraordinary thing for the well-established Republican party to have to form a club, but it was necessary to separate the real Republicans from the Len Small Republicans who had taken over the party. J. Frank Leonard, who had been mayor of Kankakee from 1893 to 1895, was president of the club, which started with 124 loyal Republicans. Its founding principles were those which Len Small did not follow -- candidates nominated by popular vote instead of by delegates, public institutions not being used to promote the interests of individuals, the good of the party being more important than the success of an individual, Republicans able to be candidates without asking the consent of a boss, and clean politics and fair treatment.

Other local Republicans named as part of the "anti-Small" faction in 1898 and 1899 were former mayor John H. Brayton, former county clerk William F. Kenega, former sheriff Peter Brosseau, former sheriff Arthur J. Byrns, former mayor and school superintendent Frank Hatch, Charles Sadler, Sid Durfee, Jay Hamlin and I.B. Hanna. Today, they among the names of the most prominent men in Kankakee's history.

The shakedown of state employees by Governor Tanner and his political organization went on for the entire four years he was in office, and it was in every state facility, not just at the Kankakee institution. Every state employee who made at least $60 per month was assessed five to ten percent of his or her pay. In Chicago, Judge Eldridge Hanecy, who ran for mayor in 1901 and lost to Carter Harrison Jr., was part of this scheme.

The *Chicago Tribune* reported that as soon as Tanner took office, he called his department heads together to organize the shakedown. Other political big shots there were Col. J.R.B. Van Cleave and Col. Thomas Scott.

Len Small took another step up the ladder when he ran for state senator in 1900. W.R. Hunter ran against him in the spring primary for delegates to the nominating convention, in an effort to wrest some control of the party from Small. It took 100 ballots before the convention chose Small over Hunter. Hunter cried foul, saying Small used an adjournment to twist arms and make deals for the nomination. Small won the election in the fall -- 1900 was a big year for the Republicans. But as usual, Len Small ran far behind the rest of the ticket in the fall.

He kept his position as head of the asylum while serving as state senator.

Len Small was at the center of another scandal that shook the state asylum in 1902. One issue, known for years but now suddenly a scandal, was his shakedown of state workers for campaign contributions.

Small must have known his shakedown of employees was underhanded by the way he handled the "assessments." Small had two salary checks made out for each employee -- one was for 90 per cent of the salary, the other for 10 per cent, and the smaller check was endorsed to Len Small. Then, Small signed a receipt for the full amount, which was sent to the state treasurer.

The assessments totaled $40,000 a year at Kankakee.

A.W. Huber was fired from his job at the asylum and then went to work for the Reuter Hardware Co. His story was about the day he was asked if he had paid his political assessment. Huber replied that he had not and he had no intention of doing so. He then was called into the office of Superintendent Corbus and was told, "You know what will happen if you do not pay up." A short time later, Huber was fired; John Childs was fired at the same time for the same reason.

Dr. T.R. Foster, a Kankakee physician, said he paid his five per cent assessment while on the medical staff of the asylum, up until two months before he left. He said Corbus called him into his office and said, "You know I do not approve of this practice, but I am forced to collect the money. You know what will happen if you do not pay up."

There were a lot of other revelations in this scandal -- two female patients giving birth to babies fathered by staff members; the business manager having furniture for his house made in the hospital shops; selling hospital horses below their value; inhumane treatment of patients; inadequate fire protection; and poor discipline due to politics.

And accusations were made against two of the three men on the board of trustees. William Murphy was accused of drinking and of being involved in questionable conduct with a female employee. Len Small was accused of taking hospital horses for his private use and of assessing money from employee paychecks for campaign funds.

Governor Richard Yates talked to the hospital administration and trustees and then asked the State Board of Charities to investigate.

There were lengthy public hearings with numerous witnesses. Former employee Harry Ball testified he saw Murphy intoxicated, drinking from a whiskey bottle, going to a female attendant's bedroom. Murphy denied the charges and went one step further. That night, as Ball slept in his room at the Homestead boarding house across the road from the state hospital, a sheriff's deputy arrested him and took him to jail on a warrant for perjury, sworn out by Murphy.

At the hearing on the perjury charge the next morning, Murphy testified that he did drink liquor from the hospital supplies but not to excess and not on the dates named by Ball. And he said he was caught hugging a woman but didn't go to her room. The court dismissed the perjury charge against Ball. But that night, Murphy had Ball arrested and jailed again on the same charge.

Murphy and Small were determined to see that Ball was prosecuted for his story. They had Judge John Small order Ball arrested a second time for "perjury" after Ball already had been released by another judge. Then their vendetta took a very unusual turn.

Follett Bull and Lewis Orr, Ball's lawyers, took a petition of *habeas corpus* to a judge in Chicago, arguing that their client could not get a fair trial in Kankakee because of Len and John Small. Len was a witness against Ball and John was the only local judge left to hear the case. The writ was granted by a Chicago judge.

Len Small then pulled a dirty trick that was typical of the tactics he pulled throughout his life. As Ball sat in a Kankakee jail, waiting to be taken to Chicago, Len Small got a local saloonkeeper to put up the bail for Ball. Lawyer Charles Campbell came to get Ball out of jail. Ball declined, preferring to remain in jail.

If Ball had left on bail, the writ of *habeas corpus* would have been invalid. Small would have had Harry Ball in his grasp, ready for more Kankakee justice. Instead, Ball waited for a Chicago deputy and was taken to Chicago, where a judge dismissed the perjury charge.

Ball sued Small, Murphy and treasurer Cornelius R. Miller for $50,000 for false imprisonment. The case went to trial in February 1904 and was dismissed.

Len Small admitted he used a hospital horse to sow oats on his farm. He said that the state allowed transportation expenses between home and the hospital for trustees. He had used his own horse ten times for the very short distance from his home to the hospital. This was compensation. The state horse was in his pasture, he admitted.

And Small testified that he was a candidate for state office, so state hospital employees under him stuffed envelopes and did other political work. He said he was not aware if any work was done on state time.

The accusation that employee George Irwin was paid to spend weeks in Chicago to do political work was admitted -- but since it happened years ago, it was dropped.

Superintendent Corbus testified that five percent of paychecks were taken from employees who earned more than $50 a month. This was for political purposes, Corbus said, and the idea came from Len Small.

The state board reported its findings to Governor Yates. It basically dismissed all the charges of cruelty, bad food and more. It found no fault on the part of the hospital for two patients getting pregnant and giving birth.

The board found that the hospital did mandate five percent from employees' pay for political purposes. It said it would not interfere with that, only suggesting it be voluntary.

It found that Small did not usurp the superintendent's authority in hiring. And the panel found that political work by employees was "greatly exaggerated."

It found that Murphy was drunk and did collect money from attendants to buy liquor. And then it commended his work and recommended his retention.

Even then, Len Small thought he was above the law and didn't mind admitting it. Small admitted the charges against him, knowing he would be immune. He was right. Governor Richard Yates benefited from the campaign work and the money assessed from employees, so he was not going to do anything about it.

Three members of the State Board of Charities -- Judge John Gibbons, Julia Lathrop and Dr. Emil Hirsch -- made a public statement that they were disgusted with the whitewash given to the administration.

Another grand jury investigated hospital fraud charges against Small in 1903 but it did not indict. The investigation was based on stories in the *Kankakee Evening Democrat* written by reporter Thomas Bonfield Jr.

Another grand jury was convened after another scandal at the hospital in May 1906. The focus was the cruel treatment of patients. A former employee told the *Chicago Tribune,* "It is necessary to show the patients that they cannot run things. A good beating when they first visit the hospital is usually enough. No matter how crazy a man is, he is apt to remember his lesson." Attendants do not tell on each other and patients are not believed.

The grand jury hearings went on for weeks, with several dozen witnesses testifying. Dr. Macia Berlin-Weinberg, a Chicago dentist who was a patient for a few months in 1900, testified that she was attacked by attendants on three occasions. Once was for refusing to use a stiff old toothbrush. Another time, she asked for a glass of water and a nurse gagged her with a sheet and dragged her to bed by her hair, dislocating a shoulder and nearly severing an ear. She cited attacks on other female patients.

Berlin-Weinberg testified that a towel used by 50 patients was changed once a week, there was unchecked disease, bread was moldy and gnawed by rats and meat was tainted. She said she once found a rat's body in her bean soup.

Three officials of City National Bank in Kankakee testified that interest from the hospital's state funds on deposit was paid directly to the personal account of hospital treasurer Cornelius R. Miller. Miller also was vice president of Small's bank and he later became a prominent figure in Governor Len Small's administration.

The investigation concluded by finding no fault and taking no action -- not surprising, since two hospital members were on the grand jury, including Miller!

The grand jury found that the female patient had been raped but the guilty man was unknown. It found no evidence of graft in the disposing of dead bodies or in the coal contracts.

It found that Miller took the interest on state funds but said that he was entitled to it as part of his pay. It found cruel treatment of patients, but so what?

The sarcastic headline in the June 15 *Kankakee Gazette* summed it up: *Grand Jury Reports They Find No Evidence -- C.R. Miller Was Entitled To Interest*

On State Funds, The Present Coal Contract Properly Let, And Everything Is Lovely.

Len Small and the political machine were *simpatico* with "Rule or Ruin." Those they could not control must be destroyed. This was true even back in 1902.

U.S. Sen. William E. Mason, a Chicago lawyer, was seeking re-nomination on the Republican ticket. Mason earned the machine's enmity by speaking out against the assessments of state workers' money for campaign funds. So Lorimer decided to replace Mason with Albert J. Hopkins, a congressman from Aurora.

Lt. Gov. William Northcutt was chairman of the Republican convention, which really was a rubber-stamp of the Lorimer machine. The convention endorsed the administration of Governor Richard Yates (who would be dumped by the machine two years later) and it chose Hopkins as the Republican nominee for the U.S. Senate. (Hopkins won. When he sought re-nomination six years later, he was dumped -- in favor of Lorimer himself, who subsequently was kicked out of the Senate for having bribed legislators to elect him).

There was dissension from some delegates but they were not given a voice. Outside the convention, in an interview with *The New York Times,* Sen. Mason said, "I will succeed myself as United States senator from Illinois. I have made no fight for delegates. If it was a straight Republican convention, it could have nothing to do with selecting a United States senator.

"Certainly a convention made up by brutally unseating regularly elected delegates and seating those selected by ballot box stuffing and boodle could have nothing in common with Republicanism. These ultimate effects will be to elect me and to defeat Mr. Lorimer for Congress."

In Illinois, never bet against the Machine. Incumbent Senator Mason lost his bid to Hopkins. Lorimer was elected to Congress.

Small had his own political scandal in 1902, even though it was not his election. In October, it was charged that Small tried to bribe James B. Dawson of Morris to withdraw his candidacy just before the election. Dawson was running against Edward C. Curtis for state representative.

The charge came from Dawson and from Senator Mason. They said Small and Curtis offered up to $5,000 if Dawson would take his name off the ballot, and that the offer was approved by Governor Yates.

In a newspaper account, E.O. Love said Len Small gave him the order to approach Dawson with the deal, and that Love would get $1,500 if he succeeded.

Dawson had two public officials from Morris sit behind a partition as witnesses so they could hear Love's proposal. They heard Love tell of a meeting at the Great Northern Hotel in which Hopkins, Small, Curtis and Yates approved the deal.

Dawson and Love went to Len Small's office at the asylum on Oct. 24 where the deal was discussed. The next day, Dawson called Small and told him that he didn't have enough money to buy him.

When the scandal hit the newspapers, Small admitted that a proposition was discussed. But Len Small responded to this charge in the same fashion that became his trademark in later years. He lied about it and then placed the blame on the other person.

Small said it was Dawson who asked for money to withdraw. Love's story now had changed. Small said Love was backing him up in the claim that Dawson had become a candidate only to extort money from the party.

Small's account in the *Kankakee Daily Gazette* told how Love had relentlessly pursued him -- to his office, to the state hospital, even on street cars in Kankakee, to ask for "reimbursement of campaign expenses" and then Dawson would take his name off the ballot. Small said he told the man on several occasions that he didn't care if Dawson remained on the ballot and he would not pay.

The story, that Small would not take the opportunity to eliminate an opponent, does not sound like the Len Small we would come to know. But the rest of his story does. Riding on a Kankakee street car with Small (according to Small's story), Dawson and Love asked for $500 to withdraw from the race. Small said his reply was, "You cannot get any expense money from me." Dawson said, "We will. There are two of us and one of you. If you do not give us $500, we will go to Chicago and tell Billy Mason that you tried to buy us off. Mason will get it published in the Chicago papers, making a big sensation, and you can't get them to publish your denial because they are all against you but the *Inter-Ocean."*

Now *that* sounds like Len Small!

In the same story, Small said he wasn't really sure that the man who said he was Dawson really was Dawson. He claimed he never saw Dawson before or since that encounter and this man may have been an imposter looking to extort money.

Curtis also claimed he never met Dawson or offered him a bribe.

No matter. Curtis defeated Dawson in the election a week later.

As governor, Tanner did the bidding of the Chicago bosses. But Lorimer's deal with traction robber baron Charles Tyson Yerkes cost Tanner what little integrity he had.

Yerkes had sought a monopoly over Chicago's streetcars and had unsuccessfully tried to bribe Tanner's predecessor, Governor Altgeld. Yerkes tried again with Tanner and he found a more amenable governor. After a bitter battle, the Illinois legislature passed a bill allowing city councils to approve their own extended contracts. This was a gift of graft to Chicago. Tanner signed the bill. When the issue came before the Chicago City Council, people showed up with lynch-ropes. Yerkes failed to get his 99-year franchises.

Tanner decided to run against Senator Shelby Cullom in 1900 rather than seek a second term as governor. He lost.

Richard Yates, the much less impressive son of the Civil War-era governor of the same name, was the choice of Lorimer for governor in 1900, Yates won.

Small became an important part of the Yates organization. Yates agreed to Small's request to be named the party's candidate for state treasurer in 1902 but that was vetoed by Lorimer, who wanted Fred Busse of Chicago.

There was intrigue in the battle for state treasurer in 1902. At a meeting in early February, Len Small and Edward C. Curtis met with Lorimer. Small was led to believe he would be the candidate of the slate makers. When it became apparent that Busse would be Lorimer's choice, an angry Len Small went to Governor Yates and complained that he had been betrayed by Lorimer. Small soon learned who was the boss in the state Republican party, and it wasn't Governor Yates.

Small dutifully deferred to Lorimer and Busse, stepping aside and waiting two years (treasurers served two-year terms and could not succeed themselves).

Governor Yates also learned just who was boss. Yates had shown a little independence, believing that he, not Lorimer, was governor. Yates wanted to make his own appointments and build his own political machine. Lorimer did not like it. When Yates sought a second term in 1904, Lorimer decided that he wanted Col. Frank O. Lowden of Oregon, Illinois, instead. Lowden, a lawyer, teacher, farmer and Spanish-American War veteran, was a new name in politics.

The fight for the nomination was a bitter one. It was a hot summer, and after 22 days and 78 ballots, the convention was deadlocked between the candidates -- Yates, Lowden and Cook County State's Attorney Charles S. Deneen.

Len Small had pledged his Kankakee delegation to Yates. Lorimer made a deal with Small to swing his votes to Lowden after Yates faltered. But Yates remained strong, ballot after ballot, leading Lowden and far ahead of Deneen. Lorimer tried to break the logjam by demanding that Small join Lowden at once.

Small said Yates had promised him the nomination for state treasurer if he stuck by him. Lorimer quickly promised the same if Small would switch to Lowden. Small agreed, promising to have his delegation vote for Lowden on the next ballot.

Meanwhile, Yates was planning strategy of his own. He could see what was happening. He knew deals were being made by Lorimer to put Lowden through. Yates met with leaders of other delegations and with Deneen. Yates said he would throw his support to Deneen. Why? Because he would rather lose the nomination than see it go to Lorimer's hand-picked choice.

As for Small, he told Yates he would keep his promise to Lorimer to switch the Kankakee votes to Lowden on the next ballot while influencing his friends in other delegations to vote for Deneen. Small's price was the nomination for state treasurer.

And that was how, on the 79th ballot, Charles Deneen won the Republican nomination for governor and how Len Small won the nomination for state treasurer.

Both were elected in the fall.

It was this action that split the Republican party into two warring camps for decades to come. Up until now, Lorimer was the Republican boss. Now, there was a competing faction, with people like Charles Deneen and others in later years (such as Edward Brundage) who would challenge boss politics.

Len Small stuck with the bosses, even as he played both sides. Small helped bring to the statewide Republicans what he had brought to the local Republicans in Kankakee -- division, strife and factional warfare. He didn't care.

How Len Small operated was shown in the election of 1905 through a series of stories in the *Kankakee Daily Gazette*.

Len Small wasn't a candidate in 1905. His brother John was the candidate for circuit judge. John was on the ballot because Len put him there.

John Small had been a county judge from 1894 to 1897 and then was elected to a six-year term as a circuit court judge. He got that nomination in 1897 in an underhanded way. Charles Starr, who had been a judge for 40 years, did not campaign for re-nomination because he felt a judge was above such politics. Unfortunately, he didn't count on the trickery of the Smalls. Starr wasn't stupid but he did believe in a man's word. Just days before the convention slated candidates, Len Small had personally assured him he would be re-nominated, all the while Len was scheming against Judge Starr on behalf of John, lining up delegates.

John Small won in 1897 and he ran for re-election in 1903. Even though John was an incumbent, the Smalls had to use trickery to get him re-nominated. Len "persuaded" the Republican Central Committee to disregard the Iroquois County convention's choice in order to place John on the ballot. The feeling against the Smalls was so strong that party leaders convinced John to withdraw his candidacy. John claimed he was pulling out because of his health but he resumed his law practice without interruption.

When Judge Charles Garnsey died in 1905, Len Small decided that John would run in the special election. Other attorneys who wanted to run were pushed out by Len Small through threat and intimidation. His tactics were so blatant and crude that again a revolt was made by fellow Republicans and others in the district against what they saw as another power grab by Small.

Albert O. Marshall, a 64-year-old Joliet lawyer who had been a judge from 1894 to 1902, was persuaded by people in the three-county judicial circuit to run against John Small. Marshall, a Civil War veteran who wrote a book about his battlefield experiences, was a highly respected man.

The attacks on Marshall in Small's *Kankakee Daily Republican* amounted to no more than deriding him for having held several offices in his career, even though these were few and primarily on Joliet school boards. That charge was quite a stretch for Len Small, considering the number of offices he already had held at public expense by that time. In his hometown of Joliet, the *Joliet Daily Republican* (controlled by Congressman Howard Snapp, a political boss and friend of Small) never wrote a bad word about Marshall until this campaign.

The *Gazette* was a Republican party newspaper and it had both criticized and defended Small in print over the years. But it announced that, for the first time in its 38-year history, it was not endorsing the Republican nominee -- "good citizenship rises above party" -- and so it would not support John Small.

The *Gazette* was joined by the *Joliet Daily Herald, Joliet Daily News* and other newspapers in the district in bitter opposition to John Small's candidacy.

Interestingly, Kankakee's *The Evening Democrat* newspaper did not oppose John Small. In fact, it found him acceptable. The newspaper, which for years had bitterly criticized, ridiculed, mocked and attacked the Smalls, now was silent. When John Small ran for judge in 1903, *The Evening Democrat* said, "As a jurist, he is a pygmy, a mere dwarf." It added that Small showed "bad temperament" as a judge and showed no community spirit off the bench. Most of Kankakee's attorneys would not endorse him.

Indeed, Small had a poor record as a judge. He had 38 cases appealed and 15 were reversed. To avoid further reversals, Small granted new trials to a number of defendants who had appeared before him. Compared to the other two circuit judges, this was a terrible record.

But in 1905, *The Evening Democrat* had no quarrel with John Small's candidacy. It was an unbelievable position for such a virulent anti-Small publication. *Gazette* editors claimed the Smalls had bribed *The Evening Democrat* and other area newspapers. The *Gazette* had problems with other behavior. It said that when Len was a candidate for state senator in 1900, John (who was a judge at the time) went to a local polling place and sat in the voting booth next to the ballot box, where he was not lawfully allowed, as Len and his men allegedly brought in people to vote illegally. John Small refused to leave when asked by Kankakee Police Chief Sylvester Jackson. The *Gazette* quoted John Small as telling the police chief, "By (expletive), I'm pretty near as big a man as you are" and "Do you know who I am?"

While a judge, John Small accepted free passes to ride on the railroads, a possibly illegal gift from corporations that might appear before his bench. John Small had been a lawyer for the Chicago Southern Railroad.

In May 1900, Judge Small adjourned his court for a week so he could go to the party's state convention in Peoria where he and Len followed Lorimer's orders to nominate Yates for governor. In accepting the Republican nomination in 1905, John Small acknowledged the judgeship was a "political job."

A charge of bribery and an offer to have court cases "fixed" was made against Len Small in this election. The accusation was made by William R. Hunter, who had tangled with the Smalls previously over the direction of the local Republican party.

Hunter was the Illinois Central's lawyer for Kankakee County, so he knew what he was talking about. At the time, there were six personal injury cases pending in the circuit court against the Illinois Central, seeking a total of $180,000 in damages. Len Small approached an officer of the railroad and said that if the company would convince Hunter to support John Small for judge, "he would make a contract with the railroad company regarding their lawsuits, that they should get a *fair show.*" The emphasis was Hunter's.

The implication from Small was obvious to both the railroad official and to Hunter -- in exchange for Hunter's support of John Small in the election, Judge Small would rule in favor of the railroad in these cases.

"I was called into the office of the railroad company and I was told by said official that Mr. Small was willing to make such a contract, and I was asked what I thought of such a proposition," Hunter wrote in the *Kankakee Daily Gazette* on June 30. "I asked the official if Mr. Small would not also make a written contract to the effect that the plaintiffs in these damage suits, the crippled railroad men, the widows of the men killed on the track and their orphan children would get a fair show in the trial of their cases before his Honor John Small. The official said that Mr. Small said nothing about that proposition. You can readily understand what Small meant when he said *fair show.*"

Hunter continued, "I then and there denounced Mr. Small and his brother as low-minded, wicked men who were seeking to trade and barter justice for poltical support, and this has engendered in the breasts of those gentlemen the bitter feeling which is manifested by the articles in the *Republican* of June 28, to which neither one of them had the courage to sign his name."

Len Small responded to Hunter's comments in the *Gazette* by lying about it and placing the blame on the other person. Small wrote a letter to John Drennan, district lawyer for the railroad, saying that it was Hunter who made the proposition.

John Drennan did not believe Len Small.

Drennan wrote back, telling Small his accusation was "astonishing to me in the extreme." Drennan said Hunter "has always been one of our most faithful, efficient and trusted local attorneys." Drennan said Hunter would not have the authority to make any such agreement. Only Drennan or someone higher in the corporation could make such a deal and, Drennan added, no such deal would ever be made.

Over the years, those who would not support the Smalls were vilified in print and in public. John and Len sought the support of Hunter, even though Hunter had been opposed to the Smalls for years. Hunter was a respectable citizen and prominent Republican whose endorsement would be significant. When Hunter declined, the Small's newspaper printed a story critical of Hunter. It was that article that prompted Hunter to write his story in the *Gazette* as a reply.

Hunter's *Gazette* column went on. "Len Small has been around telling my clients that if they could line me up for John Small, he would guarantee that they would get a fair deal in court. I have resented this on every occasion. I still resent it, and feel that these gentlemen have no higher opinion of the sacredness of the functions of a judge than they have of buying and selling the votes of the gutter snipes to whom they pay their ill-gotten gains."

During John Small's previous term as a judge, Hunter said, "When a man got sued, the first thing he did was to either go to see Len Small or ask his attorney to see him, so that he could get a fair show. The people of this county earnestly believe that Len Small advised his brother while on the bench to decide the cases, and that they were decided according to the political affiliation of the party."

And Hunter further said that State Treasurer Small was "trying to use the power of the State Board of Equalization and Board of Review to compel some of the corporations in this city to line up their employees for brother John."

"If Mr. Small can fool the people into voting for John, he will then have control, together with his partner Mr. Curtis, a majority of the banks in this county, the power of the state treasury, the hospital patronage, county fair, etc." Hunter wrote. "He has his hand in the county Board of Review, endeavoring to influence it to the best of his ability in assessing the property the people and excepting the property of his friends. He bargains for and promises all the offices of the county years in advance -- master in chancery, state's attorney, county judge, sheriff, treasurer and others. Give him control of the circuit court and Mr. Small and his adherents will feel double secure, and with Brother John on the bench, the average lawyer remains silent, even though he feels that he should speak and protest against their conduct, and the fear that Brother John might by some accident become judge again has kept many of them silent. The power that Mr. Len Small now has in this county has caused many of our citizens to remain silent, lest they might lose trade or have difficulty in their financial operations. There are a few men in this county who have the courage to speak out and tell the truth about these gentlemen, regardless of the consequences, and it is about time that free American citizens should rise and assert their rights. The man who votes for John Small next Saturday is blind to his own most sacred interest. He aids in giving the Smalls one more club with which to silence and throttle the common people, and will undoubtedly regret it when it is too late."

W. R. Hunter

John Small

Albert O. Marshall, the Independent Party candidate, beat John Small, the Republican Party candidate, by a wide margin. There was no Democrat candidate on the ballot because the Democrats and Republicans made a deal to combine for John Small, according to the *Gazette* and the *Clifton Advocate.* Marshall had no party organization behind him. He had no one to lean on to squeeze votes. He made no promises, deals, bribes or intimidation.

Albert O. Marshall was a distinguished jurist. A school in Joliet is named for A.O. Marshall.

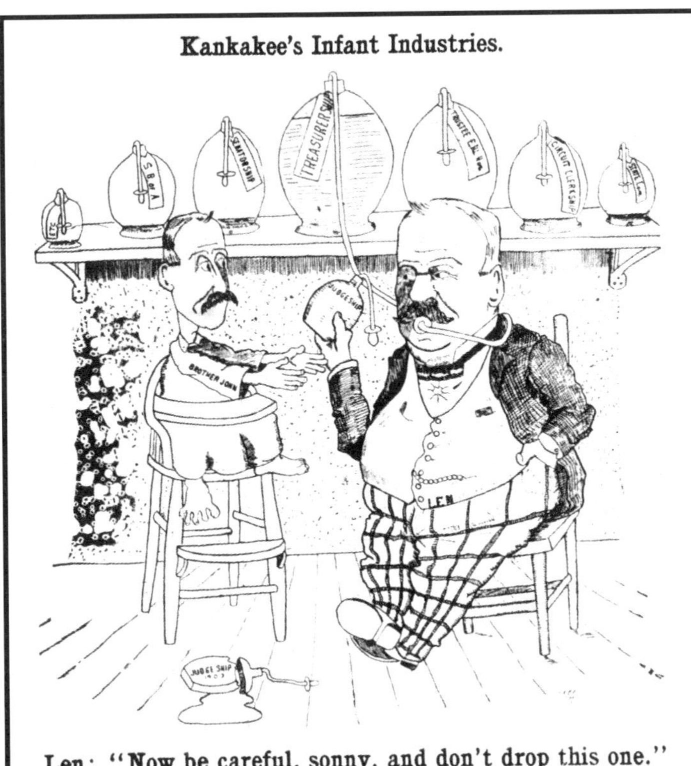

Len: "Now be careful, sonny, and don't drop this one."

Kankakee Daily Gazette, June 26, 1905.

Len Small bottle-feeds political power to brother John.

Kankakee Daily Gazette, June 27, 1905. Ed Curtis and Len Small, and John Small as Len's puppet, controlling banks, post offices, the district fair, the state hospital, the state treasury, newspapers and apple orchards in Southern Illinois. It said John Small's election would give the Machine control of the circuit court.

Chapter 5

Ambition and Manipulation, 1907 - 1919

Len Small kept his hands in local politics, making sure he was in charge of his local power base, even though he was state treasurer. A local newspaper charged in 1907 that Small "packed" grand juries with his own choices so they would not investigate any possible crimes he committed.

This is another example of something happening in little Kankakee in an early era that would be repeated on a bigger scale years later.

"For the past eight years, the Small organization has been in control of the board of supervisors," the March 23 *Evening Democrat* wrote. "There are at least 15 members of the county board who will do the bidding of the Machine and party Boss

"Why should Small want to control the supervisors? It is for control of the grand juries. The supervisors select the grand juries. The grand juries investigate crimes and misdemeanors. For the last eight years, every grand jury sitting in Kankakee has been composed of men under the control and who worked at the dictation of Small.

"In other words, every grand jury is packed."

The newspaper asked, "For what purpose? It can be said frankly and truthfully, to stave off any investigation that might come up. Fear of the law leads men to take desperate chances. Without a packed grand jury, unpleasant indictments might be returned."

The Evening Democrat cited examples of Machine men who chose grand jurors on behalf of Small and Curtis.

Small threw out a phony campaign issue as the March 1907 primary drew near. A principal issue, he said, was "Shall the Sabbath desecration be continued at Gougar's Grove all next summer?"

The grove was a popular picnic area and sometimes people drank liquor there on a Sunday picnic. This was before Prohibition. Liquor was legal. This activity supposedly shocked Small, who a few years later thought it was all right for Chicago gangsters to push bathtub gin illegally (even on Sundays).

The Evening Democrat noted that township elections had nothing to do with picnics at the grove, an area owned by William Gougar, a supervisor not part of the machine. The newspaper said Small's issue was an attempt to hide the real issues, a few of which were: "Shall grafting be continued? Shall Len Small be permitted to keep the thousands of dollars interest on state money? Shall the grand juries of this county continue to protect Ring politicians? Shall men be elected to office who are controlled by Len Small?"

Len Small's newspaper, the *Kankakee Daily Republican,* was always full of irony. No more so than in 1908 when Small decided to back former governor Richard Yates against incumbent Charles Deneen. For months, the newspaper berated Deneen almost every day, hurling terrible names and accusations. The main focus was the local state asylum, since Deneen ultimately was responsible for it as governor. Deneen was accused of being part of patient abuse, strange deaths, immoral conduct by employees and even an "increased death rate" using questionable figures. This was election-year dirty politics. All the accusations that were made when Small was on the asylum board, which the *Daily Republican* denied, now were true with Small off the board and his rival as governor.

The *Daily Republican* quoted Yates as saying that Deneen's administration was "a compound of extravagance, favoritism to special interests and individuals, indifferent to the public good and heartlessness unspeakable to the defenseless wards of the people house in our state institutions." Maybe the newspaper forgot that until recently, Len Small had been chairman of the state hospital board.

A large *Daily Republican* page-one headline even screamed that a 25-cent tip Deneen gave to a railroad porter on a state trip was charged on his expense account. Can you imagine, after what Len Small did, being accused of being a crook by his newspaper? Can you imagine, with what Len Small took, being accused of misusing state funds by giving a poor porter a 25-cent tip?

And can you imagine the July 20, 1908 *Daily Republican* story accusing Deneen of taking $243,000 from Organized Crime gamblers in Chicago, during a previous term as state's attorney? This was eerily similar to real charges in Len Small's future with one exception -- Deneen's office earned a percentage of fines and fees, legally paid by the state, not illegally paid by gangsters.

Deneen was cast as a devil in the *Daily Republican* in 1908 -- until August, when Deneen won the Republican primary over Yates -- and then the *Daily Republican* endorsed Deneen, all the while continuing to denounce him.

In August 1910, the newspaper charged that Deneen had a "slush fund" where he levied assessments from employees in state institutions -- the same thing Len Small did and admitted to when he was on the state hospital board. The source of this charge against Deneen was Frank L. Smith.

And you will never guess one of the biggest issues on which Small and the *Kankakee Daily Republican* attacked Deneen. It was Deneen's "scheme" to build hard roads in Illinois!

A May 11, 1908, *Kankakee Daily Republican* story said that Deneen's "desire to ruin the farming community by the construction of hard roads is enough to condemn him without any other charges being brought."

"In these days of agricultural prosperity, money lenders cannot get a death-grip on the farms unless the governor can get through his hard-roads scheme, which would place a mortgage on every 160 acres on each side of a road that could not be lifted by the average farmer. The governor yet cannot understand why the farmers of this county talked of ropes when his legislative committee came to Champaign some years ago to inaugurate the hard roads boom, but everybody here can," the newspaper wrote.

A July 14 story said hard roads were opposed by farmers and were "wanted only by one or two classes who are moved by a selfish or financial interest." It said township road commissioners could make "good roads" and the state should not make "hard roads." It said "every little mud hole after a rain is the signal for a torrent of abuse...and there is no greater modern miracle than the rapidity with which our roads dry up after a rain." The long article condemned those who wanted paved roads. It cited this math: If 1,000 men built 50 miles of paved roads each year, it would take 2,204 years to build 72 miles in each of the state's 1,660 townships.

Grading roads after a rain and letting them dry hard was what the *Daily Republican* preferred and it referred to this several times as "the Chebanse idea."

Years later, Len Small bragged that he was "the hard roads governor" who "pulled Illinois out of the mud." Apparently, he needed that mud to sling.

A side note: When I got out of college in the 1970s, I took a job as a reporter for *The Daily Times* in Ottawa, a Small newspaper (yes, I worked for Len H. Small, the governor's grandson, who was a very nice man). Ben Samek, a LaSalle County Board member from Peru, told me he did not like what the newspaper printed. "Len Small stole all that money so he could buy newspapers to call **us** crooks!" he angrily said to me in 1977.

Senator Lorimer and Senator Shelby Cullom arranged a political job for Len Small after Small left the state treasurer's office. They used their political pull to have President William Howard Taft appoint Small as assistant U.S. treasurer for the Chicago district. Small's qualifications were questioned and enough suspicion was raised that the president put off the appointment for awhile. Treasury Secretary Franklin MacVeagh in particular did not want Small. Even though Small was a banker and former state treasurer, MacVeagh thought it would be an appointment more of politics than merit. A number of senators also raised objections and the president considered pulling the nomination. But Taft gave into the pressure from the two Illinois senators and Small got the job in June 1910. As a result, Small sided with Taft over Theodore Roosevelt for the Republican presidential nomination in 1912 -- a bitter battle that resulted in a party split and Taft's defeat.

Len Small probably started thinking about becoming governor when he was peddling milk from a wagon in Kankakee as a young man.

It was talked about in 1902 when Small tried to get the nomination for state treasurer. It was mentioned again in 1904 and 1906, when he did win the election as treasurer.

By 1907, Small was a genuine candidate for the Republican nomination for governor in the 1908 election.

The Evening Democrat's April 22, 1907 edition carried the large headline, *Len Small For Governor; This Is Not A Joke.* The story said Small would fight Governor Deneen for the nomination and Edward C. Curtis was his campaign manager.

Small went with a local contingent -- Edward C. Curtis, Charles Robinson, Cornelius R. Miller, Edward Jeffers and Kankakee Mayor Fred Mann -- to a political gathering Springfield in October 1907 to assess and promote Small's candidacy.

Len Small really had no chance. Instead, he and the Machine worked against Deneen in support of the weak former governor, Richard Yates.

Small was to have had a spot on the state ticket if Yates had won the nomination. The *Chicago Examiner* said of the possible slate, "In the proposed arrangement, it is understood that Len Small is to have charge of the war chest. Small was state treasurer when there were no fool laws nor pledges to keep an honest man from getting all he could out of the job, and on the best information he got over $200,000 for his two-year-tenure."

But Deneen was too strong to be unseated, despite any pressure from the Republican machine of William Lorimer.

Lorimer made Tanner and Yates governor but had been thwarted in his attempt to elect Frank O. Lowden governor in 1904, when Charles S. Deneen won the nomination and election. Lorimer was again disappointed when he unsuccessfully tried to use Yates to deny Deneen re-nomination in 1908.

Boss Lorimer was determined that 1912 would be more successful.

Lorimer thought he could unseat Governor Deneen in 1912 as he did Governor Yates in 1904. Len Small was Lorimer's candidate for the Republican nomination against Deneen, representing Lorimer's "Lincoln Protective League." The Republican party in Illinois was terribly split for many years between regular Republicans and the Chicago machine. Lorimer had started the Lincoln Protective League in order to run candidates against regular Republicans and claim the party for himself.

It was in 1912 when Len Small really learned the value of owning his own daily newspaper. Up until then, Small used his *Kankakee Daily Republican* to promote his interests locally, advancing the candidacy of himself and others and savaging his opponents. But in 1912, he used it in a big way to promote his gubernatorial hopes.

Small became a candidate for governor in late 1911. On Jan. 2, 1912, a number of Small's people showed up at the secretary of state's office in Springfield and announced they would camp in line until Feb. 9, the first day that nominating petitions could be filed. They did this so Len Small's name could be first on the primary ballot. Small said being first would mean an additional 40,000 votes because that many people automatically vote for the name at the top.

Secretary of State James Rose was shocked. This was not done in those days. But he let them stay. Among those who showed up Jan. 2 were State Sen. Edward C. Curtis, Kankakee County Sheriff Dan Lee, *Daily Republican* representative H.B. Deselm and a few Lorimer aides. They pledged to have someone representing them in line, in shifts, so they would be first.

To be sure of this, Small filed a lawsuit against the secretary of state to insure that his name would be first on the ballot.

The *Kankakee Daily Republican* called Small "Lorimer's candidate."

The campaign for governor began in earnest on Jan. 2, 1912.

From January 1912 until the primary election on April 9, hardly a day went by without the *Kankakee Daily Republican* printing a story on page one with screaming headlines about Len Small's candidacy.

The barrage began even earlier. The Nov. 3, 1911, edition had these headlines to just one story: *SMALL'S CANDIDACY IS GAINING STRENGTH EVERY DAY ALL OVER THE STATE; From Galena to Cairo and from Danville to Quincy, He is Regarded as the 'Man of the Hour;' KANKAKEEAN IS THE MOST TALKED ABOUT MAN FOR GOVERNORSHIP; In Chicago, as Well as in Almost Every City, Hamlet and Village in the State, Len Small is Deemed the Logical Candidate.*

The headlines got bigger and more effusive every day. Shameless was the only word for it. Orson Welles could have made a movie called *Citizen Small.*

The Feb. 13, 1912, *Kankakee Daily Republican* had boxcar headlines across the top of page one, *LEN SMALL OF KANKAKEE NAMED FOR GOVERNOR.* The entire front page had stories about this, with a huge picture of Small. The reader might think Small had been elected governor, or at least had won the Republican nomination for governor. No, this was a story from the renegade Republican convention in Springfield, orchestrated by Lorimer and Lundin. This was not a "nomination" that placed Small on the Republican ballot; it was a "nomination" by the Lincoln Protective League to be on the ballot for the Republican nomination.

"It would be impossible to depict the scene which greeted the mention of Len Small when Senator Edward C. Curtis of the 18th Congressional District, in a ringing voice that penetrated every corner of the great auditorium, placed the name of Mr. Small before the enthusiastic convention. The scene was like the great

KANKAKEE DAILY REPUBLICAN

VOLUME XXIV — KANKAKEE, ILLINOIS, SATURDAY, MARCH 30, 1912 — NUMBER

'SMALL WILL MAKE THE BEST GOVERNOR ILLINOIS EVER HAD'

—CHAIRMAN JEWELL AT DANVILLE

TRUST PRESS PASSES OUT THE ORDER TO WAGE WARFARE AGAINST LEN. SMALL, THE FARMER CANDIDAT

Chicago Tribune and Its Hirelings Trair Their Batteries on Kankakee Man as the Winner.

VERMILION AND EDGAR COUNTIES SWING INTO THE LEN. SMALL COLUMN; CRUSHING DEFEAT FOR DENEEN

Opera Houses at Danville and Paris Are

DIKE BREAKS; WATER FLOODS COUNTRY; MANY LIVES ARE LOST; GREAT DAMAGE DONE

DENEEN CAMPAIGN IS IN A STATE OF COLLAPSE

Cry Now Is Anything to Beat the Downstate Man Whose Sweeping Victories Are Sure

Readers of the *Kankakee Daily Republican* in 1911 and 1912 would be living in the same fantasy world as Len Small if this was the only newspaper they read. Above is one of the front pages (March 30) from Len Small's first real campaign for governor, in 1912.

demonstration in the Chicago national convention when the name of James G. Blaine was sounded by Senator Thurston, when men went wild and 30 bands played and pandemonium reigned supreme," the story went. "Mr. Curtis undertook to ride the storm, but no man on earth could have mounted the crest of the wave. At the mention of Len Small's name, men were on their feet and cheering like soldiers in the din of battle. Sen. Curtis' voice was lost in the maelstrom that gathered about the Man Of The Hour, and when the next governor of Illinois was borne to the front of the stage, there followed a demonstration which the writer feels utterly unable to describe."

Was the writer Leslie Small, son of the candidate, who became editor a year later? The writer was not too objective.

"It was an enthusiastic burst of patriotism, affection for the man and loyalty to his cause that would have turned the head of any man, but the man from Kankakee stood before the throng, apparently unmoved by the greatest demonstration ever given a private citizen in the history of Illinois politics."

After many comparisons of Len Small to Abraham Lincoln, William Hale Thompson spoke to endorse Small. At that time, Thompson was just a protégé of Lorimer and Lundin and no more than a candidate for the Republican nomination for a seat on the Cook County Board of Review.

Then, The Man Himself spoke. Never known as a great speaker, Small's speech was brief but ironic. He said, "I believe in honest politics, where a man's word is as good as his bond. Oh, for the old time Republican honesty of the days of Lincoln, Grant, Oglesby, Logan and Tanner, when truth, friendship and loyalty counted for something, and when lying, deceit and trickery were condemned, when men, yes, even governors, had red blood in their veins."

With that, "Men grabbed banners and marched up and down the aisles, women occupying the boxes waved their handkerchiefs and the great convention was a scene of the wildest confusion. The mention of Len Small's name was all that was needed to arouse the delegates. He was the one man more than all others in favor with the convention."

Small spoke more, after the crowd calmed down. "We are the most important campaign since the Civil War." He explained that reformers and socialists were the threats. The "trust press" of Chicago also was the enemy, he said.

"Bedlam" broke out when William Lorimer came to the podium. "Whatever one may think of the merits of the principles advocated by Senator Lorimer, the truth was apparent to those who witnessed the scene that Mr. Lorimer is more than a mere popular idol with the 3,000 men who jammed the big Chatterton opera house to the doors. That he is fairly worshiped by those men, that many of them no doubt would give up their lives for him, that they would put every other human consideration in this world to one side for the sake of helping him, that they would endure anything humanly possible to show their remarkable devotion and loyalty to him -- these things were written plainly in the bedlam that shook the big playhouse."

Whew! Maybe Leslie Small didn't write this for the *Kankakee Daily Republican.* Maybe William Lorimer wrote it.

The newspaper declared that Len Small was nominated for governor. But you have to read the pages and pages of newspaper ink closely to see that this was just the convention of the Lincoln League, Lorimer's organization that called itself the "true" Republican party. That is why the convention could so strongly condemn incumbent Republican Governor Charles Deneen.

But being allied with the disgraced Lorimer didn't help Small.

Lorimer had been under investigation for nearly three years, and wouldn't be expelled from the Senate until July, but only Len Small failed to see at this point that Lorimer was a liability. Small's loyalty to the Chicago boss was so strong that they campaigned together frequently in late 1911 and in early 1912.

The *Kankakee Daily Republican* continued to hail Small and denounce Deneen from January through April 9. Small traveled to nearly every county in the state, and every day's edition chronicled the adoring throngs that greeted him. Before the election, the *Daily Republican* said the primary election was "the greatest political battle in the history of Illinois politics."

But the *Kankakee Daily Republican* had a circulation of 4,215 in 1912 and wasn't seen by many people outside of Kankakee County.

Deneen campaigned in Springfield on March 29 and again compared the cost of coal at the Kankakee asylum during Small's reign to the six years after Small was removed. Each year, the bill was $25,000 to $30,000 less than it was when Small was giving the contracts to Lorimer's company. Deneen also reminded voters that the state did not receive one cent of interest on its deposits in Small's two-year term as state treasurer.

"Who received the interest on public funds when Mr. Small was treasurer?" the governor asked. "The records can be raked with a fine tooth comb and the interest referred to cannot be found."

Another candidate for the Republican nomination for governor in 1912 was Cook County State's Attorney John Wayman. He said Small was not a Republican candidate but a Lorimer candidate, and Lorimer was the "real candidate" who was seeking a Small victory as a means to "vindicate" his reputation. He mocked Small's image as the "farmer candidate" by saying, "The only ground that Len Small can claim to be the farmer candidate is on the theory that he is interested in farming out the Republican Party to Lorimer."

Wayman added, "The history of Illinois for the last few years shows that the present disorganized state of the party is due to the mismanagement of its leaders and due to the factional warfare between William Lorimer and Charles Deneen. The party is bigger than both Lorimer and Deneen, and big enough to throw them aside. This is not a fight to see Lorimer triumph over Deneen, nor to see Deneen triumph over Lorimer, but a fight in which the Republican party is going to triumph over both of them."

On April 9, 1912, Small lost the Republican nomination to Deneen by a two-to-one margin. In November, Deneen lost the governor's job to Democrat Edward Dunne.

The crushing defeat in his own party's primary might lead a sensible candidate to conclude that being tied to Lorimer and the Chicago Machine was a liability. But not Len Small. Really, he had no where else to go. Without the backing of the Machine, he would have had no backing at all.

Len Small was connected to the corrupt Thompson even before Thompson became mayor in 1915, and even when Small was a bigger name than Thompson. This was because Small took his orders from Lorimer, and Lorimer controlled both Small and Thompson at that time.

A lesson Len Small learned early was that he needed a newspaper for a mouthpiece if he wanted to get ahead in politics. Medill McCormick had the *Chicago Tribune,* William Randolph Hearst had his newspapers and Joseph Pulitzer had his newspapers, among several examples. Len Small and a few other investors -- including Edward C. Curtis, Cornelius R. Miller and Ed Jeffers -- bought the *Kankakee Daily Times* in 1903 and renamed it the *Kankakee Daily Republican.* The newspaper became Small's mouthpiece, for better or for worse.

A Dec. 26, 1914, story in the *Kankakee Daily Republican* boosted the unknown Thompson's candidacy for mayor. The story was headlined *A Good Thing For Chicago; Mr. Hale Thompson For Mayor.* It started, "The election of Wm. Hale Thompson for Mayor of Chicago would be a great thing for that city. Thompson would make the ideal mayor. He is honest, able, energetic, a popular man and a good fellow. If there is any one thing that Chicago needs more than another, it is the kind of a city government they would get under the administration of a man like Thompson." The article goes on and on in the same vein. How would a rural editor in Kankakee know about an unknown Chicago politician? It was because Thompson was Lorimer's man, so that made him the candidate of Small and his newspaper.

The stories continued in the Kankakee newspaper about William Hale Thompson, how he had many friends in Kankakee, how great he was (*All Chicago Singing Praises Of William Hale Thompson* was the June 16, 1915 headline). It even carried a story about Mary Mackenzie of Kankakee, who was Thompson's teacher 26 years earlier at Metropolitan College in Chicago (where he was a great guy).

Of course, it was natural that the top headline in the *Daily Republican* on May 17, 1915 was *Thompson Camp Backs Len Small For Governorship.* The "camp" included Lorimer and Lundin. It would be another five years before they succeeded.

A story reported that on May 20, 1915, Thompson, along with "his chief political advisor" Fred Lundin, spent most of the day conferring with Small.

Thompson had been in office only a few months when the front page of the July 22, 1915 *Kankakee Daily Republican* proclaimed in big headlines, *Thompson's Eye On The Presidency -- Chicago Mayor Quizzed On Report of G.O.P. Candidacy, Says Good Chance -- 'He's A Big Man' -- Political Adviser Fred Lundin Says Thompson Is Big Enough Man To Fill The Job.*

The story was datelined from San Diego, Calif., where the same newspaper story had Thompson announcing his candidacy, then demurring that he was not a candidate, then telling the reporter, "Ask Lundin."

This paragraph was interesting: "The report is supposed to have emanated from a complimentary phrase used Monday night by a speaker who introduced Mayor Thompson before the Illinois Society of Los Angeles as 'a man big enough to fill the Presidency and one who would soon.'"

What do you want to bet that the "speaker" was Len Small, taking turns in promoting each other's "groundswell" support for higher office?

At the Kankakee fair's Republican Day on Sept. 9, 1915, Small's featured celebrity guests were Chicago's new mayor, Big Bill Thompson, House Speaker Joseph Cannon, Frank L. Smith, Fred Lundin and a number of lesser politicians. Kankakee's fairs for years featured Thompson as its honored guest. Thompson's high point was at the 1920 fair, when he spoke in favor of Small's bid for governor.

In a *Daily Republican* story about a political rally in Watseka in March 1916, Small's "unbiased" reporter described Thompson as "the biggest and best mayor Chicago ever had."

Thompson spoke to a large crowd at the Majestic Theatre in Kankakee on Aug. 12, 1918. The *Daily Republican* described the crowd as large and wildly enthusiastic. Thompson was running as a candidate for the Republican nomination for U.S. Senate. A brass band met Thompson at the Illinois Central station and paraded him to the Schuyler Hotel and to the theatre. He was introduced by the chairman of the event, Len Small.

Also speaking was Frank Ayers, a Chicago lawyer. Ayers assailed multimillionaires and corporations who owned newspapers and who controlled businesses and the government for their own profit. No, he wasn't talking about Len Small, he meant Medill McCormick, an owner of the *Chicago Tribune.* McCormick was Thompson's opponent and he went on to defeat Thompson by a wide margin.

"The *Chicago Tribune* has been fighting Len Small because Len Small is an honest man," Thompson told the Kankakee audience that night.

Small maneuvered his way to become chairman of the Illinois Agricultural Board in 1915 to tighten his hold on political ties to farm groups.

Small looked to 1916 to again run for governor. A front page headline in the May 17, 1915 *Kankakee Daily Republican* was *THOMPSON CAMP BACKS LEN SMALL FOR GOVERNORSHIP.* Working hand in hand, the July 22, 1915 Kankakee newspaper headlined a story, *THOMPSON'S EYE ON THE PRESIDENCY,* even though Thompson had been mayor of Chicago for only a few months at that time.

But Lorimer and Lundin called the shots, and Len Small was not their choice for governor in 1916.

Instead, Small was the machine candidate for state treasurer in 1916 and he was elected. That was the year Lorimer finally got his man, Frank O. Lowden, nominated and elected governor of Illinois.

Lowden was a very wealthy man. He was a successful farmer and lawyer before he married the daughter of George M. Pullman, the railroad sleeping car tycoon. Surprisingly for a Lorimer candidate, Lowden proved to be a very good governor. He pushed through the Civil Administrative Code of 1917, which radically reorganized state government. His civil service reforms brought honesty and public confidence back to state government. His list of accomplishments as governor is very impressive.

Lowden was the governor who saw that bonds were issued to pay for his program of paved roads -- a program that Len Small continued, and for which Small would take full credit.

Lowden was considered a candidate for the presidency in 1920. He might have won the presidential nomination. But the honest Lowden refused to turn over state patronage to Fred Lundin. Thompson and the Chicago machine's work against him in the Illinois presidential primary was one of several factors that scuttled Lowden's prospects. Still, Lowden was one of three candidates (along with Leonard Wood and Hiram Johnson) in a deadlocked convention before leaders in the party's "smoke-filled room" settled for the unimpressive Warren G. Harding.

Many observers believe that if Lowden had played ball with the Thompson machine, he may have been elected president of the United States in 1920.

At the 1924 Republican national convention, Lowden was courted for the vice presidential nomination and he refused it. It was rumored that he did not want to have to endorse Len Small for governor.

When Len Small was state treasurer in his first term from 1905 to 1907, he kept the interest on state deposits. This amounted to about $200,000.

This was theft -- keeping interest money that was earned from deposits that didn't belong to him -- but Small argued a loophole in the law to his advantage.

The statute under embezzlement said it was illegal for a public official to "use, by way of investment or loan for his own use, except as authorized by law, with or without interest, any portion of the money, bonds, mortgages, coupons, bank bills, notes, warrants, orders or other funds or securities entrusted to him for safe-keeping or disbursement."

Small didn't deny he kept the interest on state deposits. He argued he was entitled to it, above his handsome salary as treasurer, because the statute was a "negative law" and so was "inoperative." He kept the money, just as he had done with the interest on state hospital deposits.

He said several previous treasurers had done the same. He was right.

There were no calls for a real investigation, and the Republican state administration in Springfield was not interested in prosecuting a man who had done so much for their own campaign coffers.

John Smulski followed Small as treasurer in 1907 and he campaigned on the promise of returning interest funds to the state. It was front page headlines in Kankakee's *Evening Democrat* when he kept his promise. "Len Small, our own distinguished citizen, didn't turn over any interest money," *The Evening Democrat* story said. "No, he pocketed the entire amount and instead of returning it to the state, has purchased high-priced automobiles, farms, banks and other things too numerous to mention."

Smulski turned over interest money to the state "because he was honest enough to know that the money did not belong to him and he had no right to it." *The Evening Democrat* continued. "Len Small stuck $200,000 down into his jeans because he thought he could not be caught and forced to cough up.

"That's the difference between the two men. Both are professing Christians. Smulski didn't have the announcement of his conversion broadcast through the public press," a reference to a very public altar call Len Small made that year when evangelist Billy Sunday put on a huge tent revival in Kankakee.

"Still, this little mollycoddle, who has been sending bad odors up from Kankakee because of his political intrigues and the corruption instituted by his machine, wants to be governor of Illinois."

Legislators changed the law in 1908 because of Small's chicanery. The new law specifically read:

"The state treasurer shall deposit all moneys received by him on account of the state within five days after receiving same, in such banks in the cities in the state as in the opinion of the treasurer are secure and which shall pay the highest rate of interest to the state for such deposits. The money so deposited shall be placed to the account of the state treasurer."

It meant interest money earned on state deposits belonged to the state.

As Small took office as state treasurer in January 1917, the first thing he did was to declare that "Illinois is broke." Small claimed that, for the first time in Illinois history, the state could not meet its January payroll to pay state employees. He blamed the Cook County treasurer, who he said was withholding money from the state in order to earn interest for the county.

Small's tenure was marked with criticism that the treasurer was quick to put money in the bank but slow to pay it out. The state legislature passed a law that required local taxing bodies to send their state money every month. This way, the money earned interest for the state, not the local counties and schools. On the other hand, companies doing business with the state had to wait months to be paid. This, again, was to keep money in the state treasury to earn more money for the state.

Or, more accurately, to earn more money for Len Small and Edward Curtis.

After Small left the treasurer's office in January 1919, he continued on the state payroll in a fairly well-paying position as an assistant treasurer (examiner of securities). The job paid $6,000 a year, which was big money in those days (perhaps twice the average annual income for ordinary Americans). This job led Small to keep his hands on state money, as we will see later in this book.

Small kept that job until July 1, 1920, when he became a candidate for governor.

"If there has been a time during the last 20 years that Small hasn't been getting public money for doing nothing, the records fail to disclose it," the *Kankakee Daily News* said in August 1920. "Building up an immense fortune in money taken from the taxpayers has been his specialty. Starting in politics, with no other means of support, he has accumulated great wealth. Small has often said 'Politics is my business' and he has made his business pay. His capacity and his selfishness are so well known that no one expects him to do anything which entails personal work or the spending of a dollar -- except in politics."

Small's election judge was arrested in the April 1919 local election. John Savage was the judge in the Fourth Precinct, known for years for questionable election practices. When Savage refused to turn over the ballots to the town clerk, Sheriff William Riley arrested him. Three of the four Small candidates for the county board lost.

Chapter 6

The Campaign for Governor, 1920

The trouble that came to Len Small after he became governor, concerning his handling of money as state treasurer, was not a surprise. The public knew about the allegations for months before the 1920 election.

But there was more to this than it was. It was a scandal that should have been, but it wasn't.

When Small left the treasurer's office in January 1919, he kept a considerable amount of interest money. As he prepared his run for the Republican nomination for governor in 1920, he suddenly remembered this money -- and on April 23, he paid the state $143,585 in interest that he "forgot" he had been holding as state treasurer for a year and a half after leaving office.

He tried to keep it quiet. The news didn't come out until August.

When the story did come out, the public was presented with some interesting information. Here is how it was laid out.

Small became treasurer on Jan. 8, 1917. He did not make a report on interest earnings for the next 21 months, not until Sept. 30, 1918, when he deposited $306,424 in interest. When he left office on Jan. 13, 1919, he had made no other report.

The next interest report was on April 23, 1920, when he deposited $143,585. He said this was for the period of Oct. 1, 1918, to Jan. 13, 1919.

Holding this money for 15 months earned Small another $11,000 to $14,000 in interest on the interest, for himself. He did not turn this interest on the interest over to the state.

The state law said "the state treasurer shall deposit all money received by him on account of the state within five days after receiving the same in such banks." This was part of the law passed after Small's first term as treasurer ended in 1907, to prevent anyone else from doing what Small had done. His successor in 1919, Fred Sterling, made monthly deposits. Sterling turned in $604,735 in his first 16 months, compared to $450,010 by Small in two (actually three) years.

In the middle of the 1920 campaign, a side show act played out in the circus that was Len Small's life.

Len Small received a "Black Hand" letter on June 27 threatening death to him and his family unless he paid $40,000. The "Black Hand" was a shadow group of Sicilians who operated an extortion racket in this manner. It was small time and it nearly was over by the early 1920s when the Mafia became the more organized, more profitable and preferred operation of Sicilians.

The letter was full of misspellings and poor grammar, so much so that it may have been intentional to make authorities believe it was written by ignorant immigrants. It turned out that the extortionists were not Sicilian. And they were not too smart. Their crude letter might really have been an indication of their ignorance.

William Allers, a farmer from the Manteno area, came into Small's office at the First Trust & Savings Bank in Kankakee on June 29 and asked Small if he had received a Black Hand letter. Small was surprised. He had, and he dismissed it as a crank letter from a local asylum patient. Small said he had gotten another Black Hand letter eight years earlier and his father had received one several years before that. Small asked Allers what he knew about it.

Allers said one of his farm hands, Byron Caudell, had written it. Allers saw the letter on a dresser at his farm and heard Caudell talking on the telephone to Neucomb Palmer about sending it to Len Small. Caudell had quit his job and left the farm on the day before sending the letter.

Small and his son Leslie went to Chicago to see Mayor Thompson to get experienced police detectives to track down Caudell and Palmer.

The Chicago and Kankakee police didn't need to work too hard. They staked out the road near Momence where the extortionists told Small to drop the money. Since Caudell had stolen Allers' car, the vehicle and Caudell were tracked down in Spring Valley on July 4. Police picked up Palmer at his house.

Palmer and Caudell were taken back to the Kankakee County jail. They were indicted on Oct. 8. Caudell livened things up by escaping from his confinement at the Kankakee State Hospital on Oct. 11, removing an iron bar from his window and running away, barefoot and in pajamas. He was caught the next day in a cornfield near Cabery by farmers Walter Wright, Louis Farley and Charlie Falter.

Caudell went to court and pleaded guilty to stealing the car and was sentenced to 1-to-20 years in the penitentiary. Palmer was not charged.

Col. John Clinnin (a genuine colonel who commanded men in battle during World War I) spoke at a large anti-Small political rally at the Majestic Theatre in Kankakee on Sept. 8. A number of speakers were featured at this rally.

Clinnin called Fred Lundin "the real head of the organization" and Thompson "the smoke screen." Clinnin said, "A band of ruthless politicians under the leadership of a man of mystery in the person of Fred Lundin of Chicago have undertaken to capture the executive, legislative and judicial branches of our government. They seek to control the public offices and the Republican party of the state for the purpose of perfecting a state-wide Tammany."

More bad news for the candidate came out the next day when Ed Schumaker, a labor union leader in Kankakee, branded Small as "unfriendly to labor." Schumaker said 90 per cent of Kankakee's union members opposed Small, and that his newspaper supported anti-labor candidates. Small strongly denied it.

The battle for the Republican nomination for governor in 1920 wasn't just between two rival candidates of the same party seeking a nomination. Once more, it was a war between two factions seeking control of the party. The battle was between the Thompson-Lorimer-Lundin machine, with Len Small as its candidate, and the regular Republicans represented by Lowden, with Lt. Gov. John Oglesby as its candidate.

Oglesby, like Yates, was the son of a Civil War-era governor of Illinois.

The first face-off came in May 1920 when the state central committee met in Springfield and the machine succeeded in making Frank L. Smith chairman. Thompson savored his victory over Lowden, which virtually left the outgoing governor with very little political power in the state.

Both Smith and Small wanted the nomination for governor, the lifelong dream of both men. The machine picked Small for governor and Smith for the U.S. Senate.

Len Small was the machine's candidate because he was "always obedient, always subservient, always ready to perform willingly and capably for Poor Swede and Big Bill," according to Lloyd Wendt and Herman Kogan's *Big Bill Of Chicago.*

The *Daily Republican* was more subdued in pushing Small's nomination in 1920 than it had been in 1912. The first mention in the newspaper was on March 25. It was the middle of June when the newspaper began to ramp up toward the Sept. 15 primary, again with the daily stories of the many politicians and newspapers who endorsed his candidacy and who said so many nice things about him. This time, the Kankakee newspaper did not turn into The Daily Len Small Campaign Sheet. It didn't have to -- 1920 was going to be a Republican year, and the party's choice was in the hands of the machine, not the voters.

One characteristic of Small's campaign was that he needed a villain to fight. It wasn't enough for him to campaign on his record and his promises. He needed an enemy to vilify and to show the voters his virtue in opposing such a villain.

Even though Governor Frank Lowden was not a candidate, he was made a target. Small and Thompson portrayed Lowden as the "boss" trying to get his own man Oglesby elected governor. That was more hypocrisy from Small -- Lowden endorsed Oglesby primarily to counter the Chicago machine, but it was Thompson, Lorimer and Small who were the political bosses.

Lowden said the extraordinary circumstance that the Chicago machine might put Boss Small in the governor's office led him to do something he did not want to do -- endorse his own slate. "It is not one of persons but of principles," Lowden said. "It is the issue between free and representative government, responsible to the people, and a Tammanyized government controlled by a boss interested only in the aggrandizement of the Machine. It is the issue between this Tammany government, which has bankrupted the treasury of the city of Chicago, which is in default to the city's creditors...and which has piled up the city's debt by millions upon millions. It is the issue between this tax-eating, tribute-levying Thompson-Tammany rule and a frugal, efficient, economical, patriotic government administering the affairs of the state."

Lowden continued, "In Chicago, a machine has sought to fasten a stranglehold on the city by paying enormous fees to favorites, according undue privileges to heelers, awarding contracts at fat prices to henchmen, and by importing into the Republican primaries thousands of Democratic floaters who are temporarily Republicans for revenue only, this Tammany organization now seeks to seize the government of the state, its legislature and its courts."

Lowden joined with other state Republicans who did not want their party in the control of men who he called "a menace to the future of Illinois...and now holds the business, political and educational activities of Chicago by the throat."

In July, the downstate *Lacon Home Journal* said Small was "pretty near the last man in the state that the *Journal* would support for the governorship. His record doesn't suit us at all, and it is hoped that a crimp will be put into his aspirations that will shelve him politically for all time to come."

Big Bill Thompson toured the state with Small, campaigning as if Big Bill himself was the candidate. It was like Big Bill to always be the center of attention, even at a Len Small rally. Thompson and Small condemned Lowden in the strongest terms at every stop. It might seem an unwise strategy to attack Lowden, a very popular governor, rather than running against Oglesby. And it also might seem an unwise strategy for Small to remain so closely tied to the boss politics of Thompson and the disgraced Lorimer. It almost did not work.

The primary election was Sept. 15. But the results were disputed, with charges that the election was stolen in Chicago.

Outside of Cook County, Oglesby won 84 counties while Small won 16. Oglesby had an 86,000-vote lead outside of Cook County. When the Machine found out how many votes it needed in Cook County, it found them. Small was declared the winner.

Oglesby filed suit, asking the court to declare 15,000 votes in 300 Chicago precincts invalid. These precincts went heavily for Small, and Oglesby charged fraud. Oglesby's lawyers also asked for a canvass of the entire vote in Chicago.

Examples given by Oglesby's people are the classic Chicago voting patterns that have gone on for more than a century -- people voting more than once, ghost voters, people brought in and allowed to vote illegally. Big Bill's Machine pulled out all the stops for Len Small. Every Chicago politician today knows the plan.

Even with the Machine's vote fraud, Small led by only 5,430 votes. Nullifying the votes in the disputed precincts would give the nomination to Oglesby.

Shelby Singleton, secretary of the Citizens Association, said the voter fraud needed a grand jury investigation. "In different precincts which it has investigated, it has found evidence of almost every conceivable violation of the laws enacted to guard the integrity of the ballot. Proof has been found of illegal registration, as many as 70 people being illegally registered from one shady hotel. The names of persons thus unlawfully registered have been voted by gangs of gunmen who drove from one polling place to another. Wholesale thefts of ballots have been perpetrated by judges and clerks of election."

Facing the possibility that the State Board of Elections or the courts would rule against him, Small took out petitions on Oct. 1 to have himself listed on the ballot as an independent candidate.

Small publicly denied this was happening, claiming he was a loyal Republican who would support the party's nominee. But Thompson made sure all of the Machine's candidates took out petitions in case they were disqualified for the Republican ballot.

Lawyers for both sides presented their cases to the Chicago Board of Elections in a hearing that turned out to be a farce, as the chairman gaveled Oglesby's lawyers into silence again and again. The Chicago Board of Elections declared Small the winner without waiting for the results of the court hearing.

The judge in the court case was James T. Burns, an Irish-born man whose family moved to Kankakee when he was a child. Burns had been the subject of one of Len Small's vicious political attacks several years before when he dared to enter local politics. Burns was a genuine war hero with service in the Spanish-American War and World War I. He was a judge in Kankakee County and sometimes worked in Cook County courts.

At the time, Judge Burns was the Democrat candidate for attorney general against Edward Brundage.

Small made an official statement on the controversy: "I have been honestly nominated by the Republicans of Illinois as their candidate for governor, but in spite of this, a desperate attempt is being made by the *Chicago Tribune* and the *Chicago Daily News* to nullify the will of the majority of Republicans of Illinois by cheating me out of the nomination, which I have fairly won."

The *Chicago Tribune* editorialized: "Confronted by legal action to investigate charges of fraud in the recent primary election and eliminate fraudulent votes from the returns, Len Small asserts there is a conspiracy on foot to steal the nomination from him. If Mr. Small believes there were no serious and even decisive frauds in the primary, which gave him a majority in Chicago, why should he brand the effort to reveal the truth as a conspiracy against him? If there were no frauds, an investigation or court action can throw out no votes and will leave Mr. Small the nomination without question."

Judge Burns ruled against Oglesby on Oct. 6, saying his lawyers had not shown sufficient evidence to disenfranchise all those voters. But Burns said his primary reason was that a county judge didn't have jurisdiction over a board of election commissioners.

The State Board of Elections then declared Len Small the winner of the nomination, barely a month before the election. The total was 377,005 for Small and 369,108 for Oglesby.

Small acted like the slim 7,902 margin was a landslide. He threw a big party and rally at the Majestic Theatre in Kankakee on Oct. 11. Congressman William B. McKinley, who had beaten Frank L. Smith for the nomination for senator, was there. So was Secretary of State Louis Emmerson, Congressman (and former governor) Richard Yates, State Treasurer Fred Sterling and a lot of other big shots. But it was Len Small's town and Len Small's night.

In announcing his candidacy, Small listed a few of the principles of his campaign, which really were Thompson-Lorimer principles. He believed the United States should not join the proposed League of Nations and should sever all ties to the foreign entanglements that brought us into World War I. He favored cooperatives, which he said gave "better prices for producers and consumers by eliminating combines, speculators and profiteers." He favored a program to build hard roads across the state, a program that already was well underway. He favored a strong

Navy and a bonus to veterans but opposed the draft. He favored reforming the tax system to exempt those with incomes below $5,000 from paying income tax.

And he also promised to eliminate the Public Utilities Commission.

The Public Utilities Commission was created by the legislature in 1913 to regulate utility rates. No one wanted this commission abolished -- except Mayor Thompson and his candidate for governor, Len Small.

Small's general election opponent was a former U.S. senator, Col. James Hamilton Lewis.

Lewis came to Small's hometown of Kankakee on Oct. 14 and told a crowd that Small's election would be "a stain on the state and an insult to the honor of Illinois. Mayor Thompson created Mr. Small as a candidate for the mayor's personal political uses by methods at the polls that destroys states and makes anarchists of honest citizens. You are asked to deliver the state of Illinois to a man who is the candidate of the mayor of Chicago."

Lewis came to Kankakee on the same train that brought Len Small home. Small extended his hand to the former senator and greeted him warmly. Lewis took Small's hand and exchanged greetings in an icy manner. As Small walked on through the car, Lewis said to a companion, "I cannot enthuse over meeting a man whose nomination I consider one of the greatest infamies ever placed upon the people of Illinois."

Lewis proved to be a tough campaigner who did not mince words. In downstate Paris on Oct. 16, Lewis said, "Our state is becoming known as the cesspool of American politics. This condition is getting such that missionaries should be brought into Illinois to rescue it from heathenism."

He called Thompson "a new Napoleon" who was running Small as his puppet since he never could be elected statewide himself.

"If I am elected," Lewis told the crowd, "the nefarious practice of making millionaires of state treasurers through their loaning state funds privately will be stopped."

The issue of Small's illegal handling of state money as treasurer was brought up by another opponent, John Maynard Harlan, the independent candidate for governor.

Harlan said on Oct. 17 that Small owed the state another $350,000 -- in addition to the "late" interest payment of $143,585 Small made in April. Harlan used figures based on what Small turned in as treasurer, compared with what Sterling turned in, taking average interest rates into account. As things turned out in the lawsuit the attorney general filed against Small the following year, Harlan grossly underestimated what Small still owed the state.

Small made his reply to Harlan's statements in an Oct. 20 rally in Mt. Vernon. He called Harlan a liar and said he never withheld a single penny as treasurer. Small said he was the best state treasurer Illinois ever had, and said Harlan was "a paid assistant to the Democrat candidate, who is again indulging in his characteristic malicious lying and libelous attacks."

"Harlan is evidently doing his best to earn the attorney fees that, it is reported, are being paid him by great combinations of greed and wealth that are profiteering off of the people and which know my election as governor will interfere with their plans to further fatten their purses," Small said.

"He knows that as treasurer of the state of Illinois, I made the best record that has ever been made by any state treasurer," Small said. "Following a Democratic state administration of four years, I took over the treasury when it was practically empty, with many hundreds of thousands of dollars in unpaid bills. I turned over to the treasury in interest in funds during my two years term the sum of $450,000, which was more than double the amount ever paid over by any treasurer before that time.

"The insinuation that I have failed to account for any public funds or that I have kept any of the interest money belonging to the state of Illinois is a lie. Every dollar of interest collected on state funds was carried on deposit in banks the same as other state funds in the name and to the credit of the state treasurer and never to my personal credit."

Small threw a little more mud at Lewis in a speech on Oct. 31 as the campaign entered its final days. "The one regrettable feature that I deplore is that my Democratic opponent has seen fit to degrade himself by appeals to religious and race prejudice instead of discussing frankly the things he stands for as governmental policy. This attempt to fan the fires of religious bigotry and of race hatred constitutes a most dangerous assault on American institutions."

Small was no more specific than this. There is no evidence in Lewis' career or in any speech in this campaign that Lewis made such appeals.

Lewis was a skilled orator and he got a laugh from the crowd in Carlinville when he said of Mayor Thompson, "I have often thought it was appropriate that he should go to a town where there is an insane asylum to get his political servant."

Lewis' reputation in history is that of an honest man. When there was talk of removing Small from office on the issue of ineligibility in 1921, Lewis was asked if he would accept the office since he came in second in the voting. Lewis said no, he did not receive the majority of votes and did not want the job on a technicality.

The Kankakee Daily News had a few things to say about Small's candidacy. An editorial in the Aug. 31 edition took a swipe at Lorimer, Thompson, Lundin and Small. It said Small was "affiliated with the worst element in the Republican party. Just as he made a bosom friend of one of the very few men who was ever convicted on charges of political bribery, he makes a friend of the man who hung up the most notorious and unenviable war record of any citizen in the United States during 1917 and 1918. And as governor of Illinois, he would be owned body and soul by the Chicago gang of crooks and would be a mere mouthpiece at Springfield for Thompson and Lundin."

A Sept. 1 editorial said Small "poses as a reform candidate on a platform written by the most crooked gang of politicians Chicago has ever seen -- a platform repudiated by the state convention -- and whose supporters find themselves outside the regular party ranks."

The next day, an editorial began, "Having traveled the rounds of all public offices that could be made financially profitable to himself, Len Small now desires to become governor of Illinois. Beyond question, he sees an opportunity to further enrich himself through the spending of $200,000,000 in Cook County and Illinois during the next four years. Small is a blooming perennial as an office seeker. Twenty years he has spent in public office, and during all that time has been of benefit only to himself. He has never engaged in a constructive work, and the meaning of statesmanship is unknown to him. A single object from which he has never deviated is that of lining his pockets with gold. His rapacity and greed have always marked his work as a politician. He has never denied taking interest money which belonged to the state."

Tax dodgers, profiteers, greedy public utilities and everyone else who conspired to cheat the public were avowed enemies of Len Small.

But Small's honesty in his own tax matters became an issue in 1920. Small swore to the county assessor that he owned three Holstein cattle, valued at $90.

"When this schedule was made public, the people of Kankakee were amazed," the *Chicago Daily News* reported in August. "For years, they have watched a splendid herd of about 50 Holsteins driven to pasture and pointed to them with pride as being 'Len Small's registered herd, one of the finest in the land.' These Holsteins still are going to pasture, and now the hunt is on to discover the owner, as no one appears to pay taxes on them. The value of the cattle supposed to belonging to Small is estimated at $20,000. Mr. Small is considered by his neighbors to be a millionaire, and when it was shown by his sworn schedule that he has only $1,000 in the bank and that the value of all his personal property is only $4,300 including three automobiles, valuable household furniture, etc., Kankakee expressed its astonishment."

The newspaper said Small's personal property for taxable purposes was $8,970 -- not the $4,485 that Small claimed. It cited a number of questionable tax figures claimed by Small's newspaper, his brother and his son.

The *Chicago Daily News* also said assessments on the Smalls' property were not entered in the regular book of records in the Kankakee courthouse; it was in an addendum to the book, and was found only after a lengthy search by reporters. The newspaper said Small's assessment was kept hidden from the public record and had been changed after the reporters' inquiry.

The *Daily News* asked, "If Len Small pays taxes on only $4,485 worth of property, who are 'the rich tax-dodgers?'"

The question could be asked in another light. If Len Small could steal a million dollars of state money and not pay income tax on it, then just who did he consider a rich tax dodger?

Len Small, Mayor Thompson and their political organization frequently condemned socialism, an especially unpopular philosophy in America in this post-war European and Russian Bolshevik era.

But hypocrisy has always been the hallmark of socialists and it was the hallmark of the men behind the Lincoln Protective League. The organization was founded by Thompson, Lorimer, Lundin and Small to promote American values. A condemnation of socialism was one of its tenets. Socialists were against the principles of Abraham Lincoln, as espoused by the Lincoln League.

But how socialist were the views the Lincoln League?

One of Len Small's main issues in 1920 was on taxes: "Len Small demands a more even distribution of the burden of taxation, and punishment of the rich tax-dodgers who attempt to evade paying their just share of the expense of government."

This sounds high minded but has a ring of the "hate the rich and successful" hypocritical philosophy of the socialists, and just enough of their demagoguery to make it sound good.

Small's campaign promise to abolish the Public Utilities Commission, to eliminate the state regulation of utilities, was part of Small's plan to "fight millionaires" and "greedy corporations" who cheated the public with high rates.

Edward D. Shurtleff was one of the candidates for the Republican nomination for governor in 1920. He came right out and assailed Thompson and Small for what he called a socialist platform. Shurtleff said their plan to confiscate war profits was a socialistic view, especially their view that normal post-war appreciation of farmland and other business could be declared as profiteering. He also called Thompson unpatriotic.

The *Hoopston Herald* in July 1920 said the issue in the governor's race was "Thompsonism and socialism against 100 per cent downstate Americanism." It added, "Len Small should get the vote of all that class who regret the victory of the allies over Teutonic barbarism and invasion of defenseless little nations. The issue is clearly designed, whether the seeds of socialism or those of Americanism, the Third International of Moscow or the Constitution of the United States will germinate on this soil."

Oglesby told a crowd in Monmouth on Aug. 24 that Len Small and Frank L. Smith were campaigning as socialists in Chicago and as conservatives downstate.

Small answered his critics in an Aug. 8 speech in Elgin, railing again against the newspapers and the public utility companies. "This is not a campaign, as the public utilities candidates claim, of our platform being socialistic or of Mayor Thompson trying to get control of the state of Illinois, but it is a campaign for the rights of the people on the one hand, and the greed of organized wealth that is robbing the people on the other hand."

His speech went on to promise to abolish the Public Utilities Commission and added, "I am in favor of cooperative buying and selling, which will insure to the producer a fair price for his labor and commodities and save to the consumer the extortionate profits of corrupt combines, speculators and profiteers."

In his 1924 platform, Small repeated many of these themes. He included an "excess profits tax" for people who succeeded too well and a confiscatory inheritance tax. He opposed injunctions in labor disputes and favored protective tariffs.

It did not sound like conservative Republican policy.

Like all socialists, they said one thing and did another.

As the 1920 campaign for governor got underway, Mayor Thompson assailed Governor Lowden in the strongest terms at every opportunity.

Wasn't Small the Republican nominee for governor, and wasn't Lowden the incumbent Republican governor? Wasn't the Democrat nominee James Hamilton Lewis? Yes to all those questions. Were Thompson and Lowden on the ballot? No, they were not.

That was typical of this strange campaign. Even though Small was the candidate, Thompson had as big a presence as the candidate.

"Whenever Len Small and Big Bill shared a platform, the candidate, a sad-faced man in a rumpled suit, always made a short, dull speech, ending 'I'm sorry to be taking up your time, for I know you want to hear the greatest mayor Chicago ever had, the greatest man in the United States,'" Wendt and Kogan wrote.

One of the main themes Thompson used was that Lowden did not keep a promise to reform the Public Utilities Commission and give "home rule" to Chicago over its utilities. In other words, Thompson expected Lowden to give Chicago free reign in setting utility rates. It was why Thompson supported Lowden four years earlier. When Lowden didn't do it, and when Lowden endorsed his own candidate over Thompson's puppet, Thompson went on the attack.

"Had you taken your ignoble leave of public life without attempting to perpetuate the misgovernment and pernicious policies which have placed such stupendous burdens upon our people of Chicago, as well as of the state at large, I would have been the last person to say or do anything to prevent our people from forgetting you as soon as possible or to keep the foul blot placed by you upon the escutcheon of Illinois from fading away in the light of a better day," Thompson wrote in an open letter to Lowden in August. But, he added, Lowden forgot his campaign promises to free Chicago from the authority of the Public Utilities Commission and instead allied himself with the *Chicago Tribune* and *Chicago Daily News*.

Thompson appeared at the Kankakee fair in August 1920 to large crowds and he toured the state for Small. The campaign rhetoric in the primary campaign sometimes became shrill and desperate.

Small accused Governor Lowden and Lt. Gov. Oglesby of trying to "wreck" the Republican party by opposing his candidacy. It was the regular Republicans against the Lincoln League Republicans, and it was the Machine that thought it had the legitimate right. The Machine was incensed that Oglesby would ask for a recount in the Sept. 15 primary in which he lost to Small by a narrow margin. A frantic Small screamed that Lowden was trying to "steal" the nomination away from him.

It isn't unusual for politicians to act shocked at opponents' opinions or behavior of which they themselves are guilty. In August 1920, Len Small's newspaper printed a story about a rumor of a "slush fund of millions of dollars from the public utility interests" to be used by Lowden on behalf of Oglesby to defeat Small. And, of course, Mayor Thompson felt obligated to comment on this phony story. Thompson said money from rate increases were going to a campaign fund to defeat Small, the people's champion who would fight the utility companies.

Thompson and Small were not shy in expressing their views. This was from an Aug. 31, 1920 story in the *Kankakee Daily Republican* about a Thompson speech in Bloomington: "Characterizing the Lowden-Oglesby Public Utilities ticket as a 'privilege-seeking crowd supported by the traction barons and criminal profiteers,' Mayor Thompson spoke for the candidacy of the Small-Smith ticket last night in Bloomington." Among those in the Lowden-Public Utilities profiteering crowd, he added, were the *Chicago Tribune* and *Chicago Daily News.* And again, Thompson compared himself, Small and Smith to Abraham Lincoln.

Not surprisingly, the *Chicago Tribune* would not endorse Len Small. The strongly partisan Republican newspaper endorsed Democrat James Hamilton Lewis. It said Small was a "Thompson-Tammany Republican" which is one of "individual rather than party principles." The newspaper said it "believes this organization has exploited and looted the city of Chicago for purely selfish ends. It believes this organization is eager to control the state administration in order that it may extend its field of exploitation."

In an Oct. 15, 1920, story, the *New York Times* wrote that Small's candidacy "has impaired the true Republican principles of the state. By doing so, it has injected an element into the state election which stains the state Republican ticket."

It was a big Republican year in 1920. The real battle had been for the Republican nomination, which was tantamount to winning the election. Small was elected in November, beating Democrat James Hamilton Lewis by 512,000 votes, or 60 to 34 percent in a field of ten candidates. Still, Small ran 200,000 votes behind the president in Chicago. There were reports of vote fraud in Chicago, with as many as 60,000 votes stolen in Chicago.

Chapter 7

Len Small Becomes Governor

"Now followed an administration which for waste, mismanagement, inefficiency, intrigue, manipulation and downright disregard of the public interest has few parallels in the history of the United States." Author Carroll H. Wooddy, University of Chicago, 1931.

Governor Small started his administration with the same confrontation and controversy that marked his entire career. The programs he pushed got a lot of opposition, as did the manner in which he pushed them.

And six months after he was inaugurated, the governor was indicted on charges that he embezzled more than a million dollars while he was state treasurer. That story is told in chapter 9. This chapter deals with other events in his first few years as governor.

Governor Small did not waste much time in trying to put across the wishes of the Chicago Machine, as ruled by Thompson, Lundin, Lorimer and himself.

Three of the governor's top priorities were to dismantle effective commissions and replace them with boards to suit his political motives.

These were the Public Utilities Commission, the Civil Service Commission and the Tax Commission.

On Nov. 17, 1920, just two weeks after the election and nearly two months before he would take office, Small gave a press conference in which he said his first priority would be to end the Public Utilities Act and enact the Thompson Plan.

Except, Small said he did not know much about the utilities commission that he so strongly opposed.

"I haven't studied the act and I don't know whether the present commissioners are supposed to remain in office for a certain period so that their calendar may be cleared of pending cases, or whether they pass out of office automatically with the arrival of the new administration."

The Thompson Plan was to bring "home rule" to Chicago, a euphemism that meant Thompson would have dictatorial control over the utilities, including the streetcar franchises and anything else he could get his hands on. It was one of the main promises of Thompson and Small.

The governor-elect also announced that approval of all patronage jobs would go through City Hall, to be handled by Mayor William Hale Thompson and state party chairman Frank L. Smith.

Indeed, one of Governor Small's first acts was to fire all the members of the Public Utilities Commission and replace them with new members. Frank L. Smith was named chairman. This might seem like a strange act for a governor who pledged to eliminate the commission.

Small did have the legislature abolish the Public Utilities Commission but he replaced it with the Illinois Commerce Commission, a nearly identical body that was stacked to his political advantage. That story is told in chapter 8.

Governor Small made an effort to change the state Tax Commission.

A number of citizens and groups had spent 30 years trying to reform the tax system to make it fair. The old tax board was composed of 25 people, elected from the different congressional districts. It was rife with politics and corruption. Some corporations had unusually high tax rates while others were unusually low, depending on payoffs. Progress stalled over the years to change the system until the Tax Commission was established in 1919 during Governor Lowden's administration. The new Tax Commission had only three members, appointed by the governor and answerable to him. They were considered experts, not petty politicians.

Governor Small said the system needed to be reformed, even though the present system had been enacted less than two years earlier. Small said his plan would get more tax money from the rich, who had been evading their share. The governor said billions of dollars were being hidden from the tax assessors, and making these wealthy "tax dodgers" pay would make the tax burden fairer for all taxpayers. His plan was to centralize all local taxing power under a state Tax Commission.

Small's plan called for a new commission to be appointed by the governor. The new commission would be expanded from three to seven members, and these would be high-paying political positions with the opportunity for huge patronage.

The governor's critics had a different view of Small's idea of "reform." They did not like the idea that the new Tax Commission would have added powers, including the power to go into local tax assessments of individuals and corporations going back 10 years. The purpose, according to Small's critics, would be to intimidate and harass in order to get people into line politically. Individuals and corporations who were friendly to the political organization, or who paid bribes, would get lower tax assessments. The others would have their assessments raised. Centralizing taxing power this way would give the governor and his organization unlimited power and enable Small to build a more powerful machine on a statewide level. This was the claim of his critics.

The bill would put companies "under the heel of the political machine," according to John Glenn of the Illinois Manufacturers Association. Local boards of assessors would "become nothing but clerks under the direction of the state tax commission."

Small said he needed the power to find the tax cheats being hidden by local assessors. He said the world war brought an unusual increase in prices, and more taxes had to be collected to meet these costs.

"This can be done by the enactment of legislation to place on the rolls millions upon millions of taxable property heretofore concealed by rich tax dodgers, who systematically evade payment of their just share of the expenses of this government under which they accumulated their riches," Small said.

Some legislators thought Small's real motive was to grab power. They could not swallow what Governor Small was trying to do with the tax system and they did not like the strong-arm tactics used by the bosses in Chicago.

Mayor Thompson and Fred Lundin came to Springfield on June 14, 1921 to twist a few arms. They set up headquarters and had legislators file through one at a time, cornering and pressuring members. Trading votes for the tax bill in exchange for other pet legislation was offered. Jobs and other favors were promised by the boatload.

More often than not, their tactics had an opposite effect. Republican State Sen. Otis Glenn of Murphysboro said to the press, "For God's sake, if you wish to save Governor Small, get Mayor Thompson and Fred Lundin out of town on the first train."

William Weber, a member of the Cook County Board of Assessors for 22 years, broke with Thompson on this bill. He called the tax commission bill "a most dangerous bill" and not a home-rule bill as Thompson was characterizing it. "I can't see how it is getting close to the people when you take their taxing and assessing power away from them and take it to Springfield," he said. "The bill, instead of getting more taxes from the tax dodgers, will only add more expenses to every taxpayer. It will mean a new group of assessors and reviewers."

The final blow against the bill came when it was revealed that the governor's men were trying to bribe members to vote his way. Rep. John MacNeil of Olney said that Julius Johnson, secretary of the Public Utilities Commission, had offered him patronage and other considerations if he would vote for the civil service and tax commission bills.

"I have Johnson's proposition here in his own handwriting," MacNeil told his fellow lawmakers. "There is enough taint, corruption and stench here to murder this bill and the Republican administration. Johnson ought to be fired tomorrow morning or Governor Small ought to resign."

Rep. Truman Snell of Carlinville said Johnson offered him the job of assistant commissioner of the utilities board if he could deliver votes of fellow Southern Illinois representatives on the civil service and tax commission bills. Snell said Frank L. Smith, chairman of the Public Utilities Commission, was there for the discussion.

"I have personal knowledge of what has been tried tonight and particularly by this man Johnson," said State Rep. Homer Tice of Greenview, who had been a supporter of Small's legislation. "I now say to Governor Small and his lieutenants here that I am through. It's too strong for me and I can't stomach it."

Johnson asked Snell if he could deliver the votes of representatives J.L. Hammond of Anna and Frank Morrasy of Sheffield. "Johnson came to me and asked me if I could vote for these two bills (tax and civil service)," Snell said. "He asked me what I wanted in exchange for my support. 'If you will vote for tax and civil service and deliver Morrasy and Hammond, you will be made an assistant utilities commissioner.' He said he'd come back in a few minutes." Johnson did come back -- with Frank L. Smith. Snell had heard enough and the conversation ended before Smith could say anything.

The charges of bribery stunned fellow legislators. It brought up memories of past disgraces, including the Allen bill and the Lorimer bribery for the Senate seat.

"Not since the time of Charles I in England and the revolution in our own country has such a suggestion of dictatorial usurpation been heard," the editorial in the Sept. 22 *Chicago Tribune* said. "Lundinism as revealed by the conduct of the Thompson machine in Chicago and the Small organization in the statehouse is determined upon absolute and irresponsible power or downfall."

There was one representative who loudly objected to the accusations -- Lee O'Neil Browne of Ottawa, a man who proved his own corruption many times over his career. The nearly hysterical Browne denounced Snell, especially for Snell's mention of the Lorimer scandal. Browne said that if he had it to do over again, he would still vote for Lorimer to be senator.

Of course, Governor Small said he was shocked to hear of attempted bribery. He said he would look into the matter. That same day, MacNeil walked into the governor's office and repeated his statements and had the governor's secretary put it in writing. Rep. Earl Searcy of Springfield and Rep. William Maucker of Rock Island also gave statements to the governor.

Rep. Searcy and Rep. Bayliss L. Barber, both from the Springfield area, were promised that ownership of the state fairgrounds would be transferred from Sangamon County to the state of Illinois if they would vote for the civil service and tax bills. The transfer would include $500,000 for improvements to the fairgrounds.

"I desire to inform the members of the House that I have not authorized any persons or employees connected with the state government to make any pledge or promise for any vote, for or against any measure before the legislature, and shall make a searching inquiry into the charge made against the employee referred to and shall direct such action as the facts and justice warrant for the honor and dignity of Illinois," Small said.

However, the majority of the House was upset enough with the entire matter to defeat the tax commission bill by a vote of 99 to 46 on June 18, despite the best pressure from the Machine and a last minute personal appeal from Governor Small. Thompson and Lundin sat in the gallery and watched their measure go down to defeat.

Legislators called for the resignation of Julius Johnson as secretary of the Public Utilities Commission. Several also called for Governor Small's resignation.

Governor Small accepted Johnson's resignation -- and then appointed him secretary of the new Illinois Commerce Commission, with a raise in pay.

The tax commission plan was dead but Small was able to replace the commissioners with his own people. Col. Joseph Sanborn was a genuine hero of the Spanish-American War, the Mexican border war and World War I, as well as being a commander in the National Guard in a 40-year military career. After a bitter legislative battle, Small ousted Sanborn and replaced him with Percy Coffin, a political hack who had been bouncing around the Thompson administration in a number of positions. Coffin resigned from the Tax Commission in October 1923, under pressure, after being accused of many charges of graft, including taking a $10,000 payment from a paving company. He also was charged with neglect of duty and unfair assessment of farmland. The charges against Coffin were most vocally made by William H. Malone, a fellow member of the Tax Commission who soon would have his own trouble with the law. Coffin also was caught up in the "expert's fees" case.

Governor Small tried again in 1923 and in 1925 and failed. He tried for a constitutional amendment and that did not succeed.

Governor Small next went after the Civil Service Commission.

One of the highlights of Governor Frank Lowden's administration was the enactment of the Civil Administrative Code of 1917. His reforms replaced political patronage with a merit system and made government a little more honest.

That changed when Len Small became governor. Small wanted to eliminate the merit system and bring back political patronage and the spoils system.

State Sen. John A. Wheeler of Springfield sponsored the legislation to eliminate civil service, commonly called the Wheeler bill. The bill really came out of the Thompson-Lundin-Small Combine as a means of grabbing thousands of additional jobs for their own distribution. It was not too cleverly disguised, and the battle was not one of ideals, it was one of politics and who would vote with the Machine.

Governor Small gave some high sounding demagoguery on why he supported the Wheeler bill -- coal miners with experience underground will be better inspectors than a student with a high civil service score, experienced farmers will manage state farms and grow better crops than younger men, a dollar's worth of service for a dollar spent, and so on -- but the governor's real purpose was seen in other parts of his statement.

"To accomplish this purpose, state employees must be loyal to the people, efficient and competent," the governor said. "Experience has shown that the civil service law has not in all cases aided in attaining that end (a dollar's worth of service)...the man we will need cannot be secured through civil service examination. Administrative officials should not be denied the right of selection between applicants for employment."

R.E. Blackwood, secretary of the Civil Service Reform Association, called it a "patronage plum" that would take 3,000 merit jobs and give them to the political spoils system. Blackwood said, "Apparently no one in the Lundin-Thompson-Small organization has the courage to stand out before the people and advocate a straightforward attempt to repeal the state civil service law. They choose rather to undermine the service by exempting all important positions and leaving the impression with the people that there is still a law."

Leaders of the Chicago Woman's Club met with legislators to oppose the governor's bill, citing the 3,000 civil service jobs lost to the "spoils system."

The independent Legislative Voters League opposed the governor's bill. Its president, Clifford Barnes, said the bill "would not only wreck the employment machinery of the state but would virtually destroy its merit system. It is essential that the civil service system, which has been built up by years of effort and has substantially increased the efficiency of the state government, should be strengthened rather than abolished."

The first thing Governor Small had to do was to fire the commissioners and replace them with his own cronies. He appointed Helen Griffin, wife of Grant Park banker Ernest B. Griffin, to the Civil Service Board. She saw that Monroe Curtis (nephew of Mrs. Griffin and son of Edward C. Curtis) was given a civil service job as an assistant administrative auditor without an exam. (In ill health in April 1968, at age 83, Mrs. Griffin shot herself to death in her Kankakee home).

Isidore Levin, secretary of the commission, was removed in 1921. Levin was not going to go quietly. He made a number of accusations against the governor regarding state jobs that summed up a lot of what other sources were saying about the issue.

Levin said the Wheeler bill that killed civil service was passed, ironically, by legislators who were bribed with non-merit jobs for their vote. He said Small used the opportunity to place a number of relatives on state payrolls, along with cronies and their relatives. Levin said Small made numerous "temporary" appointments that were not so temporary.

In the statement Levin made when he was fired, he said he was told by Charles Purdunn, president of the Civil Service Board, "The governor is planning to cut out all the examinations, issuing temporary permits, and to mange the civil service so that only Small men will get the jobs, and they do not trust you to go along with the Small crowd."

"The Small commission is requiring oral interviews so that the competent applicants can be worn out with the extra expense and the crooked oral interviews," Levin said. "I say emphatically that C.A. Purdunn, Michael F. Walsh and Mrs. Griffin have conducted oral examinations for the sole purpose of passing the henchmen of Small and failing the others. The so-called examinations have been given at Kankakee without advertising them according to law. Persons have been appointed to permanent places with eligible lists in force. Every eligible list that could be killed was killed. Purdunn has advised the department heads how to evade the law. I have not signed a pay roll for months."

Levin went on: "Mr. Purdunn promised me a job paying me as much, if not more, than I am receiving now, if I will step aside and give up the secretaryship so that the governor can place his own man in my stead. I would rather be reduced to starvation and live in the gutter than to deliberately violate the civil service law."

A number of appointments made by political rather than by merit were cited. Levin said he criticized the political appointment of Lawrence Becherer and was told by Purdunn that Becherer was a Small favorite. "I replied that the governor has no authority under the law to make this appointment. He flared up and said, 'Do you mean to tell me that the commission can tell the governor what he can do?' I replied, 'The governor is expected to obey the law as much as any other person.'"

Levin, who had served as secretary under governors Dunne and Lowden, said it always was the policy that an attendant who beat a patient would never get his job back. But since Chauncey Jenkins became head of the department, several such attendants had been reinstated after a politically-connected call was made.

Small took items off a list of examinations that should have been left there, he cancelled eligible lists, he held up exam results so he could appoint his own "temporary" workers to jobs, he made appointments without the signature of department heads. Levin said only enough examinations were given "to help make some sort of a show" and the eligible lists were frozen. "With no examinations and no eligible lists, temporary permits can be issued for the governor's henchmen," he said.

Levin issued an examination call, and Small eliminated 13 of the positions. Levin said he was told by Leslie Small "that his father wanted only people upon whom he could depend, and when he had an administrative measure he expects every officer and employee to lobby for it and not be opposed to it."

An example was in July, when the director of the Kankakee State Hospital gave oral examinations to four people who had not filed an application. This was done on the orders of Leslie Small, Levin said.

Levin said Governor Small was making numerous appointments where he had no authority because these jobs were under civil service.

In February 1922, R.E. Blackwood went to the state's attorney in Sangamon County to see the records of the Civil Service Commission and he asked for a grand jury to investigate the abuses. Complaints had been piling up for months from all over the state. Blackwood first went to the commission for the records, something he previously always was allowed to do. With Small as governor, access to the records was denied.

One of the most lucrative sources of graft and patronage for Mayor Thompson and Governor Small was the parks system in Chicago. The state's Supreme Court declared the Park Civil Service Act of 1911 unconstitutional, on a technicality. The House and Senate passed a new law to meet the constitutionality and to protect 3,500 civil service jobs and pensions. The votes were unanimous.

However, Small vetoed the bill. By trading favors for votes (with lawmakers who had their own interest in Chicago patronage), Small was able to get the legislature to sustain his veto. Small took the civil service jobs in the Chicago parks departments and gave them to Mayor Thompson to distribute as patronage to political supporters.

Lee O'Neil Browne led the fight to sustain Small's veto.

State Rep. John Gibson of Chicago said Small's veto was "an attempt to grab jobs and build up for the fight they see coming in 1924." State Rep. Lottie Holman O'Neill of Downers Grove said, "It is nothing short of a calamity to defeat civil service. Instead of trying to weaken it, we should fight to strengthen it and protect merit employees from the schemes of politicians."

The Illinois League of Women Voters attacked the governor's civil service policy at its convention in the Congress Hotel in Chicago on Nov. 20, 1923. Mrs. Murray Nelson told the 300 delegates that Governor Small was "a tyrannical overlord of the spoils system throughout the state" and had not held a single state civil service examination in the past year. Governor Lowden held 296 examinations in his four years, she said.

Mrs. Nelson said 3,500 jobs were taken off civil service by Small. "Are we helpless under this return to the feudal system? This is the situation of the overlord and the trembling serf."

State Rep. Howard Castle, a Republican from Barrington, was so upset with the governor's heavy-handed methods that he wrote an article, “Executive Usurpation In Illinois,” for the August 1921 issue of the Legislative Voter's League newsletter. He cited the ramming through of Gotthard Dahlberg, a Chicago Republican, as speaker of the House, on orders from Thompson and Lundin in Chicago. This was done through promises of patronage, Castle said, and "if the promise of patronage proved insufficient, the governor's emissaries are reported to have gone further and to have threatened to oust from the state service some friend of the member whose vote was sought, unless he could see his way clear to support the governor's choice for speaker."

The result, Castle said, was that state work was tied up for five weeks while Speaker Dahlberg consulted with Mayor Thompson and Governor Small about appointments to committees. Certain committees had to be stacked with specific members who would be loyal to the agenda of the governor on key bills.

And, Castle added, the administration's methods turned away even some who had supported him. "The governor is reported to have named the very important Appropriations Committee in its entirety and to have chosen many of the committee chairmen. The governor's bills were given precedence over all others. With little or no consideration in committee, these measures, many of them lengthy and complicated, were pushed to passage with no adequate explanation. Under a practice long established, bills were not placed in the order of placing them on the calendar but according to the Speaker's whims. These conditions prevailed in both houses until two weeks before the close of the session, when a reaction set in and three of the governor's bills were defeated."

Castle gave three reasons for the reaction. First, a coalition judicial ticket won the June elections, showing that City Hall could be beaten. Second, "the lobbying methods used by the governor's appointees became so objectionable that members who, up to that time had gone all the way for him, revolted." Third, Lundin and Thompson used the Speaker's room as their office, as they called in members and tried to strong-arm them to vote for the governor's bills. This worked to alienate, rather than to convince them.

And Small continued to do as he pleased, ignoring the merit system. In 1924, Dr. Homer Curtis, a veterinarian in Polo, was sent pledge cards and told to sign up voters for Len Small. He thought his job as an assistant state veterinarian was protected by civil service, since he passed the examination and got his position under Governor Lowden's administration. When Dr. Curtis didn't send the pledge cards in, he was warned twice by letter before receiving a third letter telling him he was removed from the list of assistant state veterinarians.

The employees hired through patronage dragged down all the departments in the state. A legislative committee investigating it reported in 1923:

"Probably in every department of the state government there were employees who were not devoting their full time, or even a fair share of it, to the work of the state. This situation caused a breaking down of the morale of the employees in the departments when the hardest workers failed to receive equal compensation to those who were notoriously neglecting their duties."

Carroll H. Wooddy observed in 1931, "The integrated type of administrative organization through which Lowden had made possible notable economies now afforded Small the opportunity for the construction of a powerful spoils machine, of which he took the fullest advantage. Relying for personal popularity upon the construction of a system of hard roads throughout the state, a program which had been initiated by Governor Lowden, Small proceeded to employ the vast resources of the state government for political ends. The civil service system went by the board and a great majority of the administrative posts of the state were turned over to the spoils-men. State purchases were turned over to the governor's son, Leslie, as director of purchases and construction."

Eighty per cent of state employees were under civil service and a substantial number of those workers were taken from civil service to patronage when Small became governor. "Under the administration of that governor, the whole merit system was subjected to a type of manipulation which rendered the legal safeguards of little or no significance," Wooddy wrote.

Small and Thompson used these state employees as their own personal army who would work for their re-election.

Governor Small addressed his legislative defeats in a speech he made at a rally with Mayor Thompson at Riverview Park in Chicago on July 23. Small's speeches were predictable, in the sense that they all hit the same foes, bragged about the same qualities and pushed the same buttons as would any demagogue. This time, he said, "Perhaps never in the history of this state has such an aggregation of special interests combined to defeat the will of the people. The *Chicago Tribune* and the *Daily News*, the mouthpieces of organized wealth and greed and of the criminal profiteer, lied about the object of those bills and did everything they could to defeat them. And when the bills failed to get enough votes to carry, they said Governor Small had been defeated by the legislature. My friends, I want to say to you that those bills were not offered or supported by me because they were in the interest of Governor Small. They were supported by me because they were in your interests, they were right and fair in the interests of the people. It was not Governor Small who was defeated, it was the people of Illinois who were defeated by the big interests working through the legislature."

He then went on to explain why the attorney general was persecuting him, not forgetting to mention the *Tribune,* Senator Medill McCormick, "the vicious political ring" in Sangamon County and the cement trust and the traction barons, adding that "standing up to them is almost like taking one's life in his own hands."

The Legislative Voters League, which monitored the voting records and the conduct of state lawmakers, published a report in February 1924 that was severely critical of Governor Small's methods. It cited what it called "the vicious efforts of the Small administration to dominate the legislature."

It called the passage of the governor's bill for a $100 million road bond "one of the most elaborate and tireless propaganda campaigns the state has ever seen."

Independent lawmakers not controlled by Small were the only thing preventing the Small administration from "running wild" with spending, the report said.

"With the Senate controlled by Governor Small and with the enormous power of state patronage and all the other resources of the administration constantly exerted to achieve its ends, the problem of those forced was how to hold in check the elements of misrule. Having concentrated his efforts upon the Senate at the election of 1922 in order to head off threatened impeachment, Governor Small had lost control of the House, which was organized independently by the election of David E. Shanahan as speaker for the fourth time. Under Speaker Shanahan's experienced leadership, the independent forces were reasonably successful throughout the session in preventing bad legislation and in holding down appropriations, although the executive power was used in a more systematic way to influence legislation than ever before at Springfield."

The report contrasted appropriations between Small and his predecessor: $13.9 million under Governor Lowden in 1917, $23.4 million under Governor Small in 1923.

The league also had words for the governor's mauling of civil service.

"The most discreditable occurrence of the session was Governor Small's veto of the park civil service bill and the success of his effort to prevent the House from passing the bill over his veto."

Small demonstrated the power he and City Hall wielded by grabbing a state senate seat in the November 1922 elections.

The Chicago political machine has always been adept at stealing elections. Up until 1931, it was the Republicans; since then, it has been the Democrats.

Small himself was elected in this manner in 1920.

The state senate race in Chicago's First District in 1922 was between Democrat Norman MacPherson and Republican Adolph Marks. Marks was the candidate of Mayor Thompson and Fred Lundin. MacPherson won the election on first count by 43 votes, and his victory was confirmed by a canvass by the Chicago Board of Elections. But after the State Board of Elections reviewed the results, enough votes were thrown out to make Marks the winner.

Martin J. O'Brien, Democrat chairman in Chicago, had the canvass carefully watched because he feared fraud. The Republicans had Judge Frank Righeimer preside over the canvass in Chicago, hoping he would throw out a precinct on a charge of fraud and give the election to Marks. But the judge ruled that the senate was the place to present any evidence of fraud and have a recount.

That didn't happen. The state board took control of the vote counting.

It renewed talk of impeachment of the governor, from a large number of officials in both parties.

Edward Brundage gave his legal opinion of what the board did. The Republican attorney general said, "They wanted that seat and they took it. That's all there is to it. The state canvassing board has no authority except to review the figures submitted to them by the clerks of the several counties of the state. It is not a court. It cannot count ballots. And it cannot go into the question whether the votes were counted correctly in the several counties." The state canvassing board, he added, was created only to put together votes for candidates whose districts include more than one county. Secretary of State Louis Emmerson agreed with him, as did former attorney general Patrick Lucey who cited a Supreme Court ruling to back up his view.

The Democrat's managing committee in Cook County demanded a grand jury investigation and criminal prosecution of Governor Small. Part of its resolution read, "The action of the state board was taken in defiance of the law as repeatedly interpreted by the Supreme Court of the State of Illinois. And can be considered in no other light than a deliberate attempt on the part of the unspeakable Small to increase his voting strength in the state senate to such a number as will preclude the possibility of his removal through the medium of impeachment proceedings which have been threatened ever since his acquittal by a petit jury in Lake County."

The resolution "denounces the act of Small and his confederates as a willful and outrageous violation, not alone of their oath of office, but of the statutory law of Illinois."

Congressman A.J. Sabath said that if Small could throw out one precinct, he could throw out more, and "no Democrat would be safe." Democrat official Dennis Egan said Small's action was "the most dastardly act in the history of Illinois politics."

Illinois Democrats promised a fight on four fronts: in addition to the request for a grand jury and impeachment of the governor, they asked the Supreme Court to intervene and they asked the state senate to rule on admitting the rightfully elected member.

It was another battle won by Governor Small. Adolph Marks gave the governor the one-seat majority he needed.

That same month, 25 members of the governor's own party signed a statement objecting to Small's tactics of "persuasion and coercion" in his attempt to become a "czar" that dictates to the legislature. The 25 state senators did not like Small's heavy-handed rule, not even the move that took a seat from a Democrat. The statement of the Republican state senators did not comment on any issues such as impeachment or senate officers, it only said it wanted the independence to organize itself along its own lines in an ethical way.

There were three scandals in Chicago at that time that touched the Small administration. One was the "expert fees" rip-off and two involved Chicago schools.

Mayor Thompson and his boys in City Hall cheated Chicago taxpayers out of $2.2 million in 1920 and 1921 in fake "expert fees." Thompson's "City Beautification" program involved the purchase of land for street-widening and bridge building projects. Several real estate "experts" (Thompson cronies whose expertise was in graft and fraud) collected millions of dollars for their advice on the project.

One of the "experts" was Ernest Lyons, who was paid $668,468 over three years. Lyons paid Percy Coffin, head of the state tax commission, $50,000 to assist in appraisal of property in connection with street improvements. Coffin admitted to grand jury that a large amount of money was kicked back to Thompson's campaign fund. Coffin also was on the payroll of White Paving, which monopolized city paving contracts. Michael Faherty, president of the Board of Local Improvements, and H.B. Detweiler, secretary of White Paving Co., were accused of fraudulently obtaining $28,000 in contracts for improvements to the Michigan Avenue bridge.

Indicted in 1923 were Faherty and Coffin and three real estate experts, Arthur Merigold, Frank Meece and Edward Waller, and realtor Arthur Brautigan. State's Attorney Robert Crowe made a deal with Coffin, and charges against Coffin, Faherty and four others were dropped. Coffin was not out of a position for long. In January 1924, he was named by Fred Lundin to the choice job of public administrator of Cook County.

The case slowly made its way through the justice system. In June 1928, Thompson and the others were convicted and ordered to pay $1.7 million. That judgment was reversed by the state Supreme Court on Oct. 25, 1930.

The first school scandal involved the firing of Chicago School Superintendent Charles Chadsey in 1919. A lawsuit was filed and Judge Kickham Scanlan reinstated Chadsey. The school board refused to allow Chadsey back into his office. The matter went back to court and the school trustees were found in contempt of court by Judge Scanlan on July 26, 1920. School board attorney William Bither and eight members of the school board were sentenced to jail.

Bither was the most severely punished. He was sentenced to five days and a $500 fine. The six men on the school board were given lesser jail sentences and fines, and the three women on the board were just fined. All remained free on appeal.

The Appellate Court upheld the contempt ruling on Jan. 28, 1922. A rehearing was denied on Feb. 6. The very next day, Governor Small pardoned Bither and the school board members. None of them had spent a day in jail.

Small's explanation had a familiar ring.

"The judge entered a finding in harmony with the mayor's enemies and again imposed Chadsey upon the school system. The whole matter is a political case growing out of a political issue, resulting in a political trial and a political finding and decision based upon political bias." Small added that the "integrity of further litigation therewith is questionable" because the case was prosecuted by Attorney General Edward Brundage.

Judge Scanlan said the governor had no authority to grant pardons in this case. It was not like a criminal conviction, he said, it was a case of someone having contempt of a court order. A pardon was a violation of the separation of powers between the executive and the judiciary. "If such a power as that were given the governor, our courts would soon be destroyed," Judge Scanlan said.

The state appealed Small's pardons to the Supreme Court. Special Assistant Prosecutor Angus Roy Shannon's brief to the court contained this incredibly prescient observation:

"Logically, if under this executive power, the governor has the right to pardon in cases of contempt of court, he also has the right to pardon in cases of contempt against the legislature.

"Is it too fantastic to assume that in some future decadent stage of our beloved state's history, there might be a governor who was indicted for a crime; that when finally the case was dragged to trial, certain witnesses necessary to prove the facts refused to testify though produced in court through legal process; that the court adjudged them guilty of criminal contempt and sentenced them to incarceration in jail; that the governor pardoned them before they sought review by this court of that sentence; that thereafter the legislature convened and the governor was impeached, and on the trial of the impeachment, with the chief justice of this court presiding, witnesses necessary to prove the facts refused to testify, though produced before the senate through legal process; that these witnesses were found guilty of legislative contempt and sentenced to incarceration; that the governor immediately pardoned them; that the trial of the impeachment resulted in a consequent paralysis of functioning power and amounted to naught -- is it fantastic to so assume?"

That is pretty close to what happened in the next two years, with Small's pardons of Newmark and Boyle and with *quo warranto* (see chapters 12 and 19).

What made Shannon's observation so amazing was that it came in April 1922. Small was indicted but his trial had not started.

Shannon continued, "Yet such is the extent of power which the governor is claiming. It, of course, is not alone repugnant to the judicial power of self protection but also to the legislative power of self protection, free from executive interference."

Shannon's brief to the court hinted at Governor Small's previous assertion that he held powers similar to a king. Shannon attacked the governor's view.

"This form of government was and is diametrically opposed to the old English government, where the king was the original sovereignty. The courts of England were his. He created them. He was ever present in them. The system was one of executive justice. The king was the head of the judicial system. Each indignity to his courts or defiance to their authority or disobedience of their orders was against him, their creator, and he, being the one injured, had the power to forgive -- the right to pardon. That was the system in England until the constitutional revolution of 1688. It is all foreign and repugnant to our system of government. We have no scheme of executive justice. We have no courts created by a king. We have no king."

The brief closed with the statement that "The alleged pardons of the governor pleaded in this cause are null and void."

The Illinois Supreme Court agreed and did not recognize the pardons.

The Supreme Court refused on Dec. 8, 1922 to grant a rehearing of the contempt cases, and Bither went to jail the next day.

When Scanlan ran for re-election in 1921, Lundin's and Thompson's forces turned out the full power of the political machine to defeat Judge Scanlan because he ruled against the Thompson-Lundin school board. City Hall admitted the vendetta and Scanlan acknowledged it. Scanlan won the election.

The second school scandal involved Thompson, Lundin and the Chicago school board. They were accused of stealing a million dollars from the school district in kickbacks from contracts, phony billing and fraud in the purchase of property. One typical example of their theft was in the purchase of the site for Wendell Phillips High School. The property had been offered to the school board for $65,000 and the board rejected it. The property then was bought by Charles A. White, vice president of Lincoln State Bank, for $65,000. A week later, White (the former state legislator who took a bribe to make William Lorimer senator in 1909) sold it to the school board for $95,000. The property for the Forrestville school was bought in a similar manner.

The phony school contracts included false invoices (including to some companies owned by Lundin), over-billing and shaking down everyone who did business with the school district for campaign contributions. It was Lundin who approved all contracts and it was Lundin who picked the members of the school board. One of the school board members was Michael Moynihan, who also had been appointed to the Illinois Commerce Commission by Governor Small. Moynihan's company sold phonographs to the school district for two-and-a-half times their retail value. Central Metallic Door Co., a company owned by Lundin, got the contract for all doors for school buildings.

Thirteen people were indicted in September 1922, including Moynihan and

Bither.

As the case progressed, witnesses wouldn't cooperate with the grand jury and several were sentenced for contempt. Private detective Robert Cochrane told the grand jury and Chief Justice Michael McKinley that it was none of their business who hired him to harass grand jurors. He went to jail. One of Cochrane's operatives, Ben Newmark, lied to the grand jury. He disappeared before he could be arrested. Two coal company officials also could not be found to tell their part in questionable expenses in the coal contracts.

Joseph Span and Charles Driscoll, indicted for bribing a state representative and a state senator to raise the school tax rate and for offering bribes to school trustees to raise the pay of school engineers, were jailed for refusing to tell the grand jury who got the money.

As the jury was sworn in on Dec. 8, Bither went to jail on the contempt charge from the Chadsey case. Bither's lawyers, Charles LeForgee and Werner Schroeder, asked the judge to delay the trial until Bither's five-day sentence was up because it might prejudice the jury if they saw Bither led into court in the custody of a deputy. The judge said the deputy would not lead Bither in or sit by him.

On Dec. 21, 1922, a jury found Bither guilty and sentenced him to 1-to-5-years. Realtor Henry Kaup was found guilty and was sentenced to nine months. Both men also were fined $2,000.

"We had in mind recent pardons by Governor Small," said jury foreman William Corrigan. "We didn't know how much actual time they would serve so we added the fines to insure some punishment."

The convictions were reversed on appeal a year later. State's Attorney Robert Crowe decided not to retry the case.

Lundin and 22 others, including Bither and Moynihan, were indicted in January 1923 on further charges of school graft. The indictments came the day after Big Bill Thompson announced he would not seek another term as mayor because of the scandals.

Lundin was represented by high-powered Chicago lawyers Clarence Darrow, Charles Erbstein and Patrick H. O'Donnell. The trial of Lundin, Moynihan, Bither and the others was held in April 1923. Thanks to the oratory of Darrow and the perjured testimony of Thompson, Lundin and associates beat the rap.

Governor Small made unwanted headlines at home during this time. The first one was when he fired the tenant farmer on his dairy farm.

E.H. Satterfield was confined to his house with a severe case of the measles in January 1921. After two weeks of illness, during which his four children also came down with the measles, an angry Len Small came to Satterfield's house. "Now is a good time for you to get a new job," the governor said, according to an interview Satterfield gave the *Kankakee Daily News.* "If you work for me, you've got to work 30 days out of the month. The job on this farm requires a man to work every day, and you have not been doing it."

Satterfield said he told the governor he had worked every day since taking the job the previous September, until he was stricken with the measles. The governor replied that he didn't want to argue and told Satterfield to get out.

The Masonic lodge planned a circus in Chicago in 1922 and wanted a permit to operate paddle wheels. Thompson promised the permit and then sent a police lieutenant to Masonic Imperial Potentate Will Wade to demand $100 a night as a payoff. Wade told his fellow Shriners that Thompson was trying to shake down the Masons. It caused quite a stir. Thompson went to the monthly gathering of the Shriners at the Medinah Temple on Nov. 24 to give his side of the story. He was unable to finish his speech. He was hissed and booed off the stage by 4,000 Shriners and had to leave the hall for his own safety. An angry Thompson responded by ordering Governor Small to fire Wade's business partner, Thomas Houston, as state insurance commissioner. Small did as he was told.

In late 1924, Small forced the Live Poultry Transit Co. out of Kankakee. The business was in an industrial park a half mile from Small's house. He didn't like the smell. He used his Commerce Commission to use its muscle, since the poultry shipping yard was next to a train yard. A hundred men were thrown out of work.

And another of those bizarre side stories that popped up in Len Small's life happened in March 1923. Chicago Police Chief Fitzmorris and Detective Hughes said they had information that West Side gangsters had imported a gunman from Denver to kill the governor for $10,000.

The governor said he was unconcerned. He appeared in public as usual and without guards. The story was reported in the March 22 *Kankakee Daily Republican.* It was just a few paragraphs long and was never mentioned again.

It was another bizarre incident that made no sense. Why would gangsters want to kill Len Small? He was the gangsters' best friend. Did Chicago gangsters need to import a hit man? And from Denver? Denver was not known as a stronghold of professional killers. No guards after such a threat? No further mention? Was Len Small in a habit of fabricating crazy schemes as a smokescreen every time he needed to divert attention from a new scandal?

State Sen. James Barbour sued Governor Small for $50,000 for slander in April 1924. Barbour (yet another Republican who was considered a political enemy by Small) was a special prosecutor in 1923 for the trial of Rock Island mobster John Looney. Barbour was successful. Looney was convicted on several charges, including murder, and went to the penitentiary.

Governor Small made speeches accusing Barbour of illegally being paid twice by the state for his work -- once as a state senator and again as a special prosecutor for the state's attorney. Barbour said his fee in the Looney case was paid from a special fund, collected from local citizens to clean up vice in Rock Island.

"It comes from ill grace from a man like Small to charge anyone with the theft of state moneys, much less an innocent man," Barbour said.

Small defended his charge by saying that once that private money was turned over to the state's attorney's office for the prosecution, it became state money. (An interesting argument, from a man who apparently did not think that interest earned on state money in state bank accounts belonged to the state).

After some angry exchanges between Barbour and Small's lawyers in preliminary hearings in December 1926, and after a jury was chosen, Judge William Gemmill asked Small and Barbour to try to work something out. Barbour dropped his lawsuit.

Chapter 8

Frank L. Smith and the Utilities

Colonel Frank L. Smith of nearby Dwight was another unsavory character in a mob of such people surrounding Lennington Small.

Smith, born in 1867 in Dwight (30 miles west of Kankakee), was in banking and real estate there. He made his fortune through the Keeley Institute in Dwight, a world famous resort for curing alcoholism. It made its founders -- Dr. Leslie Keeley, John R. Oughton and Curtis Judd -- tremendously wealthy. They needed to invest their profits and chose Frank L. Smith to start a real estate firm. This also made the ambitious Smith tremendously wealthy.

Smith made so much money that he founded the First National Bank of Dwight, which also was called The Frank L. Smith Bank. He had architect Frank Lloyd Wright design the building which was built in 1905. It still stands today and is still a bank.

Smith also owned a local baseball team, named after himself -- The Frank L. Smiths, which actually was a pretty good semi-pro ball club.

He called himself Col. Smith for most of his life, even though he was not a colonel and was never in the military (in 1896, Governor Tanner appointed Smith a "colonel" of some kind on his staff. It was a reward for raising large sums of campaign money).

Here's a local story that says something about Smith's character. When he decided to tear down his house in Dwight to build a new one, he kept one room of the old house intact from the wrecker's ball. This way, his new mansion was built as an "addition" to his old mansion, so this very rich man didn't have to pay for a building permit for a new house.

Smith was an egotistical self-promoter who kept himself in the local newspaper constantly with advertising (for both his businesses and himself) and with endless political statements and announcements. He was a constant frustrated candidate for political office. He didn't own the *Dwight Star & Herald* but he might as well have owned it, from the adoration it gave him, in a situation similar to Len Small and his *Kankakee Daily Republican.*

But Smith went beyond local bombast. He aspired to statewide and national office and he was wiling to sell his soul to get it, so be became closely politically allied with Len Small, William Lorimer, Fred Lundin and Big Bill Thompson.

"Between 1920 and 1928, Smith, Small and Thompson became inseparably linked as a trio in the public mind, representing well-nigh the lowest level of governmental performance," wrote Smith biographer Carroll H. Woody in 1931.

When Smith ran as Lundin's candidate for the nomination for senator in 1920, he campaigned on the Lundin platform, one that he had opposed at the state convention. "Lundin declared that this inconsistency clearly convinced him of Smith's utter lack of principle," Woody wrote.

Smith had his own shady record in Dwight. He went to the state legislature to oppose a bill that would have ended a contract system that was a help to a brother-in-law. As a congressman, Smith used influence to have the federal government buy the former buildings of the Keeley Institute in Dwight for use as a veteran's hospital, and Smith made a big commission on the sale. Smith also was involved in the failure of the Lorimer bank. Smith helped Lorimer dispose of bank shares, and his friends ended up with worthless securities while Smith and Lorimer fared well.

Smith's temperament was not unlike that of Len Small. Both men showed their petty side even when in high office. Smith held grudges, even snubbing Governor Charles Deneen at a railroad station after Deneen refused a political favor years earlier. One of the first things Smith did in 1921, after becoming a part of the Small administration, was to have James Lyon removed as public administrator of Livingston County and Ralph Bradford removed as head of the Bureau of Fish and Game Conservation. Both were from Smith's home county and had refused to support him for governor in 1920.

This behavior hurt no one but Smith. The pattern was repeated time and time again, as Smith figuratively shot himself in the foot by alienating many important people in the state, out of pettiness, ruining future favors and chances.

"Opposition he could not endure, and to be thwarted threw him into a state of anger almost pathological in its intensity," Woody wrote.

Frank L. Smith began his political career by running for circuit clerk and losing in 1896. Smith desperately desired to become governor of Illinois. He ran for statewide office in almost every election year beginning in 1904, and his ambition, desperation and inadequacy was apparent to the voters.

He may have been best known locally for all the campaigns he lost. He ran unsuccessfully for the nomination for lieutenant governor and governor and congress numerous times over his lifetime. Voters could smell the desperation on him.

Smith's non-stop personal publicity campaign for 20 years finally convinced enough voters to elect him to a two-year term in Congress in 1918. He wanted to be the Chicago machine's choice for governor in 1920 but it picked Len Small. The machine picked Smith as its candidate to run for the nomination for the U.S. Senate. His Republican opponents were William B. McKinley of Champaign and Col. B.M. Chipperfield of Canton. McKinley won the nomination and the election.

As soon as Len Small took office, he pushed through one of Mayor Thompson's major goals, one of the reasons why Small was placed in the governor's chair. That was the "reformation" of the state's Public Utilities Act.

The background for all this went back to 1916, just after Big Bill became mayor. Big Bill wanted his own piece of the utilities pie. The "Thompson Traction Plan" was to create a transportation authority board to consolidate the streetcar and elevated rail lines and fix a five-cent fare. It would have given the city ownership of the profitable streetcar companies, taking it away from private ownership.

Members of the Public Utilities Commission would not go along with Mayor Thompson's plan. So the city of Chicago sued the commission. Chicago lost, even after taking the case to the highest court in the state. The Illinois Supreme Court ruled on April 19, 1917 that the Public Utilities Commission was constitutional.

So how did the Chicago political machine outmaneuver the Supreme Court? The first thing was to get Thompson's man, Len Small, elected governor.

When Small became governor, he fired all the members of the Public Utilities Commission and replaced them with Thompson's people. Frank L. Smith was appointed chairman, and the new commissioners were Cicero Lindley, Patrick Moynihan, Hal Trovillion and James Sullivan. Julius Johnson was named secretary.

Small decided to abolish the Public Utilities Commission and replace it with a new agency that had the same powers but now with expanded authority. For this, he needed the approval of the legislature.

Abolishing the Public Utilities Commission was not some sneaky move that Small pulled once he became governor. It was a campaign promise and a big part of his inaugural address, where he referred to it as "Thompson Traction Plan."

But it wasn't until his inaugural address that he gave the details. Control over utilities would go to cities that had control prior to the creation of the Public Utilities Commission. Utilities elsewhere in the state would be regulated by a newly-created commission created by the governor.

Building and owning public transportation utilities was not something that was practical at the time for many cities other than Chicago. It was a gift to the city of Chicago and it came on the direct orders of Mayor William Hale Thompson.

The governor said the changes were needed to take power from a state commission and give local control to the communities, a strange view for a state official. But it did not do this. The bill abolished the Public Utilities Commission and replaced it with the Illinois Commerce Commission. The ICC controlled utilities outside municipalities or in municipalities that did not adopt the Home Rule.

Even though Small said this was a fulfillment of a campaign promise, it really was just the opposite. Small had promised to repeal the public utilities law and bring home rule to Illinois cities. His ICC incorporated more than 80 sections of the old law in the new bill. An amendment by State Sen. John Dailey of Peoria eliminated the home rule clause.

Small's real purpose was to gut the state commission and replace it with a new commission that took orders from Thompson and the other Chicago bosses.

Small called it the "Home Rule" measure. He wanted to make it look like he was giving something to local communities rather than have it be seen as a huge giveaway to Thompson and Chicago.

Minority Leader John Devine of Dixon saw this and campaigned against it.

The Republicans held the majority in the legislature, and most of the lawmakers wanted to cooperate with the new governor and his agenda. The legislature approved doing away with the Public Utilities Commission and creating the Illinois Commerce Commission. Frank L. Smith became the first chairman of the Illinois Commerce Commission on April 6. The new commission was divided into nine sections, each with a chief, all answerable to the ICC board.

A lot of legislators later regretted voting to change the commission, after they saw how Len Small was using it for political purposes. "I am ready to take back all the arguments I have made in favor of the commission and its predecessor, the utilities commission," State Sen, John Dailey told the legislature in June 1923. "It has failed because of the influence of politics and of utilities.

"The great power of the state, the ruler of all parties and all factions, is Samuel Insull. He is the damning power, garroting over the state and paralyzing the moral life of Illinois. He is the uncrowned king of Illinois."

State Sen. Otis Glenn of Murphysboro followed. "Samuel Insull is not the uncrowned king. The ruler of Illinois is King Len, the Small. The last man that King Len the Small appointed to the commerce commission was a man who was bribed to turn his own judgment to influence the jury at Waukegan. That man (William Smith) was bribed, just as much as if he had been given money. This unfit man sits on the commerce commission."

Julius Johnson was named secretary of the ICC. He was City Hall's unsuccessful candidate for the nomination for state auditor in 1920.

When Governor Small was lining up votes in the state legislature to abolish the Public Utilities Commission, Johnson went around making every promise he could in order to bribe legislators to vote Small's way. In one instance, a downstate legislator was promised "anything he asked for" by Johnson if he could convince other legislators to vote Small's way. This form of persuasion was done on the pending utilities, tax and civil service bills, told in chapter 7.

This type of dealing has always been business as usual in Illinois politics, and still is. Illinois officeholders freely use patronage to reward friends and punish enemies. Len Small used this tool as much as anyone ever has in Illinois.

One of the men Governor Small appointed to the Illinois Commerce Commission was Chicago's Second Ward Boss Daniel Jackson. Jackson was the Mob's man in charge of gambling operations in almost every speakeasy in Chicago's black neighborhoods.

Edward Litsinger, running against Big Bill's candidate for the County Board of Review in 1927, said in a campaign speech that "the Three Musketeers are Big Bill, Len Small and Frank L. Smith. The right way to pronounce it is the Three-Must-Get-Theirs."

Smith ran for the Republican nomination for the U.S. Senate in 1920 and lost to William B. McKinley. Smith ran for the nomination again in 1926. He never wanted the job; his lifelong ambition was to be governor. But the party bosses in Chicago slated him for the senate race and he did what he was told.

Smith beat McKinley for the nomination in 1926 by spending a huge amount of campaign money. How he got this money proved to be his undoing.

The nation's biggest utilities baron was Samuel Insull. He was the president of Commonwealth Edison and he also held large interests in Peoples Gas, Public Service Co. and a number of railroads and streetcar lines. Insull was a backer of Thompson's "traction plan" to control the rail and streetcar lines.

Insull virtually invented the holding company. His pyramid scheme in taking over smaller companies, manipulating stocks, issuing junk securities, pocketing fraudulent fees and more, earned him $150 million. But the collapse of his empire a few years later during the Great Depression ruined 600,000 shareholders and led to the enactment of federal legislation to prevent this sort of fraud from happening again. Insull fled to Istanbul and was extradited. He was put on trial on numerous counts of embezzlement, mail fraud, stock fraud, anti-trust violations and more. Insull was found not guilty because his machinations were too complex for prosecutors to make understandable to juries.

Insull contributed $125,000 to Frank L. Smith's 1926 senate campaign. That was on the record but sources at the time put the figure at several times that amount. (The figure equals perhaps $10 million in 2009 dollars).

Another utilities magnate who contributed heavily to Smith's fund was Col. Ira C. Copley. His title came from being on the staff of governors Altgeld and Deneen and from service in the National Guard.

Copley owned Western United Corp., a group of natural gas, electric, streetcar and mining companies. Col. Copley knew Col. Smith from their term in Congress together. Like Len Small, Copley felt the need for his own newspaper. He bought newspapers in his hometown of Aurora, and in Joliet, Elgin and Springfield. Copley Press eventually owned 10 dailies and 19 weeklies in Illinois and California. He also endowed Copley Memorial Hospital in Aurora.

Copley and Insull were unfriendly competitors, with Insull unsuccessfully trying to acquire Copley's properties for years. Smith's ICC brokered a deal between Copley and Insull and the territories they would divide.

Clement Studebaker Jr., president and chairman of the board of Illinois Power & Light Corp., Illinois Traction Co. and South Bend Watch Co. (and an officer in the Chicago & South Bend Railroad, and the Studebaker Motor Corp.) also gave heavily to Smith's campaign fund.

Smith shook down other executives of state utilities for money for his campaign for the U.S. Senate nomination in 1926. Smith far outspent his opponent, defeating McKinley for the nomination. Smith won in November.

McKinley died shortly after the election. Governor Small appointed Smith to serve the remaining three months of the senator's term. But because Smith took money from executives he was regulating, the U.S. Senate would not admit Smith, citing fraud and corruption in his election. When Smith came back to the Senate a few months later to take the seat to which he was elected, the Senate held a trial and affirmed its decision to keep Smith out.

Senator Jim Reed of Missouri, chairman of the committee that would decide whether or not to accept Smith's certification of election and admit him to the Senate, said, "The evidence demonstrates such fraudulent conduct as to show his unfitness. It also discloses enough to make it a justifiable conclusion that his appointment comes from and springs from his election, and that it never would have been made except for that election, an election which, the evidence discloses, was wickedly and fraudulently accomplished. It is that which taints and challenges these credentials here presented."

Arkansas Senator Thaddeus Caraway claimed Insull gave Smith $500,000 and that Insull offered newspapers $100,000 to support Smith in print. Caraway also claimed that payoffs to campaign funds followed favorable rulings from the ICC.

Caraway said there was a connection between Copley's contributions to Smith's campaign and the ICC's action in the sale of Copley's utilities.

Copley was questioned by the senate committee. It was a crime in Illinois for an officer of a utility to give money to a member of the commission. But no charges were brought against Copley. The senate committee wanted to ask why Studebaker, a resident of Indiana, gave so much money to an Illinois candidate but Studebaker could not be found during the hearings.

It also was a criminal offense for Smith, as chairman of the ICC, to accept a contribution from a utility company official. Smith could have faced a $1,000 fine and six months in jail, but of course, he was not prosecuted.

Smith did not give a good defense at the senate hearings. His claim, that the ICC reduced utility rates by as much as $44 million over the previous six years, did not fly. Utility rates had been at record war-time highs just before Smith became chairman and it was argued that the reductions should have been another $50 million deeper. A few smaller utility companies had taken the ICC to federal court to protest their rate reductions. Illinois Bell Telephone was one that won its protest. But Insull never protested the amount of his rate reductions.

Smith never offered evidence that the money did not influence him, and the senate committee took that as a default admission of guilt. And Insull did not come to the defense of Smith.

Rather than put on a legitimate defense of his actions, Smith "threw up a smoke screen of legal technicalities, sophistries and refinements which, if entertained, will sanctify the fraud of the present and open wide the door to every trickster, bribe giver, ballot box stuffer and corruptionist who may in the future come here with a certificate, howsoever obtained," Sen. Reed said.

A *Chicago Tribune* story from Washington reported an exchange between an Illinois man and President Calvin Coolidge, where the man said that George Brennan, the Democrat candidate, also accepted a contribution from Insull. Coolidge responded, "But Brennan wasn't regulating Insull's properties, was he?"

"It seemed to me unthinkable, after those confessions had been made, which seemed to me criminal, that the state of Abraham Lincoln had an electorate which had sunk so low that it was willing to go before the world and say, 'This is the man we want to represent us in the U.S. Senate,'" Julius Rosenwald said before Reed's committee. Rosenwald was a wealthy clothing manufacturer and part-owner and chief executive of Sears-Roebuck Co. His Rosenwald Fund has provided more than $70 million for African-American education, Jewish charities, public schools, universities, museums and more over the decades. Rosenwald was a principal founder and financial backer of the Museum of Science and Industry in Chicago. Rosenwald did as much as anyone at the time to wedge Frank L. Smith from the governmental scene in Illinois.

Meanwhile, Pennsylvania Senator-Elect William S. Vare faced the same problem. He was a congressman and the undisputed political boss of Philadelphia. He was in league with mobsters like Waxey Gordon and Lucky Luciano. Vare's 1926 campaign for the U.S. Senate was scandalous from top to bottom. Governor Gifford Pinchot refused to certify the election and he testified at Senate hearings. The Senate also refused to seat Vare.

Newspaper editorial writers all across the country gave their opinions.

"No more daring or brazen example of low politics and crooked business has come to light in recent years than the connection of Samuel Insull with the sensational primary of Illinois," the West Virginia *Charleston Gazette* wrote on Aug. 4, 1926. The *Cleveland Press* on July 30, 1926 wrote, "Does anyone think the financial group headed by Samuel Insull spent money to nominate Frank Smith just because he was a good fellow and would represent all the people of Illinois? What do they expect? They expect substantial dividends on their political investments. They want legislation that will enable them to get personal franchises." *The Nashville Tennessean* on Aug. 4, 1926 wrote, "A sense of propriety would forbid Smith's accepting any favors from these selfish and predatory interests. Yet his services have evidently been so satisfactory to them that he is able to obtain their financial support in seeking higher office."

The Raleigh News & Observer on Aug. 5, 1926 wrote that it was "first cousin to bribery when something like $500,000 is spent by public service corporations to nominate the head of the Commerce Commission, whose action has been entirely pleasing to the traction interests." *The Ohio State Journal* wrote on Aug. 7, 1926, "Insull wanted more than simple justice, so like all those who would destroy government by the people and set up government by privilege, he tried to buy what he wanted." The *Norfolk Virginian-Pilot* wrote on Aug. 2, 1926, "Mr. Insull's money was peculiarly the money that Mr. Smith's position made it impossible for him to accept. That it was handed over in currency suggests that both Mr. Insull and Mr. Smith were aware of some impropriety. Properly speaking, it was a callous flouting of the elementary rules governing the relations of public utility commissioners with the owners of the utilities that they were commissioned to regulate. A public official unable to sense the enormity of such an act cannot be regarded as the type of man needed in the United States Senate."

Two other assessments were very brutal. The *Memphis Commercial Appeal* on Aug. 4, 1926 said Insull was worse than bootleggers and gunmen in Chicago. "Insull has done more to hurt Americans than the deadliest gunman that ever shot a victim in the back. Mr. Insull and his associates in Illinois have done more to encourage bolshevism, communism and anarchy than all the wild orators that have ever preached in the country. Mr. Insull and his crowd have committed a high crime against the Constitution of the United States, and the crime is as mean, as vicious, as it is high." And on Aug. 6, 1926, the *Milwaukee Journal* wrote of Smith's claim that the money placed him under no obligation: "No obligation? Well, that's just fine!! What kind of a man takes $200,000 and feels no obligations?"

The *Springfield Republican* said, "The truth is that the Senate has never struck a stronger blow for decency and purity in elections of the states of the Union.

The repercussions of this act must be worth dozens of statutes limiting or regulating candidates' expenditures in senate elections. The Smith case will serve notice that hereafter, no candidate can debauch public morals without incurring the grave risk of being thrown out when he attempts to pass through the Senate's door."

Senator Reed summed up in the *Congressional Record* on Jan. 19, 1928: "It is a plain, bald, naked question we are going to settle -- that is, whether seats can be bought in the United State Senate in the interest of those who have had the right to decide as to the life and death of the interests contributing the money.

"There are certain things so plain that you need the guideboard of no law to tell you they are evil," Reed continued. "If this man is to be seated, let us hang over the door of the Senate, 'Seats For Sale.'"

The *Chicago Daily News* commented on Nov. 1, 1926, "Frank L. Smith has succeeded mainly in registering his uncomprehending astonishment at the discovery that moral forces count in politics."

The scandal broke after the primary and before the general election. Smith's refusal to step aside for a more honorable Republican candidate caused a huge rift in the Republican party. But because 1926 was a big Republican year (and perhaps because all the testimony had not yet aired in Senate hearings), Smith won the general election. And, like Len Small, he used a victory at the polls as a "vindication" of the criminal charge against him. (And, as with Kankakee and Len Small, the local media and museum in Dwight does not mention Frank L. Smith's disgrace).

Governor Small said he would not accept the decision of the U.S. Senate in excluding Smith. He would back Smith again in the next primary election. It was reported that Small was considering appointing William Lorimer to fill the remainder of Smith's term until a special election was held. Remember, Lorimer had been kicked out of the Senate in 1912 for having bribed his way in!

It took another year but Smith finally gave up trying to claim his Senate seat. He handed his resignation to Governor Small on Feb. 9, 1928. TIME magazine reported, "The gesture was not a humble one but the first half of a defiant one. Twiddling his fingers over another sheet of paper, Governor Small completed the gesture by appointing Col. Smith to succeed himself in the Senate vacancy. Then the gesturers planned to have Col. Smith re-elected next November by the people of Illinois."

Yes, Governor Small appointed Frank L. Smith as senator after the vacancy arose from Frank L. Smith being denied the seat on corruption charges! The Senate was not amused by this gesture.

Smith ran again for the Senate nomination in April1928 but lost big. That was the year of the Pineapple Primary, detailed in chapter 21. Len Small also lost that election for nomination for a third term as governor.

The "colonel" from Dwight never took the Senate seat to which he was elected.

Smith campaigned for office again, running for a congressional seat in 1930 that he hoped would lead to the governor's mansion in 1932 (when he would be 65 years old). He came out on top among a field of 23 candidates in the primary but lost the general election by a large margin.

Smith died at his Dwight home on Aug. 30, 1950. The large front page story in the *Kankakee Daily Journal* referred to him as "former United States Senator Frank L. Smith." It wrote glowingly of his many accomplishments but did not mention his scandal or the fact that he never really was a senator.

Frank L. Smith -- like Len Small, George Ryan, Dan Rostenkowski and many other Illinois politicians over the past century -- never understood just what it was that he did wrong. To explain this, "the blame again must be laid upon the accepted practices of Illinois politics, for it was in this school that Smith's political conscience had been trained," Carroll H. Woody wrote in 1931.

Frank L. Smith was, Wooddy said, "A third-rate aspirant for first-class honors."

Wooddy had another insightful observation, not confined to just his generation: "If the Illinois electorate is dead to the appeal of merit, if it prefers to be deluded by false issues, blinded by slogans and debauched by well-financed machines, if it erects precinct intriguers and small-town bosses into the stature of statesmen, if it prizes party regularity above civic virtue, why should the blame rest upon the puppets with whom this deluding game of politics is played? The faults of Smith, the individual, we may palliate as the logical result of the system which produced him."

When uninformed voters allow special interests and political machines to take control, "it is hardly surprising that government tends to fall into the hands of politicians of the type of Thompson, Small or Smith."

"One cannot read the story of Smith's career and emerge with any notably high opinion of the man. For statesmanlike vision, for genuine political principles, for lofty character, even for a considerable measure of intelligent judgment, one looks in vain"

Chapter 9

The Governor Is Indicted

Len Small and Ed Brundage did not like one another.

Brundage first was elected attorney general in 1916. Brundage was a Republican but he became an enemy of the Chicago political machine. Mayor Thompson slated Richard J. Barr of Joliet to be the party's nominee in 1920. Brundage aligned himself with the Lowden faction and he won the primary and re-election in 1920.

When Small became governor, he severely slashed Attorney General Brundage's budget. This, according to the legend promoted by the Smalls -- and cited by many historians and authors -- is why Brundage indicted Small for embezzlement. It was a "vendetta," a trumped-up "persecution" of the governor.

Nothing could be further from the truth.

First, it must be understood why Small cut the attorney general's budget. It was the typical fashion of Len Small, Big Bill Thompson and Fred Lundin to reward friends and punish enemies. Brundage's budget was cut by $1.5 million.

But the motive was more than to just punish Brundage. It was meant to cripple the office by cutting off money to prosecute the Prohibition laws.

And to cut off money to investigate and prosecute the governor.

Brundage's budget included $150,000 for enforcement of Prohibition laws and this specifically was cut from the budget. The friends of the governor and the mayor in Chicago, who were becoming very rich by supplying bootleg booze, did not want the law enforced. Small and Thompson did not plan to disappoint their friends with the pinstripe suits and the bent noses.

Enforcement of liquor laws in Chicago became entirely the responsibility of federal agents. There was no money to prosecute bootleggers -- and besides, most of the Chicago police force was on the payrolls of the various gangs.

A lot of other state departments received drastic cuts by Governor Small, cuts totaling $7 million. Not all of these cuts were sustained.

Brundage knew exactly why his department was being cut. He had been looking into allegations of embezzlement on a massive scale by Small when Small was state treasurer. Len Small had known for months that he was being investigated by the attorney general's office. Small's motive in making the drastic cut "was to shut off the sinews of a successful prosecution.

"Word was sent to me several times by emissaries of the governor that if I would dismiss the civil suits against him, he would approve any appropriations to my office the legislature saw fit to make," Brundage later said.

Small must have been dumfounded, finding a man he could not bribe.

The budget cuts were announced by Governor Small on July 1. Exactly one week later, Brundage made the public announcement that he was convening a special grand jury to look into Small's activities as state treasurer.

Even though the attorney general had been conducting an investigation for months, it was not known to the public until July. The swiftness of the timing between the cuts on July 1, convening a grand jury on July 8, and the indictments on July 20 is what led Small to claim that it was revenge. It is what has kept that story going all these years.

We know why Small cut Brundage's budget. But why did Brundage decide to investigate the allegations against Small for his actions in a previous state office? That story has not been told, but it was simple and obvious and it was not sudden.

Brundage had no other choice, in order to do his job as the state's top law enforcement official, in light of the evidence brought to him.

The facts are that Small was indicted for embezzling more than a million dollars while he was state treasurer. He went on trial in Waukegan and was acquitted. But there is more to the case than that -- a little matter of jury tampering explains the acquittal. But before we get into the details of the trial, let us look at the details of how Len Small stole all that money, as laid out by the prosecutor and as explained in the grand jury findings. Here is how Brundage explained it -- from various accounts at the time, and two years later, in a speech when he had all the facts, including many facts not available at the time of Small's trial.

The whole matter of Small's theft came to light as soon as Edward Miller became state treasurer in 1921. He found that the state received no money from interest on deposits for the first five months of 1920. He also found a record of $10,000,000 deposited in the Grant Park Bank, and it had been loaned without the securities to back it up.

Miller took his information to Attorney General Edward J. Brundage. A quick look into the matter caused Brundage to question whether the Grant Park Bank was legitimate. When Brundage found out state money was being loaned at 6 to 8 per cent interest, while the state treasury was being paid 2 per cent, he decided it bore further investigation.

Brundage called a grand jury in Sangamon County to investigate Small's actions as state treasurer.

The scope of Brundage's probe went beyond Small's two-year term as treasurer from 1917 to 1919. The grand jury was looking into the acts of all treasurers from 1915 to 1921. This included Fred Sterling and Andrew Russel.

When Miller first went to Brundage, he asked for legal advice. He wanted to know if the ledgers, daily cash book, draft register and cancelled checks of the state treasurer were public property or private property. Brundage replied that, of course, it was public property. Miller said he was told the outgoing treasurer kept possession of the records.

"Things are all wrong in the office," Miller told Brundage. "Everything is wrong, and especially the transfer receipt."

Brundage asked Miller for the transfer receipt. It showed $10,052,000 of listed securities, showing money in 360 banks across the state. At the bottom was listed $10,000,000 in Chicago for "safe keeping," dated Jan. 7.

Brundage asked Miller if he had demanded the $10 million from outgoing treasurer Fred Sterling. Miller said yes, but was told to "see Len. He has it."

Brundage went on. "At that time, Len Small had just taken his seat as governor. His second term as state treasurer expired two years earlier.

"Mr. Miller told me further that he had seen Len Small, who admitted that he had the $10 million and added that 'it was all right.' Miller still insisted upon having it in his possession, and the governor promised to deliver to him the securities. My advice to Miller was not to sign the transfer receipt until the securities were delivered, as his securities would be liable if he failed to obtain possession of the ten million dollars."

A week later, Miller was called and asked to meet with the governor at the state capitol. Vernon Curtis was there. The governor pulled a small package from his pocket and gave it to Miller, saying, "Here are your securities."

Miller opened the package and found bank notes from the Swift and the Armour packing houses, totaling $9.9 million. Miller asked about the $100,000 shortage.

"Mr. Small looked up to Curtis and said, 'That's so, Vernon, we must make that up.' The two held a whispered conversation and the governor said, 'I will loan $100,000 to Curtis to make up the shortage,'" Brundage said.

"From the desk he drew forth a note of the late Senator Edward C. Curtis, payable to himself and endorsed by him, and bonds of the American Thread Co. aggregating the amount short. He then remarked to Mr. Curtis, 'You had better give Miller the certificates of deposit.' Curtis drew from his pocket 20 certificates of deposit of the Grant Park Bank, E.C. Curtis & Bro., proprietors, aggregating $10 million. The peculiar thing was that the certificates of deposit presented to be in the hands of the state treasurer were in the possession of the maker of the certificates. Usually, the note giver does not retain the note after making it."

Miller went straight to the offices of the Swift and the Armour companies and demanded payment of the notes. The company officials were surprised to learn that the loans came from state money. They had been told by Edward Curtis that he represented a number of banks that wanted to invest in packing house securities.

The packers said they could not pay the entire amount that was due but would repay them in monthly installments, adding seven per cent additional interest. Miller agreed, collected the interest, and turned it in to the state treasury.

Brundage and Miller sent investigators to Grant Park to look into this "Grant Park Bank." They found no one in this town of approximately 600 people who had heard of the bank.

Some of the old-timers remembered a Grant Park Bank but they said it was dissolved in 1898 when Alonzo Curtis and his sons established a national bank, known as Grant Park Trust & Savings Bank.

That proved to be exactly right.

Miller's investigators went to the Kankakee County courthouse and found that the Grant Park Bank ceased being on the tax records in 1898. They also found no mention of the "bank" in the assets of the estate of Edward Curtis, who died in March 1920.

Investigators discovered that Edward Curtis opened an account at the Fort Dearborn National Bank in Chicago on April 21, 1917 -- just three months after Len Small became state treasurer, and just as quarterly receipts from the county collectors began coming in. Curtis put the account in the name of the "Grant Park Bank" and deposited $2,000.

The Fort Dearborn National Bank was made the depository for the Cook County treasurer to deposit taxes collected for the state.

As soon as Curtis opened this account, he went to the Dwight & H.M. Jackson printers in Chicago and had 500 certificates of deposit and 500 deposit slips for the Grant Park Bank made, along with a "Grant Park Bank" rubber stamp.

Curiously, Curtis told the printer not to give the name of the Grant Park Bank to Rand, McNally & Co, who published a bank directory -- because "it was not in the banking business."

Len Small then began his part of the scheme. He told his chief deputy to open a state account to be designated as a "safe account." He then wrote a draft against the account for $50,000, taken from money in the Fort Dearborn bank and payable to the Grant Park Bank.

The Fort Dearborn bank credited the state's $50,000 draft to the Grant Park Bank's account. On the same day, Edward Curtis used the money to buy a cashier's check in the amount of $50,000, payable to himself. Curtis took the check to the Live Stock Exchange National Bank in Chicago and bought the short-term notes of the packing houses. Upon doing this, he immediately received a check payable to himself for the four-and-a-half per cent interest. The agreement was that the principal and interest would be paid to Curtis.

The money laundering scheme continued in amounts of $500,000 to $1 million, until the amount totaled $10 million in this phantom "Grant Park Bank."

State investigators had to make an exhaustive search to get the records of these transactions from the Live Stock Exchange and the Fort Dearborn banks and from the Swift and the Armour companies because investigators were unable to get the records the easy way, from the state treasurer's office, since Len Small had taken them when he left office.

Small took "the ledger, daily cash book and draft register and all of the checks and drafts issued by him as state treasurer," Brundage said. "He had left not one scrap of paper by which his account as state treasurer could be audited and the amount of interest earned on the public funds in his custody definitely ascertained."

Small made only two interest payments into the state treasury -- $306,424 on Sept. 30, 1918 and $143,585 on April 23, 1920, which was 15 months after leaving office.

"This interest was not placed in the treasury when received by him, as required by law, but was used by Small until the end of his term, and after," Brundage said.

When Small's two-year term was up, he got his successor, Fred Sterling, to appoint him as a "securities expert" to look after the Grant Park Bank account. Sterling owed Small because Small's political power put Sterling in office.

The money continued pouring into the Grant Park Bank until it hit a high of $18 million in July 1919.

What Brundage didn't know at the time -- and didn't find out until after the trial -- was that on the same day Small left the state treasurer's office in January 1919, he loaned $6.5 million and drew $233,236, which was six months interest in advance. He used this money in 1920 to replace state money he had taken for personal use.

"Why was this interest collected the last day of Small's term and paid into the treasurer's account?" Brundage later asked. "The reason is simply that during the last year of his administration, he had withdrawn for his personal use, and that of his co-conspirators, more than $750,000.

"Half of it had already been paid back from interest on state money invested with the packers, and on the last day of his term, they still owed the treasury this $443,000, which must be paid before turning over the office to his successor, or the conspiracy would be discovered."

Brundage continued. "Briefly, here is how Small used this money. In June 1918, he purchased $60,000 of Armour & Co. bonds, paying for them with funds taken from the state treasurer's accounts through the medium of this Grant Park Bank. We have his receipt for these bonds, signed by his own hand.

"During the fall of 1918, Small purchased and had transferred to him 1,373 shares of stock of the Ridgely National Bank, Springfield. This stock was paid for by checks of, or drafts on, E.C. Curtis, aggregating $254,005, which was in turn paid out of funds withdrawn from the state treasurer's account through this same Grant Park Bank.

"On one occasion, the Springfield bank drew a draft on Curtis for $111,833 in payments of stock issued to Small. His draft was paid at the First National Bank of Chicago with funds drawn that same day from the state treasurer's account at the Fort Dearborn bank. For all of this stock, we have Small's receipt signed by his own hand.

"On another occasion, he and his co-conspirators took $100,000 from the treasurer's account and with $50,000 of it purchased various stocks and bonds at the National City company in Chicago. We do not know what was done with the other $50,000.

"Again, in December 1918, $100,000 was withdrawn through the medium of this Grant Park Bank and $100,000 of American Thread company bonds were purchased at the National City company. You will recall that when the conspiracy was exposed in 1921 and they were having difficulty in making up the $100,000 shortage in securities, Small loaned to Vernon Curtis some American Thread company bonds to help make up the shortage.

"Then, in September 1918, Small went through the motions of paying nearly $307,000 into the treasury as interest on public funds collected by him and which he had failed to pay into the treasury. Small had never denied the charge that the money was not actually paid until the last day of his term, when his friend E.C. Curtis paid it for him out of interest on state money invested with the packers, which itself already belonged to the state. What monumental effrontery it was to pay the state with its own money?

"Small and his co-conspirators used for their own personal use more than $750,000 of state money and paid it back during the last few months of his term, almost if not entirely from earnings on other state moneys. The total amount of public moneys manipulated in this manner was more than $28,000,000. If reinvestments be included, the amount reaches the staggering total of over $65,000,000.

"The rate of interest paid on these loans ranged from four-and-a-half per cent to eight-and-a-half per cent, the average probably being around seven per cent. The total amount of interest earned on these public moneys from April 21, 1917 to January 11, 1921 was $2,185,000. Internal checks which were presented to the jury at Waukegan showed that some of them were deposited in the First Trust & Savings Bank of Kankakee, of which Small was president. Some were used to return money withdrawn for the personal use of the conspirators and the balance was deposited in the Grant Park Trust & Savings Bank, of which E.C. Curtis was president."

"All of the public moneys of the state, except a small fraction, were invested through the medium of the so-called Grant Park Bank," Brundage said. "At one time, the legitimate banks had in their custody only $3 million, but this Grant Park Bank, presumed to be in a town of 600 inhabitants, had $10 million at one time."

The amount of interest earned on state deposits and reported to the treasury during the four years of Len Small's and Fred Sterling's terms was $1,046,131. And the amount of interest earned on state deposits during that same time by the Grant Park Bank was $2,185,000, according to Brundage.

"Treasurer Len Small had in his possession a total of $23 million of public money and paid in as interest upon that sum an average of about 1.85 per cent. The money invested in packing house securities paid the war time rate of interest, from 6 to 8.5 per cent," Brundage said.

After State Treasurer Edward Miller told his story to the attorney general, Brundage said to him, "Mr. Miller, do you realize that this is a criminal conspiracy to loot the public treasury?"

Miller replied, "I presume it is." Brundage asked Miller if he was willing to present the evidence to the state's attorney of Sangamon County. Miller said yes.

State's Attorney C. Fred Mortimer was "utterly amazed" when he saw the evidence. A grand jury in Springfield was convened in July 1921, consisting of 18 farmers and five men from the city.

Among those testifying were State Treasurer Edward Miller, who told the same story he told to Brundage and Mortimer. He said Small deposited $10 million in the Grant Park Bank, which then bought $4.5 million in short-term notes of Swift & Co. and $5.5 million of notes of Armour & Co. The interest rates on these securities were about eight per cent. The interest was paid to Edward C. Curtis.

Also called before the grand jury were Fred Crowell, treasurer of Armour & Co., and W.W. Sherman, assistant treasurer of Swift & Co. The Chicago meat packers who took the loans said they believed the loans were from the Curtis bank. They claimed innocence about state deposits being loaned fraudulently.

Subpoenas also were served to George M. Bennett, a former business partner of Alonzo Curtis; Kankakee County Clerk Henry Groenewoud; Alice Cornell, former secretary to Edward C. Curtis; Henry Luehrs, assistant state treasurer under Small; Harry Whittemore, a former Kankakee County assistant state's attorney.

The grand jury also called Norman Griffin, cashier at Grant Park Trust & Savings Bank.

Griffin told the grand jury that the Grant Park Bank was started as a private bank in the general store of Alonzo Curtis in 1890. After Alonzo died, sons Edward and Vernon incorporated it in 1898 as the Grant Park National Bank (which became the Grant Park Trust & Savings Bank in 1908).

All the while, Griffin said, the private "Grant Park Bank" continued to exist (somewhere) in the same building. This was Small's "conclusive" proof that the bank was legitimate; it also was Brundage's proof that the private bank was a ruse.

Griffin said he worked only for the legitimate Grant Park Trust & Savings Bank, and Edward Curtis was the only person who worked for the private bank.

Griffin told the grand jury that the Grant Park Bank had no building, no room, no furniture, never advertised it was open and had no sign to let the people know it existed. It never solicited business from the people of Grant Park (population 459 in 1920) as the other two banks in town did. Its only client was the state of Illinois, with deposits courtesy of State Treasurer Len Small.

After adjourning for a few days, the grand jury resumed on July 20. It must have been an uncomfortable scene the day before, when Small and Brundage found themselves sitting just a few feet apart on the same train to Springfield.

Governor Small issued several emphatic denials or any wrongdoing. His statement on July 12 said, "The schemes and slanders of the character assassins who are the tools of the rich tax dodgers and the traction barons, and those who have been prevented by my veto from looting the state treasury, will not deter me from doing everything in my power to carry on the principles upon which I made my campaign and which I reiterated in my inauguration address. I promised that I would give the people a dollar in value for every dollar of their money spent. I have succeeded in reducing the cost of roads many thousands of dollars a mile and I have vetoed $7 million in appropriations, cutting out items which were not necessary to the welfare of the state."

At the same time, Small started his own investigation, demanding that Brundage furnish paperwork showing every dollar spent by the attorney general's office. Small was looking for anything in an attempt to have Brundage removed from office.

Len Small, Vernon Curtis and Fred Sterling were indicted on July 20, 1921, on six counts of embezzling state funds, conspiracy to defraud the state, and for operating a "confidence game." They were accused of stealing more than a million dollars.

Judge Ernest Smith set the bond for Small and Sterling at $150,000 each. Vernon Curtis' bond was set at $100,000.

The indictment said, "Len Small as treasurer did wickedly, willfully, unlawfully and feloniously embezzle and fraudulently convert to his own use, steal, take and carry away the said money belonging to, and then and there, being the property of the state of Illinois."

Another count charged the governor with the embezzlement of "bonds, mortgages, coupons, bank bills, notes, warrants, orders, funds and securities" and accused Small of converting these securities to his own use.

The conspiracy and confidence game indictments charged that Small, Sterling and Curtis got together to plan their theft of state funds.

The grand jury also submitted a report recommending that the legislature conduct an exhaustive investigation into the handling of public funds, and to enact legislation to prevent future malfeasance. Just as loopholes were tightened after Small's ended his first term as treasurer in 1907, the law needed to be tightened after Small's second term.

In returning the indictments, the grand jury cited the law that said the state treasurer was required to deposit money within five days of receipt into banks that were secure and that paid the highest rates of interest.

"We find that both the letter and the spirit of the law were violated," the report said.

It continued: "Instead of loaning the state moneys to all secure banks of the state without discrimination and to such of them that paid the highest rate of interest, only a portion of that money was loaned in accordance with the provisions of the statute. For the purpose of circumventing these provisions, an ingenious scheme was devised and closely adhered to."

Brundage said the daily balances of the state treasury were carried on the books under two primary funds, one in a "vault fund" and the other in a "safe fund." The vault fund contained money deposited in legitimate banks throughout the state. The money in the safe fund was money deposited in the phony Grant Park Bank. The vault fund total always was much less than the amount in the safe fund.

The books of the safe account were not kept in the treasurer's office, he added. Brundage didn't know where they were kept -- or where they were now.

Brundage said the Grant Park Bank was "purported to be owned by a single individual and did not transact any banking business whatever, as it had no depositor other than the state of Illinois, yet it was given huge deposits of public moneys by two former state treasurers, Small and Sterling. The average deposits of state moneys carried by this purported bank were $10 million.

"The evidence shows that money was taken from the state treasury, generally in lots of $500,000, and deposited in the so-called Grant Park Bank, which thereupon issued and delivered to the state treasurer certificates of deposits for the amounts received, but without any collateral security. In other words, the only evidence of indebtedness and the only security held by the treasurer for the loans aggregating $10 million were paper obligations of a fictitious bank."

In other words, the certificates of deposit printed by Curtis were bogus.

"The moneys so received were used in purchasing at a discount short-time notes issued by Swift & Co. and Armour & Co., two large corporations engaged in the packing business in Chicago. These transactions netted the purchasers of the notes large profits. If any portion of the profits so realized was paid into the state treasury, it was less than 2 per cent. The evidence shows that most of the banks receiving public moneys paid into the state treasury on public funds during the administration of Messrs. Small and Sterling less than 2 per cent per annum.

"Records of the treasurer's office for July 10, 1919 show the manner in which public funds were handled. On that day, the vault fund was debited with $7,977,500 of which sum $4,477,000 was deposited to approximately 300 banks throughout the state, and $3,000,000 in private banking institutions, while the safe fund was debited with $18,000,000."

Given the facts of the state's case, the grand jury returned the indictments.

The indictments should have come as no surprise to anyone. Small's record as treasurer was well known. It had been discussed in public for years. Both of his opponents in the 1920 campaign for governor, John Maynard Harlan and James Hamilton Lewis, brought it up several times. Even Small addressed the issue during the 1920 campaign, denying he kept any of the money he had deposited.

But as usual, Small said it was all a plot by political enemies. He blamed everyone he could, but singled out the attorney general.

"Attorney General Brundage, leader of the conspiracy, has succeeded in obtaining this indictment, simply because of the personal fury I aroused in him because I refused to permit him to take from the taxpayers' pockets $1.5 million for the upkeep of his personal political machine," Small's lengthy statement included.

"So Mr. Brundage not only desired my political assassination, but he proceeded with the machinery at his hands to accomplish that fact. The *Chicago Tribune,* spokesman for all the interests, gladly lent the aid of its powerful press to spreading the broadcast of Mr. Brundage's propaganda.

"Brundage came to Sangamon County, the only county in the state where he had any hopes of securing an indictment against me. While it may seem amazing that any grand jury could do this thing, still I am not surprised that a Sangamon County grand jury, dominated by an organization protecting the most vicious criminals and law violators to be found in the state of Illinois, has taken this action."

Sangamon County is where the state capital of Springfield is located.

"The *Chicago Daily News,* owned and edited by Mr. Victor Lawson, not only a tax dodger of record himself but spokesman for the millionaire tax dodgers of Chicago who refuse to bear their just proportion of taxes, rushed to the aid of Mr. Brundage and the *Tribune.* The public utility interests, offended because I have kept my pledge for the home rule and the abolition of their former tool, the Public Utilities Commission, gave what support they were able to give to Mr. Brundage's effort to besmirch my name and my record. The traction interests, who know the present governor of Illinois will reduce street car fares from 8 and 10 cents to 5, if it is humanly possible, gladly joined with Mr. Brundage and the other interests to annihilate me.

"I am absolutely innocent of every charge they make."

But even as the grand jury was doing its work, Governor Small was trying to bribe a member of the grand jury by offering him a state job.

Yes, Small later was accused of tampering with the jury at his trial in Waukegan in June 1922 -- but this charge accused Small of trying to bribe a member of the Sangamon County grand jury that indicted him in July 1921!

The story came out on Nov. 29, 1921, in the *Chicago Journal, Chicago Daily News* and *Kankakee Daily News.* It had been mentioned several months earlier. This story brought the accusation up again, with more details.

The newspaper stories said that William "Buck" Evans, a grand jury member, was approached by a Small "zealot" who offered a bribe for not returning the indictments. It was rumored that former judge Chauncey H. Jenkins was the man. Jenkins denied it. Jenkins claimed that Evans approached him for a state job and threatened to ruin Jenkins in the press if he didn't get the job.

Jenkins, appointed by Governor Small as state director of Public Welfare, was one of three Springfield politicians who put up their property as surety on Small's bond when the governor was arrested.

Jenkins claimed the newspapers printed the story to prejudice the jury pool. However, Mortimer told Small's lawyers about the accusations several weeks earlier and took no action so he would not prejudice public opinion against Small.

The NEWS First

THE KANKAKEE DAILY NEWS

Member United Press

VOLUME TWO — KANKAKEE, ILLINOIS, SATURDAY, JULY 23, 1921

SMALL TO USE MILITIA

SMALL'S LAWDEFIANCE SEEN AS SERIOUS BLOW TO CLAIM OF INNOCENCE

Refusal to Take Chance With Justice Held One of Series of Blunders Which Will Have Ill Effect.

CONDUCTOR'S ORDERS MUST BE OBEYED

RULING OF APPELLATE COURT IN SPRINGFIELD THIS WEEK.

SINN FEIN OPPOSE ACCEPTANCE OF PREMIER'S OFFER

WOULD PREFER RESUMPTION OF HOSTILITIES TO POTENTIAL DOMINION HOME RULE.

DRILLING OF OIL WELLS IS SLOW WORK

DRILL HAS PENETRATED BUT 24 FEET BELOW THE SURFACE.

GOVERNOR DETERMINES PHYSICAL RESISTANCE IF WARRANT IS SERVED

Adjutant Dickson Advises Chief Executive That Military Forces Can Report in Twenty Minutes to Protect Him.

Springfield, July 23.—State troops were ready today to report on twenty minutes' notice to protect Governor Len Small from arrest.

IF IT'S NEWS IT'S IN

The NEWS First

THE KANKAKEE DAILY NEWS

Member United Press

VOLUME TWO — KANKAKEE, ILLINOIS, TUESDAY, JULY 26, 1921

MUST ARREST SMALL

"There is No King in Illinois," Says Jurist

DESPERATE FEAR SEEN AS CAUSE OF SMALL'S FIGHT AGAINST COURT

...sible Result of Trial Held Responsible for Threatened Use of Militia to Protect Self from Arrest on Warrant.

(BY A STAFF CORRESPONDENT.)

SMALL BEING USED AS TOOL

HEALY HOME, VAN'S SIDING DESTROYED

HOUSE AND PRACTICALLY ALL ITS CONTENTS ARE BURNED.

UNDER CHARGES OF EMBEZZLEMENT

LEN SMALL

SOVIET WILL FIGHT FAMINE IN RUSSIA

THOUSANDS DYING DAILY FOR WANT OF FOOD AND WATER.

The mills of the gods grind slowly, but they grind Small exceedingly.

JUDGE SMITH ORDERS WARRANT PLACED WITH SHERIFF FOR SERVICE

Aged Jurist Quotes the Law to Show That Every Effort Must Be Made to Serve Governor.

Springfield, July 26.—Judge E. S. Smith today held Governor Len Small amenable to arrest on warrants charging embezzlement of large sums of state funds.

Overruling the contention of Small's attorneys that the governor is immune from arrest by virtue of office, Judge Smith said:

"THERE IS NO KING IN ILLINOIS. THE GOVERNOR IS LIABLE TO ARREST."

Chapter 10

The Governor Is Arrested

"The King can do no wrong."

-- Small's lawyers' legal basis and argument in court as to why Len Small could not be indicted or arrested for any crime.

The process is simple. A public official is indicted, he surrenders, is processed, he puts up his bond and he is released.

Not Len Small.

He decided to turn this ordinary procedure into a circus side show, with himself as the head clown, and then he complained that the audience was laughing at him.

When the indictments were returned, Sangamon County Judge Ernest Smith issued the customary arrest warrants for Len Small, Fred Sterling and Vernon Curtis.

Len Small was the only one to put up a high-profile fight against the arrest warrant.

Governor Small made it clear that he was not going to comply. He said he would not be arrested and he would not be put on trial.

The day after the indictment, Small claimed he was immune from arrest because, as governor, he was above the law. He cited the state constitution for his reasoning, claiming that one branch of government (the judiciary) could not interfere with another branch (the executive).

To prevent his arrest, Small said he had "the power to call out state troops to hold off the sheriff's deputies at the point of the bayonet."

What is more, Small said that defying the indictments was "not a personal privilege but an exemption in the interest of the public welfare, and to perpetuate the independence of the executive department."

And in keeping with the governor's regard for the public, he said he would avoid arrest because "chaos in state government" would result if he was arrested.

"How could a government function without a head? How could the laws be executed without an executive? How could the laws enacted by the legislature be either in force or enforced without a governor?" he said.

In other words, the state of Illinois could not function without Len Small. He was doing us a favor by refusing to be arrested and tried.

"Now suppose the governor submits to arrest," Small continued. "Suppose he refused to give bail. Suppose he is imprisoned, but although imprisoned he is in the state and still governor. While under arrest, he might very naturally refuse to act in his official capacity. The governor, being in the state, the lieutenant governor cannot act as governor, and so the executive function is suspended, the body is without a head. Chaos will reign."

The governor then made a very ominous threat.

"Again, suppose the court orders the sheriff to arrest the governor and that the sheriff tries to carry out the order of the court, but the Constitution makes the governor a commander in chief of the military and naval forces of the state, and the officers and members of these forces are sworn to obey their commander in chief. Should the sheriff attempt to use force in arresting the governor?

"The military, obeying their commander in chief, resist the attempt. What is the result? One independent function of the government, trying by physical force to overcome and reduce to subjection another equally independent branch. The House is divided against itself. Anarchy may follow."

Small continued his "suppositions" by saying that if a governor is convicted, he had the power to pardon himself.

It was all so incredible -- Governor Small's claim that he could not be arrested for a crime because he was above the law; and if the sheriff attempted to arrest him, he could call out the military to fight the sheriff's deputies; and that if he was convicted, he could pardon himself.

The governor made it clear, on several occasions in his own *Kankakee Daily Republican,* that the use of military force to protect himself from arrest was a real possibility. When asked how far the governor would go, a top aide told the *New York Times,* "He'll go the limit."

The governor backed up his words with a show of force. Small's own newspaper on July 22 noted, "The presence of several National Guard officers in uniform in the state house was considered significant in some quarters today, inasmuch as the opinion of the governor's counsel holds that he has it in his power to muster troops to protect him from arrest if such a move is considered necessary."

When Adjutant General Frank S. Dickson appeared at the state house in uniform, he said he donned the military regalia because he expected to visit state troops in annual encampment at various camps.

This could have been a much more serious situation than some had anticipated. The *Kankakee Daily News* observed that the governor could use martial law to seize the state's court records. Martial law would suspend court proceedings, and Springfield might have to remain under martial law until Small's term expired, the newspaper added. It imagined this scenario:

"The spectacle of holding the capital of the state under martial law would make Governor Small and his administration the laughingstock of the nation, toward which end it is galloping even now. Even if he should call out the militia for active duty to protect him against a lone sheriff with a warrant, it would present a laughable spectacle. The visitors to Springfield would time their sight-seeing to witness the imposing sight of the governor leaving the mansion for the state house with a company of soldiers at his heels. Visitors to the capitol building would find soldiers in the corridors to search them and wave them away from the sacred portals of the executive offices. There would be soldiers around the mansion, pompous officers with polished sabers, polished puttees and boots. Truly, regal splendors of the royalty and king, which the governor, along with Big Bill and Fred Lundin, claim they despise in their campaign speeches. And when he went to Kankakee, would he have them put on a special car for his bodyguard? Would the democratic home of Kankakee's farmers look like a military camp? And if the governor and his soldiery went on to Chicago to get orders from Fred Lundin, would they be quartered in the hotels?"

Curtis and Sterling submitted themselves to arrest and booking at once, as is the procedure, and they made bail. On Aug. 24, Sterling paid the state $391,386 in interest on state funds that he had kept as state treasurer -- seven months after leaving office. Sterling claimed this was just a late accounting on his part and not a payback of stolen money. In Sterling's two-year term as treasurer, he had turned in $996,121 in interest. Even so, State's Attorney Fred Mortimer said Sterling's $391,386 payment was not enough.

Small made it clear that he wasn't going to surrender. And with his armed militia around the capitol, he made it clear he wasn't going to let the sheriff come to arrest him. He hinted that troops at Camp Logan could be called at any time.

And Governor Small suggested that he might call out the National Guard to put Springfield under martial law and round up his political enemies!

"I would be proud of doing anything in my power to drive away from the shadow of our state house the vicious and the depraved," Small was quoted in the July 25 edition of his own *Kankakee Daily Republican*.

The story continued: "And in this sentence, there may be meaning. For some of Governor Small's friends have been urging him to clamp the city under martial law. As commander in chief of the state military forces, he could then direct the purging of the town. An entertaining counter, certainly, to the indictments."

The decisions, Small said, would depend on the decision of Judge Ernest Smith about a governor's immunity from arrest. Hasty action by the court, according to Small's lawyer George Gillespie, would be "Mexicanizing the state of Illinois."

Not everyone thought Governor Small had the authority to call out the troops for such a purpose. One vocal critic was Col. Franklin A. Denison, a Chicago attorney who was a former commander of the 8th Illinois National Guard Infantry and the 370th U.S. Infantry during the war. Denison said any troops ordered to Springfield would be under the orders of the county officials, specifically the sheriff.

"There is no question of this being the fact," Denison said. "The Constitution provides without qualification that the military shall be in strict subordination to the civil power and the state law provides specifically that troops ordered out to suppress riots or similar disturbances shall report to the sheriff of the county or the mayor of the city in which the disturbance occurs. As for the governor's right to call out troops to prevent the service of a warrant upon him, I can find nothing in the law that would authorize such a step. The Constitution is specific in limiting him to calling out troops 'to execute the laws, suppress insurrections and repeal invasion.' There has been no allegation that any of these developments threatens at the present time.

"Furthermore, there is no doubt that if troops ordered out were directed to do an illegal act, the mere fact that they were ordered to do it would not excuse them from responsibility for that act. If, for instance, a soldier were ordered to fire upon a deputy sheriff in the performance of his duty, that soldier could be held for murder."

Col. Denison suggested that Gen. Dickson seek legal advice. A number of other lawyers expressed the same opinion. One said that "if a governor should call out troops to protect his person from arrest, he would be in effect leading an insurrection."

It may have been such advice that made Small back down from his threat.

In an irony of history, Governor Small (like Governor George Ryan) had a former governor (Joseph Fifer) among those representing him in court.

Former Democrat congressman James Graham also was on Small's legal team. Graham advised Small to resist arrest, to call out the National Guard, to place Springfield and Sangamon County under martial law and to arrest local political opponent Richard Sullivan and try him before a military court!

Governor Small met with Adjutant Gen. Frank Dickson about calling out the National Guard to prevent the sheriff from arresting him.

"Adjutant Frank Dickson was strutting around the state house in full uniform following a conference with Small, during which he told the governor the state militia could be called out in 20 minutes after the call was issued," the *Kankakee Daily News* reported on July 23.

Judge Smith listened to the lawyers' arguments about executive immunity. He had a few questions of his own.

"The contention made here, if it prevails, would mean that the governor can, during his term of office, commit whatever crime he pleases and would be answerable to nobody until he gets out of office," the judge said. "It would seem that for four years, the governor could commit any violation of law. I am not saying that the governor would do it, but that is the result of the argument."

Judge Smith asked Graham a hypothetical question: "Do you mean to say that if the governor of Illinois should go out on the streets of Springfield and commit a murder, he could not be arrested and tried for it?"

Incredibly, Graham replied that if that happened, the governor "could not be touched until after he had served his term as governor."

Judge Smith asked, "Suppose the governor should be re-elected, he would be exempt for eight years?"

Graham replied, "Don't you see that by his re-election, the whole people would have passed on his case?"

The judge had enough of this ridiculous sparring. "The people are not the courts. That is a question for the judiciary to pass on," he said.

Fifer said, "To incarcerate your governor is a flesh wound, but to break down the institutions founded by our forefathers, that is blood poison. I don't know what may happen. But when I pull aside the curtain, I tremble for this country."

Judge Smith indicated he did not appear worried about the future of the country in this matter. "The action pending here, and which somewhat distresses the court, has no relation whatsoever to any official conduct," the judge said. "The offense charged is not one committed as an act of the governor, and the argument presented support that the governor during his term of office may commit any crime he pleases and be answerable to no one. That is a dangerous assumption."

The lawyers argued before Judge Ernest Smith on July 21 that Len Small was not subject to arrest because he was governor, with Graham basing the defense on an Old English doctrine, "The King can do no wrong."

The judge was outraged at this argument. "'The King can do no wrong' is an old monarchial doctrine, but in this republic, that doctrine has never reached the application of elected officials. Our governors are not born kings. They were not born with halos around them."

A *New York Times* account went, "Judge Smith referred to Governor Small's attitude as that of a King above his subjects, and declared that there was no counterpart in Illinois to the title of King."

(This incident came back to embarrass Graham in April 1922, when Illinois Democrats held their convention in Springfield. One section of the platform condemned Governor Small for his "king can do no wrong" defense. Graham was a delegate and he had a "pained expression" when the phrase was introduced. Graham made a motion to strike the wording from the resolution but he could not find anyone to second his motion).

"The 75-year-old jurist, with eyes gleaming and jaws coming together with a snap, ordered the clerk of the court to place the warrants for Small's arrest in the hands of Sheriff Mester," the *Kankakee Daily News* wrote. "Then, for Mester's benefit, he quoted from the law to show that the sheriff must make every effort to serve the warrants or he is liable to punishment for non-performance of duty.

"Judge Smith declared that the governor will violate the law should he carry out his threat of calling state troops for his protection. 'The governor has no right to call the militia for his personal protection,' he declared."

Judge Smith continued: "We have been fortunate in the charges and conduct of our elected officers, but never has it been suspected or intimated that they are not capable of committing a crime before, during or after their terms of office. Our governors are not born kings. They are not surrounded by a halo at birth that has given them immunity from arrest. Our governors are liable to arrest."

Small's lawyer's tactic was to argue that impeachment should be the process, not criminal charges. Impeachment was not likely with a Republican majority in Springfield.

But the judge did not buy into that tactic. The Constitution provides for impeachment, the judge added, but that is for malfeasance in office, and not the proper remedy for a criminal act. The judge also did not like the talk that Small would call out the state militia to protect himself from arrest.

"The governor may call out the militia to enforce the law," the judge was quoted in the *New York Times.* "It has been said that he may call out the militia to prevent service of writs on him. This does not impress the Court with great force. The governor cannot call out the militia to prevent the procession of law. The only purpose for which the militia can be called out is to aid the civil authorities in enforcing the law, not to break the law, not to set aside the judgment of the judiciary.

"This question hardly merits discussion because it is almost beyond the pale of possibilities that any but a tyrant would really and seriously think of calling out the military power of the state, or of attempting to do so to prevent the execution of a mandate of the statute of an order of the court which is subject to review of a higher court," the judge said.

Such an unlawful order would be the same as if no order were issued, he said. The judge also saw through Small's tactic to delay criminal prosecution until he was out of office so that a statute of limitations would expire.

Another of Small's threats came up in court. "Mr. Fifer said that the governor might be thrown into jail and while there might pardon everyone but himself," the *New York Times* account added. "The governor might pardon others and empty the jails," the judge replied, but "he could not pardon himself."

Governor Small returned to Springfield on July 24 but with bodyguards -- National Guard Col. A.F. Lorenzen and Capt. Carlos E. Black, in full uniform. Also with Small were lawyer Albert Fink, Percy Coffin, Cornelius R. Miller and W.H.H. Miller. They were met at the station by Chauncey H. Jenkins and State Sen. John A. Wheeler.

On July 25, the day before the judge was to rule on whether Small would have to submit to arrest, Co. C of the 4th Illinois Infantry was ordered to report to the armory at Springfield. They were told to be ready for immediate service. The governor held a long conference with Col. A.F. Lorenzen but no order was given.

Small eventually backed off his threat to call out the militia. The *Kankakee Daily Republican* said the threat "has caused a feeling of panic among the vice interests of Springfield. Under the office-holders controlled by the Dick Sullivan machine, bootleggers, gambling houses and other vicious resorts have been permitted to operate without molestation. The vice interest's terror has been inspired by the thought that military control of the capital would be followed by a cleanup that would drive out every sink hole in the city. This would automatically shut off an annual revenue of approximately $500,000 for certain politicians who countenanced present conditions."

Judge Smith ruled on July 26 that Governor Len Small was not above the law. The judge said Small was not immune from arrest and that warrants should be served. However, the judge granted a special privilege to the privileged governor. He said Small would be permitted to make his appearance to the court at his convenience "within a reasonable amount of time."

Sheriff Henry Mester notified the governor that warrants were being held. He went one step further, adding, "I may go over for an interview with the governor later, but no attempt will be made to embarrass him." Mester said he would exercise "tact" and would not "force" the arrest of the governor.

Instead of seeing this as being conciliatory or a compromise in confrontation, a "close friend" of Governor Small "laughed heartily" at the sheriff's comments, according to a July 26 story in the *Kankakee Daily Republican.* Small was quoted as saying, "He will find me right here, and everything will be just as it is right now."

He was daring the sheriff to come and get him. Small still refused to submit himself to the court's procedure. He continued to argue that he was immune from arrest.

While publicly saying he would submit to arrest if the sheriff came to get him, Small evaded the sheriff. Small refused to allow his secretary to meet the state's attorney, who had called with an offer for Small give his bond informally to avoid any inconvenience. When the state's attorney asked if the governor would be in his office, the secretary said that Small had left Springfield for Kankakee. Small then went to Chicago to seek advice from Big Bill Thompson, Fred Lundin and others. Once again, Small happened to be on the same train to Chicago as Brundage.

Small finally notified the Sangamon County sheriff on July 27 that he could be served the warrant in his Chicago office. The sheriff told Small to come to Springfield.

Small used this to proclaim that the sheriff had "cold feet" and was afraid to make the arrest.

Governor Small's had several attorneys during this time. The attorney who gave him the legal advice and acted as his spokesman in this matter was Albert Fink -- the same lawyer for William Lorimer in his trial for banking fraud in 1914 and the same lawyer who would act as Al Capone's attorney in his tax evasion case in 1931.

Yes, Fink was the mouthpiece for William Lorimer, Len Small and Al Capone.

It was a legal maneuver on Fink's part. The governor would remain in Chicago while his lawyers filed a writ of *habeas corpus* in a Chicago court. Fink said he could find a "friendlier" judge in Chicago.

Fink hoped this would force the state to show immediate proof why the governor should be required to submit himself to a criminal trial. If the writ was granted, the indictment would be nullified and the state could not put Small on trial unless it obtained a new indictment based on new evidence. The legal trickery was part of the Small playbook.

But although there were plenty of Chicago judges friendly to City Hall, those who looked at the petition from Small's lawyers could not get past the "king can do no wrong" argument and Judge Smith's scathing ruling.

It was Governor Small's notion that if he was arrested in a certain county, the trial would have to be held in that county. If he had to go on trial, Cook County was the place he preferred.

Meanwhile, Sheriff Mester said he would not go north to arrest Small.

"I will not go to Chicago to serve the warrants on Governor Small," Mester said. "I am sending a telegram to Mr. Fink, advising him that Governor Small may give bond in Springfield at his convenience."

Mester told the *New York Times,* "It is not my present intention to use force."

The *Times* reported that Small "has had several husky guards in attendance both at the State House and mansion ever since the indictments were returned." If the sheriff showed up, it added, the bodyguards would be supplemented by state militia.

Even though Small said he was making himself available to Sangamon

County Sheriff Mester -- in Chicago, 200 miles from the sheriff's jurisdiction -- he changed hotels on July 27. The next day, his whereabouts were unknown, although the *Daily Republican* reported he was in conference at the house of Albert Fink.

Lawyers for the notorious Carl Wanderer, who was to hang for murder on July 29, were frantic. They were waiting on their request for a reprieve from the governor but no one knew where he was.

There was no question of Wanderer's guilt. Small was found and he issued a reprieve to September, when Wanderer was hanged. This was one murderer who was not pardoned by Governor Small.

A humorous incident happened in the middle of all this. Sheriff Mester received a telegram from Frank Minkler, a deputy sheriff in Great Barrington, Mass., asking if there was a reward offered for the capture of Len Small. Minkler thought he spotted the Illinois governor in his state and he wanted to know if it was worth his while to take him in.

"I have a man under watch who resembles Small's picture and he is a man keeping shady," Minkler wrote. "The man and picture have a resemblance hardly to be mistaken." Mester replied that there was no reward.

The Kankakee Daily Republican printed on July 29 a new list of "reasons" why "they" were seeking the governor's destruction. First, because the governor "thwarted the attempt of the cement trust to rob the people of $54 million in building 4,800 miles of hard roads." Second, because the governor "vetoed needless appropriations of the people's money, mounting to $7 million, of which one-tenth, or $700,000 was for Attorney General Brundage." Third, because the governor "stands for legislation which will save the people of Chicago the difference between 5 and 8 cent street car fares, which amounts to thousands of dollars per day." Fourth, because the governor "advocates passing a law which will reduce taxes by placing the $12 billion in wealth which is now dodging taxation, on the tax books." Fifth, because Governor Small "refuses to permit his office to be used as a vehicle for Medill McCormick's gluttonous political ambition."

Even though Sheriff Mester said he would not come to Chicago to arrest Governor Small, the governor continued to keep his whereabouts a mystery. He went further by heading out on a "hard road inspection tour" through a number of counties across the state. It began on July 29 and continued until Aug. 3. The man who declared himself the "honest protector of the people's money" promised miles and miles of new hard roads and new armories for Kankakee and Danville.

A minor accident was blown into superhuman heroics by Small's *Kankakee Daily Republican.* The governor's limousine skidded into a ditch near Momence on Aug. 2 "The governor leaped from the machine and held it up until others in the machine scrambled to safety," according to the brief news account.

The governor continued to avoid Springfield. On his "hard roads tour" in Danville on Aug. 3, he dared Mester to come and arrest him in Vermilion County.

"They know why they do not want me arrested outside of Sangamon County, ruled as it is by the rottenest political ring in the history of the state," Small said. "This ring furnishes protection to 300 of the lowest dives, where murder is often committed, and from which the boss collects tribute."

Governor Small finally returned to Springfield on the evening of Aug. 7. Sheriff Mester said he would wait a day or two. If the governor had not surrendered by then, Mester said he would go to the governor's office but not take the arrest warrants along. "They will be served right here in my office," Mester said. "Everything is in readiness for him to come in and arrange his bond."

Sheriff Henry Mester did everything he could to make the arrest a smooth, dignified and private matter. It was Small who insisted on obstruction, obstinacy and public embarrassment of himself.

By Tuesday, Aug. 9, the sheriff was convinced that Small had no intention of coming in privately. He went to the governor's office at 11:30 a.m., hoping to catch him leaving his office for lunch. "There is nothing to do but to arrest him in spite of his protests," Mester said. "We have given him a chance to come over voluntarily and arrange his bonds and he has refused."

Because of all the legal wrangling, and on legal advice, Mester did not want to arrest the governor in his office while he was conducting state business. It was the idea of Small and his lawyers that the whole case would be thrown out of court if the warrants were improperly served -- and they thought serving warrants while the governor was in the performance of his duties would do the trick.

Sheriff Mester waited in the hallway, calmly smoking a cigar. But Small did not go out to lunch. Mester told a reporter he was prepared to wait all day. By the end of the day, his patience was stretched as thin as it would go. He went into the governor's office. The report of the confrontation was taken by the governor's stenographers, and the account here comes from both the *Chicago Tribune* and from the *Kankakee Daily Republican.*

"Well, how d'ye do, Governor?" Mester said.

"How are you today?" the governor replied, as he rose and shook the sheriff's outstretched hand.

"Pretty well, thank you, Governor," said the sheriff. "I thought I would come and see you about those warrants, and see whether you had made arrangements to come and give bonds and save trouble."

"You haven't got the warrants with you?" asked Governor Small.

"No, sir," said the sheriff.

"I don't see how I could do that," the governor said. He then read a long prepared statement on his position, repeating his argument that he would not submit to the jurisdiction of the judiciary because it was against the constitutional separation of powers.

When Small finished his speech, the sheriff said, "Well, on the other hand, under my oath of office, I am supposed to carry out the orders of the court."

"You are responsible for your acts, not the court, not at all, the court not at all," shouted the governor. "You and your bondsmen are responsible for your acts."

After an uncomfortable pause, the sheriff went on, "Well, I will have to serve the warrants. I thought I would come over first and see if you would file bonds."

"No," said Governor Small.

"I would be in contempt of court if I did not do it," the sheriff said.

The governor said nothing. The sheriff said, to no one in particular, "I get hit both ways. Well, I guess I'll have to take it."

Sheriff Mester felt embarrassed. He looked around the room and then said, "It's not a very nice job. It makes it kind of bad. The public will say, 'You have the warrants now, why don't you arrest the governor?' It sets a kind of precedent."

"You have neither power nor right," Governor Small replied. "If the court told you to hang Judge Gillespie and you did it, you would be guilty of murder."

Mester smiled. "Well, a court wouldn't issue that kind of an order. It would be unreasonable."

"It would not be any more unreasonable or unusual than what you are trying to do," Small said.

"Well, I am not well enough posted on the law to answer those questions. The warrants came into my hands to be served," the sheriff replied. "I came over to see whether you would come over and submit. We are trying to accommodate you the best we can. If you feel like taking that stand -- that is what I came to see you about."

The governor said there was nothing else he could do. The sheriff asked whether the governor would come if he arrested him. Small replied he would "do whatever is necessary to fulfill my obligations" to the people of the state.

The governor dared the sheriff to arrest him. The sheriff said he would not arrest the governor in his own office and that he would wait for him to come out. George Gillespie, another of Small's lawyers, also encouraged the sheriff to make the arrest there. The sheriff said he would not, citing his own legal advice about arresting a governor while he is in the performance of his duties. After bantering back and forth, the sheriff said he had nothing against Mr. Small and was only doing his duty in serving the warrants he was given.

"Here is your prisoner," Gillespie said. "Why don't you arrest him?"

"I never told you there would be any physical encounter," Governor Small said. "I will say to you that I was not going to get into any fist fight with you."

The frustrated Mester replied, "And I am not going to get into any fist fight with you. There is no necessity. If you will tell me you will come over there, I will arrest you in the courthouse. I am not looking for notoriety. If you will say you will come over to the courthouse, I will arrest you there."

Small said, "Well, I will tell you, I go home pretty early to dinner, about 5 o'clock. Why don't you just come over to the house there and arrest me?"

Mester said he would do that. Mester asked again if he understood correctly that Small was still refusing to submit to arrest. Small said yes.

Sheriff Mester left the governor's office. The reporters followed him to the governor's mansion.

Just after 5 p.m., Sheriff Mester was escorted into the library of the executive mansion.

"Governor Small, I have three warrants for your arrest," Mester said. He read each of them, and then said, "In the name of the people of the state of Illinois, I arrest you."

It was the first time a sitting governor had been arrested in state history.

(And the only time, until Governor Rod Blagojevich was arrested by federal agents at his Chicago home on Dec. 9, 2008 and taken away in handcuffs).

Gillespie handed the sheriff a bond that already had been prepared. The bond put up property valued at $150,000. Across the bottom, Small had written, "This bond is given by Len Small, governor of the state of Illinois, under protest that he is not subject to arrest during his term of office as governor."

Sheriff Mester said he did not know if what the governor offered was acceptable. The sheriff's bond had been drawn and was waiting at the sheriff's office, and needed nothing but the governor's signature.

A frantic Gillespie tried twice to force it on Mester. The sheriff said he needed the state's attorney to rule on whether it was sufficient. After a heated argument on the part of the governor's lawyers, Mester remained unmoved. He insisted he was going to take the governor.

A worried and unsmiling Len Small put on his hat and walked out of the executive mansion past a crowd of reporters and photographers, in the custody of the sheriff.

The governor, accompanied by his son Leslie, his son-in-law Arthur E. Inglesh and two of his attorneys, was taken to the courthouse. Hundreds of people had gathered around the mansion to see the governor led out by the sheriff.

It was a humiliating experience, as the governor took his "perp walk" before reporters and the public. And it was totally unnecessary, brought about only by Small's refusal to obey the law and the order of the court. Small could make his "constitutional" argument, but once the court ruled against it, he should have complied. President Nixon took the same stand with his tapes, but he did give them up when the court so ruled.

At the courthouse, State's Attorney C. Fred Mortimer greeted the governor. "Ah, this is the first time I have had the honor of meeting you, Governor, but I am sorry it is under these circumstances."

Governor Small made no reply.

Mortimer approved the bond. It was signed by the governor, with the words "under protest" added. Then the governor was on his way back home.

"The bond was signed and accepted and Governor Small hurriedly left with his retinue," said the *New York Times*. "He pulled his hat tightly down on his head and looked neither to the right nor the left as he strode through the lane of spectators which had been opened for his exit. There were no plaudits from the populace, who apparently realized that even a 'King' can be arrested, after all."

"It was on the cards as arranged by the governor's enemies, it seemed, that Len Small should be drawn through the streets of the capitol as a felon," the news account in the *Kankakee Daily Republican* said.

"Men and women crowded into the sheriff's office, while outside others fought for places at the windows and a sight of the rare spectacle staged for their benefit by Sheriff Mester," the article continued.

"Well, boys, it's all over," Sheriff Mester said to the newspapermen. "I'm glad it's all over. It was a mighty unpleasant job."

"Len Small is arrested," the *Belleville News Democrat* editor wrote, "the same as any other man who is accused of committing a crime...notwithstanding the fact that he happens, through an accident of politics, to be the governor of the state, to the eternal disgrace of Illinois. We believe that he is guilty, as guilty as can be. He took the money, every dollar he is accused of having taken, and then some.

"No man can get hundreds of thousands of dollars of public money mixed with his own private account without realizing that there is a mistake somewhere and without knowing that the accretion is not his. Len Small paid back $200,000 during the last campaign under political pressure and under duress of expediency, which he confessed was the state's money that he had in some way unbeknownst to himself mysteriously mixed with his private bank account. He is guilty to a moral certainty, whether they will ever be able to prove it on him in court or not. He will try to evade punishment through appeal to technicalities, resort to trickery, the use of political pull and shin-plastering with the free use of boodle. Thieves who steal that much are never sent to the penitentiary.

"Len Small says that the big interests are after him because he has been a people's man in the governor's office. He has been Bill Thompson's man and not the people's man at all. He is giving the state the rottenest administration it ever had, and he must go some to beat Dick Yates and Jack Tanner and Matteson.

"The Len Small incident will have one good influence on American politics. It will teach every crook in office, no matter how high he is up or expects to rise, the arm of the law is long enough to reach his collar and to yank him down from his high horse if the right prosecutor gets after him. It teaches that the 'divine right of kings' does not obtain in America. We have no superior beings on our soil who are privileged to commit crimes like the crazy bastards who occupied the throne of France before the revolution of 1789. Len Small may be the king of the Kankakee County Fair, but not the king of Illinois."

The day after his arrest, Small left Springfield, saying he did not know when he would return.

"I want to inspect some more roads," he said.

In every controversial incident in his life -- and there were plenty of them -- Governor Small issued his own statement of defense. A lengthy one was printed on the front page of the Aug. 11 *Kankakee Daily Republican*. Small rounded up the usual suspects, enemies old and new. Part of Small's long statement included the following:

"I have never evaded arrest upon the framed-up charges in my indictments in the many counties of this state which I have since visited. I have gone about the state freely on the performance of my duties, subject to the apprehension of any sheriff or other officer in any one of such counties. The sheriff of Sangamon County was closely advised of my movements and could have ordered my arrest in any county where I happened to be, if he so desired.

"No molestation has been attempted, except in gang-ruled Sangamon County. Here, the ruffianism of corrupt politics has threatened the orderly processes of government. Here the ring would subordinate proper lawful function to its improper and lawless purposes. Notwithstanding pretensions of decency, my enemies maliciously staged a spectacular arrest under circumstances intended to humiliate me and disgrace the people of our state. Even though the sheriff stated he had not thought that I would evade arrest, nevertheless the capitol of the state was besieged and surrounded by an army of deputies drawn from the slums of the city of Springfield.

"When I was finally arrested in the executive mansion, the sheriff pre-emptorily refused to examine or accept a bond with ample surety which I presented, and forcibly took me from the executive mansion and paraded me through a mob which had been assembled to jeer and insult the governor."

But it was Small who invited the sheriff to his house to arrest him there. If Small had gone to the courthouse, as the sheriff wanted, the arrest and bond could have been done discreetly, without any need for a public scene.

The *New York Times* on Aug. 10 observed, "The curtain was rung down on the farce, which has amused the entire nation ever since Governor Small's indictment on July 20, toward the end of what was the most farcical day of the governor's whole game of hide and seek with the law."

Indeed, it was a farce. Newspapers across the nation followed the story of the governor who thought he was above the law and who ran from the law for several weeks.

Within a few days, Small was back in Chicago, receiving the choreographed adulation to which he was accustomed in Big Bill's town. Thompson and Small led an entourage of 200 automobiles from Chicago on a tour of the Dixie Highway. Miss Kankakee was there. As the parade made its way through Illinois towns, a few hundred more automobiles joined the party, and each town's beauty queen was introduced at each stop.

A big picnic celebration for Governor Small was arranged at Emington at the end of August. Small's speeches over the years were pretty much the same, with amazingly little variance, except for the insertion of the name of a new enemy who was to blame for everything.

This time, it again was the spiel about holding sacred the public trust, "the welfare of humanity above the mighty dollar of the profiteer," the enemies out to get him because he was not controlled by the rich. He added something about his current troubles.

"Little did I realize what it would cost for a man who had been elected to a public office to oppose the profiteering of the great cement trust, which I am told controls the output of 95 per cent of the cement of the world," Small told the Emington crowd. "Little did I realize how those great money combinations were welded and interwoven and dovetailed together."

It was the "cement trust" that was among those behind the indictment, Small said. He claimed he was building hard roads for $28,000 a mile instead of the $40,000 the "cement trust" wanted to charge the state.

These figures are false, as we will see in chapter 23.

"The interests which believed they could continue to reap a large profit, aided by the *Chicago Tribune* and the *Daily News,* put up a hard fight," Small told the crowd. "They tried to force us to proceed with the high prices. In many places, they induced Automobile Associations, Chambers of Commerce and other well-meaning organizations to pass resolutions, urging us to proceed to build roads regardless of cost."

Small prevailed over these foes, he said, and hundreds of miles of roads had been built to date.

"The *Chicago Tribune* and other cement trust propagandists have done everything in their power to misrepresent our work. They have kept large forces of experienced trained writers and editors slurring our work and belittling what we are accomplishing.

"Perhaps never in the history of this state has such an aggregation of great interests combined to defeat the will of the people."

Small's lengthy speech at Emington was quoted in his own *Kankakee Daily Republican* on Sept. 2, with the writer making this observation: "It was apparent from the start that Governor Small was looked upon as a champion of the people's cause; that in him rests the only hope of protection against a criminal profiteering octopus which is seeking with mighty tentacles to strangle the happiness and freedom of the common people."

Small attacked a new enemy in his Emington speech. He said "babies in Chicago were dying for want of milk because of the great corporations which run the milk through a pasteurizing machine and deliver it to the consumer" at high prices.

He didn't forget to mention the cement trust and traction barons.

The *Chicago Tribune* reported the same speech as the governor telling the farmers he was keeping his promises to them, and a regular excoriation of the *Tribune,* the *Daily News*, Medill McCormick and Edward Brundage, "who has men on his payroll who never did a lick of work for the state but who went out to do his political bidding whenever Brundage told them to."

The news story in the Kankakee newspaper noted, "At times, Mr. Small's anger reached a point where he would become almost choked with emotion."

The Governor's Mansion in Springfield -- where Len Small was arrested by the sheriff on Aug. 8, 1921 -- the first Illinois governor arrested while in office. Photo by Jim Ridings

Chapter 11

The Governor On Trial

From the day he was indicted, Governor Small demanded a speedy trial so he could prove to the public that he was innocent.

But also from the day of the indictment, Small did everything he could to delay the process. It began with running away from the sheriff for several weeks and went on for months with claims of immunity, motions challenging the legality of the grand jury, motions to quash the indictments, motions to dismiss based on technicalities, change of venue and continuance after continuance, until it finally went to trial nearly ten months later.

Failing to kill the indictment by arguing that the governor could not be indicted or prosecuted, Small's lawyers now thought the best way to beat the rap was by getting a change of venue.

Small's lawyers filed papers on Aug. 16, 1921 for a change of venue. Judge Smith and any Sangamon County jury would be prejudiced against Len Small, Small's lawyers said.

Lawyers for the governor filed 100 affidavits with the court, from people in the county who said they thought Small could not get a fair trial there. Mortimer countered with 2,002 affidavits from people who said he could get a fair trial.

The governor's lawyers succeeded in getting a change of venue on Oct. 10. The prosecutor and the judge in Sangamon County did not like the claim that the governor could not get a fair trial in their county. But they did not object, in the pursuit of justice. Of five suggested counties, Small picked Lake County, the home turf of Fred Lundin. It was close enough to where the Chicago gangsters lived, and that was an important consideration for Small.

The trial was set for November, but Lake County Judge Claire C. Edwards said on Oct. 11 that he could start the trial "next Monday" if both sides agreed. Small attorney Werner Schroeder said he was ready for trial anytime. Brundage said the same thing. Four days later, Governor Small said he would fight any delay by the prosecution. "I want the trial to start at the earliest possible moment," he said. "I am ready for trial. The case cannot come to trial too soon to suit me."

Still, the legal wrangling by Small's lawyers went on for months.

Another amusing side note happened in October 1921. R.C. Leuth and A.W. Calkins, who were appearing in *Smiles of 1921* in Wichita, Kansas, asked R.W. Long, editor of the *Wichita Eagle,* to settle a bet. The Illinois case was a national story and the two had a wager on Len Small's height. The editor sent a telegram to Kankakee, and the governor agreed to be measured. A *Kankakee Daily Republi-*

can representative measured Small, "and his correct height was found to be five feet nine and one-half inches tall, for that is his height with his shoes on, and he wears them most of the time."

Attorney General Brundage filed civil lawsuits in November 1921 against five former state treasurers to recover an estimated $2.5 million in interest money due to the state. The five were state treasurers between 1909 and 1921 -- Governor Small, Lt. Gov. Sterling, Auditor Andrew Russel, William Ryan and Edward Mitchell. This lawsuit was separate from the criminal proceedings.

The year 1909 was significant because it was in 1908 that a law was passed to prevent the underhanded dealings of Len Small in his first term as state treasurer from 1905 to 1907. This law required the treasurer to deposit money in Illinois banks that paid the highest rate of interest.

"Pounding his desk for emphasis, Governor Len Small, before departing for his home at Kankakee at noon today, repeated his demand for immediate trial and called upon the prosecution to explain the delay in transferring the records in the case against him from Springfield to the trial court in Waukegan."

This was the lead paragraph in the Nov. 3, 1921, *Kankakee Daily Republican* story. The prosecution was engaged in paperwork to transfer the Sangamon County sheriff's bond to a regular bond, in order to send the case to a different county, and Small "made no attempt to curb his ire" in objecting to any delay caused by this.

But almost immediately, Small and his lawyers started their own series of delays. They thought these objections would cause the indictments to be dismissed.

The first was filed on Nov. 26. Their motion sought to quash the indictments on the arguments that the indictments charged the governor with no crime, that the governor is not charged with profiting personally, that the grand jury was not lawfully selected and that the indictments were written in a flawed manner.

Judge Edwards heard arguments on the motions on Dec. 5, the date the trial was to have begun. Some of the legal arguments from Small's lawyers were perplexing. They still argued that the governor was immune from arrest and prosecution, even though another judge ruled against him and even though another motion claimed he was not charged with violating a specific law.

Other arguments were beyond perplexing. One motion read. "The indictment fails to charge that money or property entrusted to Governor Small when he was state treasurer was the property of the state." And, "The indictment fails to allege the purpose for which the money was entrusted to the treasurer." Also, "That the pretended fiduciary relation between the principal and Len Small, as the agent, servant, employee or officer of such principal is not shown."

Lead counsel Charles C. LeForgee argued before Judge Edwards on Dec. 5 that the governor couldn't get a fair trial anywhere in Illinois. LeForgee threw in a number of other arguments trying to quash the indictments.

Lake County Judge Claire Edwards ruled on Dec. 29 that Small would stand trial on conspiracy to embezzle two million dollars of state funds. The indictment consisted of nine counts, with four of the original thirteen counts knocked out.

Governor Small made a New Year's Eve statement on the last day of 1921, and it was a little more heated than his regular slash-and-burn style. It was in response to a reporter's question that Small might be prosecuted in Springfield on additional charges if he was acquitted in Waukegan.

"I would be surprised at nothing the contemptible, cowardly, sneaking character assassins, who know there is not a word of truth in their charges, do. They know they can never prove a single charge, so long mouthed. They hope, of course, to throw all the filthy mud that their slimy fingers can pick from the dirty gutters to blacken my character, as by continuous misrepresentation and falsifications they would prevent me, if possible, during my term of office, from performing the important duties of the office of governor. But the real purpose is a conspiracy to gain control of the state legislature."

Brundage's response was to laugh at the governor's standard vitriol. He also said that some of Small's rambling statement, along with a pamphlet Small circulated in Lake County to the prospective jury pool, bordered on contempt of court.

Pre-trial motions started on Dec. 5, 1921. Small drove to Waukegan from Fred Lundin's home. The first motion argued by LeForgee was to quash the indictments. It developed into sensational accusations from both sides. The state claimed that Small's lawyers had knowingly introduced a false document. The defense claimed the state had altered the document in question.

LeForgee introduced the minutes of the Sangamon County Board for 1920 and 1921. He was trying to show that a meeting adjournment made the selection of the grand jury invalid. The minutes for the Tuesday, Sept. 14, 1920 meeting noted it was adjourned until "Thursday morning." LeForgee argued that "Thursday" was an undetermined date, and the board term ceased, so its appointment of a grand jury was not valid. The state's copy showed "Sept. 16" entered after "Thursday morning." LeForgee claimed his copy had been given to them by the county clerk before the alteration. Sangamon County Clerk Charles Byers admitted that his records had been altered as a "correction." It was a point scored in Small's favor. But it did not invalidate the grand jury.

Judge Edwards ruled in favor of Governor Small on a few points, based on technicalities. The judge ruled that the indictment charging the governor with operating a confidence game was flawed and he dismissed it. Prosecutors wanted the conspiracy charge tried first, believing it was their strongest case. In order to insure this, the state had to drop the embezzlement charge. Small's lawyers objected -- they wanted the embezzlement charge to go to trial first but they could not stop the state if it wanted to drop the charge. In the end, just the conspiracy indictment stood.

Small claimed the state's case was falling apart. But the primary reason for most of the counts being dropped or dismissed were technicalities.

"A missing word, the position of a name, three errors in drawing indictments, and the shuffling of a pile of papers accounted for the victories won by the governor today," the *New York Times* reported on Dec. 30.

"The foreman of the Sangamon County Grand Jury signed his name in the wrong place on the back of an indictment charging Governor Small, Lieutenant Gov. Sterling and Mr. Curtis jointly with embezzlement of $700,000. Judge Edwards quashed the indictment because of the foreman's error," the *New York Times* reported. "A typist left the word 'feloniously' out of a count charging the trio with operating a confidence game. The charge was quashed. Two counts in the joint conspiracy indictment failed to allege the special injury supposed to have been done the state. They were quashed. Another count in the same indictment failed to allege commission of an overt act in furtherance of the alleged conspiracy. It was quashed. The clerk of the Sangamon County circuit court, in affixing consecutive numbers to the indictments, happened to pick up the one charging Governor Small with embezzling $500,000 first and gave it the first number. Therefore, Judge Edwards ordered this case tried first, and rather than comply, the State dismissed the indictment."

Further motions asked that Small and Curtis be tried separately. Curtis said the sensational publicity given to Small hurt his own chances for a fair trial. The prosecution wanted both defendants to stand trial together. Judge Edwards ruled on Dec. 31 that Small would be tried separately and first.

Sterling did not ask for a change of venue.

Judge Edwards set Jan. 9 as the date for the trial to start. Further legal wrangling kept pushing back that date. On Feb. 4, Judge Edwards set March 6 for the trial to start. But on March 6, the governor asked for another delay. He said his road building program needed his immediate attention or else a thousand men would be out of work. Prosecutor Fred Mortimer called the request a "mockery of the trial." But after a long argument, the judge moved the trial date to April 3.

Edward Brundage said Small had another motive in seeking this delay. He said Small did not want evidence or testimony from the trial to get in the newspapers just before the April primary elections.

The governor used some of that time for a political tour, in advance of the primary, to Freeport, Dixon and LaSalle, where the *Kankakee Daily Republican* reported huge, adoring crowds. Before a packed crowd at the Luna Theatre in Kankakee on March 30, Small led a rally for local candidates. In his hometown, his newspaper could not find enough adjectives to describe the love and affection he received from his worshipful following.

On April 3, just as jury selection was about to start, the governor's lawyers tried another tactic to delay the inevitable. They challenged the legality of the entire jury pool since only men were put on the list. It was the custom at the time that only men were jurors in important cases. The 19th Amendment to the Constitution, giving women the right to vote, was less than two years old. Schroeder's objection took the court by surprise. It had never before been raised in Illinois. Schroeder framed this as protecting the constitutional rights of women but the real purpose was an attempt to protect Small from going to trial. If the judge upheld this objection, proceedings would be delayed until September when the county board was set to meet to draw up another list of prospective jurors. A few days were eaten up with this argument but Judge Edwards did not uphold this challenge. A compromise was agreed upon. The prosecution and defense selected three people to select jurors from a list. The twelve jurymen who had been waiting for the trial to start were dismissed. The proceedings were continued another two weeks. It was agreed by both sides that no women would be picked for the jury. So much for the defense of women's rights.

Small succeeded in delaying the start of the trial until after the April primary elections. Nevertheless, candidates backed by the Small-Thompson machine lost.

Motions before the court were still being made in early April 1922 as the state still was trying to obtain the records of the Grant Park Bank, the Grant Park Trust & Savings Bank, and Small's First Trust & Savings Bank of Kankakee, which had been subpoenaed weeks earlier.

One of the prosecutors was James H. Wilkerson, who later became a federal judge. Wilkerson was known for a career of honesty and integrity. It was his integrity that sent Al Capone to the penitentiary for a lengthy term. Federal prosecutors made a deal with Capone in 1931, where the Mob boss would plead guilty to income tax evasion in exchange for a two-year sentence. Judge Wilkerson rejected the plea bargain, to the astonishment of the deal makers. Capone charged his plea, went to trial, was convicted and got an 11-year sentence from Wilkerson.

Wilkerson questioned Norman Griffin on the witness stand on April 6, 1922, in an exchange that is astounding to read.

Griffin, cashier of the Grant Park Trust & Savings Bank (and brother-in-law of Edward C. Curtis), told the court that the records of the Grant Park Bank, and some records of the Grant Park Trust & Savings Bank, were accidentally burned a year earlier by a janitor who mistook them for waste paper.

Wilkerson asked Griffin about Grant Park's bank records for 1917.

We don't have them, Griffin said. What about 1918? No, not 1918.

Well, then, what records do you have?

"Some time in 1921," Griffin said.

Wilkerson asked what happened to the other records.

They were burned in February 1921, Griffin said.

Who destroyed them?

"I don't know, exactly," Griffin replied. Then he gave a name, exactly -- Edwin Lakey, the janitor for the bank.

"Narrate a little more the circumstances, explain how a janitor would have access to the papers of a bank with authority to destroy them," Wilkerson asked.

Griffin explained that in February 1921, a new burglar alarm system was being installed in the Grant Park Trust & Savings Bank. Everything was removed from the vault and taken to the basement, Griffin said. "A good deal of the material, of the older material, was inadvertently burned in the furnace, and that is the reason I state that part of the material was at that time destroyed. I don't know how much."

February 1921 was exactly when Edward Miller and Edward Brundage were investigating the dealings of Len Small and the Grant Park Bank, and Len Small knew this.

At whose direction did Lakey burn the bank records? Wilkerson asked.

"Well, I don't think at anyone's direction," Griffin replied.

Where is the janitor now? asked Wilkerson

Uh, Lakey died three or four weeks ago, Griffin said.

"The papers from the vault that you sent to the basement, did these include some drafts?" Yes, Griffin replied.

"Now, you have been given on this memorandum, certain drafts during

1917 and 1918. You were unable to find any of these, were you?" Wilkerson asked.

"Yes, sir."

"A draft is rather an important document in the business of a bank, isn't it?"

"Yes, sir, I think it is."

"It might relate to matters involving litigation which would not be barred by the statute of limitations for ten years, wouldn't it? You know that as a fact, don't you?"

"There might be," Griffin responded.

"And yet, under these circumstances, you sent original drafts to the basement," Wilkerson inquired.

"No, I did not say I sent them there," Griffin said.

Then who sent them? Griffin said he didn't know.

"Well, how do you know they were sent there, then?" Wilkerson asked.

Griffin remained evasive and confusing. "There are a lot of drafts filed in the vault previous to that time, when this was remodeled, and a great deal of that was carried to the basement and never returned from the basement. I don't know just how many of them. I did not do very much of that work myself. I don't know just what was taken down. I was there at times."

Wilkerson tried to pin him down. Who had charge of this? I don't know. Who did the physical work of moving it? I don't know, the janitor did part of it. The man who is dead? Yes. Anybody else help him? Mr. Ruge, the assistant cashier. Did Ruge tell the janitor to burn these? No, I am sure he did not. Then who did tell him? I don't think anybody told him.

Wilkerson pointed to a certificate of deposit for $175,000 issued to Fred Sterling. "Don't you have some special place where you keep those?"

"Well, I suppose they were in the vault," Griffin said. "I don't remember any particular certificates mentioned there."

Griffin couldn't remember much at all, even certificates of $150,000 and more. This was at a bank where a big deposit from a customer might be $50.

Grant Park Trust & Savings Bank (the legitimate bank).
The other "Grant Park Bank" had no building because it did not exist.

Even more amazing was Wilkerson's inquiry concerning transactions between the Grant Park Trust & Savings Bank and the Continental & Commercial National Bank of Chicago. The records produced by Griffin did not match all the records from Continental, and those on both books did not always match figures. Griffin had no explanation.

After the examination of the witness, Wilkerson said he had been practicing law for many years and this was the most "extraordinary" case he had ever seen, where the books of a bank could not be produced, and allegedly were burned by a janitor.

Wilkerson also questioned Louis E. Beckman that day. Beckman, cashier at Small's bank (and a future mayor of Kankakee), told an equally evasive and astounding tale. Wilkerson wanted to know about Len Small's bank records from Jan. 1, 1917 to July 20, 1921.

Beckman said he could find no record at the bank of any accounts in the name of Len Small -- or Small's wife, Small's son or Fred Sterling. Len Small, who had been president of the bank since it was founded, did not have an account until November 1921, according to Beckman.

Wilkerson could not believe what he was hearing. Neither did Judge Edwards, who interrupted the examination. "Let me see if I understand the question," the judge asked. "You did not find anything, only since November 1921?"

Beckman said yes, Len Small apparently did not have an account in his own bank. After some more legal waltzing around the issue, Luther Bratton objected to continuing on this route. Bratton, a powerful Republican lawyer and politician from Kankakee County, was the attorney for Small's bank.

"What books have been kept by this bank during the period mentioned, showing the account with depositors?" Wilkerson asked.

"Well, we have a ledger there with our accounts, a loose leaf ledger," Beckman replied.

"How frequently are summaries made showing the status of the accounts in the bank? You make a summary, do you not, at stated intervals?" Wilkerson asked.

Bratton objected again, saying this was a matter for the state auditor. The judge ruled the line of questioning was proper.

Wilkerson asked if the loose leaf ledger had an index. Beckman said it was entered alphabetically. This led to an argument between Bratton and Wilkerson about inspecting the bank's records, with Bratton maintaining than an inspection of all the banks' records was a "fishing expedition."

Kankakeeans could read the amazing testimony of Beckman and Griffin in the *Kankakee Daily News,* but not in Small's *Kankakee Daily Republican.*

C.H. Burnett, vice president of Waukegan National Bank, was appointed by Judge Edwards to examine the books of the Grant Park and Kankakee banks. This was because officials from both banks produced so little material of what had been subpoenaed, so the judge sent Burnett to the source to dig for himself.

"Governor Small cannot charge that this is more conspiracy of his enemies, because only his own friends had access to the bank's records, and it is going to take a lot of explaining to a jury and public to get them to believe the explanations about the conflagration in the furnace of the Grant Park institution or that Governor Small did not carry an account of any kind in the bank of which he is the president," the *Kankakee Daily News* noted.

Small's forces tried to throw another monkey wrench into the proceedings in late April, when the Lundin-controlled Lake County Board passed a resolution demanding that Sangamon County immediately pay the first week's expenses of the Small trial. The very affluent Lake County claimed the first week cost $3,000 and that put a financial strain on the county.

Sangamon County, which was in good financial shape, was offended that another county thought it wouldn't pay its tab after the proceedings were over. Mortimer said this was the first time in Illinois history that one county asked another for payment before a case was finished. He told Judge Edwards that his county would pay every penny. The judge said he would ignore the board's resolution.

Jury selection began on April 24. Judge Edwards granted requests that no jurors be drawn from Breton Township, which included a bitter anti-Small faction, or from Grant Township, Fred Lundin's territory.

The first 100 prospects were excused within two days.

More talk of jury tampering was made even before Small's jury was selected. It concerned Henry Garey, an automobile salesman from Waukegan, who was examined as a potential juror on May 5. The defense liked Garey very much and wanted to seat him. The state wanted to reject him. In questioning that morning, Garey said he had no opinion about the case and said he had not discussed the case with anyone. In the afternoon, Garey admitted he did have an opinion. "A change has come over me since I came here," Garey said in the afternoon session. "I can't explain exactly what."

The judge held a conference in his chambers with Garey and both sets of lawyers to see why this potential juror changed his mind. Garey said a remark he made in the hallway -- to a defense lawyer who was not "officially" listed as part of Small's team -- was overheard by a prosecutor and was "misunderstood." Garey said he and other potential jurors had talked about the case.

Other "talkative" potential jurors were questioned, particularly one who got in touch with defense lawyers. Even at this point, prosecutors said they were looking for pro-Small people "planted" in the jury pool. That same day, Charles Melville, a motorman from Highland Park who had been accepted as a juror, was dismissed when it was revealed he had expressed an anti-Small opinion. Another excused juror, Robert Fagan, had called defense lawyers to tell them about Melville. Wilkerson asked Judge Edwards to look into this, wondering why Fagan ran to Small's lawyers with his story instead of going to the judge. Wilkerson wanted to know if Fagan was Small "plant."

The jury selection process went through 425 prospects before settling on the final juror on May 10. The jury consisted of Alexander Smith, a ditcher from Rosencrans; George Martin of Highland Park, a grain elevator foreman; William Barnard of Lake Forest, landscape gardener; John B. Fields of Antioch, former taxi driver; Frank Reardon of Waukegan, steel and wire employee; W.C. Repkow, substitute postal clerk; Ralph Peterson of Highland Park, hospital fireman; George Beckman of West Deerfield, brick maker; Lawrence Buss of Hainesville, laborer; August Larsen of Highland Park, gardener; John E. Larsen of Waukegan, retired oil dealer and farmer; Hans Johnson of Waukegan, steel mill worker.

Just before the last juror was chosen, LeForgee tried to throw another wrench into the machinery by asking the judge to declare the 1908 treasurer law unconstitutional. It was part of LeForgee's "ten points of law" on which he wanted the judge to rule before accepting the jury. The prosecution strongly objected to this being introduced at this time Judge Edwards ruled against LeForgee's motion.

Finally, the actual trial was ready to begin. Opening arguments began on May 11, 1922. State's Attorney Fred Mortimer laid out the case in his lengthy opening statement -- that Len Small was a banker who was state treasurer from 1917 to 1919, and who deposited millions of dollars in a fictitious "Grant Park Bank" in a conspiracy with Edward and Vernon Curtis to defraud the state out of two million dollars in interest. This conspiracy and fraud continued when Fred Sterling succeeded Small as treasurer. He said the Grant Park Bank had no building, no employees and existed only on paper for the purpose of fraud. He spelled out how this scheme was done (as was explained in chapter 9).

Mortimer also explained the law that required the state treasurer to deposit funds that would pay "the highest rate of interest." Mortimer said he would prove that Small deposited state funds in his friend Curtis' bank, had it loaned to Chicago meat packers at 8 per cent interest, paid the state just 2 per cent, and pocketed the difference. Mortimer said payments on the loans were made out to Curtis, not to the bank. This was a "money laundering" scheme to conceal that some of the money was going to Len Small.

Mortimer told the jury that he could prove that Small personally profited from these loans. He said he had a note from Armour & Co. for $500,000 which paid $24,333.33 interest. That interest was paid to Continental & Commercial National Bank in Chicago, which issued cashier's checks to Edward C. Curtis in the amounts of $10,500 and $13,833. That money, Mortimer said, was used by Len Small to purchase securities.

"He used $10,500 with the Hanchett & Co. to purchase bonds," Mortimer said. "The bonds were delivered to Mr. Small personally, and he got his change by a check issued by the bond company for $448.33." The check was endorsed by Len Small, and the receipt for the bonds was signed by Len Small, Mortimer added.

The opening argument of Charles LeForgee contained an interesting counterpoint. He maintained that the governor could not be convicted "because that excess of interest was never in possession of the state of Illinois, and it was never obtained by Curtis from the state of Illinois."

LeForgee argued the Grant Park Bank was a legitimate private bank, and it allowed Curtis "more liberty of operation" than his state bank. At that time, LeForgee noted, private banks were legal. LeForgee said the amount of interest paid from money in the Grant Park Bank equaled the amount of interest paid from state deposits in all the other banks combined, and the principal was repaid.

LeForgee said Chicago banks paid two per cent interest and would not put up collateral for the funds because of the uncertainty of the length of time the money would be on deposit. So, he said, Small set up a "safe fund" at an institution that would accept large quantities of money and provided security. That institution was the Grant Park Bank.

The certificates of deposit from the Grant Park Bank were the security required, LeForgee said.

LeForgee didn't deny the Grant Park Bank loaned money at five to eight per cent while paying the state two per cent. But he said the money in the "vault fund" in another 400 banks across the state also loaned money at five to eight per cent while paying the state two per cent, and no one accused them of a conspiracy.

And, he added, if the Grant Park Bank was not real, how could it pay all that money in interest to the state?

While Small denied he profited personally, the law said "the state treasurer shall be personally responsible for the faithful performance of his duties under the law and for a proper accounting of all money paid to him as state treasurer."

Just as Small's first term as state treasurer brought about a change in the law, passed to prevent the treasurer from keeping the interest money on state deposits, his second term as treasurer brought another change, a law passed in 1919 to prevent treasurers from depositing state funds in "private" banks, and requiring that all money (including all interest) be turned over to the state.

This, Small clearly did not do. But he said his actions came before this law was passed. He was only partially right, since his scheme continued through the term of his successor.

Brundage explained that Small deposited state money in two funds, the "safe fund" and the "vault fund." Brundage said the "vault fund" was the total in legitimate institutions in the state and was less than the amount in the "safe fund." The "safe fund" was the total in the so-called Grant Park Bank. Money was carried on the books in a "safe fund" to hide the fact that Small, Curtis and Sterling were loaning out state money for their personal profit, with Curtis issuing phony certificates of deposit in the fake Grant Park Bank.

Brundage said the "safe fund" and the "vault fund" amounted to keeping two sets of books.

The state claimed that the Grant Park Bank was a fraud, created by Small and Curtis to launder money from state deposits. It was Brundage's contention that the bank existed only on paper and was used only for the purpose of loaning money on state deposits for personal gain.

To defend himself, Small's lawyers had to establish that the Grant Park Bank was legitimate. In preliminary hearings in January 1922, LeForgee, asserted that the Grant Park Bank was a real bank because the state accepted a million dollars in interest earned by the bank during the terms of Small and Sterling.

"The bill (indictment) states that Illinois accepted $1,000,000 in interest in state funds, and still it claims it is a fictitious bank," LeForgee told Judge Edwards. "If it was, why did the state accept the huge amount of interest? Just why the sovereign state of Illinois saw fit to do business and gain profit from a false institution is beyond me."

Of course, the "state" and the "bank" doing business with one another both were Len Small.

Small's lawyers also claimed the Grant Park Bank was allied with the Grant Park Trust & Savings Bank, which Edward Curtis owned.

Incredibly, Small's lawyers claimed that the grand jury testimony by Norman Griffin "conclusively" proved the Grant Park Bank was legitimate -- and they then said that the Grant Park Bank suddenly ceased on April 4, 1921. This would have been three months after new laws went into effect on Jan. 1, laws enacted because of Treasurer Small's financial legerdemain.

The prosecution asked how such a successful bank that recently had $10 million in deposits could just close. (Prosecutors may have hesitated to say "close its doors" since the "bank" had no doors.)

LeForgee opened his address in court by telling the jury that the prosperity of 1917 and 1918 brought a lot of revenue to the state.

"So as this money accumulated in the state treasury and grew to large proportions during the latter part of Governor Small's tenure of the office of state treasurer, there came the question to the defendant, 'What are we going to do with all this money? Am I going down through the state and put $20,000 in this bank and $20,000 in that bank and examine the abstracts of title to Tom and Bill Jones land and the affairs of that institution?' Why, there wouldn't be enough vault space in the state treasury to take care of $8,000,000 worth of securities scattered throughout the state in innumerable banks."

"And the question confronting the defendant was what are we going to do with the accumulation of money? Why, gentlemen, there was created the safe fund," LeForgee said. The purpose of the safe fund, he added, was to loan large quantities of money "rather than to allow it to lie idle in the treasury."

Some of the arguments LeForgee made sound incredible now. He said Chicago banks were paying one-and-a-half to two per cent interest, so the treasurer went to a miniscule bank in a miniscule town, and the bank just happened to be owned by his friend.

"There was Curtis," LeForgee said. "He was at the head of a chain of banks numbering 15 to 18 in the state of Illinois. He was a man of large affairs. He knew securities." Curtis, he said, issued certificates of deposit that were backed with collateral security. The Grant Park Bank was no different than other banks in the state that held state money and it was not the only private bank that held state money, he said.

LeForgee told the jury that the Grant Park Bank never lost a penny of state deposits. And the bank returned more interest, both in dollars and in percentage, than any other bank that held state deposits.

But the argument the state made was that Small and Curtis personally profited from state funds loaned at higher percentage rates, regardless of the interest rate returned to the state.

One of LeForgee's main arguments was that excess interest earned by the Grant Park Bank did not belong to the state. He said his was "good business acumen" on the part of the bankers to make such a good profit. That also may be true, but it had nothing to do with the allegations.

The *Kankakee Daily Republican* put its own spin on everything, including LeForgee's statement to the jury. "The senior counsel of the governor's defense told of the defendant's humble beginning in life as a milkman and of his later employment as a grader on railroads. Step by step, he traced the governor's career and sought to impress on the jurors that they were privileged to consider the present exalted position of the governor in arriving at judgment."

LeForgee spoke to the "lifelong friendship" between Len Small and Ed Curtis. When Curtis became speaker of the Illinois House, Small went to Springfield as his personal secretary. Curtis was Small's mentor, helped him get ahead in politics and LeForgee said, Curtis tried for 20 years to make Len Small governor.

"Prior to 1921, any man in the state of Illinois had the right to open a bank and do a banking business," LeForgee told the jury. "So do not get too firmly fixed in your mind that this is a fictitious bank."

The original Grant Park Bank, which began in a general store, legally continued even after Curtis started the Grant Park National Bank, LeForgee said.

That was at the heart of the case. Was the Grant Park Bank a legitimate bank, and did Small and Curtis personally profit from state deposits funneled through it?

LeForgee presented an interesting, if flawed, argument on May 15. He said, essentially, that Small did not steal any money from the state treasury because the excess interest money withheld from the state never went into the treasury. The law says that the treasurer cannot put any money in or take any money out of the treasury without the added signature of the state auditor, LeForgee contended.

"When does money become the property of the state of Illinois?" Leforgee asked the jury. "Under the law I have just stated, it cannot become the money of the state of Illinois until the auditor has OK'd its passage into the treasury.

"The money obtained was never in the possession of the state, Never, never, never. And their charge of obtaining money by false pretenses is an utter legal impossibility." Even if the prosecution's evidence is true, LeForgee said, "it is utterly impossible to obtain a conviction because the excess was never in the possession of the state of Illinois and it never was obtained by Curtis from the state of Illinois."

Some revealing testimony was given early in the trial when Harry Luehrs testified on May 15. Luehrs had been assistant state treasurer since 1915 but had worked in the office since 1905, appointed when his fellow Kankakeean Len Small first took office.

Prosecutor Edward Pree asked Luehrs about the "vault account." Luehrs said this consisted of perhaps 250 banks holding state funds. He said these records were kept in a loose leaf ledger. The ledger listed the names and locations of the banks that held state deposits, the number of certificates and the dates and amounts in each bank.

Where is that ledger now? Luehrs said he didn't know.

What became of the ledger after Small left office?

"I think I sent it to him," Luehrs said.

Pree asked if the treasurer's office currently had any records of interest paid by banks during Small's term. Luehrs said no. Pree asked if Luehrs ever had these records in his office. Luehrs said yes, he had the monthly sheets -- which also were sent to Small after leaving office.

Pree asked about other books or records. Luehrs said a book called the "tickler" showed the distribution of cash in the treasury on each particular day. There also was a draft book, showing the record of drafts issued by the treasurer.

Where are these books now? Luehrs said he didn't know, but he probably sent them to Small when he left office.

Did you have cancelled drafts in the office during Mr. Small's term? Yes. Where are they now? Presumably, they were sent to Mr. Small, Luehrs said.

"Have you any records in your possession in the office of the state treasurer in Springfield or any other place whereby you can ascertain the total amount of money loaned out by the state of Illinois to the different banks of Illinois during Mr. Small's second term?" Pree asked. No, Luehrs replied.

Luehrs then was asked about the "safe account" and the "vault account." Luehrs said "safe account" transactions were recorded in the "tickler." No particular bank was listed in the records but all drafts were made payable to the Grant Park Bank. Luehrs said Small instructed him to make the drafts to the Grant Park Bank.

"What, if any, plan or system of notifying the respective banks that had state moneys deposited, with reference to paying interest on state deposits?" Pree asked.

"A notice was sent to each bank about the last day of each month," Luehrs replied.

"Was there any reference at the bottom about returning that notice with remittance?" Pree asked. Yes, Luehrs responded.

"Did you ever send out any of these notices to the Grant Park Bank during Small's second term?" asked Pree. No, said Luehrs.

Why not?

"I have not any recollection on that question," Luehrs said.

"Did you have any conversation with Mr. Small in reference to the sending of notices of that kind to the Grant Park Bank?"

"I have not any recollection. I may have been told not to send them. I don't know."

Luehrs was asked if he ever saw the securities or collateral kept in connection with the Grant Park Bank deposits. He said no.

He was asked if saw the collateral for the other banks in the state that held state deposits. Luehrs said not for every bank, but he did see all the records that were kept in Springfield.

"During Mr. Small's second term as treasurer, what, if anything, was done with the interest moneys received at Springfield?"

"They were sent to the bank at Kankakee, the First Trust & Savings Bank," Luehrs said.

Luehrs said the Grant Park Bank held about $12 million. The total held in all the other 250 to 300 banks combined equaled the same amount. He also said that funds going into the Grant Park Bank continued through Sterling's term, all the way to September 1921.

Pree then entered into evidence a "tickler" book from Fred Sterling's term. Under further questioning, Pree got Luehrs to admit a number of things. Luehrs said he did make out drafts to the Grant Park Bank during Sterling's term. He said he handled drafts from Small to the Grant Park Bank, some were $500,000 each. He said interest money from the other banks in the state was sent to the Rockford National Bank. He said there was no "safe account" prior to Small taking office and that the "safe account" was started at the Grant Park Bank by Small himself. He said he never saw the Grant Park certificates of deposit but was told by Small that they were in Chicago. He said he saw the records of the "vault account" of deposits in other banks but not the records of the "safe account" in the Grant Park Bank. He said the Grant Park Bank was the only bank in the "safe account." He said he did see certificates from the other banks. He said he never examined the collateral of the Grant Park Bank -- not until 1921, when Edward Miller became treasurer and got the certificates from Len Small.

And after Small left office as treasurer, what position did Small hold with the office? Examiner of Collaterals. And what were his duties? To approve collateral put up by the banks.

Luehrs also said the treasurer's office at Springfield never received any interest from the Grant Park Bank in Small's or Sterling's terms.

Under cross examination, Luehrs told LeForgee that other treasurers also had some records sent home with them. Luehrs said he did not consider the "tickler" book of daily balances to be part of the state's official records. LeForgee argued that this book was not a public record and should not be admitted as evidence. The judge ruled against him.

Pree asked Luehrs about draft ledgers with the Continental & Commercial National Bank and with the Fort Dearborn National Bank. These also were sent to Small, Luehrs said.

Questioning Luehrs three days later, prosecutor James Wilkerson got this startling admission -- during Len Small and Fred Sterling terms, three million dollars was left in a permanent account with the banking firm of Dunlap, Russel & Co. in Jacksonville. This firm was owned by Andrew Russel, who was state treasurer from 1909 to 1911 and from 1915 to 1917. At that time, Russel was state auditor. No interest was paid to the state from that three million dollar deposit.

Edward Dunlap of Ayers National Bank of Jacksonville testified that the books of Dunlap, Russel & Co. were destroyed after it merged with the Ayers bank in 1921.

Andrew Russel later was convicted of bank fraud and sent to a federal prison in Michigan, where he died. The conviction stemmed from the failure of the Ayers National Bank in 1932, where Russel's overdrafts totaled $1.3 million.

The state introduced notes totaling $11.5 million from Armour & Co. F.W. Croll, Armour's treasurer, identified checks from Armour for $400,000 in interest, paid to Edward Curtis. Nowhere on the transactions did the name of the Grant Park Bank appear. Checks were mailed to Curtis at Grant Park Trust & Savings Bank. Albert Colby of Armour testified that his company never had any dealings with the "Grant Park Bank."

Croll told the court that he could afford to pay Curtis a higher rate of interest than he paid to banks because Curtis, as an individual, did not require a deposit be left in a bank. The extra he paid Curtis was equivalent to what he lost when a bank required that some of the money be left in the bank at no interest to Armour.

LeForgee fought the introduction of this evidence, saying that these were deals between Curtis and Armour and did not show interest being taken from the state. Wilkerson countered by saying this was important evidence, proving that the money loaned to the packers was the state's money. Judge Edwards allowed the evidence.

The state called witnesses from the Continental & Commercial National Bank and from the Fort Dearborn National Bank to testify about transactions with the Curtis brothers.

Cudahy Packing Co.'s assistant treasurer, John Wagner, told the court he dealt directly with Edward Curtis and never heard of a "Grant Park Bank." Wagner said he had no dealings with Governor Small.

W.W. Sherman, assistant treasurer of Swift & Co., testified about borrowing funds from the Curtis brothers. He also said he never had dealings with a "Grant Park Bank." In fact, he said he never heard of the bank.

As Sherman left the witness stand, Governor Small got up and shook hands with him, in front of the jury. Judge Edwards warned the attorneys to control the conduct of their witnesses.

Also introduced was evidence that Small and his Kankakee bank bought $60,000 in Armour bonds and $30,000 in Whiteside County bonds, which Wilkerson said came from interest on state deposits.

More evidence was a check for $10,500 from Armour & Co. -- an interest payment on its loan -- which was made out to Edward C. Curtis, then signed over to Len Small and used by him to buy Franklin County bonds.

Marshall Jackson, president of the stationary company in Chicago that produced the Grant Park Bank ledger, rubber stamp and certificates of deposit in 1917, testified that Vernon Curtis told him at the time that the Grant Park Bank did not need to be listed with the Banker's Directory because it "is not going to be engaged in the banking business and there is no occasion for any bank number." Jackson said Curtis also told him not to mail anything to the Grant Park Bank but to the Curtis Trust Co.

None of the men from the packing houses had any direct contact with Len Small during these transactions. But Howard Rice, a former auditor with the Fort Dearborn National Bank, told the court that he did.

Rice identified cashier's checks from the Live Stock Exchange National Bank that had been deposited by Ed Curtis into the account of State Treasurer Len Small in the Fort Dearborn bank.

It was Ed Curtis' name on these deposit slips, not the name of the Grant Park Bank. And it was this money in the Fort Dearborn Bank that was loaned to the packers.

This, the prosecution said, connected Len Small to the entire scheme. It no longer was a matter of Ed Curtis making loans.

The state showed the loans were made by Curtis, not by the Grant Park Bank, and the interest was paid to Curtis, not to the Grant Park Bank. Money to reimburse the "safe account" was deposited by Curtis into Small's Fort Dearborn account (via the Live Stock bank), not into an account in the Grant Park Bank.

And ledger pages from the Fort Dearborn bank, where the Grant Park Bank had an account, showed only $250 interest was earned by the Grant Park Bank during the four years of Small and Sterling as state treasurer.

Continental & Commercial National Bank, Wilkerson contended, did not allow Curtis to set up an account there in the name of the Grant Park Bank because Curtis could not show the bank existed.

The prosecution showed how Governor Small even used his wife as part of the scheme. Records from Continental & Commercial Trust & Savings Bank showed it sold to Mrs. Small on June 24, 1918 six per cent convertible gold debentures from Armour & Co totaling $58,010. The prosecution traced this money to a transaction between Grant Park Trust & Savings to Continental. And on June 9, 1919, Edward Curtis bought 100 shares of stock in the Illinois Central Railroad in the name of Mrs. Small and 100 shares in the name of the wife of Lt. Gov. Sterling -- all with money made from interest on state deposits.

State Treasurer Edward Miller was on the stand June 1. He said when he became treasurer in January 1921, he found $10 million missing. He asked outgoing treasurer Fred Sterling and was told that Len Small had it. Miller said when he asked Small for the money, Small gave him $9.9 million in Armour and Swift notes.

The defense had contended that Small had nothing to do with the transactions with the packers. So how did he have Armour and Swift notes?

At the same meeting, Miller testified, Vernon Curtis gave him certificates of deposit on the loans, from the Grant Park Bank.

When Miller told Small that he was $100,000 short, Small and Vernon Curtis had a private conversation. Small gave Miller $100,000 worth of temporary securities: $80,000 on notes signed by E.C. Curtis and two mortgages totaling $20,000. A week later, Leslie Small gave Miller a cashier's check for $100,000 from his Kankakee bank in exchange for the other notes and securities.

Miller also related an interesting bit of advice Len Small gave him just after the election. Small advised Miller to have his bond signed by individuals, not by a surety company.

"He said that the personal bond would require no investigation or examination by the signers of the bond, and he thought and expressed the idea that the surety company would want to investigate and examine the affairs of the office," Miller said.

And he related a very interesting conversation he had with Fred Sterling. "Sterling asked me what I intended to do regarding the other collections of the securities turned over to me," Miller told the court. "I replied that I intended to collect them. He then said, 'Ed, be careful about what you do. We are all friends of yours, and you can't do anything without hurting some of us.'"

On June 7, nineteen residents of Grant Park were called to the witness stand. They all testified that they lived in Grant Park all their lives and knew most of the other people in town, but none had ever heard of the Grant Park Bank. They had never seen a building, a sign or paperwork about such a place. One of the witnesses was Elroy Streeter, a director of the Grant Park Trust & Savings Bank, who had his insurance office on the second floor of the bank building. Streeter never heard anything about a "Grant Park Bank." Walter Brice, a farmer and a former business partner of Edward Curtis, testified he had never heard of the Grant Park Bank.

Norman Griffin, cashier of the legitimate bank in town, repeated for the jury his story of how the bank's records for these crucial dates had been burned by a janitor. Griffin did add something new, under questioning by Wilkerson -- he said the Grant Park Bank was never acknowledged as a banking institution by him in the annual reports he made for his own bank to the state auditor from 1917 to 1920.

Arthur Ruge, Griffin's assistant, was put on the witness stand but he proved to have a remarkable lapse of memory about practically everything.

Charles Hayden, a director of Grant Park Trust & Savings Bank, had been with the bank since 1907. He said he had heard of the "Grant Park Bank" back in the 1890s but did not know it had done any business in recent years. C.B. Streeter, another director, testified that the Grant Park Bank ceased operations in 1897.

The last witness for the state was Donald Currier, an expert who tied together the financial transactions of Small, Curtis, Sterling, the bank and the packers. It was technical, dry and sometimes numbing. But he made the state's case. In all, there were more than 7,000 pieces of evidence and more than 100 witnesses.

The trial really had few great courtroom theatrics. Documents were introduced as exhibits, witnesses testified about bank certificates, loans and so on. The public soon got tired of it and attendance was never great.

Even the jurors started showing disinterest. The jury threatened to go on "strike" on May 24 unless they could stay out later at night. Their elder bailiffs put them to bed at 9 p.m. and the jurors wanted them replaced with younger bailiffs who would take them out in the evenings. One juror asked the judge to hold court on Saturday. For the three-day Decoration Day weekend, the judge gave them just the holiday off.

The jurors rebelled again on Sunday, June 4. Eleven jurors wanted to attend a baseball game at Antioch while Arthur Larsen, the twelfth juror, wanted to go to a Viking Club picnic at Gurnee. An argument ensued and the 11 jurors telephoned Judge Edwards and asked him to lock up Larsen while they went to the game. Edwards ordered all 12 jurors to go to the ball game. Larsen claimed he had a headache, so the trip to the game was called off. Later in the day, bailiff John Whalen took the jurors for a walk near the Lake Michigan harbor. Some of the jurors rented fishing equipment and were about to go to the end of the pier, but the elderly Whalen would not walk that far. The disgruntled jurors had to fish in shallow waters.

The following week, Judge Edwards divided the jury into two groups so there would be a choice of whether to go out at night or sit home and play cards.

On June 10, the jury rebelled again. Homer Cook, a younger bailiff who was added to the staff a few weeks earlier, was removed at the request of the prosecution. Jurors demanded to be taken to Judge Edwards' house on a Saturday evening and they protested the removal of Cook. The judge did not reinstate Cook.

Waukegan continued to be bored by the slow moving parade of bankers, papers and numbers in the courtroom. "Around the courthouse, the trial is completely eclipsed by Sheriff Green's search for a convenient spot to hang a prisoner, sentenced to die a week from Friday," the Associated Press noted.

The condemned prisoner was Capone gangster Ignatz Potz, scheduled to hang June 16 for the murder of a policeman who was in pursuit of the bootleggers.

The state rested its case against Governor Small on June 19. The next day was spent on 19 defense motions to strike from the record most of the state's exhibits and much of the testimony. The judge ruled against the defense on almost everything.

Charles LeForgee shocked the courtroom by announcing he did not plan to put on a defense.

Small's trial lasted nine weeks. The first three weeks took up jury selection and opening arguments. The prosecution's case took six weeks. The defense case took only minutes. LeForgee rose and said, "The defense is entirely satisfied to rest on the evidence of the prosecution itself."

In closing arguments to the jury, Edward Pree criticized Norman Griffin for having a lapse of memory while being questioned by the state, but remembering everything while being cross examined by the defense. He shouted, "There's something rotten in Denmark and don't forget he is a brother-in-law of Vernon Curtis, a co-defendant in this case. I never saw anything so rotten as his testimony on this witness stand. If I had it in my power, I would send him to the penitentiary for that performance."

Fred Mortimer said the conspiracy between the defendants went on for several years until Edward Miller became treasurer "and the people found out what had been going on." Mortimer got quite excited in his summary.

Referring to Small and the Curtis brothers, Mortimer said, "These three martyrs were going to help the state. Oh yes, help the state? By God, they were helping themselves. That's the story.

"Well, they say Len Small didn't get the money. No, Len didn't get any of it. Not any? Not any? No! Not a chance! Here are his buddies, Ed Curtis and his brother Vern Curtis, doing what? Loaning the people's money at from five to eight and a half per cent and paying the state of Illinois, they say, two per cent. Yet they say it was an honest transaction and we say it was a disgrace and a dishonor in the history of Illinois and your land and my land.'

Mortimer compared the bankers to bootleggers. "All this bank had was a label."

In his closing argument, Wilkinson called Small a "war profiteer" and said the governor's lawyers insulted the intelligence of the jurors by trying to make them believe these financial transactions went on without Small's knowledge.

"To argue to this jury that the treasurer of the state of Illinois did not know that the money which was deposited in his account in the Fort Dearborn bank by E.C. Curtis was money of the packers which was obtained by Curtis in the way in which Curtis obtained it, is to make of E.C. Curtis a man so black in character...to violate a law with reference to handling public moneys, an unpardonable sin of base treachery and of faithlessness to his friend," Wilkinson said.

The governor's attorneys -- Alexander Beaubien, Werner Schroeder and Charles LeForgee -- made the closing arguments for the defense.

Beaubien told the jury that Small returned every penny that was deposited and that the state did not prove that Len Small personally profited from the loans to the meat packers. "The state's case is built on flimsy, circumstantial evidence, rubber stamps, witnesses who are not in a position to know the facts and experts who do not expert."

Schroeder continued the argument that the whole case was a politically-motivated persecution of the governor. He said the verdict would mean retaining Governor Small's good name and honor or destroying it.

"There have been poured into your ears such words as 'damnable' and 'rotten' and 'graft,'" Schroeder told the jury. "That is the construction and the interpretation which the three gentlemen who spoke for the prosecution have put upon the acts of these men, the Curtises, Small and Sterling. Our interpretation is that they were the honest acts of an honest man."

LeForgee's closing speech was a long and somewhat shameless appeal to patriotism, saying that Curtis was a hero whose bank paid the state every time it needed its cash to pursue the great world war, nearly crediting Curtis with winning the war single-handedly. He even quoted George M. Cohan's patriotic songs in making his point

The case went to the jury on Saturday, June 24, 1922. An hour and a half later, they returned with a verdict of "not guilty" after taking two ballots.

The courtroom exploded in yells and cheers from the governor's family and friends. Ida Small made her way through the crowded courtroom to her husband. The governor "put one arm around her shoulder, while the tears streaming down her cheeks, she gently pressed her husband's hand."

The governor then walked to the jury box. He shook each man's hand, saying, "I thank you from the bottom of my heart and so does Mrs. Small."

"We would have been in sooner, but we wanted to stay out long enough to make it look right," the *Kankakee Daily Republican* quoted a juror as telling a defense attorney. "Not one of the jurors thought it worthwhile to examine any of the 7,000 exhibits introduced by the state," the *Daily Republican* reported.

A few of the jurors told the press that their verdict came from the state's failure to prove that Small personally profited from the deal.

Friends of the governor mobbed him with congratulations. As they left the courthouse, his followers formed a caravan that drove from Waukegan to Kankakee for a victory celebration.

Governor Small's house at 1525 W. Station Street was the site of a large party and reception that Saturday evening. Ida Small, who had spent the previous nine weeks by her husband's side in the Waukegan courthouse, also was by his side in the reception line on the front porch for more than an hour.

Late in the evening, as the last of the visitors was being greeted by Governor Small, Mrs. Small told her husband that she was feeling faint. She stepped inside and sat down. Mrs. Small suffered a stroke and went into unconsciousness. She died Monday morning, June 26.

When the doctors told the governor there was no hope for his wife, he said, "Thank God she lived to see me vindicated. It was the happiest day of her life."

Governor Small was in a state of shock when his wife passed on. He needed a sedative and a lot of sleep before he was able to face making funeral arrangements.

Ida Small

Mrs. Small's sudden death surprised everyone. Any expression of criticism of the verdict by the public and the press died when Mrs. Small died. The only expressions were those of sympathy, even from nemeses such as Ed Brundage and the *Chicago Tribune.*

But there were some expressions of anger and bitterness.

Kankakee Doctor E.G. Wilson and the *Kankakee Daily Republican* flat out blamed Brundage and other political enemies for Mrs. Small's death. "Guilty of murder in the first degree" was the quote attributed to "public opinion" in a June 27 news story that was more an attack on the governor's enemies than a tribute to Mrs. Small.

Chicago's American said "her life paid the price of the despicable political conspiracy led and fostered by the *Chicago Tribune."* Chicago's Corporation Counsel Sam Ettleson said Mrs. Small's death was "nothing but murder, done by dirty politics."

Mrs. Small's funeral was the biggest Kankakee had seen up to that time. Mayor Thompson and Fred Lundin were among the many dignitaries who came to Kankakee. Most of the state officials came from Springfield for the funeral.

Six months after the trial, Circuit Court Judge Norman Jones struck down part of the 1908 treasurer law. Jones, who would become the Democrat candidate against Small in 1924, ruled that the legislature did not have the power to designate where state money would be deposited, or to designate the rate of interest. It did not strike down the pertinent part of the law that said the treasurer could not keep the interest for himself. Small, somehow, declared this ruling as a "vindication."

Four months after the trial, Judge Claire C. Edwards announced he would be a candidate for election as an Illinois Supreme Court justice. Governor Small supported his candidacy. Edwards did not win.

Chapter 12

Jury Tampering: Did the Governor's Gangsters Bribe His Jury?

Len Small's acquittal was hailed as a vindication by the governor and his supporters. And it was immediately questioned by those who could not believe it.

Was he found "not guilty" because the jury believed the governor really didn't steal a million dollars from the transactions made by the fictitious "Grant Park Bank" or was it because the prosecution couldn't prove Small personally profited from the scheme?

Or was it because the trial was "fixed?"

Governor Small and his supporters celebrated an honest victory in court. His supporters in Kankakee today maintain that stand.

The evidence does not support a verdict of an "honest victory in court."

The fight made by the governor and his men started even before the indictments were returned. We have seen the alleged bribe offered by Small to Brundage to stop the investigation. We have seen the alleged bribe offered to a member of the grand jury to not vote for the indictments.

We have seen the governor's efforts to evade justice by running from the sheriff, his threat to call out the militia, his argument in court that he was above the law, and we have seen the many legal maneuvers to have the indictments quashed or the charges dropped. But that wasn't the extent of his efforts.

An important legal maneuver was to secure a change of venue from downstate Sangamon County to Lake County, the home of Fred Lundin. Small already was tied to the Mob, and already had started eight years of selling pardons and paroles to criminals. Waukegan was an area that Al Capone and his mobsters could influence. It would be easier for the governor's gangsters to get to jurors there than in rural central Illinois.

Once the trial was set for Lake County, Small's men tried to taint the jury pool. The method was explained by Roger E. Chapin, a probate judge and member of the Sangamon County Board. He knew what was going on, first-hand.

"Immediately upon the transfer of the case to Waukegan a county-wide canvass was arranged to ascertain the attitude of every person in Lake County toward Len Small to aid in eliminating prospective jurors who were unfavorable to him," Judge Chapin wrote.

"This canvass was made by baking powder salesmen who came into Lake County in great numbers to sell baking powder from house to house. They offered with each can of baking powder a free portrait of the purchaser's choice, of the picture of George Washington, Abraham Lincoln or Len Small. At that time the feeling for or against Small was pretty strong and the salesmen could tell very clearly whether the household was on Small's side or against him by the reaction to this offer. The baking powder salesmen's tabulations were used in selecting or eliminating jurors."

One of the men behind the "baking powder survey" was William J. Stratton, a Republican boss and county chairman of Lake County. Stratton also was influential in getting Small his change of venue

Through his political position, Stratton was able to get a variety of patronage jobs, including state game and fish warden.

As a reward for his help, Small created the Department of Conservation and he named William J. Stratton as director. The opportunistic Stratton plastered his name on everything he could, all across the state, as a preparation to running for statewide office.

Stratton was among those who urged Secretary of State Louis Emmerson to run against Small in 1928. This way, Stratton could run for secretary of state. At the same time, Stratton was seeking Small's endorsement.

Small didn't endorse him but he offered a deal for his support over Emmerson. Stratton decided his chances were better with Emmerson. He bet on the right horse, and won with Emmerson in 1928.

It must have been tough for Stratton to be called a "back stabber" by someone like Len Small.

Stratton's son, William G. Stratton, was governor of Illinois from 1953 to 1961. He went on trial in 1965 for income tax evasion and was acquitted.

While the prosecution was making its closing arguments in court, the *Daily Republican* on June 22 reported, "The Governor himself is happy and laughing, as he always is when confident that another great battle has been won."

That night, Small took his two grandsons to the circus in Waukegan. "The Governor's face has been wreathed in smiles ever since friends from all over the state are here to congratulate him on what they believe to be certain failure of the state to secure a verdict," it was reported in the newspaper the next day.

That doesn't sound like a man on trial for his political life, worried about the outcome of his trial.

That is because gangsters had gotten to the jurors and bribed and intimidated them into a verdict in favor of the governor.

The allegations at the time were that a lawyer connected to the governor went to City Hall in Chicago. Two mobsters, Umbrella Mike Boyle and Cornelius "Con" Shea, were contracted to "fix" the jury. Ben Newmark also was involved.

Boyle was the head of the Electrical Workers Union in Chicago and a part of Organized Crime. He got his nickname by carrying a folded umbrella, into which payoffs and collections were dropped. Shea was a labor racketeer and murderer.

Chicago gangsters Eddie Courtney and Eddie Kaufman paid visits to the jurors after they were selected for the Small trial. They offered money and the promise of state jobs, and when that wasn't enough, they used intimidation.

Following Courtney and Kaufman to keep an eye on their work was Walter Stevens, called the "dean of Chicago gunmen" for the 60 murders he committed.

The prosecution put on its case for six weeks. When it came time for the defense, LeForgee told the judge his case would rest on what the prosecution had presented.

The judge and prosecutor looked surprised. No defense?

No, Len Small did not need to put on a defense when he had the jury in his pocket. Despite the evidence against Small, the jury did not take long in coming to a "not guilty" verdict on June 24, 1922.

It was a classic scene that would be copied in future movies about fixed juries in Mob trials.

Jurors already had their bags packed on the final day of the case, even before closing arguments were finished. They went into the jury room and did not look at a single exhibit of evidence before coming to their verdict.

Within two months of Small's acquittal, most of his jury had jobs on the state payroll. John B. Fields, a former cab driver from Antioch, was named deputy game warden for the Kankakee district. It was William J. Stratton who escorted Fields from the jury box after the verdict.

Walter Repkow and Frank Reardon were appointed state highway patrolmen. William Barnard and Lawrence Buss were given jobs with the state highway department. Jury foreman Alex Smith got the job as drainage inspector at the massive Stateville penitentiary under construction. George Martin was given a job in the state game department.

Homer Cook, a county bailiff who watched over the jurors, had another job at the same time -- this one on the payroll of Len Small as a game warden for the state. Lake County Clerk Lew Hendee also got an additional paycheck for a second job as a state game warden, given after the trial.

Lake County Sheriff Elmer Green, who had custody of the jurors during the trial, was named superintendent of prisons in December 1922. The *Chicago Tribune* reported that the job was "given to Green as a reward for the friendship he manifested toward the governor during his trial."

"Green and Small were said to have reached a complete understanding during his trial. The sheriff was reported to have used extraordinary care in rounding up the venire men for the Small jury," the *Trib* wrote.

The job had been held by John Whitman, a Lowden appointee. Whitman was demoted to warden of the Joliet penitentiary.

Ben Newmark, one of the hoodlums who “influenced” jurors, was rewarded with an appointment as assistant state fire marshal in January 1923.

And another curious thing happened in early 1922, as jurors were being selected for the governor’s trial. The *Waukegan Daily Sun,* which had been very anti-Small for years, suddenly began publishing editorials claiming that the charges against the governor were false and nothing but persecution. The language of the editorials was exceedingly strong, and quite an about-face for this newspaper.

It was circulated across Lake County for all prospective jurors to read.

Coverage of the pre-trial proceedings was biased toward Small. Other reporters who were not pro-Small were suspect, in the eyes of the *Sun* editors. "It would look as if the interests in question had paid representatives here to misinterpret the proceedings in order to prejudice the public against the governor," one *Sun* editorial said.

It was right about the paid representatives. But, the "interests" were the governor's people, and the intent was to prejudice the public in Small's favor.

The rival *Waukegan Daily News* thought it very strange, especially the wording, which did not fit the editor's style of writing. The *Chicago Tribune* disclosed that 1,000 copies of the editorials were mailed to newspapers and to others from the governor's press office in Springfield, with a Springfield postmark, even though the envelopes had the return address of the *Waukegan Sun*. This led the *Waukegan Daily News* to observe that this was "conclusive evidence it is propaganda to which the *Sun* has loaned itself for one reason or another. One wonders why."

The reason became clear on Aug. 19, when William Smith, editor of the *Waukegan Sun,* was appointed by the governor to the Illinois Commerce Commission at a big salary.

The *Waukegan Daily News* ran an affidavit from a man who heard William Smith's brother Frank say they had been paid $10,000 to print pro-Small stories before the trial.

Within months of the governor's acquittal, there was talk of how the jury was "fixed." And all those jurors getting state jobs added fuel to the fire. Lake County State's Attorney Ashbel V. Smith started making an investigation and gathering evidence. He took his case to a grand jury in March 1923.

William Riley, proprietor of an Antioch speakeasy, told the grand jury that he paid Fields $350 to vote for an acquittal in Len Small's trial. He said Courtney and Kaufman gave him $1,000 to bribe jurors.

Bank records showed that Riley received his payment on the date he said.

Joseph Hahn of Channel Lake told the grand jury that after he was served a summons to report as a prospective juror, he got a visit from Riley, Courtney and Kaufman. They made him an "offer." Hahn got scared and begged off the jury.

After telling their stories to the grand jury, Riley, Hahn and William Musch were put under guard in a Highland Park hotel, after receiving kidnapping threats.

The grand jury also heard testimony that six of the Small jurors were taken to Krueger's roadhouse outside Waukegan during the trial, where women and bootleg booze were "the featured entertainment."

Leslie Small, the governor's son, and Arthur Inglesh, the governor's son-in-law were brought before the grand jury to tell of their connections to mobsters involved in the jury tampering.

After the governor's trial ended, Courtney and Kaufman paid a visit to Leslie Small in Springfield. The state alleged that the gunmen were seeking payment from Small for their work. Con Shea came with them.

The auditor of the St. Nicholas Hotel in Springfield produced records for the grand jury, showing the three hoodlums were registered on Feb. 6, 1923.

Leslie Small's story to the grand jury was that the gunmen complained to him that representatives of the prosecutor tried to get them to work against the governor's case, offering them "beer running privileges" if they did. The gangsters instead offered their services to the governor, Leslie said, and he interpreted their visit as an attempt to make points with the governor so they could ask for a favor in the future. Leslie sent them to Werner Schroeder in Chicago and Schroeder ordered them out of his office, he said. Schroeder was questioned about the meetings with the mobsters and he backed up Leslie Small's story.

Leslie Small was asked why two jurors were given jobs as state policemen. Small said it was because they had been fired from their previous jobs. State's Attorney Smith provided evidence that the men quit to take the state jobs, and had not been fired.

Two mobsters almost shot it out in the hallway of the courthouse during the grand jury proceedings. Harry Paygman was a one-time "investigator" for the Chicago police, as was his underworld pal Ben Newmark. Paygman was coming out of the courtroom after testifying when he was spotted by Fred "Frenchy" Mader, who was subpoenaed in this case. Mader made "an uncomplimentary remark and gesture" and Paygman replied, "If you come outside, I'll fill you full of lead." A deputy separated the two gangsters.

Paygman had testified against Mader in 1922 when Mader was on trial for the murder of a Chicago policeman (Lt. Terrence Lyons was gunned down by gangster from a passing car). Mader and six other labor leader-gangsters, including Big Tim Murphy and Con Shea, were acquitted after two trials.

Mader was president of the powerful Chicago Building and Construction Trades Council in 1922. Mader got his position through the strong-arm tactics of Big Tim Murphy, a fellow mobster and labor racketeer who controlled several labor unions. Mader was convicted of extortion in 1915 and sentenced to three years in prison for threatening and shaking down local businessmen. Mader also was known for beating union workers who ran afoul of his rules. Mader went on trial again in 1922 for bribery, extortion, bombings and having a gang of thugs beat and intimidate other union workers in his business of shaking down contractors for a percentage of the cost of the construction of buildings in Chicago. Mader was convicted and sentenced to one year.

A number of others, including several officials close to Lundin and Thompson, were called before the grand jury. William Smith, former *Waukegan Sun* editor and now Illinois Commerce Commission director, was called.

Judge Claire Edwards told the grand jury of the gravity of the accusations before them. "The charges you are to investigate are serious," he said. "They strike at the very fundamentals of representative government, the jury system."

On April 3 1923, the grand jury indicted three men: juror John B. Fields and Chicago gangsters Eddie Courtney and Eddie Kaufman. The 14-count indictment contained conspiracy, obstruction of justice and bribery charges.

Lake County Sheriff Ed Ahlstrom waited with a warrant in a DuPage County courtroom, where Kaufman was supposed to appear on a bootlegging charge. When Kaufman didn't show, the sheriff trailed Kaufman's bondsman to several places in Chicago until finally arresting Kaufman in front of a gambling joint at 63rd and Halsted streets. Kaufman called his attorney, W.W. O'Brien.

Kaufman's $5,000 bail was signed by Russell E. Edwards -- the brother of Judge Claire Edwards.

After several more days, Courtney went to W.W. O'Brien and agreed to surrender. He was booked and made bail.

The state contended that the gangsters got to nine of the men who served on Governor Small's jury.

Riley was held in protective custody as an important state witness. He was constantly moved from hotel to hotel to keep him out of the reach of Mob machine guns. Riley also had an indictment returned against him for his part in the bribery.

The grand jury called mobsters Ben Newmark and Umbrella Mike Boyle. Testimony from other witnesses implicated the two men in the bribery of the jurors. It was alleged that Newmark handled some of the money and had registered as "John Smith" in the Salvation Army hotel, which was the governor's headquarters during the trial. From there, Newmark was said to have supervised a number of private detectives from the Cochrane Agency of Chicago who canvassed the jury pool.

William Pinnow was one potential juror who was approached with the offer of a bribe. William J. Stratton was questioned about his part in the jury fixing. Hubert Nortney, a speculator in the hog market, was subpoenaed for his alleged part as the go-between for Courtney, Kaufman and Shea with Schroeder and Leslie Small.

Cornelius R. Miller admitted to the grand jury that a $50,000 "defense fund" had been raised for the governor's trial, and investigators wanted to know if any of this money was used to bribe jurors.

Republican State Sen. Rodney Swift of Lake Forest had his own comment on the fundraising done by Miller in Lake County. "The meanest, most disreputable band of assassins ever gathered together was also brought in. I saw them in the streets of my town, laughing and arrogant. They bribed one of our men. They paid one of our editors. They debauched our county. The report is that $100,000 went into Lake County."

Judge Claire Edwards issued bench warrants for the arrest of Newmark and Boyle after the two ignored subpoenas to appear in court.

Authorities searched for Newmark and Boyle. Boyle gave himself up on May 5 but refused to talk to the grand jury on grounds he might incriminate himself. After refusing to answer any of the 86 questions put to him, the court granted Boyle immunity. Boyle still refused to talk. Judge Robert Welch told Boyle that his constitutional rights were assured by the grant of immunity. Boyle still refused, so Judge Welch found Boyle in contempt of court on May 26 and sentenced him to six months in jail. Boyle remained free on appeal.

On March 25, Judge Claire Edwards assigned a bodyguard to protect grand juror William Thomas of Highland Park, a salesman for Western Electric Co. Thomas was one of three grand jurors who were threatened if they did not "lay off Mike Boyle."

Newmark gave himself up on May 15. One of his lawyers was Michael Ahern, who in 1931 would be one of Al Capone's lawyers.

State's Attorney A.V. Smith asked the judge to sign a waiver of immunity for Newmark. Ahern shot up and objected. An angry Judge Welch asked Ahern, "Do you want this court to understand that you object to your client being granted immunity? Why, he hasn't even been taken into the grand jury room yet." Ahern sat down.

The judge couldn't understand a lawyer objecting to the court freeing his client from any penalty. But then, perhaps the judge didn't understand that gangsters do not testify, immunity or not.

Newmark was granted immunity and then was asked the same 86 probing questions put before Boyle. Newmark kept mum. Judge Welch found Newmark in contempt on June 4 and gave him six months, suspended while on appeal.

Len Small saw the claim of jury tampering this way: "This is just a continuation of the persecution by the great profiteering interests for whom the *Chicago Tribune* is the recognized mouthpiece and from whom Attorney General Brundage takes his orders."

Small saw just about everything that way.

The governor's statement was: "What a deplorable condition exists when men of impeachable character are summoned and compelled to sit on a jury and try a case, and then after giving an honest verdict based on the evidence are hounded and persecuted, lose their jobs, their families are repeatedly visited by so-called detectives who are sometimes of the most vicious elements, and then finally are indicted on evidence thus obtained through the powerful influences of the attorney general and the *Chicago Tribune,* representing the great profiteering interests. This is another example of Attorney General Brundage obeying the orders of the *Chicago Tribune* and using disreputable testimony to destroy and disgrace innocent men."

And, he added, "These interests realize that I stand in their way in my efforts to protect the people from being robbed."

He meant he was saving the state from being robbed on road contracts, not that he was saving the state from being robbed by him and his Chicago pals.

If there was any "fixing" of the jury, Small added, it was done by Brundage "and his band of crooks and criminals."

Just how -- and *why* -- a *prosecutor* would "fix" a jury to come up with an *acquittal* was something that Small didn't explain.

Perhaps Small was referring to a story he ran in his own newspaper, in which Kaufman said he was in jail at Waukegan the previous December, charged with rum running. Kaufman claimed Brundage visited him in jail and "offered him a brewery" if he would make a false confession that he tried to secure jurors favorable to Small. The newspaper also discounted the testimony of key witness William Riley. The newspaper claimed that Riley, who had been busted for liquor violations, was offered a deal from Brundage to have the charges dropped in exchange for false testimony about bribing jurors.

By the time the trial of Fields, Courtney and Kaufman began in early July 1923, Newmark and Boyle had vanished. The state put out a reward for their capture, since they were under a six-month sentence for contempt.

Leslie Small testified that he was approached by gangsters Courtney, Kaufman and Shea in Springfield. Small said one of the gangsters told him he had been arrested and his truck and supply of beer were confiscated. This was a loss of $7,000 or $8,000. Small said the gangsters told him that Brundage offered to give them back their truck and beer if they would testify against the governor.

Judge Jacob Hopkins ruled Leslie Small a hostile witness. A two-hour conference was held in the judge's chambers and little more of Small's testimony was allowed.

Since Newmark and Boyle could not be located to testify, Smith asked the court to allow a confession made by Kaufman admitting that he and Courtney did bribe jurors on orders from Newmark and Boyle. Kaufman's lawyer, W.W. O'Brien, objected.

William Riley testified that the two gangsters gave him $1,000 to bribe jurors, and he gave $350 to Fields. Riley also said he and Kaufman offered prospective juror Joe Hahn money and a state job if he got on the jury and acquitted Small.

Thomas Sommerville testified that Courtney and Kaufman had offered him bribe money and the promise of a state job if he got on the jury and sided with the governor. Small's lawyers claimed that Sommerville was insane, since he spent three weeks at the Elgin mental hospital in 1920. This necessitated an examination, and three doctors testified that Sommerville was sane and could be believed.

Prosecutor A.V. Smith said, "Courtney, Kaufman and Shea went to Curtis, Schroeder and Leslie Small demanding money. They threatened to expose the jury bribery if they didn't get it. They offered to get out of the state and not testify if they did get it."

The trial ended on July 17. No defense was presented and none of the defendants took the stand. In their closing arguments, the defendants' lawyers argued that the trial "was a political conspiracy to further blacken the name of Governor Small."

The jury took one ballot before finding all three defendants not guilty. William Wilmington, jury foreman and mayor of Round Lake, refused to talk to reporters. The 12 jurors shook hands with the lawyers and the defendants. All refused to talk to the press.

Newmark and Boyle surfaced after the trial was over. Boyle was captured on Sept. 3 while sleeping in a Wisconsin roadhouse near Oconomowoc. Newmark gave himself up on Oct. 1, on advice from his lawyer, who thought he had a loophole but needed Newmark in custody before he could use it. Newmark drove up to the Lake County jail in a shiny new automobile. He had a suitcase full of silk shirts and enough cigars to last the winter. He greeted the sheriff with a smile.

A United Press reporter quoted Boyle as saying, "Why should I worry?"

Why, indeed?

Both Newmark and Boyle were jailed on their six-month contempt sentences.

But Governor Small shocked the state on Oct. 22 when he commuted the sentences of Newmark and Boyle.

Yes, the gangsters who bribed a jury to acquit a crooked governor, and who went to jail for refusing to answer to a grand jury about it, were freed by the crooked governor.

Small had decided to free the two gangsters but waited until the state Supreme Court went out of session to issue the pardons. Small said he consulted with Samuel Ettleson, a former state senator and legal counsel to Mayor Thompson. Newmark once worked for Ettleson.

Small hid out in his Kankakee home as the announcement was made.

Governor Small issued a written statement, saying the pair "were deprived of their constitutional rights and had been arbitrarily imprisoned contrary to the clear provisions of our state constitution."

Small's statement went on, saying the contempt sentences given to Newmark and Boyle were "a miscarriage of justice" and "a last step in a series of determined efforts directed by the political enemies of the governor to punish him for having vetoed excessive appropriations and for having protected the people from criminal profiteering." It was "part and parcel and in furtherance of a conspiracy of political enemies of the governor to discredit and bring into disgrace those who have been and are opposed to them politically."

The governor was concerned about the fallout. There were calls for the Supreme Court to overturn the pardons, but the justices had gone home, and a governor's pardon is not subject to court jurisdiction.

Robert Welch, the judge who sentenced Newmark and Boyle, was now off the bench and practicing law. He said it was his opinion that the governor did not have the authority to pardon someone from a contempt sentence -- it was a separation of powers issue, the executive interfering with the judiciary. Attorney General Brundage agreed with that argument and he filed an appeal to nullify the pardons.

Remember the pardons Governor Small gave in 1922 to the members of the Chicago school board on their sentences of contempt of court? The Supreme Court ruled those pardons invalid "since the offense originated in the court." State's Attorney Smith cited that precedent in this case and said he would take it up with the Supreme Court when it reconvened in December.

The day after the pardons, Boyle was back on the job at the union hall and Newmark spent a few minutes in the office where he drew a big paycheck in a do-nothing job as an assistant fire marshal.

Small's action was "just short of incredible," the *Chicago Journal* said.

"Is it possible that the governor does not understand how this action will appear to the people of Illinois?" the newspaper wrote. "He has done more damage to his reputation by this one act than all the attacks of his factional enemies have accomplished. Here are two of his henchmen, active in his behalf, who refuse to tell what they know about a case which resulted in the acquittal of the governor on a criminal charge -- and that governor braves the wrath of the Supreme Court to keep those henchmen from being punished for their silence! If Small's bitterest enemies had plotted to destroy his standing with the people, they could not have designed anything more deadly than this."

The state Supreme Court decided in June 1924 that it would not rule on the motion challenging the governor's pardoning right in this case. The contempt charges against Newmark and Boyle were dismissed.

Former Governor Lowden weighed in with his opinion. "Why do we have courts? Of what use is judicial machinery? The writ of contempt is one of those powers without which the court is impotent to enforce its own decrees or to ask respect from anyone. The power to pardon is a power granted to the governor to correct injustice when it is too late for the courts to act. Humanity demands that the power reside somewhere to correct such injustice, but it never was intended to supplant the powers of the judiciary."

Here is the account from TIME magazine, Nov. 5, 1923: "The great game of politics is played everywhere, but nowhere with greater zest than in the state of Illinois. Governor Small, who had previously been state treasurer, was indicted for embezzlement of state funds in 1921. He fought trial for nine months, but when it finally took place, 1922, he was acquitted. Subsequently, three of the jurors and the sheriff who had charge of the jury at the trial were given places on the state payroll. In 1923, a saloon keeper confessed having given a cash bribe to one of the three jurors. They were indicted. Two other men, one a labor leader, the other a detective, were subpoenaed to give evidence. They declined to talk on the ground that it might incriminate them. The state granted them immunity. They still refused to talk. They were sentenced to six months in jail for contempt of court. They jumped bail, one was recaptured, the other gave himself up. They went to prison. Last week, Governor Small pardoned them. There is little doubt that he had no legal right to do so, but the state Supreme Court will not convene until December and nothing can be done meanwhile. This act, said the *Chicago Daily Tribune,* 'adds a cubit to Small's colossus of nerve . . . The executive clemency is extended to jailed citizens whose virtue is their silence on the methods by which a governor was acquitted of embezzlement.'"

Ben Newmark worked for a private detective agency and later worked for State's Attorney Robert Crowe as an "investigator." Crowe's reputation in history is mixed -- he had some successes as a prosecutor and never was directly tied to corruption, but he did have connections with unsavory characters. His chief assistant, William McSwiggin, was cut down by machine gun fire from a passing car as he was coming out of a Cicero tavern with two gangsters on April 27, 1926. The gunmen were sent by Al Capone.

An accusation in June 1921 that the state's attorney's office was in league with the underworld angered Crowe, and he ordered raids on six major joints on June 18. More than 200 people were arrested. But the big prize of the night, Pat O'Malley's place at Polk and Clark streets, was empty when police arrived. Newmark was in charge of the raiding squads at the time and he tipped off O'Malley.

Newmark often used his inside information from Crowe's office to tip off gangsters before raids.

Ben's brother, Dan Newmark, was a robber with a long record. In 1921, Dan had two fellow gangsters rob his own sister, in her home at gunpoint, of $20,000 in jewels.

Ben Newmark was arrested on Nov. 10, 1924 and charged with counterfeiting. He was accused of being the leader of a ring that printed counterfeit Liberty bonds and treasury savings stamps. After a lot of legal maneuvers, Newmark escaped conviction by testifying against his other counterfeiters.

Ben Newmark was getting ready for bed on the night of April 22, 1928. His wife had gone to bed earlier but she was still awake as her husband sat on the edge of the bed while taking off his clothes. The Newmarks had a party in their home that night and the last of the guests had just left. Through the bars on the bedroom window, someone pointed a shotgun and fired into the room. Newmark was still alive when the police arrived. He tried to say something to his wife but could not.

Ben Newmark died on his bedroom floor.

Police questioned Santo Jemalli but let him go for lack of evidence. Jemalli recently had been released from Leavenworth penitentiary, where he served a sentence for counterfeiting war bonds. It was the same rap for which Newmark had been arrested. Newmark got off by testifying against Jemalli and the others, and it was thought that Jemalli "hit" Newmark for revenge. Jemalli told police he didn't even know Ben Newmark.

Frank Biege, a Capone gunman, was questioned in October 1929 about the Newmark killing. Biege's wife told police her husband may have been involved in the murders of Newmark, McSwiggin and at the Moran garage on St. Valentine's Day. It didn't check out.

"At one time or another, Newmark had a hand in just about everything you could mention. His connection with gambling was notorious," an investigator told the *Chicago Tribune* after the slaying.

Chapter 13

The Civil Suit: The Governor's Second Trial

At the same time the state was preparing criminal charges against Governor Small, it also was preparing a civil lawsuit.

A criminal conviction could have sent the governor to prison. A civil suit was needed to recover as much of the embezzled funds as possible.

Brundage filed the civil suit on Nov. 26, 1921. Small, Sterling and Curtis were named in this lawsuit, as they had been in the criminal charges filed the previous July.

Illinois was a national spectacle. Its governor and its lieutenant governor both were former state treasurers and both were under indictment for stealing between one and two million dollars from the state treasury.

But if Governor Small thought his troubles were over when a jury acquitted him on the criminal charges in June 1922, he was wrong. Legal work on the civil suit was well under way. Both sides once again prepared for a fierce battle.

This time, it was former Senator Lawrence Sherman who used ancient arguments in court on Small's behalf. In September 1922, Sherman cited Alfred the Great and the Doom Book (based on the admonition from Leviticus to judge fairly). He also said the state treasurer was bound to "take and safely keep" state money and the treasurer had "no constitutional obligation to account for the manner in which he handles that money."

The treasurer only needs to pay back the money, Sherman argued.

Sangamon County Circuit Court Judge Norman Jones ruled on Dec.16, 1922 that the civil suit would go to trial. In this same ruling, Jones declared part of the 1908 law unconstitutional, where the law indicated the selection of banks by the treasurer; the ruling upheld the part of the law that said interest on deposits belonged to the state.

The governor's lawyers continued their strategy of delays. In March 1923, they asked Judge Jones to postpone any hearings until July because the governor simply was "too busy," primarily with road building contracts and with his duties as commander of the state militia. This was after the governor failed to meet a March 5 deadline for filing an answer to the charges. Assistant Attorney General Clarence Boord objected to any delay and asked the judge to hold Small in contempt of court for ignoring the deadline.

Judge Jones scolded Small for missing his deadline but did not hold him in contempt. "We cannot go along this way and permit any defendant, no matter how prominent he may be, to delay the courts unreasonably."

Boord told the judge that Small had months to prepare a plea "and yet, Mr. Small has the unparalleled effrontery to say under oath that he has not even had the time to consult with his counsel as to what the pleadings he should now file. It would seem that Mr. Small is simpleminded or that he thinks the court a fool."

In May, the governor vetoed a $75,000 appropriation to pay for the prosecution of the civil suit. His veto of $513,200 from the attorney general's $997,240 budget included the entire $250,000 law enforcement budget of the attorney general. Brundage could not muster enough votes in the legislature to override the governor's veto. The *Chicago Tribune* headlined its story, *Veto Stands, As Small Defeats Law And Order.*

There was bitter argument on both sides, in a state divided by powerful factions. State Rep. Euclid Rogers of Springfield, who also was pastor of Central Baptist Church, was the most vocal. He said "the world is tired of kings," as he laid into the way the governor fought the state's charges.

"In the whole history of government here, never was such wholesale bribery," he said. "It has been reported to me this morning that bids were given here and there. I can't believe that any member of this house has a palm which is itching like the palm of Cassius in the Roman senate to conceal his honor by accepting paltry gold. I can't believe that any member of this house is in the market.

"It has been reported repeatedly that denizens of the underworld stepped forth from their lairs to assist in the governor's acquittal at Waukegan, and we can hear in tones loud and clear from the chambers below they shall receive their reward. Is this veto in the interests of the people? Doesn't it strike you that it was spawned in a heart of hate, a hate that poisons the heart and addles the brain? The matter is bigger than Governor Small or the attorney general. In the name of justice, I protest against this veto. Enforce the law or lose your liberty."

In November, Sangamon County Circuit Court Judge Frank Burton ordered that the civil case against Small would go to the county's master in chancery for hearings. This was over the strong objection of the governor's lawyers.

The hearings would determine whether Small had to account for the money he was accused of taking. If the master in chancery decided he did, then it would go to trial. If he decided the governor did not have to account, the case would be dismissed.

The civil suit had a lower threshold of a burden of proof by the state. More importantly, it had the advantage of being determined by judges in courts as a matter of law, without a jury that could be bribed.

Many of the witnesses from the criminal trial repeated their testimony to the master in chancery.

Harry Luehrs gave more of his damaging testimony. Schroeder tried a novel tactic to silence him: since a higher court ruled that stockholders in corporations are incompetent witnesses in litigation in which their corporation is involved,

Schroeder argued that Luehrs was a stockholder in the state of Illinois because he was a taxpayer. It didn't work.

Marshall H. Jackson told of how Edward Curtis ordered supplies for the Grant Park Bank but told him not report the order "because Curtis didn't want the other banks to know what they were up to." Kankakee County Clerk H.J. Groenewoud testified that the Grant Park Bank had not been on the assessment books since 1897.

The hearings went on through most of 1924, with the appearance of some of the same evidence and some of the same witnesses that had been seen in the criminal trial. New to the hearings was Ed Trobaugh, a longtime employee in the treasurer's office. He told of the treasurer's records being nailed up in a box and sent to Kankakee after Small left office. Trobaugh also said that Edward C. Curtis visited the treasurer's office twice a week to look over the books and other records -- now missing -- because he did not trust Len Small to "play square" with all that money. Curtis had the run of the office and often spoke to no one, not even Small, as he went through teller cages and record books.

Some depositions and hearings were held in Kankakee County in late June, presided over by that county's master in chancery: John Small.

Governor Small testified on July 29, going through his prepared story. Small said that he and Curtis were business partners in Kankakee, Springfield and at other places, but were not partners in the Grant Park Bank.

The next day, his lawyers found a person who said she had an account in the Grant Park Bank. It was 73-year-old Mary Campbell, who said her transactions were handled personally by Edward C. Curtis...who was her nephew. However, she could not tell the court where the bank was to be found.

On the prosecution team was Floyd K. Britten. Small's counsel was Werner Schroeder. Charles LeForgee and George Gillespie, on Small's legal team at his criminal trial, bowed out of the civil suit. Attorney Thomas Masters helped the defense prepare for the civil suit but resigned from the case because of a disagreement. He had to sue Small to get $12,000 in legal fees he said he was owed.

As the proceedings went on, Small's lawyers began to rely more and more on an argument they only briefly mentioned in the criminal trial -- placing the blame on Small's dead partner, Edward C. Curtis. All Small did was deposit state funds in the Grant Park Bank, they said, and everything after that was done by Curtis.

Brundage shot down that argument with documents showing that First Trust & Savings Bank of Kankakee purchased $60,000 in Armour & Co. bonds on June 15, 1918. The transaction went through Continental & Commercial National Bank of Chicago and the receipt was sent to Cornelius R. Miller, cashier at Small's bank and later his director of Public Works. The bonds were issued in Len Small's name. Five days before this transaction, Treasurer Small deposited $60,000 into the "Grant Park Bank." Curtis took this money and put it in the Grant Park Trust & Savings Bank account at Continental & Commercial.

On Nov. 17, 1924, the hearings came to an end. Master in Chancery Charles Briggle decided that Governor Small had to account for the interest money in question. Briggle said Small had to reveal the amount of interest earned on deposits while he was treasurer and he had to disclose his methods in operating the treasury.

Small's lawyers bitterly fought having to make an accounting of his methods -- strangely so, since that would have been the one way to prove his innocence.

Briggle ruled that the Grant Park Bank did not exist and was merely a subterfuge to manipulate the state's money. But even if it had been a real bank, he said, the transactions would have been just as questionable. Briggle said that Small had not made the proper accounting as required by law.

This decision meant that the case would go before a judge for a ruling.

Attorney General Brundage was happy with the decision, saying it proved what he had contended all along. But the decision had to be bittersweet for Brundage. He had suffered in the party's internecine warfare. His failure to win a conviction of the governor hurt his image. And the party's machine marked him for defeat. It ran Oscar Carlstrom, the state tax commissioner, against Brundage in the 1924 primary for attorney general. Carlstrom won the nomination and the election.

Brundage claimed in late October 1924 that Briggle's report was ready to be released but was being withheld until after the election to help Small and his slate of candidates. Brundage asked Judge Burton at the time to have the report released but the judge would not interfere.

Carlstrom said that if he was elected attorney general, he would dismiss the civil suit against Small -- the reason for which Carlstrom was slated for the office.

Carlstrom did not get the chance. Circuit Court Judge Frank Burton said he would rule on the chancery report in December, before Carlstrom took office. He said he had heard Carlstrom's campaign statements and was not going to let the matter drag into the next administration. This way, the state Supreme Court would have the final word, no matter who was attorney general.

Small hired four more lawyers, including Patrick H. O'Donnell and State Sen. John Dailey of Peoria, a lawmaker who would be helpful to his fate in the legislature. His lawyers asked for a delay in order to familiarize themselves with the proceedings. Judge Burton said they would have enough time before the next court date, without any delays.

Small's lawyers tried a new tactic at the next hearing on Dec. 1. They filed a complaint that both Briggle and Burton were partisan and biased and they asked that the matter be sent to another master in chancery to have the whole procedure start all over again.

Judge Burton denied the motion to refer the case to another master in chancery and he defended Briggle's objectivity. He also denied Schroeder's argument that the acquittal in Waukegan was a legal defense in the civil suit.

The governor and several members of his family were injured on Dec. 5, 1924 when their car went into a ditch south of Pontiac. The governor was severely bruised, as were his son Leslie and daughter Ida May. Leslie was driving. His car collided with a car driven by E.L. Fosdick of Pontiac. Fosdick and his wife were injured. The injuries caused the governor to miss dedicating the new Stateville prison near Joliet and bought him some delays in court proceedings in the civil suit.

The case resumed in court on Dec. 13. Assistant Attorney General Floyd Britton said Small's financial irregularities were not confined just to the loans to the packers. He said the interest payments from all the legitimate banks across the state were sent to Len Small's personal account in his Kankakee bank, and that money was paid to the state in two lump sums, the total determined by Small. Britton held a Fort Dearborn bank check for $50,000. It, like most other similar checks, had not been cleared through the state auditor's office as required by law. This alone was grounds to remove Small from office, Britton said.

Judge Burton made his ruling on Dec. 30, 1924, that Len Small was liable for the interest earned by the Grant Park Bank that was not turned over to the state. Held equally liable were Vernon Curtis and Etha Curtis, widow of Edward C. Curtis.

"This witness, ex-Treasurer Small, has testified," the judge said in announcing his ruling. "His testimony is in the form of a general denial. He has had under his control all of the evidence of the entire transaction. I wish I could believe that testimony. I have tried to. I cannot."

"There has been no evidence produced or suggested that traces one dollar of all the interest that has been received through the Curtis bank into the state treasury," Judge Burton said. "In the view of this court, that money was state funds. The state was entitled to that entire interest. Those who have collected that interest, so far as the record shows, still have it."

The judge said that every bit of evidence that would prove Len Small innocent was missing. Even a denial from Small was absent, since he would not take the stand. "There is something peculiar in this case. I never met one equaling it. In this whole record, there is an entire absence of evidence which this defendant should produce."

The Grant Park Bank, Judge Burton said, was not a real bank but a sham in which to hide fraudulent activity.

Once more, Len Small faced the possibility of being removed from office. The state's constitutional provision about ineligibility for being indebted to the state was brought up again. Impeachment was one possibility. Another was the discussion among some legislators that they would not approve the canvass of the votes for governor from the November election in which Small won a second term, and thus not declare he was "duly elected and qualified."

The governor managed to hold on by making the appeal that the chancery report was not a final decree. He was a cat with nine lives.

But Small's ambition in trying to block the case rubbed Carlstrom the wrong way. Small tried to force Carlstrom to name Werner Schroeder as first assistant attorney general. This way, Small's defense lawyer would now be in charge of the prosecution! But Carlstrom was the duly-elected attorney general and he knew how such an appointment would be perceived. He was not about to be steamrollered.

Once Carlstrom took office, he could see that the wheels of justice had to keep moving.

Schroeder filed an appeal to the Illinois Supreme Court on Feb. 14, 1925.

The high court made its ruling on Dec. 16, 1925. It affirmed the lower court ruling that Len Small must repay the state for the interest money in the Grant

Park Bank that never found its way into the state treasury.

Governor Small faced the possibility of having to pay the state one million dollars...or more.

It was a stunning defeat for Governor Small. The state Supreme Court effectively ruled that Small did steal the money when he was state treasurer.

"The evidence in this record shows beyond all reasonable doubt a liability to account," the majority opinion read. "Proof of the fact that a public official having custody of public funds loaned these funds to others with a secret arrangement respecting the payment of interest, and that in reporting interest collected, he did not reveal the source of the payments, without more, would be sufficient to justify an order to account.

"Where a treasurer or other public official has the custody of public funds, and such funds earn interest, he is required by the settled law of this state to turn such interest into the public treasury as soon as it is received by him. This is now and has always been the law in this state without regard to a statute on the subject. This liability to account for profits made on public is the same whether the interest or discount is paid to the officer directly as such or whether it comes to him indirectly as a partner or stockholder in a bank where public funds are deposited.

"Where it is established that a public official having public funds in custody deals with the trust money in his own name, directly or indirectly, every presumption is indulged against the trustee, and he is held to a strict accountability in the conversion. From the careful examination of this record which the public interests involved and the importance of the results which follow our decision demand, we are convinced that the chancellor would not have been justified under the evidence in entering any decree other than the one directing appellants to account to appellee," the majority opinion, in part, read.

The majority justices said in no uncertain terms that the Grant Park Bank was a fraud. They added, "That the accounts of the so-called Grant Park Bank were issued by Small and the Curtises to carry on transactions with the packers is established beyond all reasonable doubt."

Edward Brundage was satisfied. "There never was the slightest doubt of the guilt of Governor Small in misusing public funds while state treasurer, as the evidence was overwhelming. Now the public gets from the highest tribunal in the state confirmation of my course, and I feel the effort was well worth the struggle."

"The action of the Supreme Court justifies the prosecution of Governor Small in the criminal courts of Sangamon and Lake counties," said Lake County State's Attorney A.V. Smith. "If Governor Small took the interest money, as shown by the findings of the master in chancery of the Sangamon County circuit court and sustained by the Supreme Court, he committed a criminal act."

The *Chicago Tribune* devoted a lot of ink to the story, printing in full the opinions of both the majority and the dissenting justices.

However, Small's *Kankakee Daily Republican* gave pages and pages of text, over several days, of only the opinions of the *dissenting* judges. That's right. The *Kankakee Daily Republican* gave only the story of why the opinion was wrong, told completely from the 12,000-word statement of the two dissenting justices.

Its Dec. 17 story was headlined, *Facts In Case Ignored, Say Judges --*

Justices Duncan And Heard Hold For Gov. Small In Big Issues; Dissenting Opinion Declare Majority Of The Court In Decision Apparently Ignored All The Great Volume Of Oral Testimony And Did Not Even Make Discussion Of Any Of Evidence, Except The Mere Deductions From Transactions By The Curtises And Small, Which Are Explained Fully By Small In The Records.

The *Kankakee Daily Republican* story said that the court affirmed the ruling of Judge Norman Jones in declaring the 1908 law concerning state treasurers unconstitutional. That was not true. Jones' decision did not strike down the entire law, and the Supreme Court's ruling did not affirm any such thing.

But the arguments of the dissenting justices were not as helpful to Small as he thought. Quoted in the Kankakee newspaper, Justices Warren Duncan and Oscar Heard agreed with some pretty damning points before they disagreed with the final opinion.

"It is evident," their opinion went, "items were run through the Grant Park Bank account to conceal the fact public funds from the state treasury were being used to purchase packers' notes. The total shown in the safe account at the end of Small's term was $9,700,000, the question now before us as being merely whether there is a liability to account.

"The tabulation shows during Small's term as treasurer more than $1,000,000 in discounts was collected from the packers as a result of loans directly from the state treasury." They added, "That the accounts called the Grant Park Bank were used by Small and the Curtises to conceal their transactions with the packers is established beyond all doubt."

And, "The said alleged Grant Park Bank mentioned and described in the bill of complaint in this cause had no existence and was not in fact a bank during this period from Jan. 8, 1917 to Jan. 11, 1919, but was a mere scheme or device used by said Len Small, Edward C. Curtis and Verne S. Curtis in an attempt to give legal color to such use of said funds for investments in the notes and securities aforesaid.

"The question was also one of the questions decided or passed on by the master of chancery whose theory of the case was that Small and the two Curtises were merely the agents of the state and on the doctrine of agency he finds that there is a several liability as to each one instead of a joint and several liability."

Duncan and Heard finally came to their points in Small's favor. They said the majority of the court ignored the oral testimony and only looked at the bank transactions. They also said that Edward Curtis made the transactions with the meat packers and it was not shown that Len Small was jointly liable.

"Where a liability arises from an intentional wrongful act of several parties conspiring together, each is liable for all resultant damages." The dissenters didn't think it was proven that Small was a part of the conspiracy. But theirs was the minority opinion.

Despite the newspaper's loud proclamations of the "dissent," it hardly was an argument in Small's behalf. Even the dissenting justices agreed that the Grant Park Bank was a sham created to conceal fraud by Curtis and Small!

Justice Heard, who had been on the high court only since 1924, was hurt by this opinion and by other previous political connections to Governor Small. Heard had the vigorous support of the Small organization when he ran for re-election to the bench in June 1933, but he was defeated.

Governor Small's lawyers filed a petition for a rehearing on Jan. 2, 1926. The petition claimed that the high court ignored the governor's testimony. A total of 14 reasons for a rehearing were listed, basically a rehash of the defense arguments.

Small also argued that the judgment would bankrupt him.

The Supreme Court denied Small a rehearing on Feb. 9, and it ordered the case back to the circuit court and to a master of chancery to decide the exact amount the governor should pay.

Len Small, Fred Lundin and Arthur Inglesh met in Chicago to start a fund raising campaign to pay the governor's judgment. About 300 department heads and appointees met at the Palmer House and were told to squeeze their state employees for contributions.

The big officeholders did as they were told, but a number of state employees down the ladder did not like Lundin's order to "pay or quit." The *Chicago Tribune* cited one employee, a scrubwoman at the Watertown State Hospital at East Moline, who earned $55 a month. She was still trying to pay the cost of her husband's funeral. She was told to pay $5.50 of her monthly wages to the Len Small Fund. "She clenches her worn hands and weeps as she tells it. But she says she'll have to pay," the story said. Other employees earning more than $2,500 a year were ordered to come up with a month's wages.

Hundreds of state employees, working on state time, mailed out a million and a half letters soliciting funds for the governor, using state trucks and postage paid by the taxpayers.

At a special course in road construction held at the University of Illinois at Urbana, Frank Sheets, chief highway engineer for the state, used the occasion to put the squeeze on the construction engineers of the state Division of Highways. Sheets told them to pay $75 to $300 each, depending on their pay scale. Failure to make this "voluntary" contribution would mean a loss of their job.

By August 1926, the account in Small's Kankakee bank had reached a half million dollars.

The setting of the day for payment dragged on, as Small's lawyers conferred with Carlstrom and Briggle on just how much the governor owed. In May 1927, Schroeder pleaded with the state not to bankrupt the governor. Schroeder denied that funds were being raised to pay the governor's judgment.

The state figured Small and Curtis owed $1,025,000. Deducted from that figure was the $222,000 that Curtis had paid the treasury in interest from the deposits. However, Carlstrom made a deal with the governor. A smaller figure was worked out and approved by Briggle.

On June 3, 1927, it was announced that Governor Small would pay the state treasury $650,000. Judge Frank Burton agreed to the settlement.

The wheeling and dealing went farther than just the significantly reduced dollar figure that was reached.

In agreeing to settle with the state, Len Small was able to get a concession that he was innocent of all wrongdoing, as part of the deal.

The agreement said "that the evidence in this cause fails to establish that the defendant, Len Small, received any sum or sums of money whatsoever as interest upon public funds for or during his term of office as state treasurer, except such sums as he has already accounted for and paid into the state treasury of this state, and that the liability of the said defendant, Len Small, in this case is solely for interest received by the other defendants herein."

In Len Small's view, this decision was a "vindication" and proof of his innocence.

In reality, it was a "plea bargain" concession, a settlement with the state to end the process. It is not uncommon for white collar criminals to make similar deals with the state, agreeing to pay if they are allowed to admit no guilt.

This concession on the part of the state was another clever move on Len Small's part -- it allowed him and his family to forever claim that he was innocent. Even the state says, in a legal document, that he is innocent, see?

But there was a flaw in Small's logic and that comes from the strange stipulations that sometimes are contained in settlements and from the way they are interpreted. The settlement declared that the other defendants, Verne Curtis and Etha Curtis -- the ones who allegedly kept the interest money from the loans -- were liable but did not have to pay. Len Small, who got the court to stipulate that he did not profit from the loans, had to pay. In other words, the late Edward C. Curtis was guilty and Len Small was innocent.

But where was the money? It wasn't in the estate of Ed Curtis.

Sterling and Russel were dismissed from further prosecution.

The governor knew he would have to pay and he was happy to wrangle from the state's attorney a provision that "there was no evidence" that he personally profited. The state also was happy, now that it was able to get the money and have the case finally over.

This concession from Carlstrom was not what Carlstrom had argued before the Supreme Court. At that time, Carlstrom said Small "received pecuniary advantage from the use of state money, both principal and interest," and "that Len Small received advantage from these transactions is clear from the record." And, "that Small appropriated to his own use all of the interest from legitimate banks up to Sept. 30, 1918 cannot be possibly disputed on the facts in this case...Small may have paid in from the earnings on packers' notes an amount equal to the legitimate interest, but that he kept the legitimate interest for himself cannot be successfully denied on this record."

Governor Small issued a statement about the settlement. In it, he stuck to the same explanations he had given numerous times in the past -- except they were not exactly explanations as much as they were arguments, rationalizations and excuses.

"The terms of the settlement made in the Sangamon Circuit Court this morning expressly admits the truth of the contention I have made throughout this suit, that I have fully accounted for and paid into the state treasury every dollar of principal and interest received by me for or during my term of office as state treasurer; that I have not at any time received any interest on public funds except that interest which I have heretofore paid into the treasury; and that the sum which I am agreeing to pay is money received for the Grant Park Bank and not by me."

Small admitted that as state treasurer, he became "responsible for all the funds in the state treasury." And, he said, the law allowed deposits to be made in private banks.

"I deposited large sums in the Grant Park Bank, of which Senator Curtis was the head, receiving the best collateral, thereby insuring the safety of the state funds. The long accounting, which has just recently been completed, shows undisputedly that the Grant Park Bank paid the state more than $222,000 in interest money and that all of the principal deposited was returned to the state in full.

"By depositing the state funds in the Grant Park Bank, I as state treasurer not only received additional collateral which made the public money absolutely safe against loss, but I secured for the state a higher rate of interest than the largest banks in Illinois would pay. After years of litigation, the court held that I was jointly liable with the owners of the Grant Park Bank for all the profits which they made in loaning state funds, and the Supreme Court upheld that ruling.

"The stipulation filed today was based upon the findings of the court on the earnings of the Grant Park Bank. The decisions of the courts in this case have been to the effect that I must pay regardless of whether or not I received any interest. These decisions made necessary this settlement by me. I repeat what I have said so many times -- I did not now and never did owe the state of Illinois one cent of interest. All of the principal and all of the interest which I collected as state treasurer has been paid into the state treasury; and the state treasurer's office during my term was run for the best interests of the state, strictly according to law.

"Senator Curtis is dead. The Grant Park Bank, which loaned the public money, as all other banks loaned it, for the profit of its owners, has gone out of business. The other defendants in this case are unable to pay this judgment. If it is humanly possible, I will pay it. Despite this great hardship, I am gratified and I believe that my friends throughout Illinois will be gratified that in the stipulation it is recognized that I, as state treasurer, made full and complete payment to the state of all interest received by me, and that my liability is based merely upon a technical responsibility for what others received."

In essence, Small said that although he was liable for the excess interest that was not deposited into the state treasury, and that he agreed to pay part of it back, he was innocent of any wrongdoing.

Or, in other words, in the settlement he accepted, Len Small agreed to pay $650,000 of the money he had claimed he had not stolen.

Governor Small finally paid the $650,000 settlement on July 15, 1927. He got that money from assessing salaries of state employees and from squeezing road building contractors. He did not go bankrupt and he did not have to sell off any part of his bank or his newspaper or his farm.

The governor was smiling broadly when he walked into the courtroom with the certified check. He grinned as he passed the check among the newspapermen.

Appellate Court Judge Otto Kerner Sr. was the Democrat candidate to succeed Oscar Carlstrom as attorney general in 1932. He claimed that the deal with

Small cheated the state and that Small really owed another $650,000. One of his campaign pledges was to reopen the civil suit and get more money from Small.

Kerner won the election in November 1932. Two weeks later, Carlstrom once again dismissed the state's civil lawsuits against Russel and Sterling.

Kerner filed suit in Cook County circuit court in July 1933, asking the court to vacate and set aside the decree that settled the civil case. He called the settlement six years earlier a "fraud." He said he would go after Sterling and Russel as well. Kerner's lawsuit also asked to retry the case in its entirety.

Len Small did not like this. The case was settled, over, and he had paid the state. It was not fair to open it up and try to squeeze more from him.

Werner Schroeder filed a motion saying that the Cook County court had no jurisdiction in the matter. After an entire day of arguments in court, Judge Hugo Friend sided with Small, ruling in November 1933 that one circuit court did not have the jurisdiction, authority or power to change a ruling from another circuit court. In June 1934, the state Supreme Court agreed.

Fred Sterling died on Feb. 10, 1934 in his home town of Rockford. He was a newspaperman, and became owner of the *Rockford Daily Register-Gazette.*

There is one more postscript to this matter. On Jan. 20, 1934, Edward Brundage was found in the basement of his Lake Forest home with a bullet in his heart. His business associates said he had suffered heavy financial losses and was in poor health. But he left no note and gave no indication. He was fully dressed and his chauffeur was waiting to take him to his Chicago office. The butt of the gun had a handkerchief wrapped around it. Brundage was set to appear as an important state witness in a racketeering trial of 18 mobsters, under way in Chicago. His death was ruled "suicide."

Edward Brundage

Fred Sterling

Chapter 14

Al Capone

Al Capone has become a mythic figure, a larger-than-life legend.

The truth is, Capone was a swarthy, overweight, cold-blooded murderer who became very wealthy by bringing misery and death to others.

He was in the business of bootlegging, prostitution, gambling, drugs, extortion, murder and other horrible enterprises. Yet he has been glamorized with a cult following.

Capone's exploits were numerous and they were gruesome.

There are plenty of biographies of Al Capone, many of them excellent books. The best ones are listed in the bibliography in the back of this book. The reader is referred to those books for further details.

This book deals with Big Al Capone in his relationships with the corrupt politicians he controlled. This includes Big Bill Thompson and Big Len Small.

There is a fascination with Al Capone that is hard to understand from a rational standpoint.

It can be argued that he is the most famous Chicagoan ever, even though he was born and raised in New York. He started as a thug and a bouncer at Frankie Yale's tavern in New York. It was there that he was slashed across the face in a bar room fight, earning his nickname "Scarface."

Capone, incidentally, was very sensitive and vain about the scar that marked the left side of his face. He did not like the name "Scarface" -- he preferred his close friends call him "Snorkey," meaning sharp or elegant.

Around the world, the mention of Chicago makes many people think of Al Capone. There have been better people from Chicago, but few of them seem to come to mind for people elsewhere.

The whole gangster genre is glamorized and romanticized. These men dressed well, had lots of money, women, fast cars and blazing guns. In reality, these grotesque men were just cold-blooded murderers who would kill without giving it a second thought.

Movies had a lot to do with glamorizing this image. Al Capone was the biggest of this terrible bunch so he is glamorized the most. Unlike most tight-lipped gangsters, Capone courted newspaper reporters for publicity. Capone did open a soup kitchen in Depression-era Chicago and funded a school milk program. But he did this only to build a Robin Hood-style image. (And even this image is phony. Capone didn't buy the food -- his man in City Hall, Daniel Serritella, shook down grocers for bribes, not just for cash but for food. The food was collected by Phil D'Andrea, a Capone bodyguard).

Perhaps part of his legend comes from the fact that Capone had the mayor and the governor in his hip pocket, and they let Capone have the city to do as he pleased.

And everyone knew it. This made Capone a king, and it was why federal agent Eliot Ness and the "Untouchables" had to come to Chicago in 1928.

Incidentally, Eliot Ness and his men had limited success in their fight against bootleggers. Ness always bragged that he "got" Capone but Capone really was "gotten" by bookkeepers in the Internal Revenue Service, not by Prohibition agents. Ness earned his "Untouchable" legend because he and his squad were the only officials or lawmen in Chicago who could not be bribed!

Paul Sann, in *The Lawless Decade*, drew this portrait of the power Capone wielded: "Scarface Al rose to heights never before scaled. He was the New Power, bigger than the city and bigger than the state. He was the Mayor, Governor and Machine Boss all rolled into one. He gave the orders; the people's elected servants carried them out and kept their mouths shut. Capone's iron rule embraced not only Chicago but whatever other parts of Illinois he had the time and inclination to exploit. His authority was so great it could not be measured."

The people's elected servants who carried out Capone's orders and kept their mouths shut, of course, included Governor Len Small.

Sann said Mayor Thompson's 1927 campaign pledge of a "wide-open town," where he promised to reopen shuttered saloons "and open ten thousand new ones...sounded more like a promise to Capone than to the electorate, and it figured. The Syndicate stood behind the Thompson campaign with a fortune in cash and a formidable armed force besides."

Capone's annual income from illegal activities was $100 million, and $30 million of that went to pay off police, judges and elected officials, and that made Capone their boss. Al Capone ruled Chicago.

Capone's prominence was shown when a four-man amphibious airplane, sent by Italian dictator Benito Mussolini, flew around the world on a publicity tour and landed in Chicago on May 15, 1927. A number of dignitaries were there to welcome the aviators, including city officials, diplomats, U.S. military personnel -- and Al Capone, who was there as the *invited guest* of the Chicago police! Capone was one of the first to shake hands with the visiting aviators.

Al Capone was issued a special Cook County deputy sheriff's badge and he flashed it on occasion.

Capone was the man who personally beat gunmen John Scalise, Albert Anselmi and Joe Giunta to death with a baseball bat in May 1929 after he found they were plotting against him. When a punk named Joe Howard slapped around Greasy Thumbs Guzik in a saloon one day in May 1924, Capone went back to the place and blew the guy's head off.

The city of Chicago plays down Capone's image. But small towns in the Chicago area, desperate for any kind of notoriety, love to claim some sort of connection -- much like towns in the East that claim "George Washington slept here."

Kankakee is one of these Chicago-area towns that revel in the glory of its connection to Capone. In 2007, the Kankakee Museum gave programs on Capone's slight (and alleged) connection to Kankakee and the surrounding area. Capone was *supposed* to have visited the Club Roma on Fifth Avenue in Kankakee, *maybe.* But an elderly niece of John Giusto, the owner of the Club Roma, was contacted in 2008 by this author. She often visited the place with her family in the 1920s and 1930s and she never heard of this claim.

There is no proof Capone ever visited Kankakee. Yet, Kankakee is proud of a Capone connection, as it is proud of Len Small and George Ryan.

Until this book, practically the only place anyone could find any mention of Len Small was in books about Chicago gangsters and biographies of Al Capone. History links the governor and the gangsters.

Len Small and Al Capone did attend at least one event together, the famous Dempsey-Tunney heavyweight title fight at Soldier Field on Sept. 22, 1927. Governor Small, Mayor Thompson and State's Attorney Crowe made their celebrity appearance before the bout.

The crowd cheered Small, Thompson and Crowe. "At his ringside seat, Al Capone joined the applause, and although the officials ignored him, it must have been comforting for him to reflect that he, the man in the dark, owned all three of these men looming above him in the light, and through them exercised greater influence than any other individual in Illinois," wrote Laurence Bergreen in *Capone, The Man and the Era.*

Throughout the lawless decade of the 1920s, The *Kankakee Daily Republican* never had an unkind word for Al Capone. In fact, Capone was practically invisible to Kankakee readers. The gangsters and shootings and bombing going on in nearby Chicago got very little ink in the Kankakee newspaper, and when it did, Capone was not mentioned. Even in reporting the St. Valentine's Day Massacre in 1929, and its follow-up stories, the Kankakee newspaper was almost alone in not attributing the carnage to Capone.

The *Chicago Tribune,* on the other hand, was never shy in covering the mayhem and murder of the gangsters shooting up its city. And the newspaper gave it straight, without a care for where the chips might fall.

The Kankakee newspaper had just two stories about Al Capone during Len Small's eight-year administration, one in 1927 and one in 1928, and both stories made Scarface sound like a folk hero.

The first story told of how Capone was moving to Florida because the government was turning up the heat in Chicago. Scarface held a press conference at the Hotel Metropole at 2300 S. Michigan Ave. on Dec. 5, 1927.

"My wife and mother hear so much about what a terrible criminal I am," Capone was quoted as saying. "It's getting too much for them. I'm sick of it all myself."

Alphonse Capone:
"There are worse fellows
in the world than me,"
he said of men like
Thompson and Small.

Lennington Small:
TIME magazine
called him
"a cold-blooded crook."

"He talked from his hotel headquarters, his 'armed fortress' as it has been called. 'I'm leaving for St. Petersburg, Fla, Tuesday,' he said. 'Let the worthy citizens of Chicago get their liquor the best way they can. I don't know when I'll get back, if ever.'

"I've been spending the best years of my life as a public benefactor. I've given the people light pleasures, shown them a good time. All I get is abuse.

"Tell the folks I'm going away. I guess the murders will stop. There won't be any more booze. You won't be able to find a crap game even, let alone a roulette wheel or a faro game. I guess Mike Hughes (chief of police) won't need his 3,000 extra cops after all. The cops won't have to lay all the gang murders on me now. Maybe they'll find a new hero for the headlines."

Capone lamented his bad image. "That's what I've got to put up with, just because I gave the public what it wants. I never had to send out high pressure salesmen. I could never meet the demand."

The article continued, "Capone, who has been painted as gang chief, vice overlord and 'bad man,' told the interviewer that he never had been convicted of a crime in his life. 'Public service is my motto,' Capone added. 'Ninety-nine percent of the people in Chicago drink and gamble. I've always regarded it as a public benefaction if they were given decent liquor and square games. But it's no use.'"

The second story the *Kankakee Daily Republican* printed about Capone, headlined *Al Capone Goes Into Business,* read like a press release from Scaface's own office.

"What police have been trying for months to do -- stop racketeering and terrorism in the cleaning and dyeing business -- today has become the goal of Al Capone, the 'Big Shot' of the gangsters.

"Capone, who has been blamed for much and found guilty of nothing, has become a principal partner in the Sanitary Cleaning Shops Inc., which has a large plant now nearing completion. His sponsor is Morris Becker, a cleaner and dyer for 42 years. Becker, in a statement given out by the Employers' Association, said the alliance with Capone gives him 'the best protection in the world' from racketeers and others who he charges have threatened his business by bombs, violence and intimidation.

"Becker believes the entry of Capone into the business will put some long delayed fear into the hearts of those who Becker says have been making the cleaning and dyeing business an unhealthy one for those who refuse to fall in line with those seeking to control it."

The Master Cleaners and Dyers Association was a racket that forced cleaners to raise prices in order to pay "protection" money to the association. Not all the Chicago gang wars of the 1920s were about bootlegging, gambling and other vice. Gangsters took over labor unions and formed their own "unions" to extort money from individuals, businesses and contractors. In the late 1920s, dry cleaners became targets of gangsters. Master Cleaners was one group that beat, bombed and killed dry cleaners to force them into line. Central Cleaners, led by Bugs Moran on the North Side, was another.

These gang wars were as violent as the beer wars. On Nov. 16, 1928, John Clay, head of the Laundry and Dyehouse Chauffeur's union, was killed by gangsters who fired machine guns and shotguns through the window of his headquarters. Clay had been indicted for conspiracy and was a suspect in the gangland killing of Big Tim Murphy.

Becker refused to go along with the Master Cleaners, and thugs from the association threatened him. The Cook County state's attorney wouldn't help him so Becker had a unique and bold idea -- he turned to Al Capone. They formed the Sanitary Cleaning Shops Inc. along with Jake "Greasy Thumbs" Guzik. Capone's "association" stood up to the Master Cleaners and Dyers Association, and his sluggers were tougher than their sluggers. The opposition was broken, and cleaners were freed from gang intimidation. Capone did not make an attempt to take over the industry. Later, when asked his occupation, Capone would say, "I'm in the cleaning business." Becker had nothing but praise for his partner.

In any event, these two stories about Capone demonstrated how the *Kankakee Daily Republican* had much harsher words for local political foes like Ben Alpiner and Wayne Dyer (and the *Chicago Tribune*) than it ever had for Al Capone.

Len Small wasn't the only disreputable public figure who thought himself a hero. Al Capone also viewed himself differently.

Capone is known for many clever and witty quotes, which may or may not have come directly from the brain of this resourceful yet uneducated man. He may have had his own publicity man or a newspaper reporter writing for him. These quotes concern his being a benefit to society.

"You can't cure thirst by law. They call Capone a bootlegger. Yes, it's bootleg while it's on the trucks, but when your host at the club, in the locker room or on the Gold Coast hands it to you on a silver platter, it's hospitality. What's Al done then? He's supplied a legitimate demand. Some call it bootlegging, some call it racketeering. I call it business."

And, "Too many Americans vote dry and live wet. Too many politicians are crooks behind their mask of respectability."

"I give the public what it wants. I violate the Prohibition law, sure. Who doesn't? The only difference is, I take more chances than the man who drinks a cocktail before dinner and a flock of highballs after it. But he's just as much a violator as I am."

"Whatever else they may say, my booze has been good and my games have been on the square. Public service is my motto."

A reporter asked him about Mob violence. Capone said gangsters who killed one another did it in self defense, "the way God looks at it," in defense of their lives and in defense of their businesses.

Capone also said he never was convicted of a crime and never ordered anyone to commit a crime. He said he never robbed anyone and never killed anyone, and no one who ever worked for him every committed a crime (all not true).

You have to wonder if Capone really believed what he was saying, as Len Small believed his own words of defense.

What did Al Capone think of the politicians he owned?

"There's one thing worse than a crook, and that's a crooked man in a big political job," he told reporters in his Dec. 5, 1927 interview. "A man who pretends he's enforcing the law and is really making dough out of somebody breaking it, a self-respecting hoodlum hasn't any use for that kind of fellow -- he buys them like he'd buy any other article necessary to his trade, but he hates them in his heart."

Regarding specific politicians, Capone added, "There are worse fellows in the world than me."

Capone's name may be legendary, but it should have the same connotation as a name like Hitler, not a name like Robin Hood.

Al Capone was not sent to prison for the murders he committed or for the even greater number of murders he ordered. He was not sent to prison for bootlegging, prostitution, extortion, bribery, hijacking or any of his other evil deeds -- he was convicted and sent to prison in 1931 *for not paying income tax* on the money he made from his evil deeds.

Unfortunately for Capone, there was no Governor Len Small to pardon him after he was convicted. But it would have been interesting -- if Small was still governor, and if Capone had been convicted in a state court instead of a federal rap -- would Len Small have dared to grant Al Capone a pardon? If Small could pardon Guzik, Stevens, Potz and so many other terrible men, we can only speculate on how kindly he would have treated Scarface.

Al Capone died in 1947, at the age of 48 -- a babbling idiot in a wheelchair, his mind gone from the ravages of syphilis. That is how this glamorous legendary figure ended his days.

Chapter 15

The Chicago Mob

It was Prohibition that made small time gangs, gamblers, whoremongers and other varied criminals into big time Organized Crime.

Those who fought for "temperance" finally won in 1919 when the 18th Amendment, known as the Volstead Act or Prohibition, was approved. It outlawed the manufacture and sale of liquor. America went dry.

It was a disaster, as is frequently the result of do-gooders with good intentions. The Prohibitionists, much like the socialists of today, thought it was not only their duty to tell others how to live their lives, they felt it necessary to *force* it on others as well. It proved to be another example of what happens when good-intentioned busybodies impose their will on others, *especially* when it is something that is contrary to human nature.

Having a beer or a sip of wine, something that had been acceptable from the beginning of time, now suddenly was a federal crime, a violation of the U.S. Constitution. Federal agents with guns and axes enforced (or tried to enforce) the unpopular law with a vigor not seen in the enforcement of many other laws.

The 18th Amendment was ratified more than a year and a half before the 19th Amendment -- banning beer was more important than giving women the right to vote.

Prohibition didn't start as a liberal or a conservative issue. It wasn't a Democrat or a Republican issue. It was a moral crusade by people who thought the consequence would be an America whose men were not ravaged by alcoholism. They didn't take human nature, the law of supply and demand, and the free market into account. In their goal to take away the misery of alcoholism and drunkenness, the temperance crowd brought a whole lot of other kinds of misery to America.

With liquor outlawed, those who would supply it to an eager public made millions of dollars. They became hugely rich and hugely powerful.

And they did not hesitate to kill anyone who got in their way.

Prohibition did not make men into gangsters. It just made the gangsters richer, more powerful, and it established and solidified a system of Organized Crime that continues to plague America.

It made for a perfect combination of an event, a time and a place.

Chicago has always been notorious for its corruption.

It probably started when the first white settlers disembarked from *Da Mayflower,* set up camp at Fort Dearborn on the shores of Lake Michigan and shook down the Indians for whatever beads they had. Since the nineteenth century (with public officials on underworld payrolls and its infamous crooked elections) to the present day (with public officials on underworld payrolls and its infamous crooked elections), Chicago has been one toddlin' town (if "toddlin" is a Native American word for "corrupt").

It was during the Civil War era when forms of organized crime took hold in Chicago. There was Gambler's Row in the 1860s and 1870s, an area of gambling joints and whorehouses on Clark Street between Randolph and Monroe streets. There was Little Cheyenne, Satan's Mile and other vice areas. The Levee area on the South Side was notorious from 1890 and 1920. Randolph Street was a haven for gambling joints. The first big crime organization was led by Mike McDonald, a gangster and Democrat kingpin who was in league with Chicago mayors and police and politicians from the 1870s to the 1890s.

Hoodlums and politicians began a more organized alliance in the 1890s with First Ward aldermen Michael "Hinky Dink" Kenna and "Bathhouse John" Coughlin. The two, according to the Chicago Historical Society, "created in the 1890s a First Ward political machine based on graft and protection money from the saloons, brothels and gambling halls of the Levee district just south of the Loop." Whorehouses ranged from diseased dives to the high class and fabled Everleigh Club, all protected by Kenna and Coughlin.

Kenna and Coughlin not only gave protection to gangster Mont Tennes and his gambling operation, the aldermen virtually became partners by setting up gambling operations in brothels, saloons and other places in Chicago. A grand jury later found that Mayor Fred Busse and Chief of Police George Shippy were tied to Tennes' organization.

Big Jim Colosimo became a bigger crime boss than McDonald. Colosimo had been a vice lord for a decade before opening Colosimo's Cafe at 2126 S. Wabash Ave in 1910. Colosimo's Café was one of Chicago's top night clubs. Big Jim's big money came from his gambling joints, brothels and white slavery rings in the Levee.

This vice was so wide open and brazen that Mayor Carter Harrison ordered a crackdown in the Levee. The plan to run the gangsters out of town ended when Big Bill Thompson was elected in 1915. The criminals not only had aldermen protecting them in their wards, they now had a friend and a partner in City Hall.

As his crime empire grew, Colosimo brought a nephew from New York to help him handle it. That man was Johnny Torrio.

When Prohibition started, Torrio saw bootlegging as a great opportunity to expand the empire. Colosimo was content with prostitution and gambling. Torrio had Colosimo murdered in 1920 and took over the operation. Colosimo had a typically lavish gangland funeral and the honorary pallbearers included 10 aldermen, three judges, two congressmen and a state representative who later became a federal judge.

Under Torrio, the Mob controlled downtown Chicago and much of the South Side. To take over the Gold Coast and North Side, Torrio had rival gang leader Dean O'Banion gunned down in 1924. O'Banion's murder sparked a bloody gangland war. In retaliation, gangsters Hymie Weiss and Bugs Moran seriously wounded Torrio in a shooting in 1925. When Torrio finally recovered, he turned the business over to Al Capone. It was Torrio who brought Scarface Al Capone from

New York to Chicago in 1920 to be his Number Two man.

The level to which Chicago police, politicians and other officials were connected to the various gangs was astounding. It was estimated that 65 percent of the Chicago police force was on the payrolls of Chicago gangs. Judges and politicians drank with gangster friends at illegal speakeasies, they signed petitions for pardons and they served as pall bearers at gangland funerals. Mobsters had paid informants in the police stations, prosecutor's office and courthouse. Compliant judges gave low bonds to gangsters so the killers could get right back on the street. There was enough money to take care of everything and everybody in Chicago, thanks to the obscene profits made from Prohibition.

In July 1923, Police Chief Morgan Collins said many of his policemen were involved in selling beer and other liquor -- and not just helping the Mob or selling protection but bootlegging on their own. Collins cited examples where policemen went into joints and told the proprietor he had to take a certain amount of beer each week or be closed up.

In Chicago's famous Maxwell Street area, the vicious Genna brothers openly distilled whiskey and gin in a massive operation that was obvious to everyone in Chicago except to the law enforcement agencies. The bloodthirsty Gennas had a large distillery operation within a few blocks of the local police precinct station -- which made it convenient since it was uniformed police officers who guarded the operation for their own "protection" payoffs. The warehouse with the bootleg liquor was open 24 hours a day with no pretense of concealment.

Charles Olson, U.S. District Attorney for Chicago, released a report in December 1926 that blamed corrupt politicians and police for the success of bootleggers. He said graft in Chicago reached $30 million annually. "The booze business could not exist without the protection of crooked officials," he said. "The grafting officials who protect the bootlegger for a price are the same grafters who have always protected gambling, prostitution, dope peddling, thievery and other forms of crime. My four years experience has convinced me that the manufacture and sale of liquor can be stopped in this district whenever the government receives proper cooperation from local law enforcement officials."

Mayor Thompson had no problem with the situation in Chicago. He was more than compliant, he was a partner. And with Len Small's election in 1920, the Mob had all the biggest elected officials in the state in their pocket.

A photograph in the March 31, 1929 *Chicago Tribune* showed a dinner party from Nov. 15, 1925 on the occasion of the christening of mobster "Diamond Joe" Esposito's son. Pictured with Esposito were Sen. Charles Deneen, Judge William Morgan, County Recorder Joseph Haas, Probate Court Clerk John Devine, Judge John Richardson, political boss Thomas Healy, Judge A. Eberhardt and former Judge Charles Williams. Another published photograph showed State's Attorney Robert Crowe, Lt. Gov. Fred Sterling, Secretary of State Louis Emmerson, State Auditor Oscar Nelson and a number of judges and state representatives seated at the speakers table with Jim Genna.

In 1923, after a bootlegging conviction, Esposito took a trip back to Italy for a visit. Esposito carried with him a memento he cherished for the rest of his life. It was a testimonial scroll, with his photograph and pictures of the American and Italian flags and "a message of good will and an assurance of welcome upon his return to America." The testimonial was signed by Governor Len Small, Mayor William Hale Thompson, Senator Charles Deneen and County Clerk Robert Sweitzer.

Esposito's criminal organization, the 42 Gang, included Sam "Momo" Giancana and Paul "The Waiter" Ricca. A partner in their bootlegging trade was Joseph P. Kennedy, patriarch of the famous political family. Esposito was a rival of Capone and it was Ricca who set up Esposito for a gangland "hit" during the 1928 primary campaign.

While the incumbent Republican party suited Al Capone's needs, rival mobster Dean O'Banion found the Democrats more to his liking. The Democrat party gave O'Banion a huge testimonial dinner in 1924 at the Webster Hotel that was attended by a large number of gangsters and politicians, not so unusual since they all were working together for their own mutual benefit. Well-known gangsters there included Earl "Hymie" Weiss, Vincent "The Schemer" Drucci, Louie "Two Gun" Altiere, Cornelius "Con" Shea, Maxie Eisen, Jerry O'Connor and Frank Gusenberg. Public officials included Michael Hughes, the Chicago Police Department's chief of detectives; Police Lt. Charles Egan; county clerk and former prosecutor Robert Sweitzer; former assistant state's attorney William Scott Stewart, who then was Altiere's lawyer; Col. Albert Sprague, the commissioner of public works and the Democrat nominee for U.S. senator; and a number of other city officials. They all drank bootleg booze and toasted O'Banion.

When scandals forced Mayor Thompson to decline to run for re-election in 1923, Democrat William Dever was elected. Dever was a reformer and he turned up the heat on bootleggers and gangsters in Chicago. Capone no longer had a friend in City Hall. Looking for a safe haven outside of the city, Capone took over Cicero and Forest View, beating and terrorizing and replacing village officials until they recognized Scarface as their ruler.

William "Porky" Dillon, a thug pardoned by Governor Small, became Forest View's police chief. Len Small appointed Edward Kovalinka as precinct committeeman and Kovalinka helped deliver Cicero to Al Capone.

"Gangsters, by terrorism, vote stealing and bribery, swung a certain faction into power, and in return were given the privilege of operating gambling, vice and booze joints," is how the *Chicago Tribune* in 1926 told the story. The details also can be found in the many books about Al Capone.

"And the chieftains in the alliance of politics and vice, according to the investigators, were Big Ed Kovalinka, Republican committeeman of the suburb, and Scarface Al Brown (Capone). In the dawning of this partnership, police say, stood Kovalinka, not long before a soda jerker, then zealous for political power; a protégé of Governor Len Small, eager to prove his mettle. Joining in that ambition was Kovalinka's friend, Edward Vogel. Together they pieced out a plan and Vogel sought out his useful comrade, Louis LaCava, who was known as an outside man for the gang leader, Scarface Caponi."

Kovalinka, Vogel and LaCava named their ticket for the village election: Joseph Klenha for president, Frank Houcheck for town clerk, T.J. Buckley for town collector and Edward Carmody for town attorney.

Kovalinka and Capone called in their gangsters to deliver the election for their ticket, "and then Capone could hang out his shingles from Cicero dens and be immune from difficulties with the village police. From that day of bargaining, it is told, has come the vortex of gang warfare, against which the authorities have been rendered impotent. A hundred murders have been planned and executed. A trio of grand juries has sought the key, thus far in vain," the 1926 *Tribune* story continued.

Capone called on Torrio, "whose houses of vice have been spread from Cicero to Burnham. And Torrio called for his pander Guzik. Capone's brother, Ralph, was on hand with his intimates, Pete Pizzo, the barber gangster and Charles Fischetti."

Also enlisted to help the Kovalinka ticket was north side Mob boss Dean O'Banion.

"Gangsters -- the rum hounds, the vice lookouts and the gamblers -- came to Cicero to vote themselves, to keep reformers from voting and to see that the ballots were properly counted for the Kovalinka ticket."

"Voters could vote if they knew who to vote for. And when the polls finally closed, the entire Kovalinka ticket was declared elected. Then began the reign, according to the police, which has been the war of gangland. Gambling chiefs were brought into Cicero. Wires were connected to the big racetracks and bookmakers launched a thriving trade, the play at Hawthorne running to $50,000 daily. Slot machines and punch boards were set up everywhere."

The huge profits were split between the Mob bosses and the politicians.

Klenha appointed Ted Svoboda as Cicero's police chief. He enforced the laws but not any of the laws violated by the Torrio and Capone mobsters who owned the city.

"Women came from the east with the bodyguards and Capone sent them to the Stickney houses, paying them $20 a day and all expenses. Guzik, an old hand at the pandering trade, once pardoned for it by Governor Small, ran that end and ran it at a handsome gain, the police said," to quote the 1926 *Tribune* story. "More brothels were built in Stickney, one sheltering as many as 60 women. When the reformers came close, Capone and Guzik shifted their bawdy scene to Forest View."

O'Banion supplied the beer to the various joints while Torrio and the Guziks ran the whorehouses. It was the disputes over the much more profitable bootlegging that caused a split between Torrio and O'Banion. This was settled when Capone sent torpedoes to gun down O'Banion in his Chicago florist shop on Nov. 10, 1924.

Any political opposition in Cicero was eliminated on April 1, 1924, election day.

Capone involved his whole Mob in that election. His thugs beat a candidate for clerk and shot up his office. On election day, a dozen touring cars full of gun-toting gangsters patrolled the streets of Cicero. At gunpoint, only voters who marked their ballots the right way were allowed to vote. When one Cicero policeman objected, Capone's thugs put him in the hospital. People who worked for the opposition were kidnapped and held until after election day. Five men were killed on that day, including Frank Capone. He and Al were holding guns on voters at a polling place when Chicago police (sent by Judge Edmund Jarecki to fight the Capone terrorists) showed up and the shooting started. Frank died. Al escaped. And the Len Small-Ed Kovalinka-Al Capone Republican ticket won in Cicero that day.

Joseph Klenha was mayor of Cicero. But later in 1924, he forgot who the real boss was. Klenha ignored one of Capone's orders and Al Capone himself went to City Hall and ordered the mayor outside. Klenha came out, with a policeman. Capone beat Mayor Klenha and knocked him down the steps of City Hall. Cicero policemen looked the other way. Another time, the city council was considering an ordinance that Capone didn't like. He sent his thugs to break up the meeting, dragged a councilman outside and beat him.

Len Small, Spike O'Donnell and the Beer War

Some of the biggest and bloodiest Mob wars of the Roaring Twenties were over control of beer territories. A particularly bloody beer war started in 1923 and went on for years.

And it was Governor Len Small who got it started.

The governor did this by letting Edward "Spike" O'Donnell out of prison by commuting his sentence and making him eligible for parole. O'Donnell, leader of the Southside O'Donnells gang, was a bootlegger, armed robber, pickpocket, bomber and murderer. O'Donnell was convicted of robbing Stockyards Savings & Trust Bank in 1917.

Spike O'Donnell's commutation came through Umbrella Mike Boyle, Capone's friend who was Governor Small's Mob contact in arranging many of the pardons and paroles granted to criminals. Small was repaying Boyle for helping win an acquittal in his corruption trial.

This was an era when most cops and politicians were on Mob payrolls and it was not unusual for a high profile criminal to have his petition for a pardon endorsed by high profile politicians. O'Donnell's commutation came with the written support of Cook County Judge George Kersten, State Sen. James C. O'Brien, State Sen. Edward J. Hughes, State Sen. Patrick J. Sullivan, State Sen. Robert W. Schultz, State Sen. P.H. Carroll, State Sen. Frank J. Ryan, State Rep. Thomas J. O'Grady, State Rep. James P. Boyle, State Rep. George S. Noonan, State Rep. John F. Healy, State Rep. Michael Maher, State Rep. Arthur J. Rutshaw and Cook County Controller William J. Graham.

Officially, Spike O'Donnell was paroled to the custody of State Sen. Frank J. Ryan as Ryan's "secretary."

Spike O'Donnell's presence was necessary for the war to start. Spike was the brains and the guts of his gang. While he was in prison, the other members of the O'Donnell gang were just petty burglars and occasional freelance gunmen. They needed Spike back on the street to organize them and get the mayhem going again.

The beer war started when the South Side O'Donnells started to fight Torrio and Capone for territory. The O'Donnells hijacked truckloads of Torrio beer and began selling it in the territories of other gangsters. On Sept. 7, 1923, some of O'Donnell's gangsters were going about their regular business of using their fists to convince saloonkeepers to take their beer instead of Torrio beer. They were making

Walter Stevens

Spike O'Donnell

their point in Joseph Kepka's saloon at 5358 South Lincoln St. when a few of the Torrio gang came in to make a counterpoint. A fierce gun battle ensued, and Torrio's men (including Walter Stevens, Dan McFall and Frank McErlane) blew the head off Jerry O'Connor, a member of the O'Donnells.

Ten days later, Stevens was one of the gunmen who killed two beer runners from the O'Donnell gang. George Meeghan and George Bucher were sitting in a Ford roadster on Garfield Boulevard at Laflin Street when a passing car opened fire, perforating the roadster. The faces of Meeghan and Bucher were no longer recognizable. It could have been a scene out of *The Untouchables, The Godfather* or *Public Enemy.*

This happened while Walter Stevens was a fugitive from justice, wanted for gunning down two Aurora police officers.

A number of gangsters were questioned in the murders, including Stevens, Spike O'Donnell, Frank McErlane, Eddie Kaufman and Johnny Torrio, who surrendered himself with his attorney, State Rep. Michael Igoe. No one was prosecuted.

The gun battles and the murders kept on coming. Eight members of the O'Donnell gang were killed in this round of battles and Walter Stevens killed five of them. Spike O'Donnell was severely wounded in a drive-by shooting in 1925 by Frank McErlane.

One night in December 1923, three truckloads of beer were hijacked by Torrio's men. Two of the truck drivers, Morrie Keane and William Egan, were shot to death by Frank McErlane and their bodies were left by the side of the road.

Mobster Ralph Sheldon made the mistake of trying to run beer in the Saltis-McErlane territory in 1926. Two of Sheldon's gang, John Tuccello and Frank DeLaurentis (a cousin of "Diamond Joe" Esposito), were delivering beer to a saloon when they were kidnapped and killed. Their bodies were left in a car parked outside Sheldon's home, as a warning. A few days later, police arrested Saltis, McErlane and Stevens.

Cook County Assistant State's Attorney William McSwiggin and two gangsters were gunned down by machine gun fire from a passing automobile as they came out of Madigan's saloon in Cicero on April 27, 1926. The two gangsters were James Doherty and Thomas Duffy, who had been cutting into Capone's beer territory. But what was McSwiggin doing in an illegal saloon and why was he in the company of gangsters? The "hit" was part of the long beer war that had been raging. Capone and some of his gunmen, along with O'Donnell and some of his gang, were indicted by a grand jury but were not prosecuted for lack of hard evidence. Capone denied the hit, saying McSwiggin was on his payroll.

A grand jury did not find fault with McSwiggin. But it did find fault with Governor Len Small.

"We believe that vicious administration of the pardon and parole laws has been one of the great contributory elements in making the present existing condition," was one finding of the grand jury.

A July 26, 1926, story in TIME magazine about the political situation with Frank L. Smith and Samuel Insull also mentioned the political scene: "Meantime, Illinois had common political crockery to contemplate. At all times, of course, they have their governor, Len Small. Last fortnight they also had a special grand jury sitting to expose wholesale ballot-stealing, box-stuffing, gun play, voting the names of dead men, kidnapping, false returns and intimidation by hirelings of the Republican machine in grimy precincts of tough Chicago. This jury found fraud enough to indict 44 judges, clerks and election officials."

Judge John Lyle was frustrated by the fact that a large number of drunks and bums were brought to court but few gangsters were. Big time bookies could get out on low bail from a friendly judge but people caught making the bets were locked up. After one raid, 50 men caught in a bookmaking parlor were before his bench. Lyle reflected that he had just seen a photograph of Governor Small at Lincoln Fields race track. "It is somewhat difficult for these defendants to understand why it is a violation to bet a dollar on a horse with a neighborhood bookie and perfectly all right to bet $500 at Lincoln Fields," Lyle said.

Treasury Agent Eliot Ness: His crimebusting ways irritated Capone, Thompson and Small

The Small-Thompson Machine was up to its neck in Mob connections. In the 1927, gangster Jack Zuta contributed $50,000 to Thompson's campaign and was quoted as saying, "I'm for Big Bill, hook, line and sinker, and Big Bill is for me, hook, line and sinker." Zuta and Thompson socialized many times. (In 1930, Zuta ordered the murder of Mob-connected *Chicago Tribune* reporter Jake Lingle. To take the heat off, Capone had Zuta gunned down a few months later).

Capone contributed a quarter of a million dollars to Thompson's campaign in 1927, along with many of his persuasive campaign workers.

When Thompson won the 1927 mayoral election, the *Chicago Tribune* observed, "Thompson is a buffoon in a tommyrot factory, but when his crowd gets loose in City Hall, Chicago has more need of Marines than any Nicaraguan town."

Big Bill went to a health resort at Wedron, north of Ottawa, in 1930 and he held court like a king. One of those who visited to pay him tribute was Len Small. The ex-governor came twice, bringing a turkey and a deer he had shot. When Small left, Daniel Serritella paid a visit. Serritella, one of Capone's men in Thompson's administration, was "city sealer," the chief of weights and measures.

Daniel Serritella (left), a Capone Mob lieutenant and political friend of Governor Small, is seen here with Ralph Capone.

Serritella and his deputy city sealer, Harry

Hochstein (another gangster who broke bones in the Bloody 20th Ward working for the Mob, Thompson and Small), were convicted on May 10, 1932 of conspiracy to cheat the public. They ran a huge racket where they took payoffs from merchants to allow short-changing of customers. Capone's lawyer Michael Ahern defended Serritella and Hochstein. Serritella managed to have his conviction overturned 18 months later.

Serritella was part of the gang of suspects, along with Frank "The Enforcer" Nitti, Louis "Little New York" Campagna and State Rep. James J. Adduci, in the murder of State Rep. John Bolton, who was shot-gunned as he drove on Harrison Street at Washtenaw Avenue on July 9, 1936. State Rep. Albert Prignano was gunned down on the steps of his home at 722 Bunker St. the previous Dec. 29 on orders from Nitti.

Serritella continued in Mob activities and in government for years. He was elected a state senator amid charges of vote fraud. In April 1944, Jake "Greasy Thumbs" Guzik was arrested for vote buying in a campaign that involved Serritella.

Mayor Thompson was defeated in 1931 by Anton Cermak, an immigrant from Bohemia who had worked in the coal mines in Braidwood as a youth. Cermak, who Thompson referred to as a "Bo-Hunk with a pushcart," was no angel. He also was a Chicago political boss with gangland connections.

Anton "Ten Percent Tony" Cermak, the architect of the present Chicago Democrat Machine, sided with gangster Roger Touhy instead of with Capone. So did his police. Cermak ordered a raid on Capone's Lexington Hotel headquarters on May 2, 1931, shortly after taking office. Police confiscated material and arrested seven hoodlums.

On Feb. 14, 1933, Cermak was with President-Elect Franklin D. Roosevelt in Miami when a Sicilian named Giuseppe Zangara fired at them. Cermak was killed. It is accepted by historians that the shooting was an assassination attempt on FDR. But many other historians insist that the real target was Cermak, on Mob orders. Cermak took two slugs in the chest while Roosevelt was unharmed.

The reason for this theory? On Dec. 19, 1932, just two months before the assassination of Cermak, Chicago police raided Mob boss Frank Nitti's office, shooting and seriously wounding Nitti. It was rumored that Mayor Cermak ordered the raid and a "hit" on Capone's successor because of Cermak's political alliance with rival gangsters. Louie "Little New York" Campagna was given the job of killing Cermak in revenge for the shooting of Nitti. He found Zangara, a nut who believed he had a fatal illness and didn't mind dying in the electric chair if the Mob would take care of his mother.

No less an authority than Judge John H. Lyle believed that Cermak's murder was a Mob hit. Lyle went on the bench in 1924 and was one of the few honest judges in Cook County. He fought the gangsters bravely and fiercely, from Al Capone to Big Bill Thompson. Lyle lost the 1931 Republican primary to Thompson. Lyle and Cermak were friends. Lyle said Cermak told him that both he and Lyle were marked for assassination because the Capone Mob could not afford to have either foe in office. Frank Loesch, head of the Chicago Crime Commission at the time, also believed this was the case.

Len Small and the Mob

Len Small can properly be called a mobster, a partner with Organized Crime.

Governor Small has his own listings in three encyclopedias of crime: *World Encyclopedia of Organized Crime* by Jay Robert Nash; *Political Corruption in America: An Encyclopedia of Scandals, Power and Greed* by Mark Grossman; and *The New Encyclopedia Of American Scandal* by George Childs Kohn. All the books cross-reference Small with listings of other individual gangsters.

Len Small's indictment gets a listing in *The Complete Public Enemy Almanac* by William Helmer and Rick Mattix.

Kohn noted in his book, "The experience of undergoing judicial arraignment did not, however, deter Small. He found a way to circumvent the authority of the court. He teamed up with a notorious gunman, a lawyer turned crook and a dishonorable union official to bribe and threaten members of the jury and their families. He was, in due course, acquitted."

In Luciano Iorizzo's book, *Al Capone: A Biography,* the governor even has his own listing in the glossary of Mob figures. "Governor Len Small, governor of Illinois, a corrupt politician indebted to Torrio, Capone and others, who pardoned whoremaster Harry Guzik, among others, for a price."

Judge John H. Lyle wrote a book in 1960, *The Dry And Lawless Years* (better than the contemporary *The Untouchables* by Eliot Ness). Lyle's book wasn't just historical research, it was first-hand knowledge. He mentions that Spike O'Donnell was paroled by Governor Small so that he could get his gang of bootleggers together. Lyle wrote that "Torrio got his *quid pro quo* for financial and other contributions to the political machine headed by Governor Small and Mayor William Hale Thompson."

Lyle wrote that Torrio sent Walter Stevens to help the governor in Waukegan and "Len Small was in debt to Stevens. The hoodlum had been useful in handling various matters for the defense which, incidentally, won an acquittal. During the first three dry years, Small's administration paroled 950 prisoners. The *Chicago Tribune* estimated that about 40 per cent joined Torrio's private army."

In his book, *Mr. Capone: The Real and Complete Story of Al Capone,* Robert J. Schoenberg wrote that Johnny Torrio and Al Capone came to Len Small's aid, in gratitude for the pardons Small sold to Mob gunmen. To help his friend, "Torrio sent intimidators and bribers to Waukegan where Small's trial would be held. The bought and browbeaten jury acquitted Small on two ballots. The governor would later show himself suitably grateful."

"Small was acquitted, it was widely believed, because he bribed the jurors," wrote Laurence Bergreen in his book, *Capone, The Man and the Era.*

John Kobler's book *Capone: The Life And World Of Al Capone* tells about the work of Newmark, Boyle and Stevens. "As the governor's trial progressed, the trio undertook such delicate missions as bribing and intimidating jurors. Small was acquitted. He did not forget his deliverers."

"Their (mobsters Little Tommy Malloy and Umbrella Mike Boyle) plan was to jointly control the building trades unions in Illinois by relying upon Boyle's political connections with the overtly corrupt Governor Small -- who during his eight-year term issued no fewer than 8,000 pardons to gangsters -- and Little Tommy's strong-arm tactics," wrote Brock Yates in his book *Umbrella Mike.*

"Governor Len Small rarely needed encouragement when it came to showing leniency to powerful gangsters." And, "Torrio had good reason to want to see Small acquitted; the former farmer was notorious for pardoning convicted criminals. Torrio sent a team of emissaries with instructions to bribe the jury first, then resort to violence if need be. The effort was rewarded with success; the jurors acquitted Small. The governor's gratitude was manna to Torrio." These are just two of many Small/Mob quotes from Rose Keefe's two books about mobsters Bugs Moran and Dean O'Banion.

"So solid was he (Torrio) with the Thompson machine that he was able to secure a pardon from Len Small for Harry Guzik and his wife Alma before they had served a single day of a sentence for operating a ring that recruited inmates for the Torrio brothels," wrote Lloyd Wendt and Herman Kogan in their book *Big Bill Of Chicago*.

In *Political Corruption In America,* Mark Grossman minces no words about Len Small. The huge encyclopedia lists the 250 most corrupt politicians in history. Small, Grossman wrote, "sold pardons to the highest bidder...some 8,000 in all...making him one of the most corrupt governors in American history." Grossman wrote that Thompson, Crowe and Small would have a third party approach convicts and offer them a pardon for a price. Ignatz Potz was one example cited by Grossman. The book also links Small's run for a third term in 1928 to support from Al Capone. "Although it is obvious that Small was, indeed, one of the most corrupt, if not the most corrupt, governor in American history, his name is almost wholly forgotten."

Governor Small's connection to the Chicago Mob may come as a surprise to people in Kankakee today. It has never been a surprise to people familiar with the history of Al Capone and the Mob.

Small was not held to account for the 8,000 pardons and paroles sold or given through his administration. Pardons and commutations are the legal prerogative of the governor. This is why both Len Small and George Ryan could get away with it, no matter how low a villain was spared by the governor or for what reason. Chapter 16 on Pardons and Paroles explains Governor Small's role as a benefactor of, and member of, Organized Crime.

"It can be argued that some of America's biggest villains during the Prohibition era were not the Al Capones, Johnny Torrios, Bugs Morans, Dutch Schultzes or Frank Costellos but the political bosses in New York, Chicago and elsewhere, who used the underworld to their considerable advantage, and the many venal, conniving police

Al Capone and Albert Fink, one of his lawyers at his 1931 trial for income tax evasion. Fink also was a mouthpiece for Len Small at his indictment.

and law enforcement officials who supplemented their incomes with mobster money," wrote author Edward Behr.

"Take that first dollar from a mobster and you're his man," Judge John H. Lyle wrote. "You're in and there's no way out."

Len Small sold his soul to Big Bill Thompson, and Al Capone held the mortgage.

There was plenty of violence among gangsters in Kankakee County during the Small era. Violence between rival Italian bootleggers in 1925 put Sam Vaccero in the murky waters of the Lehigh quarry in his car with a bullet in his head. Retaliation came two days later in a shootout on the streets of Kankakee, with Alessio Tortorici and Frank Luppino blown away in a hail of gunfire. One of the gunmen was cold-blooded murderer Victore Festante, a Sicilian immigrant. Festante escaped this rap but went to the slammer for the murder of a man in a Dwight roadhouse. He died in the Joliet penitentiary in 1937. Tales of local Mafia warfare, gangland violence, kidnapping, bank robbery, train robbery, bootlegging, gambling and prostitution abound in the history of Kankakee in the 1920s and 1930s.

The Manteno State Hospital was authorized by Governor Small and the legislature in 1927, a plum for Kankakee County. Leslie Small authorized the contracts and supervised the construction. There was Mob involvement here. Two construction workers were shot on April 7, 1930 in a dispute between two Mob labor unions fighting over territory.

W.W. O'Brien was a Mob lawyer whose story may be told some day.

O'Brien was the one who made a deal with Len Small and Big Bill Thompson to trade pardons for votes during the 1932 campaign (chapter 22).

O'Brien was the lawyer whose courtroom trickery in 1919 let hit-man Walter Stevens get away with the murder of an Aurora policeman. O'Brien represented Eddie Kaufman, the gangster who bribed the jurors at Small's trial. He was the lawyer who found a judge to let psychopath Fur Sammons out of jail in order to continue a career as a Capone tommy-gunner.

O'Brien once was shot in a saloon yet refused to name the shooter, in true underworld fashion. He was nearly disbarred after bribing two state's attorneys.

O'Brien was the lawyer for gang boss Joseph “Polack Joe” Saltis, who controlled bootlegging on the Southwest Side. Saltis went on trial in October 1926 for the murder of John "Mitters" Foley. O'Brien bribed the jury (with money supplied by mobster Earl "Hymie" Weiss) to free Saltis.

O'Brien was at Weiss' side when Weiss was "whacked" by Capone's gunmen on Oct. 11, 1926. On that day, O'Brien and Weiss came from the Saltis courtroom. They and three bodyguards got out of their cars and were walking to the florist shop of William Schofield at 738 N. State St., across the street from Holy Name Cathedral. (It was in this flower shop in 1924 that Schofield's partner Dean O'Banion was gunned down in one of the most legendary rub-outs of the Roaring Twenties.) As Weiss and the others walked by the cathedral, gunmen opened fire from across the street. Weiss and one bodyguard were killed. O'Brien was wounded.

O'Brien was the lawyer for Capone gunman "Three Finger Jack" White in March 1931, on trial for murdering Chicago Police Officer Edward Pflaume in 1925. Before the trial, Pflaume's partner, Sgt. James McBride, was shot to keep him from testifying. McBride recovered and testified. White was convicted and sent to the penitentiary.

Remember Claire Edwards, the judge at Governor Small's trial in Waukegan? He was the judge whose brother put up the bail money for gangster Eddie Kaufman. Well, Claire Edwards left the bench and went back into private law practice. In October 1929, Edwards was the lawyer defending mobster George "Bugs" Moran in Lake County court. Moran was on trial for "vagrancy," a common charge at the time to harass gangsters who had no visible jobs. Edwards told the court that Moran was the respectable boss of Central Cleaners & Dyers (an extortion group that shook down cleaners for protection money). Moran was acquitted of the vagrancy charge.

Cornelius "Con" Shea was one of the gangsters involved in the jury tampering at Governor Small's trial. Shea had quite a career as a gangster and labor racketeer. He was accused of bribery, extortion, mail fraud, racketeering, conspiracy, beatings, bombings, grand theft, robbery, murder and more yet never was convicted of these crimes. But he was convicted twice of non-gangland offenses. His first conviction was in 1908 for abandoning his wife and two young children, and he was sentenced to six months. His second conviction was in 1909 for attempted murder -- he stabbed his mistress 27 times. Shea was sentenced to 25 years but was paroled after five years.

Shea muscled his way into being named the first president of the Teamsters. While president of the Teamsters, Shea led a four-month strike during which 21 people were killed (most were black strikebreakers lynched by white gangs in the Back of the Yards neighborhood) and 416 were injured. The strike ended in accomplishing nothing. It had been called by Shea after being paid by a company that wanted to ruin a competitor.

When Shea got put of jail in 1914, he became secretary-treasurer of the Mobbed-up Theatrical Janitors Union, and he specialized in beatings and bombings. Shea was among 10 labor union terrorists who were indicted in 1921 for a series of bombings.

Shea was indicted in May 1922 for the murder of Chicago Police Lt. Terrence Lyons. This was approximately the same time Shea was meeting with Leslie Small to fix Governor Small's jury in Waukegan. Indicted with Shea for the police officer's murder were Big Tim Murphy, boss of the Chicago Building Trades Council, Fred "Frenchy" Mader, president of the Building Trades Council, and several other labor union creeps.

Cook County Sheriff Peter Hoffman and Warden Wesley Westbrook had the distinction of being the only officials in the department's history who served time in their own jail while still remaining in office. Hoffman became sheriff in 1922 and was on the payroll of Johnny Torrio. Hoffman and Westbrook were paid $2,000 a month by Morris Eller to allow jailed bootleggers Frankie Lake and Terry Druggan to have deluxe private rooms with baths, conjugal visits and frequent "furloughs" to work their bootlegging racket. Judge James Wilkerson sentenced Hoffman to 30 days and Westbrook to 120 days in their own jail. Hoffman was followed in 1926 by Sheriff Charles E. Graydon, who was put in office by Mayor Thompson. Graydon was even more corrupt. Matt Kolb, chief henchman for bootlegger Roger Touhy, joined Graydon's force as a highway patrolman. Sheriff Graydon and his force helped the gangsters expand bootlegging, slot machines and all kinds of vice throughout Cook County. Capone and Guzik took over the territory in 1931 after their gunmen put six slugs in Kolb's head in his Morton Grove saloon.

What happened to some of the gangsters mentioned here? Many ended up in true gangland fashion -- but not all. A surprising number actually died of natural causes.

Edward “Spike” O'Donnell, the target of a dozen gangland assassination attempts, died on Aug. 26, 1962 at age 72 of a heart attack in his home at 8234 Loomis Ave. George "Bugs" Moran died of lung cancer in Leavenworth penitentiary in 1957. Jake "Greasy Thumbs" Guzik died on Feb. 21, 1956 of a heart attack at age 69 while eating at St. Hubert's Grill. Johnny Torrio died of a heart attack in a barber's chair in New York at age 57 on March 16, 1957. Umbrella Mike Boyle died in 1958, still vice president of the IBEW and business manager of its local in Chicago. Ralph "Bottles" Capone died Nov. 22, 1974 in a retirement home in Hurley, Wisc. at age 81. Al Capone’s lawyers Michael Ahern died of a heart attack in his home at 4536 N. Mozart St. on Sept. 22, 1943, and Albert Fink died on March 25, 1941 at his home in Tucson, Ariz.

Some died in traditional gangland fashion. Big Tim Murphy answered the doorbell at his Chicago home on June 26, 1928 and faced a hail of machine gun fire from a passing sedan. Frank Nitti shot himself alongside a railroad track in Riverside on March 19, 1943. Sam Giancana was shot to death in his Oak Park home on June 19, 1975.

One more story needs to be told, and this does have a connection to both Illinois politics and to Illinois gangsters.

Of all the names chronicled in the lawless decade of the Roaring Twenties, there is one name that usually is omitted.

It is Joseph P. Kennedy, the patriarch of the famous Kennedy Clan.

Joe Kennedy was a partner with Diamond Joe Esposito in the bootlegging racket in the 1920s. Another member of this gang was Sam Giancana, a ruthless killer who later took over as Mob boss of Chicago.

Joe Kennedy made alliances with crime bosses in Chicago, Boston, New York and New Orleans. Kennedy smuggled whiskey from foreign distillers, where it was left on the docks for the mobsters to pick up. The police were paid to look the other way.

New York's Frank Costello -- one of the biggest Mob bosses of all, and one of the Mafia figures on whom the character of Vito Corleone in the movie *The Godfather* is said to have been based -- also ran hooch with Kennedy. Costello later bragged, "I helped Joe Kennedy get rich." And Sam Giancana was quoted as saying that Joe Kennedy was "one of the biggest crooks who ever lived."

Joe Kennedy made his early fortune by trading in inside information and in stock pools -- bidding up the price of a stock, and then when the gullible investors joined the action, syndicate members sold out, leaving the suckers with losses. He also became an expert in selling short -- gambling that the price of a stock will go down.

Joe Kennedy's reward for helping re-elect Roosevelt in 1936 was the job as ambassador to England, where he embarrassed FDR and America by expressing sympathy for the Nazis. When Germany started bombing London, Kennedy gave his infamous "Democracy is finished in England" interview. That was too much for FDR. It was Joe Kennedy who was finished.

The Kennedy association with the Mob went far beyond Old Joe's bootlegging days during Prohibition. The Mob also helped elect John F. Kennedy

JFK won in 1960 by a narrow margin. A shift of 4,480 votes in Illinois and 25,000 in Texas would have given those electoral votes, and the presidency, to Richard Nixon. But with Mayor Richard J. Daley counting ballots in Chicago and Sen. Lyndon B. Johnson counting ballots in Texas, JFK found enough votes to put him over the top.

"Actually, and this goes without saying, the presidency was really stolen in Chicago, without a question, by the Democratic Machine," said mobster Mickey Cohen. "I know that certain people in the Chicago Organization knew that they had to get John Kennedy in."

Earl Mazo wrote about voter fraud in Texas and Illinois for the *New York Herald Tribune.* But even the ethically-challenged Nixon could not believe it. "No one steals the presidency of the United States," Nixon told Mazo. What is more, Nixon said he would not challenge the election results because a lengthy fight would harm America. Even "Tricky Dick" Nixon had more ethics and morals than the Kennedys.

It was during the 1960 campaign that JFK began an affair with Judith Campbell Exner, who was having an affair with Sam Giancana at the same time. JFK had Exner arrange a meeting with him and Giancana to help in the critical West Virginia primary. Giancana sent Mob lieutenant Paul "Skinny" D'Amato to West Virginia to meet with politicians. D'Amato wrote off debts at his 500 Club in Atlantic City and handed out cash payments.

According to the Tru-TV Crime Library site (formerly Court TV), Joe Kennedy told Giancana, "If my son is elected President, he'll be your man."

Kennedy used the Boston diocese to launder campaign money. Author Peter Maas used this example: if Boston-area churches took in $950,000 on a particular Sunday from collection plates, Joe would write a check for $1 million to the diocese, deduct it as a charitable contribution and receive the $950,000 in cash. This way, the church got an extra $50,000, Joe deducted the entire amount on his income tax and he could use the money to pay politicians with cash that was untraceable.

Len Small wasn't the only tenderhearted executive when it came to pardoning felons. JFK was president for less than three years, but he issued 472 pardons -- more than any president before or since.

The most egregious pardon may be the one granted to John "Jake the Barber" Factor. He was the brother of cosmetics king Max Factor, and he was part of the Chicago Outfit from Capone's era in the 1920s all the way into the 1960s. Factor became a part owner of the Stardust Hotel and Casino in Las Vegas with several other top mobsters.

The Justice Department investigated the Stardust and was about to deport Factor to England in 1962, where he was wanted for swindling millions of dollars from Britons in a 1926 stock fraud scam.

But President Kennedy granted Factor a full and complete Presidential pardon, just 48 hours before Factor was about to be deported.

Why? Because Factor chipped in a big donation to the Kennedys' secret fund for a caper to rescue the survivors of the Bay of Pigs invasion. Factor and others who paid Attorney General Bobby Kennedy were not bothered by the Justice Department. And it ended the government's investigation into the Stardust Casino, an investigation that would have revealed Stardust's connection to Giancana, Ricca, Accardo and other mobsters.

Kennedy scandals fill countless books. President Kennedy did not provide the air cover he promised to Cuban exiles at the Bay of Pigs; as a result, fear of a full-scale invasion led Castro and the Soviets to install missiles in Cuba. Kennedy's reaction was to panic and to bring the world to the brink of nuclear war. It was Soviet Premier Nikita Khrushchev who pulled back. Then there is Marilyn Monroe and the parade of other sexual conquests. Don't forget Chappaquiddick, where Sen. Edward M. "Teddy" Kennedy took young Mary Jo Kopechne for a ride on July 18, 1969. A drunken Teddy Kennedy drove the car into a pond. Kennedy managed to get out of the car but he left Mary Jo there to die. Kennedy did not report the incident to police *for 10 hours.* Instead, he went back to his motel to establish an alibi and to call his lawyers to try to find a way to get out of his trouble. Mary Jo would have lived if Teddy Kennedy had been more interested in saving her life than he was in saving his reputation. Kennedy pleaded guilty to "leaving the scene of an accident after causing an injury." He got off with just a two-month suspended sentence and one-year probation.

The Kennedys owe their fortune and the Presidency to the Chicago Outfit. From long-time Mob connections to disastrous diplomacy, sexual scandals and more, the Kennedys have (as one wag observed) consistently shown more profile than courage.

The Kennedy family today enjoys the "Camelot" myth that they invented, as they act as the multi-millionaire spokespersons for the poor.

Chapter 16

Pardons and Paroles For Sale -- To Capone And Others

Selling pardons and paroles to gangsters, murderers and other criminals was another huge scandal in Governor Len Small's corrupt administration.

As governor, Small's administration sold more than 8,000 pardons and paroles during his eight years in office -- and these included pardoning and paroling some of the most vicious killers of the Roaring Twenties.

Robert Emmett Crowe, Cook County state's attorney in the 1920s, was frustrated by sending Mob gunmen and other criminals to jail and then having them pardoned by Governor Small.

"Perhaps the worst handicap this office confronts is Len Small's pardon and parole system," Crowe said. "He lets them out as fast as we put them in. It takes us two weeks to get the guilty man convicted and it takes the governor two seconds to sign his name on a pardon blank. In 1923, for example, I put 59 burglars and 97 robbers in Joliet, and Small released 88 burglars and 97 robbers!"

The *Chicago Journal* reported that in 1923, 308 people were sent to Pontiac prison and 252 were paroled. A total of 397 people were sent to Joliet and 441 were released. "The prisons are being emptied, and nothing in the crime records shows justification for such a performance," it wrote.

After years of individual scandals involving outrageous pardons and paroles for vicious killers, gangsters and other criminals, it was revealed that the Small administration operated a "pardon mill" where convicts could buy their way out of the penitentiary.

Two grand juries accused the governor's superintendent of paroles and pardons of selling paroles, and he was forced to resign. Len Small once again escaped the prosecution or impeachment he so richly deserved.

"I do not believe habitual criminals should be released repeatedly to commit further crimes. It has been found in our populous centers that a great deal of the crime committed is by experienced and seasoned criminals who have been released under the provisions of the parole law, again to prey on the public.

"The penal institutions of the state should be operated first to protect society against the depredations of the criminally inclined, and secondly, to bring about, if possible, the reformation of those confined there."

This wasn't spoken by a critic of Governor Small's pardon and parole system. It was spoken by Governor Small in his inaugural address in January 1921.

During the many months that he was under investigation for selling pardons and paroles, Governor Small made it clear that pardons could be made by the governor for whatever reason he wanted, or for no reason, and could not be rescinded by the courts.

He also pointed out that paroles were made by an independent board and were not made by the governor. And he said the parole board was basically the same under his administration as it had been under Governor Lowden.

This was not true.

For one thing, the parole board wasn't so independent. It is true that the governor issues pardons and not paroles, but that is a technicality of law. The governor appoints the members of the Pardons and Parole Board and they listen to their boss. Secondly, Will Colvin was the only holdover from the Lowden administration. The other members were Small appointees

And the parole board had not been doing a good job before Small took office.

The parole board had been making problems for the Chicago police before Small took office. Police Chief Charles Fitzmorris asked the incoming governor in December 1920 to put a moratorium on the parole system for a year. In 1920, 157 convicts were paroled from Joliet and 99 from Pontiac, and escapes from jails averaged two per week. "The present operation of the parole board constitutes an absolute interference with the Chicago police department," Fitzmorris said. "We are hampered and harassed continuously by paroled convicts. In many cases, in only a few weeks they are out with their guns again. The crooks regard the operation of the parole law as an open door from the penitentiary." Judges Frank Wilson and Daniel Trude agreed with Fitzmorris' request.

Governor Small had his own idea about parole reform.

Governor Small was connected to Roaring Twenties Chicago gangsters through his political alliance with Mayor Big Bill Thompson and with mobsters Johnny Torrio, Al Capone, Umbrella Mike Boyle, Walter Stevens and others. The corruption of public officials and their ties to mobsters was widespread.

Len Small was known as the "pardoning governor" and many of the pardons he sold were to gangsters.

Small even went so far as to pardon cop killers.

Perhaps the most outrageous pardons and commutations issued by Gov. Small were the ones given to Spike O'Donnell, Ben Newmark, Umbrella Mike Boyle, Ignatz Potz, Walter Stevens, Harry Guzik and Fur Sammons.

Spike O'Donnell, Ben Newmark, Mike Boyle

A notorious pardon that had far reaching effects was the pardon granted to Edward "Spike" O'Donnell, leader of one of Chicago's biggest bootlegging gangs.

Bootlegger and murderer Spike O'Donnell went to prison in 1917 for bank robbery. His release in 1923 came with the blessing of a number of state legislators who lobbied in the mobster's behalf. Governor Small's freeing of O'Donnell was what started a major Chicago beer war. That story is told in chapter 15.

And, of course, there were the pardons for Ben Newmark and Umbrella Mike Boyle, two Chicago mobsters who aided in bribing the jury that acquitted Governor Small. Both were sentenced to jail for contempt of court for not cooperating with the investigation into the jury tampering -- and both were freed by pardons from Governor Small. That story is told in chapter 12.

Ignatz Potz

On Jan. 13, 1922, a group of four Torrio-Capone bootleggers were on their way from Kenosha, Wisc. to Chicago with a load of hooch. The gangsters were driving 60 miles an hour on Sheridan Road, between Zion and Waukegan. William Peterson, a Winthrop Harbor motorcycle policeman, was in full pursuit. One of the bootleggers, Ignatz Potz, shot and killed Peterson.

Potz confessed and was sentenced to death.

Len Small made the deal to commute the sentence of Capone's gunman Potz at the same time Small himself was on trial in Waukegan for corruption, and while Small was using Capone's henchmen to bribe his jury!

Governor Small saved cop-killer Ignatz Potz from the hangman in 1922 -- and he later arranged a parole for him.

TIME magazine was disgusted by Small's brazen behavior of opening the jail cell doors for murderers. It wrote in its July 12, 1926 magazine:

"Cold-blooded murderer Ignatz Potz killed a Waukegan, Illinois, motorcycle policeman to avoid arrest for running liquor. He was condemned to death. In 1922, Governor Len Small of Illinois commuted the death penalty to life imprisonment; last week he granted a parole to Potz, effective in 1930. Aside from the question of the legality of a double commutation, aside from the reason for the date 1930, aside from the friendly relations of Potz with Len Small politics, thousands of decent Illinoisans were vastly irritated because this was merely the latest of many criminals to receive favor from a governor whom decent thousands regard as a cold-blooded crook."

The governor's explanation for the Potz pardon sounds fantastic. Small said that as he and his wife Ida were riding home from Waukegan to Kankakee on June 24, 1922, just after his acquittal, Ida mentioned -- of all things on that hectic day -- Ignatz Potz!

"Oh, Len, don't ever let him hang," is what Small claimed Ida said in the car.

Ida collapsed that night and died less than two days later. Governor Small said it was the only thing his wife had ever asked of him, in an official capacity, and he was going to honor her last request.

However, Potz was scheduled to hang on June 16 in Lake County. Len Small's trial was going on there at the time. On the evening of June 15, the day before the governor's 60th birthday -- in the middle of all the turmoil of being on trial for his political life -- the governor gave Potz's lawyer more than two hours of his time, and then he granted a 60-day stay of execution.

So Governor Small was going to commute Potz's sentence before his wife had said anything. But even if you believe his story, what the governor did was to pass the responsibility for the pardon of cop-killer Potz on to his late wife!

Small's newspaper later claimed that Mrs. Potz had asked Mrs. Small to save her husband's life on the same day as Potz's lawyer was talking to the governor. But Ida didn't mention it to her husband until their car ride home to Kankakee, six days later.

So Ida's "request" to spare Potz came a week after Mrs. Potz had spoken to her, and a week after Governor Small already had saved Potz's neck from the hangman's noose.

Sparing the life of Ignatz Potz was a request from Johnny Torrio and Al Capone, not a request from Ida Small.

The state's attorney of Lake County was outraged. He asked the court to intervene, arguing that the governor's commutation was invalid because Potz's clemency petition was not in proper form. The court found in favor of Small, citing the constitutional right of the governor to pardon as he pleased, regardless of mistakes in technicalities. "His acts in the exercise of the power can be controlled only by his conscience and his sense of public duty," the court said.

As a side point, the *Bloomington Bulletin,* a minor newspaper friendly to the governor, brought a different aspect to the Potz story. It said that while Small was in the Waukegan courthouse on trial in June 1922, Mrs. Small asked her husband why there was so much hammering outside. The governor told her that gallows were being built for a hanging. It touched her heart and she asked her husband to commute the man's sentence. The story changed the circumstance of Mrs. Small's intervention, from the car ride home to the court room earlier. Whether or not this story is true, we will never know. The article, which appeared in both the Bloomington and the Kankakee newspapers, praised the governor's tenderhearted mercy and his devotion to his late wife's request "even in the face of the sterner demands of duty." Not coincidentally, the story appeared the same week that TIME magazine was condemning Small for paroling Potz.

On the other hand, when Lake County State's Attorney Ashbel V. Smith asked the governor in July 1926 to pardon local bootlegger Lester Clow, who was serving just a four-month sentence, the governor declined.

Smith said Clow was "slightly unbalanced." Small replied to Smith, "I have never exercised executive clemency in a case where an individual has been convicted of the violation of the Prohibition act. It has not been the policy of this administration to review cases where the conviction carried a jail sentence." As for Clow's mental status, Small said it was Smith's fault for not noting this instability when he prosecuted the man.

When Small was in his last days as governor, he convened a special meeting in his office in Kankakee of the board of Pardons and Paroles. Instead of letting his parole of Potz to take effect in October 1930, as he had previously decided, Small said Potz's sentence would expire effective immediately -- Dec. 21, 1928.

Cop-killer Ignatz Potz was a free man, home in time for Christmas.

Walter Stevens

We have heard from Walter Stevens before -- he was one of the gangsters who helped intimidate and bribe the jury that acquitted Len Small.

Stevens, known as "the dean of Chicago's gunmen" (for having murdered as many as 60 people) and "the immune gunman" (for being arrested hundreds of times and almost always evading jail) was a lieutenant of Maurice "Mossy" Enright, an early labor union racketeer. Stevens used bombings, beating and murder to force his way into the unions. Enright was murdered in 1920 and Stevens went to work as a "hit man" for the Torrio-Capone mob.

In his career as a gangster, Stevens began developing political connections. This helped him, as several state senators testified in his behalf, and he was able to call on Governor Small to collect on favors.

Walter Stevens was a professional murderer. One of his victims was an Aurora police officer.

It was on Oct. 29, 1918 when Stevens and another Chicago hoodlum, Frank Williams (alias William Von Gundy), were picked up in downtown Aurora by Police Officers Alfred Olin and Lester Wedemaier for stealing a car. Stevens shot and killed Olin and seriously wounded Wedemaier, then he and Williams escaped.

Stevens was one of the most wanted men in Illinois, but police could not find him.

So the police were surprised when Walter Stevens walked into the Kane County state's attorney's office on Feb. 8, 1919 and gave himself up. He was smiling. He said he had been in Chicago all the time and he said the police knew it. In fact, he had been hiding out at a policeman's home.

Stevens finally was put on trial for the murder of Patrolman Olin. The trial started on June 11 in Geneva. But Walter Stevens wasn't worried at all about going on trial for his life. He smiled as witnesses identified him as the man who murdered Officer Olin.

W.W. O'Brien, his attorney from Chicago, hatched a plot with Stevens several months before the confident gunman surrendered. It seems a friendly salesman named "A.H. Byrnes" came to Aurora, passing out cigars and introducing himself to police officers. Even Officer Wedemaier didn't recognize the man named Byrnes -- it was Walter Stevens in disguise.

O'Brien sprung this on the jury, to everyone's surprise.

Even though a number of eyewitnesses positively identified Stevens as the gunman who shot the officers (and five other eyewitnesses declined to testify after being threatened by gangsters), there were a number of witnesses, including 15 politicians, who lied to give Stevens an alibi. It was too much. The jurors either had reasonable doubt or they were compromised. Stevens was acquitted.

Stevens had good cause to be confident. If O'Brien's tricks didn't work and if threats by gangsters and perjured testimony didn't work, he knew Governor Small would save him.

Stevens shook hands with the jurors, but before he could leave the courtroom, he was arrested for the shooting of Wedemaier. The trial in May 1920 ended with a guilty verdict for attempted murder. He was sentenced to 14 years. It was his first conviction after dozens of murders and robberies.

But Stevens jumped bail. On the lam in Florida, he smuggled rum from Cuba and he murdered two more people -- all the while, back in Illinois, crooked state senators and other politicians he owned testified for him in his appeal.

Stevens went on to commit a number of murders in the Chicago Beer War in 1923. He finally was apprehended on Oct. 22 in Indiana. Governor Small signed extradition papers four days later. There was a lot of talk that the governor was going to pardon Stevens as a reward for Stevens' help at the governor's trial the previous year.

Oct 28, 1923, the *Chicago Tribune* reported, "Application for a pardon was made to Governor Small soon after Small himself was acquitted of charges of embezzlement. Governor Small is said to have expressed his belief in Stevens' innocence and to have directed his pardon board to take cognizance of the application."

It was true. In October 1922, just four months after Small was acquitted, State Rep. Lee O'Neil Browne of Ottawa and State Sen. Richard Barr of Joliet lobbied the governor to pardon Stevens. They urged a pardon, no matter what the recommendation of the Pardons and Parole Board, and no matter the fact that Stevens was a fugitive from justice.

Browne appealed to the governor again after Stevens was apprehended in October 1923. He strongly urged Governor Small not to sign the extradition paper and he again asked a pardon for Stevens.

But even though Stevens publicly bragged that a pardon was "fixed" and forthcoming, Governor Small went slow on this one. Advisors warned him how dangerous a pardon would be, especially since the newspapers were predicting it and were bringing a lot of intense, bad publicity on the governor as they anticipated a pardon. So the governor referred it back to Colvin.

A Nov. 28, 1923 *Tribune* story said, "To his friends, he confided that politicians owe him a great favor which would be repaid with a pardon before he entered the gates of the penitentiary. His application was filed and was known to have received much consideration. Members of Governor Small's cabinet attempted to influence the Chicago Crime Commission."

Kane County State's Attorney Charles Abbott, who prosecuted Stevens for the shootings of the Aurora police officers, was certain Stevens would escape justice. He told the *Chicago Tribune* on Nov. 26, 1922, "I believe he will be pardoned before there is time for his bond to be forfeited. I believe Governor Small will pardon him because the governor has nothing to lose. He is through, anyhow. On the other hand, the Thompson organization is making its last stand in Chicago. All of the crooked politicians, gunmen, burglars and thieves want Stevens pardoned, and they control votes. The state's attorney's office of Kane County will do everything to see that the verdict of 12 men who found Stevens guilty is carried out."

Kane County Sheriff Claude Poole told the *Tribune* on Nov 28, 1922 that he was still hunting fugitive Stevens. "If I can find him, I'll take him to prison. The governor can do as he likes, but the people of Kane County want this policeman killer in the penitentiary and I'll do my duty."

Walter Stevens finally entered the Joliet prison on Oct. 29, 1923.

Governor Len Small later arranged a parole for Walter Stevens, and the cop-killer walked out of the Joliet penitentiary on Jan. 30, 1925.

Federal agents were waiting at the prison gates to take custody of Stevens on the Florida bootlegging charges. But Chauncey Jenkins, friend of Len Small and Walter Stevens, explained that Stevens was on parole and therefore was a ward of the state and not subject to arrest for previous offenses.

Walter Stevens went on for several more years in his career as a killer. He died in a Chicago hospital on Feb. 15, 1931. His age was estimated at 70. The cause of death was pneumonia.

Harry 'Greasy Thumbs' Guzik

The three Guzik brothers -- Jake, Harry and Sam -- were big-time purveyors of all kinds of vice in Chicago. Their careers began when Al Capone was just a kid knocking off lemonade stands and shaking down fellow kindergarteners for milk money in New York. Their careers went through to the modern Mob era of the 1950s.

Jake "Greasy Thumbs" Guzik was one of the top men in the Capone organization. He was Capone's business manager and one of Big Al's closest personal friends. After Capone left the scene, Jake "Greasy Thumbs" Guzik, Frank "The Enforcer" Nitti, Paul "The Waiter" Ricca, Sam "Momo" Giancana and Tony "Joe Batters" Accardo were the top Mob leaders in Chicago in the 1930s and beyond.

Even today, the Guziks and other vicious mobsters are remembered in film and lore. Jake Guzik's character was portrayed on *The Untouchables* TV series (in episodes from 1959 to 1962), in the 1967 movie *The St. Valentine's Day Massacre* and in the 1975 film *Capone.* Jake and Harry Guzik were portrayed in the 1993 *Untouchables* TV series.

You get the picture. The Guziks were very big in the Chicago Mob.

Harry Guzik was one of the Mob's biggest whoremasters. The Mob nickname "Greasy Thumbs" originally was Harry's nickname, derived from the way he peeled off bills from a large bankroll. His brother Jake later got the name from handling the Mob's finances and "greasing" the way for a fix.

Harry Guzik sometimes was referred to by the original name, Cusick.

Harry Guzik was part of a "white slavery" sensation in 1907. This is a term used when young women are forced into prostitution against their will and held as captives. This was the case that brought the term "white slavery" into general use.

This white slave ring came to light after 18-year-old Mona Marshall was rescued from the Casino saloon at 2121 Dearborn St. in May 1907. Mona had been a clerk at Marshall Field & Co. when a young customer named William Balding asked her for a date. Balding drugged Mona and then sold her to the Chicago white slavery ring for $50. Mona was forced to work as a prostitute at the Casino for nearly two months, until she was able to sneak out a letter that brought the police.

Seven people were arrested at the ring's "clearing house" at 2252 Wabash Avenue.

Harry “Greasy Thumbs” Guzik was the manager of the Casino saloon.

The story scandalized the country and resulted in the passage of the federal Mann Act.

But occasional arrests and convictions never stopped mobsters from their work. Guzik was back in business very soon. He managed whorehouses for different mobsters in the Levee's red light district for several years before going into business for himself. Raids in August 1912 caught Guzik and three others, including a 17-year-old girl, in their saloon/brothel at 2033 Armour Ave. The city appointed a committee to investigate the prostitution racket in Chicago, but an attorney for the committee complained that the state's attorney's office was hampering the efforts of the grand jury to hear testimony. Guzik was named as one of those exerting "terrific pressure." Nevertheless, Guzik and his partners were indicted on the white slavery charge involving the 17-year-old girl. At the trial in November, Judge Windes acquitted them, to the astonishment of everyone. Another raid in November 1914 brought in Guzik.

Harry Guzik

Harry Guzik found it profitable to work for Johnny Torrio, as his brother Jake rose high in the Torrio-Capone mob. Guzik ran the Torrio brothels like a barracks, with 30 or more women in each one.

Jake Guzik

Harry and Alma Guzik were managing the Roemer Inn brothel in Chicago's Posen neighborhood for Johnny Torrio in 1921 when they were arrested in what became another sensational case of white slavery. The tales from this house of horror made people's blood run cold.

In this notorious incident, Minnie Oehlerking, an innocent teenage girl from Monee, about 20 miles north of Kankakee, answered an advertisement for a city job as a maid in October 1921. The ad was placed by the Guziks.

Minnie was forced into prostitution in the Guzik's Roemer Inn. After several months as a captive, the girl managed to convince one of her customers to smuggle a note to the outside. Minnie's father and several friends came and took her from the Guzik's place. The poor girl was a physical and mental wreck. Harry and Alma Guzik were arrested.

Assistant State's Attorney E.E. Wilson, who prosecuted the case, called it "the most repulsive offense imaginable."

The Guziks tried to pay off the girl's father but could not. They were convicted on pandering (white slavery) charges and sentenced to a year in prison. They appealed their conviction to the state Appellate Court, which upheld the conviction. Then they appealed to the state Supreme Court.

They also appealed to Johnny Torrio. He went to gunman Walter Stevens, and Stevens went to his good friend Lennington Small. On June 20, 1923, before the higher court could rule on the appeal, and before the Guziks spent one day in jail, Governor Small pardoned Harry and Alma Guzik.

Within a few months, the Guziks were back in the prostitution business, operating the notorious Marshfield Inn whorehouse just outside the Chicago city limits. The Guziks later were arrested at this location along with several prostitutes.

Harry Guzik and 31 others were arrested on Sept. 6, 1924 in a raid at the Blue Goose Inn in Burr Oak, another of the whorehouses he ran for Torrio and Capone. Guzik continued his long career as a Mob whoremaster.

State Rep. Lee O'Neil Browne was the lawyer representing the Guziks in their plea for a pardon on the Roemer Inn conviction. State Rep. Thomas O'Grady appeared "unofficially" on the Guzik's behalf.

Judge Harry Fisher, who had sentenced the Guziks, refused to sign Browne's letter to Small requesting a pardon.

The outrageous Guzik pardons have been cited in several books about Al Capone and Big Bill Thompson.

Robert J. Schoenberg, in his book *Mr. Capone: The Real & Complete Story of Al Capone,* wrote that Torrio saw clemency for the Guziks as a personal mission to show everyone he had clout. "How better could Torrio demonstrate his clout to colleagues...how could anyone hope to get such an antipathetic and incorrigible felon off after so unappetizing a crime? Torrio cashed in chits the Outfit had earned the year before with Governor Small's acquittal."

Schoenberg continued, "This was clout. And because it was the Outfit acting, it imparted an impression of institutional power transferable to Capone, smoothing his way at the crucial moment."

"So solid was he (Torrio) with the Thompson machine that he was able to secure a pardon from Len Small for Harry Guzik and his wife Alma before they had served a single day of a sentence from operating a ring that recruited inmates for the Torrio brothels," wrote Lloyd Wendt and Herman Kogen in their book, *Big Bill of Chicago.*

A Chicago police report in 1931 showed the white slave trade had grown five times faster than the population since Small freed the Guziks eight years earlier. Arrests for pandering had doubled.

When the *Chicago Tribune* ran a series in 1924 that exposed some of Small's scandalous pardons and paroles, the *Kankakee Daily Republican* printed a few stories in reply. One thing about Len Small, he always had an answer for everything. And his explanations mostly were very good. Sometimes it made you wonder if the *Tribune* was telling the truth or if it was telling lies in order to persecute this poor man Small. But if any incident proved that it was Len Small who was the liar and the crook, it was his explanation of his pardons for the despicable Guziks.

According to Governor Small -- as told in his *Kankakee Daily Republican* through his political allies Chauncey H. Jenkins and Lee O'Neil Browne -- Harry and Alma Guzik owned a simple "mom and pop" restaurant, and the girl who made the accusation was a waitress. One day, the girl's father showed up with a policeman. Mr. Guzik went up to them and asked them what they wanted. The father said he didn't want his daughter working as a waitress there. Mr. Guzik told the man that if he didn't want his daughter working there, then Mr. Guzik certainly didn't want her to stay. He paid the girl her wages and she left with her father. The next thing the Guziks knew, they were indicted for pandering.

The Guziks rented the downstairs of the building for their restaurant, from a man named Schafer, who owned some kind of rooms upstairs that the Guziks knew nothing about, according to Browne.

The "naïve" Guziks went to a local politician for help. He told them to hire a certain lawyer and do what he said. The lawyer told the Guziks not to take the stand and to put up no defense. They protested because they knew they were innocent, but they did as they were told. They were convicted and sentenced to prison. They took their case to the Appellate Court and lost. Then they appealed to the Supreme Court.

"While the case was still pending in the Supreme Court, friends of Guzik and his wife came to me and asked me if I would not represent them in an appeal to the Board of Pardons and Paroles," said Browne.

Browne took the case to the board, presented his argument and applied for a pardon. The Guziks and a few of their friends also gave testimony.

The state was not notified of the hearing and so did not send anyone to object.

"I might add that at least three of the witnesses who appeared for these people before the board, one of them a prominent physician, another his wife, were respectable, responsible people who had known Guzik and his wife for years and who were most insistent, not only that Guzik and his wife were innocent of the charge, but that they were not the kind of people, especially the wife, who would under any circumstances be engaged in anything such as the indictment charges them with," Browne said.

"Finally, a favorable report approving the application for a pardon was made and presented by said board to your Excellency, and your Excellency granted the pardon," Browne wrote in the *Kankakee Daily Republican.*

And just what might be the real reason why anyone was making a big deal about the Guzik pardons? You guessed it.

The whole matter, Browne said, was a "stirred up" by the Chicago newspapers "purely for the purpose of embarrassing your Excellency and attempting to create something wrong that might furnish a talking point for those who are seeking by every means known to attribute to your Excellency ulterior motives in everything that you do and to discredit you as far as possible."

This is what passed for the truth in the bizarro world of Len Small and his partners in crime.

It was not important for Browne or the *Kankakee Daily Republican* to mention that the "friends" of Harry and Alma Guzik included Walter Stevens, Johnny Torrio and Al Capone! And they did not consider it unusual for a supposed insignificant defendant, with no influence of any kind, to hire a "connected" high-powered lawyer or to apply to the Board of Pardons and Paroles before the case had even finished going though the judicial system! There was no mention of the 1907 white slavery conviction of Pa Guzik or of his whore-mongering for Organized Crime for years. It was legally logical that statements from questionable characters before the Pardon and Parole Board would be enough to overturn a decision of a jury that had been upheld on appeal. And it was perfectly sensible for the governor to accept all this without any evidence.

No, the only evidence that Governor Len Small needed came from the Chicago Outfit. It wasn't a court order that freed the Guziks; it was the order that came from Johnny Torrio and Al Capone.

(In a historic irony, the Guzik story was told in a 1993 episode of the new *Untouchables* TV series...and the fictionalized role of Minnie was played by Kara Zediker, an actress from Kankakee. Gary Houston played Harry Guzik.)

Harry "Greasy Thumbs" Guzik later had an office in Chicago's Loop, where he paid police and other officials to protect Mob interests.

As a fitting contrast to note here, the *Kankakee Daily Republican* carried these two small news items in 1925:

"Chicago, May 14 -- Lawrence Washington, negro, was hanged in the county jail at 6:08 a.m. today for killing Nunzio Mascolino, an Evanston candy shop keeper in a holdup. His fate definitely was sealed when Governor Small refused a stay."

"Chicago, June 19 -- William Sams, negro, was hanged in the county jail at 7:04 o'clock this morning for the killing of policeman Cornelius Broderick a year ago. Governor Small announced last night that he would not interfere and that the law take its course."

One might be tempted to say that justice was a matter of black and white, but green was the only color that really mattered to Governor Len Small.

Meanwhile, Harry Guzik, Walter Stevens, Spike O'Donnell and a lot of other horrible people walked the streets as free men, thanks to the money and the influence they had to convince the governor to spring them from prison.

James "Fur" Sammons

Fur Sammons

James "Fur" Sammons was "a certified psychopath and a killer and he took enormous pride in both of those facts," according to his biography on AmericanMafia.com.

In 1900, Sammons and four friends kidnapped an 11-year-old girl off the street and brutally raped and mutilated her. They broke her nose, punched out one of her eyes and stabbed her in the vaginal area with a pencil. Sammons was arrested. In court, he smirked at the girl's parents. Sammons was convicted but he was paroled after three years.

On May 17, 1903, two months after his release, Sammons murdered Chicago saloonkeeper Patrick Barrett. Sammons was convicted in 1904 and sentenced to death. Governor Richard Yates commuted his sentence to life in prison.

Sammons paid a substantial amount of money to Mob gunman Porky Dillon to buy his freedom from Governor Small.

Dillon was another criminal freed from prison by Governor Small. Dillon became a "bagman" for Governor Small, and so the bribe money from Sammons found its way into the governor's hands. On June 20, 1923, Governor Small commuted Sammons' sentence to 50 years in prison. This made Sammons eligible for parole, and one month later the governor's parole board let Sammons out of prison.

Sammons continued his violent career and was said to especially enjoy his duties as a machine-gunner for the Capone mob. Sammons was part of a gang that pulled off two huge payroll robberies.

"To him, a human life was of no value," Assistant State's Attorney Harry Ditchburne said of Sammons. "When he was given a machine gun and sent out on a job of murder, guards would be assigned to accompany him. It was their task to prevent him from taking pot shots at pedestrians for amusement."

In a crackdown on gangsters in 1930, Attorney General Oscar Carlstrom invoked a provision of the law to petition the courts to revoke the paroles of some of Chicago's most vicious criminals. Judge John Lyle sent Sammons back to prison.

It was the notorious criminal lawyer W.W. O'Brien who found a judge to let Sammons out of the Joliet penitentiary on a writ of *habeas corpus* in July 1932. This was another outrageous judicial act -- McHenry County Circuit Court Judge Edward Shurtleff basically reversed the Illinois Supreme Court! On June 18, 1931, the high court refused O'Brien's motion for *habeas corpus* and denied Sammons a rehearing. That should have been the end of it. But O'Brien went shopping for a friendlier judge and got Shurtleff (who incidentally was Speaker of the House in 1909 and helped with William Lorimer's fraudulent election). Shurtleff agreed to a new hearing -- with the same brief and the same evidence -- and freed Sammons.

Now a free man, Fur Sammons was recruited by "Three Fingers" Jack White (another bloodthirsty gangster who won a parole from Governor Small in 1923) to work for Frank "The Enforcer" Nitti in the labor union war with the Touhy gang. A few days after his 1932 release from Joliet, Sammons machine-gunned Patrick Berrell, international vice president of the Teamsters and Touhy's man in the Teamsters, and Willie Marks, a hired gun formerly with Bugs Moran's gang. Berrell had succeeded Con Shea in his position with the union.

Carlstrom's appeal of the release of Sammons was decided in December 1933 by the Illinois Supreme Court, which overruled Judge Shurtleff and ordered Sammons back to prison. Sammons stayed there until being paroled in December 1952. Fur Sammons died at age 76 on May 20, 1960, in a room in the Englewood Arms Hotel on West 62nd Street.

The pardon for Ira Perry also created quite a scandal for the governor.

Ira Perry Jr. came from a wealthy Chicago family but an evil streak led him to a career of robbery and murder. Perry committed 60 robberies, netting $200,000, and he murdered two Chicago jewelers during his career. Perry pleaded guilty in 1922 and was sentenced to a life term in the Joliet penitentiary.

He was paroled and released on Oct. 31, 1925.

Prosecutors and police were not notified of Perry's parole hearing. In fact, they didn't learn about it until Dec. 9. That's when they blew their tops.

So did the public. The president of the Retail Jewelers Association condemned the parole. State's Attorney H.E. Fullenwider filed a petition for a writ of *mandamus,* asking that Perry be returned to prison. The petition named Chauncey H. Jenkins, director of the Illinois Department of Public Welfare; Will Colvin, supervisor of paroles; Joliet warden John Whitman; and Charles Hitch, W.W. Rhoades and Charles McCall, members of the Pardons and Paroles board.

Perry's father had made a fortune by inventing an automobile lock. Their high powered attorney was Charles Erbstein, the slippery lawyer associated with Mob figures and with officials in the Small administration who got in trouble.

The Illinois Supreme Court granted the petition and ordered Perry to be apprehended. It said it was wrong to change Perry's charge from murder to manslaughter.

Governor Small issued a statement, denying there was any secrecy about the parole of Ira Perry.

Ira Perry did not get away with it, and neither did Len Small.

Perry continued seeking parole. At his hearing in October 1931, he was represented by Harry Curtis, son of the vice president of the United States. Harry Curtis was investigated in 1930 for shaking down Chicago contractors in exchange for government contracts.

Len Small's brazen acts caused hecklers at his campaign rallies in 1924 to sing a parody of *Oh Promise Me* with the words *Oh Pardon Me.*

Governor Small's Pardon Mill

The individual pardons and paroles coming from Governor Small's office became a series of separate scandals, like little hand grenades going off before the public every so often throughout Small's eight years in office. But the whole system exploded in one huge bomb in May 1926 when it was revealed that the governor was connected to a "pardon mill" that freed thousands of convicts who paid bribes for pardons and paroles.

Grand juries were convened in Chicago and Joliet to investigate the entire Illinois prison system under Governor Small.

Interestingly, the scandal came to light because of an incident at that time which involved another Kankakee man.

Charles Duschowski was as vicious a killer who ever came out of Kankakee. He and Charles Shader murdered Chicago Police Officer Harry J. Busse in 1922. They were convicted and sent to the penitentiary in Joliet. On May 5, 1926, Duschowski beat Deputy Warden Peter Klein to death in his office, and then Duschowski and six other convicts, including Shader, escaped. All but one was recaptured. The six went on trial and were sentenced to hang. The case made national headlines. TIME magazine did a story in its Dec. 6, 1926 issue, noting in the last paragraph: "Last week in Joliet, the jury announced its verdict...and soon, six forms will dangle on the gallows, unless they are saved by further legal delay by Gov. Len Small, crook-pardoner."

Duschowski and two others were hanged in the jail yard in downtown Joliet on July 14, 1927. Shader was captured in Chicago a year later, and when he was hanged in Joliet on Oct. 10, 1928, he became the last convict executed by public hanging in Illinois. The rope was replaced by the electric chair after that.

The murder of Klein was shocking enough, but it was revealed that he was a part of a "pardons for bribes" scheme. Letters implicating top state officials were found on his desk next to his bloody corpse.

The investigation led to uncovering the elaborate scheme through which

Governor Small and his associates sold thousands of pardons and paroles.

Hope House was founded in 1902 by Maud Ballington Booth of the Volunteers of America as a shelter for destitute ex-convicts. Major Michael A. Messlein became superintendent of the place shortly after it opened. When Len Small became governor and named Will Colvin as superintendent of pardons and paroles, Messlein went into business with the administration.

In February 1921, Messlein founded Major Engineering Co. Its stated purpose was "to manufacture, buy, build, sell and trade in engine pumps and to acquire by purchase and lease certain patents on pumps."

Major Engineering's real purpose was a clearinghouse where pardons and paroles were bought by the thousands by criminals in state prisons.

Messlein procured pardons and paroles for convicts who bought stock in his company. That was how the scheme worked.

And Major Engineering Co. didn't wait for criminals to come to them. Convicts behind bars were solicited by Messlein and associates.

In May 1926, Messlein claimed he had obtained more than 8,000 pardons and paroles for his "stockholders" in this manner.

It was, in the words of Attorney General Oscar Carlstrom, a "pardon mill."

Investigators went to Major Engineering's factory at 3411 Indiana Ave. and found a few idle pieces of machinery and no evidence that any real manufacturing activity had taken place there.

George "Bugs" Moran -- the gang chief who was the intended target of Capone's massacre at the garage on Clark Street on St. Valentine's Day in 1929 -- was another who bought a parole. His 1918 robbery conviction was upheld by the state Supreme Court in December 1922. He bought $300 worth of "stock" and was paroled less than two months later. Moran was paroled to the custody of Messlein and went on to another three decades of gangland violence and petty thievery.

The Touhy gang was one of the more infamous gangs of bootleggers, thieves and union racketeers of the 1920s. Joseph Touhy, in prison for the 1918 murder of a saloonkeeper, was given a pardon by Governor Small in October 1923 after his gang came up with $6,500.

Frank Parker was known as "the flying bootlegger" because he owned an airplane and used it to smuggle booze from Canada. A burglary conviction in 1914 got him a 5-to-25-year sentence in Joliet. He was out in a few years and was operating a car theft ring and several big private breweries by the mid-1920s. Parker was one of the more notable gangsters of the 1920s, with ties to several gangs, including Bugs Moran and Hymie Weiss. Parker bought his pardon from Governor Small in 1923 by "investing" in Major Engineering Co. In fact, Parker's 6,000 shares had this gangster listed in the company records as "general manager."

Arthur Carver, a former deputy warden, told the grand jury that Parker was the personal pilot for Chauncey Jenkins and Will Colvin.

A big stockholder in Major Engineering was Will Colvin, superintendent of the Pardons and Paroles Board. He owned $25,000 in stock. Arthur Dodge Warner, a member of the parole board, also was an investor in Major Engineering Co.

At that time, Messlein told investigators he was proud of the 8,000 pardons he procured for convicts.

Investigators found several letters in Messlein's possession. One letter from Messlein was a plea to Governor Small to grant a pardon to Walter Stevens.

"My Dear Governor, Knowing it will be of interest to you to read them, I am enclosing herein letters from authorities in Florida which we have received, proving the innocence of Walter Stevens of the accusations in the Florida matter which have been brought against him by some of his enemies. I am sending these copies to you so that if any mention is made to you regarding this matter, you will have the correct information before you."

Another letter to Small was dated Feb. 22, 1926: "Some months ago I mailed to you recommendations from Warden John L. Whitman for the restoration of the rights of citizenship of Anthony Lebecki and John Nozia, which young men some time ago, under my supervision, completed their terms of parole from the Illinois State Penitentiary at Joliet and received their final discharge. Not having received their citizenship papers yet, I have become concerned, lest the matter might have slipped your mind and am therefore writing again. Will you please mail papers to my care at 4064 Broadway, Chicago, Illinois, so that I can pass them on to these young men, who are anxiously waiting to receive them?"

When the letters were revealed in May 1926, Assistant State's Attorney Joseph Savage remarked, "Perhaps the young men were anxious to cast their votes in the recent primary."

Another letter revealed the attempt to free Pete McCann, a member of the vicious Egan's Rats gang in St. Louis, who was incarcerated at Menard. The letter, from John Gibbons of Institutional Supply Co. of Chicago, was to a St. Louis man who said that the members of the pardons and paroles board would be visited and the process would "require two or three trips to Springfield to get in close touch with the powers that be." The letter mentioned $10,000 as the price to free McCann.

A letter on Klein's desk was from someone named Larry to a convict named Red. Larry wrote that he would get the money and see Messlein, adding that Messlein had taken care of him. "You know he is in business with W. Colvin and he stands strong with him. I am certain Messlein can spring you."

Colvin sent copies of the pamphlet his department printed, with the explanations for the pardons and paroles exposed in a series of *Chicago Tribune* stories. He told Messlein to distribute them "where they will do the most good," in the hands of civic and church groups.

One of the convicts who escaped after the murder of Peter Klein was Walter Stalesky. He was sent to Joliet in January 1921 on a 10-to-life sentence for armed robbery. Stalesky "invested" in Major Engineering, and Messlein was working on getting him pardoned at the time.

Another letter was from Will Colvin to William F. Schofield, 738 N. State St. Schofield had been a partner of murdered Mob boss Dean O'Banion and this was the address of their florist shop. Schofield was intervening through Messlein on behalf of Michael Cunningham, in prison for a 1916 murder.

Prosecutors said Messlein was the "middleman" between convicts and Colvin in the selling of paroles.

A letter from Hugh Olcott of Marengo was sent to Ed Girard, an officer of Major Engineering. "Friend Ed: I have a friend who wants to get a fellow out of the penitentiary, and how is he to go about it? We will come in if you think we can do anything." Girard wrote back and told Olcott to come and talk about it.

Also buying stock in Major Engineering was Walter Stevens. And so, Messlein made appeals to Governor Small for Stevens' freedom in November 1923 and in September 1924. Messlein became one of the many notables who suddenly had an alibi for Stevens' whereabouts at the time of the Aurora shootings.

Lee O'Neil Browne had a letter on file, saying, "I will do anything in my power and go to the end of the chapter for Walter. I would regard no road too hard for me to travel."

Browne did not specify what extraordinary measures he was taking to free one of Al Capone's most vicious killers.

And Browne noted that he wanted to be sure that lawyer W.W. O'Brien did not take any of his credit on Walter Stevens' behalf.

Messlein wrote back to Browne, saying he presented Stevens' case before the parole board and "Mr. Colvin was pleased, as it gave him new angles in the case. The board seemed well impressed and I look for good results." Messlein said he also talked with a preacher who had letters and petitions in support of Stevens.

Messlein added that the board would act quickly if Browne could get the Florida murder charge against Stevens dismissed.

"Please let me know how the Florida matter stands, and how soon it will be finished, as Walter is getting wild again," Messlein wrote. "The board called him in the week of their meeting and had a talk with him that seemed satisfactory, but when the other men received their tickets last week and Walter's was not among them, he immediately became nervous and now feels that we are not doing things for him, so please hurry up the things you said you would do for him so we can get him out at the earliest possible time."

Both Browne and Messlein worked to get special favors for Walter Stevens during the short time he was in prison. Browne wrote to the warden for comfortable shoes, warning him not to upset Stevens. Messlein told the warden Stevens would be allowed visiting privileges from certain people.

Grand juries in both Chicago and Joliet called witnesses. Lucas Pollack of Chicago testified that his nephew, Ralph Steiner, was in Pontiac prison for car theft. Pollack said his landlord, Yellow Kid Weil, told him to go see Messlein. Messlein suggested that if Pollack bought stock in his company, freedom could be arranged. Similar stories came from other witnesses.

Claude Peters, the business agent for the janitor's union, told how William Quesse bought his pardon. He said Quesse and a lot of union members bought stock in Major Engineering. "The stock was recommended at all union meetings," he said. A number of other members of the union testified to the same thing.

Mrs. F.J. Halveland told the grand jury that Will Colvin expressly asked her for money to free her son from prison.

Mrs. Halveland said she went to Springfield to see Colvin to ask about a parole. She told Colvin she had been referred by a Chicago lawyer. Colvin told her hiring a lawyer was a waste of money.

"Is there no way I can help my boy out?" asked Mrs. Halveland.

"Yes, there is a way," Colvin replied. He paused a long time until his meaning began to sink in.

"Do you mean money?" Mrs. Halveland asked.

"Yes, I mean money," Colvin said.

The woman went to Chicago and asked her lawyer about this and the lawyer sent her to Messlein. Messlein promised that her son would be out in a month. But Messlein didn't show up at the boy's parole hearing because his mother didn't pay. The young man finally was released after serving his sentence.

The grand jury also looked into the conditions at the prisons that led to Peter Klein's murder. Joliet's Warden John Whitman told how prison discipline was broken down by graft and politics.

"It was common talk among the prisoners that it didn't profit them at all to obey the rules and gain credits under the merit system," Whitman said. The warden, who made criminal justice a career, said Klein got his job through politics, against Whitman's wishes. He said Klein was part of the problem of prison graft.

Whitman said the escaped murderers told a guard, "The guys who can get dough or political pull, those they spring. We could never get out, so we had to take a chance."

Klein had been murdered by desperate escapees who could not afford the price of a ticket out.

Whitman said Klein ran the Joliet prison, taking orders from Chauncey Jenkins in Springfield.

An affidavit was presented to the grand jury from Julius Horney, who worked as a "keeper" supervising construction at Stateville prison in 1925 and 1926. "There was general talk among the prisoners, and I have heard it repeatedly, that there was a pardon mill in Chicago. To the prisoners, it was known as Hope House. There was a general feeling among the prisoners that if they had the money they could buy their freedom. I have heard expressions repeatedly as, 'If I had one grand, I could get out, that's all it takes,'" Horney said.

"There was no discipline and no control over the prisoners," Horney said. "In my opinion, the prisoners were running the institution. If any unruly prisoner was reported, his punishment would depend on his relationship with Deputy Warden Klein. That is to say, if the prisoner was a stool pigeon of Klein's, he would not be punished but return to his fellow prisoners where he could laugh and sneer at the officer who had reported him. If the prisoner happened not to be in the good graces of Deputy Warden Klein, he would be placed in solitary confinement.

"Several prisoners have told me from time to time that it was going to be only a matter of time before they were going to get him."

Horney said Klein had prisoners spy on the conduct of the officers and guards who Klein did not like and did not get along with.

Horney said Klein did more than facilitate the selling of pardons and paroles, he also had bootleg liquor made on the prison farm and sold it to Chicago gangs, and he allowed women into the prison honor farm.

Grace Temple, a member of the Chicago school board and a former president of the Chicago Women's Club, told the *Tribune,* "The repeated pardoning of notorious criminals by Governor Small is a real menace to the city and state. These pardons are a disgrace, and I don't see how the governor can have any respect for himself. They are particularly a menace to the children, for they see only the surface -- that a governor is handing out pardons to murderers and thugs. Gradually, their undeveloped minds begin to think that murder is all right. They think that if a governor virtually approves such things by pardoning them, they must be all right."

Will County State's Attorney Hjalmar Rehn ran into difficulty in this investigation when he found that the Pardons and Parole Board had clamped down on inmates who might be called to testify before the grand jury. The convicts knew the board held their fate in its hands, and most did not talk. However, there were several convicts who did tell stories of others who had bought their freedom, as well as several convicts who claimed they paid but were not released.

Ira Perry and several of the other convicts who received the famous and outrageous pardons were named among those who had paid for pardons through Major Engineering.

Frank Enos was Perry's cell mate. He told the grand jury that Chicago lawyer W.S. McNamara was known as one of the "fixers" of paroles. Enos told Perry that he was going to get out of prison because McNamara was on his way to see him. Perry said he, too, was going to get out. Enos wondered how that could be, since Perry pleaded guilty to murder and had a life sentence. Enos said Perry laughed and replied, "I'll get ahold of $3,500 and you'll see."

McNamara told Enos he could get him a pardon for $5,000. Enos said he didn't have that kind of money but he would see what he could do. Enos scraped up $500, gave it to McNamara, and was paroled.

Not all who were granted commutations, pardons and paroles were high powered gangsters with lots of money. Tickets out of the penitentiary were for sale to anyone for a price. Among the thousands of pardons and paroles granted by the Small administration, a number of them stood out for their audacity. Here are a few, from the headlines of several newspapers of the era.

James "Yellow Kid" Weil was one of the better and more notorious con men in the early 1900s. Governor Small gave him a pardon. The reason, explained by the parole board, was that he was "an excellent model of deportment, obedience, industry and decency" while in the Joliet penitentiary. However, Walter Szalocinski was a petty con man whose record behind bars was not so good. Szalocinski was so bad that Pontiac Warden I.M. Lish had him transferred to Joliet because of his record of fighting, insolence, making weapons and general indecency.

But Szalocinski did receive a pardon from the governor in 1923. "To hear him tell it, Weil was so angelically good, the king who can do no wrong was ashamed to confine him longer in the foul atmosphere of the prison. The other fellow was apparently so satanically bad, his Excellency was afraid to keep him longer from the pure air of freedom," the *Chicago Tribune* editorialized about the two cases.

August Boetcher sexually assaulted a nine-year-old Park Ridge girl on Sept. 27, 1919. But Boetcher was a prominent dairyman with powerful friends. The local justice of the peace advised the girl's mother not to do anything. It took the Park Ridge Women's Club to gather the evidence and see the case prosecuted.

Six days after the attack, Boetcher saw the girl once more and tried to entice her into his car again. Boetcher also tried to bribe the girl's mother to drop charges.

Boetcher finally found the right person to bribe. He was paroled on Oct. 28, 1922, less than 11 months after entering the penitentiary.

Lambert McKay was convicted in 1920 of raping his 15-year-old stepdaughter. He had been sexually abusing her for two years. He was sentenced to 1-to-20 years, but was paroled after one year. His brother, William McKay, was convicted in 1919 of sexually abusing his three-year-old daughter and went to prison on a five-year sentence. He was paroled after three years; a year later, he was back in prison for more sexual offenses.

Sam Gitlitz raped a 12-year-old girl on July 2, 1920 in the boarding house where he stayed. He threatened to kill her if she talked. A week later, he was caught by the child's mother in the middle of a second rape. When doctors examined the girl, she was found to have a venereal disease. Gitlitz was convicted and sent to Joliet on Feb. 9, 1921. He was freed on parole one year later.

Patrick Palomo was convicted of raping four girls, one age seven. He was convicted and sent to Joliet on Sept. 23, 1920 on a 20-year sentence. He was freed on parole one year later.

Louis Meyer and Jack Gilhouse took two teenage waitresses for a car ride on June 13, 1917. They got the girls drunk and then beat, robbed and raped them before shoving them into the road. Both men were convicted and sentenced to 14 years in prison. Influential people started working on their behalf for a commutation or pardon, but when their case came up in December 1919, Governor Lowden refused their request. Governor Small had them paroled in 1922.

Ivan Hawk and Marvin Plfugardt took an 18-year-old girl from a Chicago amusement park on July 18, 1921, drugged, beat and raped her. She was in the hospital for seven days before she could move. Hawk and Plfugardt were arrested the next day and they were convicted in January 1922. Both were freed by Small's parole board the next year.

Tony Sansone raped an 11-year-old girl, giving her a venereal disease. He was sentenced to 10 years in 1921 and was paroled in 1925. Walter Pinkowski, a convicted burglar, raped a 19-year-old Chicago woman in her home in 1918. He was sentenced to 10 years. He escaped in 1920, was recaptured in 1923, and paroled in 1925.

William Johnston used his business office to rape two girls, ages 14 and 15. He was sentenced to eight years in jail in 1922 and was paroled in 1925. Thomas Goldberg, a paroled convict, beat a woman and raped her at gunpoint in 1919. His 14-year sentence ended with a parole in 1925.

Emilio Nicoletti raped a 19-year-old Chicago woman on Dec. 31, 1922. Five months later, while awaiting trial, Nicoletti and two other men robbed and beat a man to death. Nicoletti's 1-year-to-life sentence ended with a parole in a year and a half.

John Lundgreen was convicted of robbery and Herman Winkel was convicted of burglary in 1918. Lundgreen was paroled in 1921 and Winkel was paroled in 1923. That December, both men were arrested for burglarizing a railroad box car.

Harry Cramer, Charles Cramer, Alex Brodie and Harry Fein received sentences of 1-year-to-life for robbing the Washington Park Bank in 1916. Small had them paroled in 1922, after pressure from several legislators. A week later, Charles Cramer was wanted in New York for a gangland murder.

State Rep. Harry Weisbrod of Chicago took a pardon signed by Governor Small to the Bridewell jail in Chicago to personally spring D.W. Korshack on April 2, 1925. Korshack had spent a week in jail, on a four-month sentence for his hit-and-run conviction in which a man was crippled.

Joseph Carenassi shot and killed Joseph Muccio in Chicago in 1916. He pleaded guilty and got a 25-year sentence. He was paroled in 1925. Filippo Scaletta murdered Vincenzo Divareo in 1916, pleaded guilty and was paroled from his 25-year sentence in 1925. James McCullom had just gotten out of prison for robbery when he murdered George Terrebery in 1916. McCullom was freed when Governor Small commuted his 20-year sentence in 1925. Edward Kremhelle killed a man while robbing a Chicago restaurant in 1915. He pleaded guilty to murder and to four robberies. He was paroled from his 25-year sentence in 1925. Charles Guile murdered a man while robbing a Chicago store and was sentenced to 20 years in 1917. He was paroled in 1925. Julius Woss and Sigmund Smolek beat and robbed a cab driver in 1925, leaving him for dead on the side of the road. They went to jail and were paroled in 11 months.

Dora Waterman chopped her husband Louis to death with a meat cleaver in 1921. She was sentenced to 17 years but was pardoned in less than two. Hilda Exlund stabbed her husband Frank to death with a butcher knife in 1919. William Winters murdered his wife Julia the same year. Both Exlund and Winters were pardoned in 1924. Patrick Walsh cut his wife's throat in 1915 and was sentenced to life in prison. He was paroled in 1925.

Floyd Flood of St. Louis was pardoned by Governor Small on Jan. 21, 1926. Small said Flood was innocent of the bank robbery conviction. Flood was out of prison for less than 12 hours when he was picked up on a warrant from Clayton, Mo., for an armed robbery there.

The race riots in East St. Louis in 1917 were among the worst in American history. Dozens of African-American men, women and children were killed at random, and whole neighborhoods of houses were burned. White mobs roamed the black neighborhoods in a mad frenzy, as they murdered by shooting, beating and lynching.

Eleven white men were convicted of murder and sent to prison. They were freed by Governor Small in 1924 -- the day after the election, in which the governor won a second term. Small said the 11 murderers were "no more guilty than hundreds of others who participated in the riots" and they had suffered enough after seven years behind bars.

The 14 black men convicted for defending themselves did not get pardons.

Labor unions have had a pretty bloody history as its members fought for better wages and conditions. But its bloody history in the early quarter of the twentieth century had little to do with those basic rights and more to do with mobsters taking over the unions and going to war over control and territory.

And the big money of these union gangsters meant they could buy their freedom from a willing and crooked governor.

Electrician union boss Umbrella Mike Boyle was one of Governor Small's favorite gangsters. In addition to becoming an accomplished union thug, Boyle became an expert at fixing juries. His reputation was such that Len Small turned to him in 1922. Boyle was the go-between in smoothing the bribery of the governor's jurors in Waukegan.

Boyle's first conviction was in 1909 for conspiracy to obtain money under false pretenses, along with union thug Martin "Skinny" Madden and Fred Pouchot, sheet metal workers business agent. They paid small fines.

Boyle tried to take over Chicago's building trades in 1921 along with Little Tommy Malloy, a bloodthirsty killer who "unionized" Chicago movie projectionists through beatings and murders. A grand jury indicted Boyle and Malloy for conspiracy, in extorting money from builders to avoid labor troubles. Governor Small granted Boyle a pardon. Malloy paid off the jury in his case and walked away. Malloy continued his mob activities until "hit men" sent by Frank Nitti took off his head in a hail of machine gun fire in 1935.

Governor Small made a habit of pardoning labor union criminals. During a rash of union violence in 1915, Robert Johnson shot Axel Alex to death. He was convicted of murder. Governor Small pardoned him.

On Aug. 7, 1925, the governor pardoned six labor leaders who were convicted of conspiracy in bombings and extortion for their part in labor wars in 1919.

The six who bought their pardons were Theodore Vind, a former president of the South Chicago Labor Assembly; Emma Porter Pipes, former business agent of the South Chicago Waitresses Union; Stanley Walczak, former business agent of the Meat Cutters Union; Orville Blevins, former business agent of the Teamsters; Frank Ambroski, former president of the Meat Cutters Union; Edward Boatman, former business agent of the Teamsters. They were convicted but remained free on appeal until the Illinois Supreme Court upheld the convictions on Feb. 22, 1925. At that time, only Amborski and Boatman could be found. They spent less than six months in jail before being freed, while their fellow bombers never spent a day in jail before getting their pardons.

Bernard O'Reilly was a 23-year-old motorman with a wife and two-year-old daughter. His wife had been ill and O'Reilly needed extra money to pay her hospital bills, so he took a second job as a laborer at a building going up at 4017 Irving Park Blvd. Thomas Jakubowski, business agent for the Hodcarrier's Union, noticed O'Reilly on the job and demanded to see his union card. O'Reilly had a card for the motorman's union but not one for the laborers. Jakubowski shot and killed O'Reilly. That was on Feb. 9, 1920. Jakubowski was convicted of murder on July 6 and was sentenced to 25 years.

But the union official's friends raised a lot of money for "legal expenses" and Governor Small freed Jakubowski on Aug. 3, 1924.

Arthur Benedicto Raymond and Raymond Harrison Williams were union officers during the bloody strike of the Master Barbers Union in 1918. Barber shops were bombed, men were beaten and several people were shot. On April 26, barber Joseph Sangerman was shot and paralyzed. An hour later, the gunmen, mistaking law student Willard Porter for a barber, shot and killed him. The union thugs who did one bombing were caught and they implicated Williams and Raymond. The two were convicted in October 1918 and remained free until the state Supreme Court upheld the conviction in February 1921. Williams and Raymond went to the penitentiary on May 13. They sought a pardon from Governor Small, and he commuted their sentences on Dec. 13.

Cook County State's Attorney Robert Crowe prosecuted Fred "Frenchy" Mader, the president of the Building Trades Council. Mader used violence and threats of strikes to extort 10 per cent of the costs of new buildings from Chicago construction firms. Even though jurors were bribed and witnesses were intimidated, Mader and 49 members of his gang were convicted.

Governor Small pardoned them all before any of them served any prison time.

It was the pardons of Mader and his union gangsters that led State's Attorney Crowe to make his remark that his biggest handicap was the parole and pardon system, where Governor Small "lets them out as fast as we put them in."

William Quesse was a powerful labor boss -- president of the Building Service Employees International Union. The union was involved in a terrible labor dispute in 1920 that escalated into bombings, beatings, intimidation, extortion and bribery. In 1922, Quesse and other union leaders were convicted of conspiracy and were sentenced to 1-to-5 years in prison. Quesse was pardoned by Governor Small in 1924 before ever having to report to prison.

It later was uncovered that Quesse bribed Small to obtain his pardon. The bribery was both with money and with political work. While his case was pending on appeal, Quesse had his union members campaign for Governor Small and circulate pledge cards. Janitors told tenants to sign pledge cards or they would go without heat.

Quesse was a rich man when he died. He left the union leadership to his nephew, William McFetridge, a local union president who ran for the presidency of the international union in 1937. George Scalise, a local union president in New York, got the job because he had strong Mob ties and was the choice of New York mobster Anthony Carfano and Chicago Mob boss Frank Nitti. McFetridge finally got the top job in 1940 after Scalise was convicted of bribery, embezzlement and labor racketeering. McFetridge, a very close political ally of Chicago Mayor Richard J. Daley, later headed the Chicago Park District.

Governor Small's pardons of 20 members of the Communist Labor Party convicted under the Illinois Sedition Act caused a national scandal in November 1922.

William Bross Lloyd was a wealthy communist -- something that should be an oxymoron but never is for their leaders. He and 16 others were convicted in March 1921 of seditious acts and sentenced to five years.

"No human agency can accurately determine how long any human being shall be incarcerated. These men are not criminals," Small said.

General John J. Pershing called for Small's impeachment at a meeting of 1,500 members of the Chicago Association of Commerce. Brigadier General Charles G. Dawes, former director of the budget (and future vice president) introduced a resolution stating that Small had "besmirched the fair name of the State of Illinois and of the United States" by commuting the sentence of Lloyd and other communists. The resolution passed, as the crowd yelled "Impeach him!"

When the crowd quieted down, Dawes told them it would do no good to try to impeach the powerful governor. But by commuting the sentences, Dawes said, Small "has invaded the judicial part of the government in thus repudiating the finding of a jury of the people, the judgment of the Supreme Court of the state of Illinois and the judgment of the Justice representing the Supreme Court of the United States."

Referring to the Lloyd pardon and Klan members in state government, Pershing said, "There is little difference between the malign influence of the radical who bores from within and the malign influence of the Ku Klux Klan. We cannot shut our eyes to the activities of the so-called Invisible Empire, whose members in office disregard their public duty and allow their criminals to go unpunished."

In February 1925, the Illinois Manufacturers Association launched a drive to make the public aware and to start an official investigation of what it called Governor Small's "wholesale penitentiary deliveries."

Governor Small apparently felt so comfortable with criminals that he even hired them on his personal staff. That was the case with "Big Gus" Zeidler, who Small hired as his personal chef, just after Small had Zeidler paroled from the Chester penitentiary from a sentence for bank robbery.

Zeidler was no petty crook to be rehabilitated as a chef.

Big Gus was well known in several states as a robber, a car thief and a major "fence" for stolen goods. Zeidler worked with gangster Frank Parker in the stolen car ring.

Zeidler, Teddy Clark and Alexander McKeown robbed the Tri-City Bank in Edwardsville of $17,000 in May 1918. The crooks had a falling out. Clark objected to only getting $2,700 as his share of the loot. His body later was found in the Missouri River, with his throat cut.

Zeidler and McKeown went on trial, were convicted and went to the penitentiary on a sentence of 10-years-to-life. At their trial, May Clark, Teddy's widow, testified that Zeidler and McKeown were in her apartment at the time of the robbery. This earned her four years in prison for perjury.

Small had Zeidler paroled in May 1923 and brought him to Springfield.

When this parole became public knowledge in November, there was a great public outrage. Zeidler was arrested on Nov. 10 in the kitchen of the executive mansion.

Zeidler had been convicted of bank robbery but he never was charged with the assault on cashier R.B. Studebaker as Zeidler attempted to lock the bank employee in the vault. Zeidler was taken back to Madison County and charged with assault with intent to kill.

Will Colvin, superintendent of the Pardon and Parole Board, demanded that the sheriff release Zeidler on the argument that, as a parolee, Zeidler was a ward of the state.

"During his confinement in Chester penitentiary, Zeidler was a good prisoner," Colvin said. "He is a wonderful cook, and acted as a cook for the various prison wardens during his stay. I refused to assent to his parole until I was convinced he intended to go straight."

Zeidler was supposed to be paroled to Victor McBroom's café in Kankakee, but he was so talented as a chef that Governor Small kept Big Gus for himself.

Colvin filed suit to have Zeidler released, and he criticized the Madison County sheriff. "Common decency to the executive of the state should have caused the sheriff to exercise better judgment." Perhaps Colvin didn't remember that two years earlier, another sheriff arrested the Boss himself in the executive mansion.

Small was not going to let this pass. He hired Chicago lawyers Clarence Darrow and Patrick H. O'Donnell to fight for Zeidler's freedom. These were the same lawyers who won an acquittal for Fred Lundin on charges of embezzling money from the Chicago school system. In their writ for *habeas corpus,* the lawyers alleged that Zeidler's arrest was a political plot by the governor's enemies to embarrass him before the 1924 elections. The petition also included the "ward of the state" argument.

It was the following January when Madison County Judge Joseph David ruled against Zeidler. The judge also criticized Zeidler's new attorneys, William McNamara and Richard Westbrook, for injecting politics into the case. Westbrook had been an assistant state's attorney in Cook County until he was fired by Robert Crowe for "fixing" a case. McNamara's specialty was buying paroles for his clients.

A few weeks later, Judge Louis Reuter denied Zeidler's appeal and sent Big Gus back to the slammer. Governor Small had the last word, pardoning Zeidler again shortly after that.

The Kankakee Daily Republican ran several articles in 1924, answering the *Tribune's* stories about the pardons. Here are Len Small's explanations for the few pardons he addressed in his newspaper.

These explanations in the Kankakee newspaper were approved by Small but were attributed to Chauncey H. Jenkins and Lee O'Neil Browne. They also were put in a 48-page pamphlet, of which 300,000 copies were printed at state expense and widely distributed during that election year.

Alcide Chagnon, a Kankakee County deputy from St. Anne, raped a 15-year-old girl in a cell at the Kankakee County jail in 1919. He pleaded guilty and was sentenced to 10 years in the penitentiary. Chagnon was paroled in 1921. Jenkins justified the parole by explaining that the sexual assault was only a "statutory" one. Chagnon was 50 years old, the father of 11 children and a member of an "influential family of Kankakee," Jenkins said. "The elderly man suffered for his misconduct. In his incarceration, the two objects of the law were met. First, his incarceration furnished an example. Second, his reformation was accomplished." (Chagnon died in 1950 at age 82).

Jacob Klein was a millionaire who worked for no pay as a DuPage County sheriff's deputy for 15 years. On Sept. 20, 1921, Klein shot and killed Leon Neumann during a routine traffic stop near Hinsdale. Klein was convicted of murder and sentenced to 14 years in prison. Small pardoned him on Aug. 1, 1923, after less than eight months behind bars. Small claimed that Klein, then age 61, was ill and was being sent home to die in peace.

Ben Straka was sentenced in 1918 to 1-year-to-life. It was his seventh term in the penitentiary for numerous offenses dating back to 1907, including burglary and armed robbery. Straka was paroled in 1921, and less than three months later he shot a man during a robbery.

Jenkins said Straka was required to serve at least four years and so Straka's parole date was determined before Small became governor. This was not true. The terms of the order was that Straka was to have a hearing after four years.

Theodore Lodin was sentenced in July 1922 to 1-to-14 years in prison for perjury. He lied under oath when called as a juror in the Quesse case. He was asked if he had been part of a criminal case previously; he said no, although he had been tried for burglary. The state indicted Lodin for taking a bribe to vote for Quesse's acquittal in his first trial; that jury could not agree and was dismissed. Lodin was paroled in October 1923. Jenkins said Lodin was a sick man and his mistake was minor.

Jenkins' explanation for the parole of the previously mentioned rapists, Jack Gilhouse and Louis Meyer, was that the young men picked up two young women, "girls who could be easily led," and went out drinking and dancing at several roadhouses. Yes, they did attack the women in their car on the road somewhere, but neither of the young men had a previous record, and they have learned their lesson.

Herman Blumson swindled Chicago banks out of $200,000. He was sent to prison for forgery, embezzlement and for operating a confidence game. He was paroled in 1923 after less than three years behind bars. Blumson, alias H. Blume, alias Harold Benjamin, was president of a cereal company in Chicago. He pulled his swindles by presenting false bills of lading to various banks and then drawing funds against the figure. He ran from the law and finally was caught in Africa. He was returned to Chicago and pleaded guilty.

Jenkins said Blumson was old and ill and his release was merciful. Blumson did not pay back any of the money he swindled.

Jenkins did not offer much of a reason for freeing Arthur Raymond and Ray Williams, convicted of terrorism in the 1918 barber's union war -- he just cited the endorsement of their union for the decision.

Ernest Gringas sexually assaulted an 11-year-old girl in Chicago in July 1920. He pleaded guilty and got a sentence of 1-to-20 years. He was out of prison a year later. Jenkins said that prior to this offense, Gringas "was a man of good character, upright in his business dealings and had never been in prior trouble." Jenkins cited a Social Services report stating that women in the girl's neighborhood said the child was "snippy and impudent to her mother" and that her mother often would have to look for her when it got dark outside. Gringas good, girl bad.

Pleas Veals, a 22-year-old man with a wife and two children in Alabama, came to Chicago looking for a job. On Jan. 13, 1920, Veals attacked and sexually assaulted a nine-year-old girl in her home while the girl was playing with an 11-year-old girl. Veals pleaded guilty in May and went to prison. Within 16 months, he was paroled and sent back to Alabama. Jenkins cited a parole board member's statement that "we are inclined to believe his story, that this was a case of consent and payment."

Consent and payment with a nine-year-old girl, this is a valid defense? Jenkins said that Veals was in trouble because he unhappy here, "and we believe that down South he will get along splendidly."

Child molester August Boetcher had his parole recommended "by 125 individual letters signed by practically every householder in the village of Park Ridge."

Bertha Wiebeck came to Chicago from Pawnee Rock, Kansas in late 1919, looking for a housekeeping job that would save the family farm. Seeking information, she asked a man she thought she could trust -- Chicago Police Officer Dorsey Chambliss. Instead of helping her, Chambliss took the 17-year-old girl to Emma Ross' house of prostitution at 3525 S. State St., where Bertha was held and raped numerous times. Bertha finally was taken to the county hospital where she died on Feb. 9, 1920. Her deathbed statement named Chambliss and what he did. Chambliss and Ross were sentenced to 1-to-5-years. Chambliss and Ross were paroled in April 1923, just two and a half years after going to prison. The reason for their paroles, Jenkins said, was that the pair "had over-served their sentences." Two months after his release, Chambliss was arrested for murdering a man in a business deal in Mound City.

Hugh Shanley was paroled in August 1923 after three years and eight months on a burglary conviction. No excuse was given but Jenkins said several state legislators agreed with the parole recommendation.

William Paschel was chief clerk in the Cook County jail. He pleaded guilty in 1923 to stealing valuables left in his custody by prisoners. His 1-to-10-year sentence ended with a parole after 11 months. Jenkins said Paschel had been punished enough.

Lee O'Neil Browne

So who were these defenders of the governor, Jenkins and Browne?

Chauncey H. Jenkins was Small's director of Public Welfare, which was in charge of prisons, pardons and paroles. He was one of three men who put up Small's bail when the governor was arrested. Jenkins also was the one accused of trying to bribe a grand jury member to not return the indictments against Len Small in July 1921.

Chauncey H. Jenkins

In November 1923, Assistant District Attorney Samuel Gross and Detective Fred Stange came to the state capitol with a warrant signed by Wisconsin Gov. J.J. Blaine for the extradition of Orrin Sweatt on a number of fraud charges. Sweatt's lawyer was George Gillespie, who also was a lawyer for Len Small and for Thompson's henchmen.

Sweatt's family was a contributor to Small's campaign. Wisconsin had a hard time with the extradition papers. After much delay, Jenkins decided that the warrants and supporting affidavits were "*prima facie* evidence that no crime was committed." Wisconsin prosecutors got more evidence, only to find more delays by Jenkins in turning over a Small supporter.

When Jenkins learned the lawyer and detective were down the hall, Jenkins jumped out of a statehouse window and ran away. Stange saw Jenkins jump and run. Stange followed. He caught Jenkins. Stange said, "This is the conduct of a child and hardly that of a grown man. Why leave by a window?" Jenkins replied, "I know it. But I haven't any explanation. I can't help myself."

Governor Blaine wrote to Governor Small, asking why his paroles chief jumped out a window to evade serving justice. He did not get a reply.

Jenkins -- a former Sangamon County probate judge -- tried to get the state Republican convention in 1924 to nominate him as its candidate for Illinois Supreme Court justice. Despite the pressure applied by Governor Small and Chicago's City Hall, the delegates could not bring themselves to such an act.

Lee O'Neil Browne was a state representative and lawyer from Ottawa who was put on trial twice for bribing Charles A. White and three other members of the state legislature to make William Lorimer a senator in 1909. The legislators admitted that Browne bribed them. The jury could not reach a verdict in the first trial, amid rumors of jury tampering. Browne was acquitted in a second trial, but a member of that jury later admitted he was bribed into voting "not guilty."

Browne's lawyer in this trial was Charles Erbstein, a favorite of Chicago's high profile criminals. Browne's trial interrupted Erbstein's defense of notorious Kankakee madam Nell Clark.

It was sleazeball Browne who arranged the purchase of the Guzik pardons with Al Capone and Governor Small in 1923. Browne also strongly, and successfully, worked to have Governor Small free one of Al Capone's top triggermen, cop-killer Walter Stevens.

Browne helped clear the way in the legislature to eliminate the Public Utilities Commission and replace it with the Illinois Commerce Commission, and he gave a glowing speech on behalf of Frank L. Smith at the time.

In Small's early months as governor, Browne acted as his "majority leader" in the House on a lot of legislation Small was trying to push through, even though Browne was a Democrat. Money talked louder than party loyalty, and his standing in the Democrat party suffered greatly because of this.

Browne owned a mansion at 640 Chapel St. in Ottawa, overlooking the Fox River. On Feb. 15, 1928, he was walking along the path on the bluff with a friend when he stooped to avoid a low-hanging branch. Browne slipped and fell 50 feet into the river's swift current. His body was fished from under the Main Street bridge.

At the time, Browne was defending Harry Hill for murdering his mother and burying her in the cellar of her Streator home. The case had gone to the jury the day before Browne's death and it came back deadlocked two days later. Browne also was working to release Chicago gangster James "Ting Eye" Murray from a federal penitentiary. Murray was part of a gang that robbed a mail train of several hundred thousand dollars in 1924. Murray provided a hideout for the gang and the loot in a building at Lafayette and Fulton streets in Ottawa.

These were the distinguished gentlemen who spoke up and defended Len Small's honor in the pardon and parole scandal.

The governor addressed the scandal several times while it was front page news, even before the news of the "pardon mill" broke. But he never really said anything substantial.

At a Labor Day speech in 1925 in Granville, Governor Small said, "I believe that human rights and justice are more sacred than corporate greed. And it makes no difference to whether a man is the poorest and humblest citizen or the wealthiest man in our state. I shall try and give him justice and a fair deal as I am able to see the right."

The governor tried to assuage the public's outrage about the pardon scandal again in an interview on Dec. 9, 1925. "Almost every few days there comes to my office some poor mother, wife, brother or sister with hardly enough funds to get them back home, begging with tears in their eyes that I release one of their family," he said. "I am human and try to be sympathetic. Maybe I have erred at times in granting their pleas; probably none of us is perfect. Only last night I was appealed to, to postpone the hanging of some unfortunate fellow in the Cook County jail. I ordered the parole board to investigate and they advised me not to grant reprieve. With all that has happened in the last few days, can you imagine what would have been directed at me if I had granted one?"

The Chicago Crime Commission didn't share Small's view. Its chief, Frederic P. Vose, said in a January 1924 report, "Illinois is suffering from too free and too indiscriminate executive exercise of the pardon law. Cases of record in Cook County indicate that law enforcement in this community has suffered a serious setback in consequence not only of this disposition to pardon, but of too great a willingness to commute and parole. No fault is to be found with the system designed to give to the repentant offender and to the reformed criminal an opportunity to regain his former place in society. But there is objection to the return to the former haunts and associations of unrepentant offenders and unreformed criminals to prey again upon law-abiding citizens and decent members of society."

Governor Small was hauled before the Will County grand jury in Joliet in May 1926 to answer questions about his pardon and parole policy, and about recent troubles at the Joliet penitentiary.

He testified for two hours, and most of it was about the lack of discipline at the Joliet penitentiary, the recent escapes and the killing of a deputy warden. Small said he considered removing the Joliet warden, but defended Jenkins and Colvin and said they would keep their jobs.

The governor said he pardoned fewer criminals than previous governors and that prisoners were serving longer terms than in the past.

"As to the talk among the prisoners that if they had sufficient money, they could secure their freedom, it has always been and probably always will be the belief and talk of convicts that had they sufficient influence or money to secure the service of able lawyers, to create propaganda by securing the support of influential newspapers, they would have won their cases," the governor said. "I do not believe that any person connected with this state administration has ever accepted any money or other emoluments for paroling, or recommending the pardon, of any convicts."

Will Colvin also was questioned by the grand jury. He was asked why he recommended the parole of Ira Perry Jr.

"Yes, I remember the Perry parole," Colvin said. "It was voted by the whole board, by myself along with other members. There was a lot of evidence presented by Perry's attorney, and the state's attorney of Cook County did not appear, despite the fact that a notice of the hearing had been published in the Chicago or Cook County law bulletin. As I recollect it, the board voted the pardon because of representations made by Perry's attorney and others appearing to show Perry's confession was obtained by third degree methods."

"And that was why you voted to parole Perry?" he was asked. "Well, I had a feeling that he ought to have it, a feeling that the charges of third degree were true," Colvin replied.

"Then you voted the parole on 'feeling,' did you?" Yes, Colvin said.

Colvin also was asked about the pardon of "Porky" Dillon, who became chief of police of Forest View after Al Capone took over the town.

Chauncey Jenkins was asked about the 386 paroles granted in the first four days of the month, including 60 on Messlein's recommendation. Jenkins put the blame for prison conditions on Warden John Whitman and the blame for pardons and paroles on Will Colvin. Jenkins denied interfering with Whitman's authority at the prison. He said Klein was hired on the recommendation of Chicago Mayor Thompson. Jenkins did admit riding in an airplane with bootlegger Frank Parker.

When the Will County grand jury reported its findings, it recommended the firing of Will Colvin as chairman of the Board of Pardons and Paroles and Chauncey Jenkins as director of the Department of Public Welfare. It also recommended firing the warden of the Joliet prison, the firing of the warden of the women's prison at Joliet, and the dismissal of a deputy warden, chief clerk, two captains and several prison guards. It also recommended firing the superintendent of the honor farm and the abolition of the honor farm.

"As long as there is politics and favoritism in the management of the prison, and paroles, trouble can be expected, and reform of convicts will be hard to achieve," the grand jury reported.

The Will County state's attorney brought the report to the governor's desk and demanded that the recommendations be implemented. He said, "Conditions at the Illinois state penitentiary are a disgrace to the state and a menace to its people."

By the end of May of 1926, the scandal was becoming too much, and someone needed to take the fall. Colvin was forced to resign his position as chairman of the Pardons and Parole Board. He was replaced by Hinton Clabaugh.

Governor Small hired Colvin right back, with a high-paying appointment to the Illinois Commerce Commission.

The grand jury, Attorney General Carlstrom, the Chicago Crime Commission, and a number of civic groups called for the firing of Chauncey Jenkins as director of the Department of Public Welfare. But Jenkins was too close to the governor and he knew too much about too many things, and Small would not fire him.

When Jenkins resigned in March 1927, Small's newspaper printed a glowing story, noting how he raised the level of care at the state's charitable institutions and how he saved the taxpayers a million dollars (although it didn't say how). "Judge Jenkins' untiring work has brought achievements and accomplishments to the Department of Public Welfare, despite the handicap of vicious political attack through which he has labored," the governor said. Jenkins was replaced by Roy Ide, another one of the men who put up Small's bond when the governor was arrested in 1921. In July 1927, Small appointed Kankakee crony Clifford B. Sawyer to the board.

By the end of May 1926, Small fired John Whitman as warden, replacing him with Elmer Green. Other prison officials recommended for firing also lost their jobs. One of these men was R.S. Jones, who had been chief clerk. He was found dead in his room in the Monroe Hotel in Joliet on June 23, the day before Small was to testify before the grand jury. Jones' death was listed as suicide.

Even the *Kankakee Daily Republican* admitted the seriousness of the situation. "There has been no concrete evidence to involve either Colvin or Jenkins, the attorney general said, but the situation had become so bad in connection with paroles that he had advised the governor for his own good to make the change," a May 26 newspaper story said.

"The disclosure by the attorney general of his conversation with the governor late yesterday after the governor had gone before the grand jury, investigating prison conditions at Joliet, came on the eve of the appearance before the special grand jury, investigating an alleged 'pardon mill' here, of Colvin and Jenkins," the newspaper story continued. "Conditions were so blatant, in connection with the parole situation, the attorney general declared that he deemed it proper to advise the chief executive in the matter."

The grand jury placed blame on Governor Small, Major Messlein and Will Colvin. But the only indictments coming out of this scandal were for the seven convicts whose escape started the whole probe.

As with many of the scandals in the Len Small administration, this did not come out of the blue. There had been talk for years about the scandalous pardons and paroles coming from the governor and the bribery in the justice system.

A panel of criminologists with the American Bar Association interviewed convicts in the Joliet penitentiary in April 1922 to find out what made them criminals. One five-time-loser told the committee, "If I had $650 on my last trial, I could have beat the charge. A gang with a drag at the state's attorney's office would have squared it. A guy who belongs to a gang and who has dough needn't worry."

In December 1928, as Governor Small approached his last weeks in office, he issued a number of last minute pardons.

On the same day Ignatz Potz was freed, Governor Small pardoned four other murderers. Sam Washington killed his common law wife in 1925; his death sentence had been commuted by Small before he was granted a full pardon. Phillip Fox and Morris Steuben, who murdered cab driver Thomas Skirven in the Mob's taxi cab war of 1921, were pardoned. Paul Lindsey was pardoned from his 14-year sentence for the murder of a gas station operator.

The next day, the governor issued more commutations. Three labor racketeers who had been convicted of extortion were freed: Roy "Muckles" Shields, business agent for the Painter's Union; and Patrick Kane and Thomas Walsh, business agents for the Sheet Metal Workers Union. All three were convicted in 1922 but were in jail only a few months because of appeals. Morris Markin, former president of Checker Cab Mfg. Co., was convicted of a fraud charge in 1923 but never spent a day in jail; he fought it before winning one of Small's year-end pardons.

And the day before he left office on Jan. 14, 1929, Governor Small freed nine more murderers by commutation and pardon: Chester Bastien of Williamson County; Henry Morris of Kane County, who the foreman of his jury said "hanging was too good for the fellow;" R.E. Johnson and Al Lucas of Lee County; Roscoe Rulon of Sangamon County; Richard Weir of Saline County; James Bunn, a former police chief in Wabash County, convicted of murder in a bootlegger's war; James Davis of Franklin County; John Corder of Vermilion County. Seven armed robbers were freed by having their life sentences commuted: Leslie Cassin and John Drusch of Chicago; Owen Durling of East St. Louis; Norman Scott of Peoria; Carl Schmitz and Wilfred Schultz of Kankakee County; Herman Lewis of St. Clair County.

Just before Small left office, two members left the parole board amid serious charges. Harry Jensen, a former head of the Chicago Carpenters Union, was fired from the board. He was accused of trying to get clemency for labor union personnel in prison. Hinton Clabaugh, a former superintendent of the Chicago Bureau of Investigation, resigned from the parole board after being accused of trying to arrange clemency for wealthy convicts and for padding the payroll with cronies.

The legislature turned its attention to reforming the parole system in April 1929. State Sen. Harold Kessinger of Aurora said the parole law "as administered has been a menace to the state, a destroyer of law and order, a stimulant to crime, in a way a suggestion to criminals that if they get caught and are convicted that after 11 months they can get out, and many times they do get out." State Rep. Ralph Hoar of Elgin cited the case of Walter Stevens.

The electric chair replaced the noose in the last year of Small's term. The first to be electrocuted were three African-American men on Dec. 15, 1928 in the Joliet penitentiary, for the May 1928 murder of Lake County farmer Will Beck.

Scandals followed for years. In 1931, William Henry Harrison resigned from the parole board after admitting he took bribes. State Sen. Daniel Serritella, Capone's man in the Thompson and Small governments, was charged in 1931 with using his position to get the parole board to free various gangsters.

Questions on why numerous cases of vicious criminals being granted paroles were made for the next decade. George Scully, supervisor of paroles, was fired in December 1936 for granting questionable paroles.

Hope House was closed in 1926 in the wake of the scandal. The old house at 6086 W. Ravenswood Park reopened in 1934, true to its original purpose and with a new superintendent.

It sounds incredible that Len Small could survive so many scandals. But this was an era where big money from politicians and gangsters bought police, judges, legislators and anything else imaginable. Small held a majority in the state legislature, and the legislators owed loyalty to the governor either through promises, bribery or extortion. Small's alliance with both the Mob and City Hall in Chicago solidified his hold on power in Illinois. He beat every rap, one way or another.

In 1916, Len Small was elected state treasurer. For that term, he turned into the state twice as much in interest money as any state treasurer before him.

His natural talent for leadership brought about his election as supervisor of Kankakee Township. That was the beginning of a long and distinguished public service.

One of his early official acts was the signing of the Soldier's Compensation Act, providing 55 million dollars in adjusted compensation. That sum was distributed to 267,537 veterans of the world war in Illinois.

He was elected state senator, served one term in the senate, gained the confidence of Governor Tanner, became actively identified with the state horticultural society, was a leader in building up the state fair.

The *Kankakee Republican-News* printed a full-page, 20-panel comic strip of Len Small's life, on April 9, 1932, during another campaign.

Chapter 17

The 1924 Campaign

It was in 1923 that a serious movement began in the Republican party to find an alternative to Len Small in 1924.

Usually, an incumbent is awarded re-nomination as a matter of course. Stick with the winner, the man who has the advantage of being able to hold onto the office. But the Republican party was divided between those who held true to its principles and those who hijacked the party and turned it into a "combine" of graft and gangsters. Unfortunately, it was the corrupt element that held the power.

This situation for the Republican party in the state was the same situation the Republican party in Kankakee County had been in for a quarter of a century.

There had been talk of dumping Small since his indictment in July 1921.

However, the first serious meeting of 50 Republican leaders to dump Small was in Chicago in June 1923. Another meeting was held in August.

In October, party leaders met in Chicago to firm up their plans. U.S. Sen. William B. McKinley was there. Among the others were six possibilities, the strongest of whom would be chosen as the candidate against Small in 1924. They were Attorney General Edward J. Brundage, former Lt. Gov. John Oglesby, and state senators Thurlow Essington, Otis Glenn, John Harrison and S.S. Tanner. It was decided to draw out the process and see which man came out on top.

Dumping Small was the topic when more than a hundred members of the Municipal League met in Urbana later in the month. The *Kankakee Daily News* printed a story quoting Walter Schneider, Kankakee's city attorney, and others about the tone of the delegates regarding Governor Small.

"Criticism of the administration was general, says Mr. Schneider, particularly the fact of the governor's alliance with the criminal element," the newspaper story went. "A Rock Island alderman well expressed the sentiment when he said, 'We have just cleaned up the grafters and vice lords in our city and sent them to the penitentiary. There they will stay unless pardoned, and we are afraid that if Small is re-nominated, that very thing will come to pass, so we are against Small, and if he should win the Republican nomination, then our city will give the Democratic nominee a majority.'"

Small's gubernatorial pardons were cited as particularly damaging. Small also was criticized for using the road building program for political purposes.

It must have seemed like a bizarre situation -- a Republican convention to choose a candidate to oppose their party's incumbent governor.

Twelve party leaders (including both U.S. senators, William B. McKinley and Medill McCormick) met in Chicago on Oct. 3, 1923 and took 20 ballots before choosing Thurlow Essington as the man they would support against Small.

John Harrison, one of the men considered as a candidate, said, "All concerned realized that personal ambition in this case was of much less consequence than the necessity for wiping out the Small administration and all it stands for. Five candidates sacrificed their own political fortunes rather than see the state further humiliated by the continuation of Smallism. Illinois will be redeemed from its chaos and its good name will be restored."

Edward Brundage gave his own blunt assessment of what this meant.

"The Republican party of Illinois is face to face with a condition that means, depending on the way it is met, either defeat or renewed confidence in its trustworthiness. The party cannot be continued in power solely as an agency for private exploitation. It must stand for public service and it must return to a standard of common public honesty. Law and order must prevail throughout the state, and odious criminals must remain in the confinement to which they have been committed. Panders, gunmen and seditionists find our penitentiaries but places of temporary restraint so long as pardoning power is exercised either for personal reasons or political advantage."

Essington opened his campaign in Rockford on Oct. 10, 1923. "The people know what Small stands for and what he has done," he told a rally. "I have an abiding faith that the people of Illinois stand for decent things. The issues are clear. It is a question of whether or not the people want a decent administration -- an administration based on efficiency, economy and honesty."

Essington said he had opposed Small before, when the governor tried to defeat him for re-election in 1922. He said his opposition to Small was why few hard roads were scheduled for LaSalle County.

"The record of the Small administration in its pardons of convicted bank robber crooks, alleged jury bribers, convicted panders and the communists who were convicted of conspiracy against this government during the war, the padding of payrolls, the breakdown of civil service, defiance of courts and laws and the claim that the king can do no wrong in Illinois," Essington said.

Small's 1924 campaign for re-election began on June 24, 1922, the day he was acquitted in his corruption trial. He declared it his "vindication," a theme he repeated constantly.

The official kickoff of Small's campaign was on Aug. 15, 1923 at a gigantic rally at the Kankakee Armory. Bands played, speeches were given and the crowd was sufficiently stirred. Big Bill Thompson, recently out of office as mayor of Chicago, was one of the honored guests along with Fred Lundin. Thompson, as usual, took the spotlight off Len Small. It was Thompson who was the rally's big act. He spoke at length, promoting Len Small along with himself. Then Big Bill led a solemn parade to Mound Grove Cemetery to the grave of Ida Small.

The *Chicago Tribune's* cynical account called this the "State Pay Rollers Convention." Thompson sat next to Small "as 13 speakers eulogized Mr. Small and held him up as a victim of persecution. The cry of persecution is an unwritten plank in the platform."

The *Kankakee Daily News* reported that "Small's campaign is being run on state funds." This was from assessments from each state worker's paycheck. Those who earned less than $200 per month were assessed one-third of a month's salary. Those earning between $200 and $300 per month were assessed one month's salary. Those earning more than $300 per month had to kick in 14 per cent of their annual salary. These assessments, along with forcing state workers to campaign and pass pledge cards for Small, were made possible by Small's wrecking of the civil service system. An exact review of how much the merit system was damaged was not possible since the Civil Service System had not issued a report since Small became governor.

The state hospital workers at Kankakee naturally resented these deductions, particularly since they were paid low wages and particularly because Small had promised to include them in the state pension system and then did not support the legislation.

Taking money from state employees' paychecks and using state workers to campaign for him was the same thing Small did 22 years earlier when he was president of the state hospital board. But nothing was done about it in 1902 and nothing was done in 1924.

Small's campaign material was printed at state expense, delivered by state trucks to the post offices, and mailed at taxpayer expense.

It was "Len Small Day" at the Illinois State Fair on Sept. 20, 1923. Once again, Big Bill Thompson was at his side, and it looked more like "Big Bill Day" in Springfield.

Thompson gave another rip-roaring speech in Chicago at a Small rally on Nov. 13. In one speech, he called Sen. Medill McCormick "the puppet of the king of England," he called his opponents "crooks and liars" and he declared the death of Ida Small to be "murder." Also speaking at the rally was Capone's man, Edward Kovalinka of Cicero, and William Stratton, Small's state game commissioner.

Throughout Len Small's political career, every campaign consisted of two elections -- an election against a Democrat in the general election, only after an even more bitter primary election against a Republican. Small was seen by his own party as the corrupt "machine" candidate and the Illinois Republican Party regularly put up candidates in order to drive him from the party.

Essington campaigned across the state in his effort to defeat Small in the April 1924 primary. And he was not shy about coming to Kankakee. He got a rousing welcome in Small's home town on Feb. 11. He assailed the governor about the Grant Park Bank and the pardons of the Guziks and others. The issue, Essington said, was Small's record, "and no careless janitor can dispose of that record."

Campaigning with Essington in Kankakee was State Sen. James Barbour. He said Small was acquitted in Waukegan because the jury was bribed and then Small pardoned the men who bribed the jurors. He said that while American boys were dying in the war and Americans at home were sacrificing for the war effort, Small was acting as a "war profiteer," stealing a fortune.

The *Kankakee Daily Republican* immediately began an intense propaganda campaign against Essington. It accused him of opposing the hard roads program and it claimed that the paving of new roads would cease if Essington was elected.

As 1924 began, former U.S. Sen. James Hamilton Lewis gave his viewpoint at an Iroquois Club banquet. "The state in its home affairs is held up as being governed by criminals and embezzlers. It is held up as the political pest house of the Union. It is now scorned by the people of the state and shamed by citizens of the state."

Essington took his campaign to Grant Park on Feb. 12, looking for the Grant Park Bank. He couldn't find it and no one in town could show it to him. One old-timer pointed to an empty lot where the bank existed in the 1890s.

Governor Small made a speech in Pana that hit all his familiar campaign themes. He told how he heroically saved taxpayer money by cutting the budget, despite severe opposition from his enemies -- Ed Brundage, the *Chicago Tribune* and "the profiteers, traction barons and trust press." He bragged about the roads being built and said his indictment on embezzlement charges was done by the big corporations to keep him tied up in court. "I believe these charges are being pushed and supported by the greatest combination of wealthy stockbrokers, gamblers and criminal profiteers that have ever combined to destroy a man in this country."

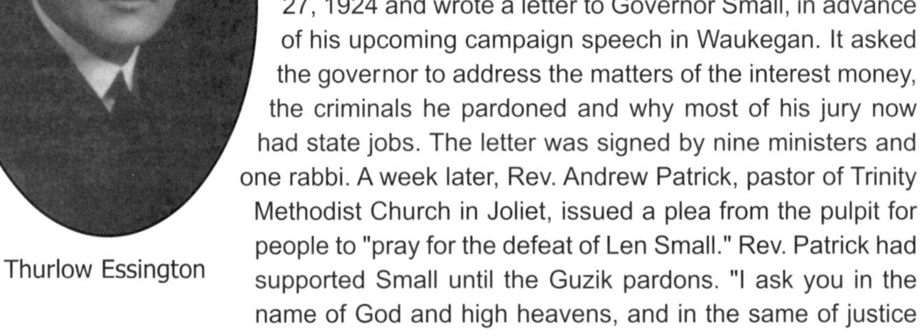
Thurlow Essington

Small asked the crowd to vote for people who would support the governor's programs. "I promise you again today, as I promised before my election, that as long as I am your governor, I shall serve you honestly and faithfully, regardless of persecutions and indictments, and I shall serve you with every particle of strength and ability that I possess."

A number of ministers from Lake County met on Feb. 27, 1924 and wrote a letter to Governor Small, in advance of his upcoming campaign speech in Waukegan. It asked the governor to address the matters of the interest money, the criminals he pardoned and why most of his jury now had state jobs. The letter was signed by nine ministers and one rabbi. A week later, Rev. Andrew Patrick, pastor of Trinity Methodist Church in Joliet, issued a plea from the pulpit for people to "pray for the defeat of Len Small." Rev. Patrick had supported Small until the Guzik pardons. "I ask you in the name of God and high heavens, and in the same of justice and the purity of womanhood, how can any person, club or organization endorse a man like Len Small?

"I ask you to place the 131,000 white crosses on the battlefields of France against the spirit that prompted the governor to pardon 16 Red radicals who were sent to prison because of their Red propaganda in trying to overthrow our government when the boys were going through hell in Europe," he added.

Small's 1924 campaign made heavy use of the "pledge cards" he had used in previous campaigns. Political workers circulated the cards, lining up voters to sign pledges to vote for Small. By November 1923, a meeting of political workers and big shots brought in 110,000 cards. Ed Jeffers, political boss of Kankakee, brought 4,500 more. William Stratton brought 4,000. Big Bill Thompson told the gathering, "If there's any patronage to give out, don't you suppose I tell the governor to give it to the men who deliver the pledge cards?"

The *Lincoln Star* told of "political feudalism" in December 1923. Employees at the Lincoln State School were expected to campaign for Small by circulating pledge cards. This was four months before the primary and was done on state time.

But the whole effort to bring in pledge cards had its own succession of embarrassing moments. Several times, Small found his own people used fraud -- imagine cheating the Boss of Frauds! Bunches of pledge cards had phony names, were signed by the same hand or somehow were not rightfully circulated. In Herscher, 83-year-old Sarah Boyd told the *Kankakee Daily News* in March 1924 that a pledge card with her signature was not right -- arthritis had taken away the use of her hands 10 years earlier.

The *Kankakee Daily News* had an especially hard-hitting editorial on April 5, 1924. Part of the lengthy column gave a personal assessment and a pretty good summary of the feelings against Small:

"A record of 25 years of schooling in the most corrupt political ring Illinois has ever seen developed a worthy graduate in Len Small. From the apt pupil who learned the devious ways of the crooked politician under Billy Lorimer, Small has become the teacher, the master of the game. Where once he eagerly absorbed the wisdom of older men in the arena of politics, and matured skill as an executive in carrying out the orders of the shrewder and more finished leaders of gang politics, Small has long since become the tutor and developed an ability for trickery which outdoes anything the old crowd could carry off in the days of long ago. As governor of Illinois, Small never rose above the political plane which established him as supervisor in Kankakee. His methods have become more bold, and any scruples that may have handicapped his political work of those days have long since been overcome. But his conception of public trust has never changed. The office of governor is only more important because it furnishes a wider scope for unquestioned talent in acquiring wealth. Through the governorship, his territory has widened. More job holders come under his control; there is much more patronage to distribute; greater sums to disburse; greater power at his command to enforce his demands. But in instinct, he is nothing more than a ward heeler with a few hungry job seekers at his heels, interested in carrying the precinct for his boss. These years of history in Illinois give Small a prominent place. Many discreditable things that have been written into it are his own misdeeds, never to be forgotten. Possibility of achievement, which often sways the acts of practical politicians through stirrings of pride and self-respect, is entirely foreign to his nature. Utterly selfish, Small has no thought about accumulation of wealth through political opportunity. And a dollar that reaches his hands has been taken out of circulation insofar as his community is concerned. His waking thoughts have been occupied with schemes for garnering the harvest that has showered upon his as state treasurer, sub-treasurer of the United States, and governor. To review the record of this man is to unfold a story of political rottenness and corruption. It is a record that can be told only in terms of reproach. There is nothing outstanding except that greed for financial and political power which must be satisfied, notwithstanding it may wreck a community or a great state."

Small beat Essington in the primary. Small had the help of the Chicago political machine, with a little extra help from the Ku Klux Klan and from Al Capone and his mobsters.

Small's Democrat opponent in the general election was Judge Norman Jones. In every campaign in Len Small's life, he claimed that his opponent was conducting a "campaign of lies" and this one was no different.

And what was one of the main issues on which Small attacked Jones? It was Jones' record on pardons!

The Democrats published a campaign pamphlet detailing Small's scandalous record on pardons and paroles. Small fired back -- even though a judge does not issue pardons or paroles.

Small's argument consisted of a full-page article in the Oct. 27, 1924 *Kankakee Daily Republican,* citing in great detail a handful of cases in which Jones wrote letters to the parole board either recommending a parole for a particular inmate up for review or at least not objecting to a parole.

It was hardly a ringing condemnation of Jones' actions, although it was intended as such. It did give an explanation into Small's view of paroles. Every prisoner, except life-termers, will get out of prison some day, the governor said. "The great horror is that of keeping the prisoner incarcerated too long," Small said.

"No human agency can determine accurately or definitely how long another human being shall properly be incarcerated for crimes," the governor once again said. "Intelligent administration reveals that the strength back of every parole law lies in supervision and aftercare exercised over the parole rather than the length of time served in a penal institution."

No mention was made of selling pardons and paroles to gangsters.

A few days later, Small's newspaper printed another lengthy attack on Judge Jones. The story was based on a speech by Small in Chicago, with a few editorial additions. Small's speech in Chicago began the usual way: "Keeping up the campaign of lies, vilification and abuse, originated against me by the *Chicago Tribune,* Judge Jones, my Democratic opponent, hopes to walk into political favor over the bleached bones of unfortunates."

Then he added, "Those who know me, my friends and acquaintances in Kankakee County where I have spent the years of my life, and those who know me politically, will tell you truthfully that Len Small, neither politically nor privately, ever committed a shameful act in his lifetime."

Small then launched into a lengthy story about the case of Charles Wright, who was arrested and tried in Judge Jones' courtroom on the charge of sexually assaulting an eight-year-old girl. Wright was convicted. Instead of a prison sentence, Jones sentenced Wright to probation.

"Do you want a man as governor with such regard for the sanctity of little children?" was Small's concluding statement in the article.

Chapter 16 details Governor Small's policy regarding pardons and paroles for child molesters, rapists and others.

Norman Jones later served as an Illinois Supreme Court justice, from 1931 until his death in 1940.

Former Mayor "Big Bill" Thompson accompanied Governor Small at a campaign rally at the Kankakee Armory on Oct. 17, 1924. Thompson accompanied Small at many campaign stops.

Martin O'Brien, chairman of the Cook County Democrats, once again raised the issue of whether Small was legally eligible to be governor. In September 1924, O'Brien said Small was barred by the state constitution because of the money he stole while state treasurer. "It was the greatest cleanup in the history of public treasury management," O'Brien said.

The firmly Republican *Chicago Tribune* endorsed Democrat Norman Jones for governor in 1924. It editorialized that just because Len Small was on the ballot as a Republican "it does not make Len Small a Republican. In our opinion, he is not a Republican. In this campaign, he is a syndicate candidate. His platform is contrary to the Republican national platform and to the principles of Republicanism. He is a discredit to the Republican party of Illinois and as his platform shows, a renegade from it and a traitor to Republican principles."

A lengthy editorial in the Nov. 3, 1924 of Small's *Kankakee Daily Republican* started with, "Tomorrow will be the most momentous day in the political history of Kankakee County." The rest of the editorial sounded the same familiar themes: "Never in the history of state politics has a man been submitted to such abuse and such bitter attacks as has Governor Len Small, citizen of Kankakee County. The big corporation-owned press in Chicago has centered all their heaviest guns on Governor Small. For more than four years, they have carried on a terrible campaign of vilification and hate in an effort to destroy a man because he has sought to represent the people and not the big corporations." And so on.

Len Small was re-elected governor of Illinois on Nov. 4, 1924. The first paragraph of the *Kankakee Daily Republican's* story was "The name of Small has been vindicated." The governor talked about his late wife and how the family name was now cleared by the voters.

It seems incredible today that, with all the scandal attached to Len Small, he was re-nominated and re-elected as governor. However, he was in control of the political machinery, the vote counting in Chicago, and it was a big Republican year. As usual, he brought up the rear in the vote totals.

In a legendary journalistic incident, the lead editorial in the *Chicago Tribune* on the morning after Small was re-elected had the headline, *It Seems Small Has Been Re-elected* -- with a long column of white space underneath.

Chapter 18

The Governor and the Klan

The Ku Klux Klan experienced a dramatic resurgence in the 1920s. Its revival happened all across America, and the Midwest was one of its strongest areas.

Governor Len Small was a favorite of the Invisible Empire.

Small claimed he was not a member of the Klan and that almost certainly is true. But he did give aid and comfort to Klansmen and he did accept the political support they gave him. He had men in his administration who were Klansmen.

Like many other side topics in this book, the phenomenon of the Klan in the 1920s is something that bears further research elsewhere by the reader.

The Ku Klux Klan started in the South after the Civil War, ostensibly as a home guard to protect traditional values, but in reality it was a terrorist group organized to brutalize, punish and keep former slaves in a subservient place. By 1871, internal corruption and a crackdown by authorities caused the group to lose its appeal, and the organization was all but gone -- even if its spirit lived on and incidents of violence continued.

However, in the 1920s, a Klan revival saw membership growing into the millions. The Klan in the 1920s was bigger that it ever had been and this was not just a Southern phenomenon. The Klan had huge memberships in the Midwest, especially in Illinois and Indiana. The KKK also had a lot of members in practically every state from Maine to California.

What was the appeal that led to the Klan resurgence?

There were a lot of factors. In the North, the Great Migration of blacks from the South, in search of better jobs, frightened many white people. The influx of immigrants and the jobs they took -- even though many of these were jobs no one else wanted -- was seen in every area of the country as a threat. Depending on your personal prejudices, the Klan had an enemy for everyone -- the Pope, Catholics, Jews, Negroes, Orientals, Mexicans, new immigrants, Bolsheviks, strikers and more.

The immorality and lawlessness unleashed by Prohibition frightened people, and the Klan promised to restore law and order and protect traditional American values, as seen by white, Anglo, Protestant citizens. It also was promoted as a fraternal, family-friendly organization.

The KKK's stock in trade was fear -- it posed as an organization that offered protection against what some people feared, and it dealt fear to those it did not like.

And this pitch worked for awhile. The Klan grew to huge numbers in the 1920s. A Klan parade down Pennsylvania Avenue in Washington D.C. in 1925 drew 40,000 marchers. Klan Day at the Texas State Fair attracted 75,000 participants. The Klan elected people to local and statewide offices all across America.

Democrat Earle B. Mayfield was the Klan's candidate for the U.S. Senate from Texas in 1922. Mayfield won the Senate seat in a crooked election and was defeated for re-election six years later.

Sen. Robert Byrd, a Democrat from West Virginia, was once a member of the Klan. So was Supreme Court Justice Hugo Black.

The Klan claimed credit for electing several governors in 1924: Ed Jackson in Indiana, Ben Paulson in Kansas, Clarence Morley in Colorado and Len Small in Illinois. Rice Means was elected U.S. senator from Colorado and he admitted membership.

The Illinois Kourier, a KKK newspaper in Chicago, boasted of the Klan's influence. "These papers (*Chicago Tribune* and *Chicago Daily News*) and other enemies of the Klan charged that Governor Len Small was favorable to the Klan and had its support. Norman L. Jones, a Democrat and the political protégé of Boss George E. Brennan, is a Protestant but upon the advice of Brennan launched a disastrous attack upon the Klan shortly before the election. Needless to say, he was badly beaten by Governor Small."

The Ku Klux Klan did have some political influence in the 1920s but the extent of that influence certainly was over-estimated by those braggarts in bed sheets.

The Klan had a wide history in Illinois in the 1920s. A Klan rally was held south of suburban Lake Zurich on Aug. 17, 1921 with 10,000 people in attendance. It was reported that 2,000 of them became members.

Another Klan meeting in a wooded area between Joliet and Plainfield on June 3, 1922 attracted between 30,000 and 50,000 people. This is about 40 miles northwest of Kankakee. Six thousand automobiles brought Klansmen from a 200-mile area. Among bonfires and burning crosses, about 2,000 people were initiated into the Klan that night.

There also were big rallies at Champaign, Urbana, Pontiac, Utica, LaSalle, Peru, Springfield, Rockford, Oak Forest and other places. The Klan was even stronger in Southern Illinois, where it virtually replaced the existing order in many areas. Many other cities had active Klan chapters. The Grand Dragon bragged in 1923 that there were 287 chartered Klaverns in Illinois, although there is no way to know if this was true.

A news item in the Sept. 3, 1921 *Kankakee Daily News* told that Klan members were in town to organize a chapter. The April 20, 1923 *Daily Republican* told of two Klan cross burnings in Kankakee. A leader claimed to have 470 members in Kankakee and 100 in Momence. He said the Klan was responsible for electing several city officials.

But the Klan could not hide its rotten core. It was run by violent and corrupt men, and it was a racket. It preached a knighthood of virtues but it dealt in violence. Klan leaders grew rich in what essentially was an Organized Crime family.

It was an organization with all the morals of the Mafia and all the brutality of the Nazis. Like the German people who submitted to the order of the state, looking for some sort of hope, people who trusted the Klan soon found themselves in the death grip of their deliverers. They thought it would be an organization that would put an end to lawlessness but found "the law and order" it produced was even worse. They saw that the violence it committed was greater than the violence that already was taking place.

Members abandoned the KKK in droves by the end of the decade. The regular citizen, who may have joined for a moral reason, saw that the organization had no morals at all. Those who may have joined it because it offered protection from their fears saw that it was more fearful than anything they had imagined. The Klan went from practically zero to millions to practically zero, all in the same decade.

A minor resurgence of the Ku Klux Klan in the 1950s and 1960s primarily was confined to the South and was based on pure racial hatred. Despite the attention it has been given by historians, it was not even a shadow of what it was in the 1920s, neither in membership nor in violence.

KKKK

Knights of Ku Klux Klan

OPEN AIR MEETING

2 Miles South of

PONTIAC, ILL.

Fri. Eve., Aug. 14

Band Concert at 7:30 P. M. by 35 Piece Band

Singing by Male Quartette

EXCELLENT SPEAKING

by the REV. APPLEGATE, of Decatur, Ill.

Plenty of good seats

Everyone Invited Regardless of Color, Creed or Sex

Refreshments Served On Grounds

The Klan advertised in Col. Frank L. Smith's hometown newspaper, the *Dwight Star & Herald*, in 1925.

Len Small was one American politician who accepted support from this growing organization in the 1920s. A politician never turns away a substantial voting block, and the foul odor coming from the KKK was not stronger than the possibly of the large number of votes it could provide.

But Small could not get too close. Despite the group's growing popularity in the 1920s, intelligent people still saw it as a terrorist organization.

Publicly, Governor Small strongly denied any connection to the KKK.

But Governor Small also did nothing to stop Klan activity in Illinois. The big rallies and cross burnings near Joliet, Champaign, Pontiac, LaSalle, Springfield, Rockford, not to mention Southern Illinois, escaped the notice of the governor. The Klan rally and cross burning in Kankakee was noted but not condemned by Small's newspaper.

A *Chicago Tribune* investigative report in January 1923 found a large number of Klansmen working in state government. A number of those identified claimed they only filled out questionnaires that came with their invitation to join the Klan but did not take the oath. One of these men was George D. Sutton, personal secretary to Governor Small.

Charles Mutters, custodian of the state fairgrounds, was a Klansman and he set up a Klan gathering on the fairgrounds. Elmer Lindley, a member of the State Fair bureau, was identified as a Klansman, along with several engineers in the State Division of Highways: Donald Marshall, R.J. Demond, C.H. Newman, Arthur Bushman, F. Herbert Wharton and Gordon Sallec.

Governor Small was criticized for allowing the Klan to use the state fairgrounds and other state property for their demonstrations.

The state legislature called Governor Small to testify on June 7, 1923 to explain his connection to Klan activities on state property.

The governor was asked point blank by Rep. Reed Cutler of Lewistown, "Are you a member of the Ku Klux Klan?"

Small laughed and said, "I don't know what they are or what they stand for. I have never been asked to join."

The governor said he didn't know who gave the Klan permission to use the grandstand or the coliseum on the state fairgrounds.

Albert Livingstone, secretary of the Illinois Senate, said he didn't know about anyone giving the Klan permission. State Rep. Thomas O'Grady of Chicago called Livingstone a liar and the two almost got into a fight.

But Livingstone's entire attitude seemed sympathetic. He said the Klan barred no one on account of religion or race. State Rep. Adelbert Roberts, an African-American Republican from Chicago, shot back, "I am an American citizen and a college graduate. Please bring me an application for membership in the Ku Klux Klan tomorrow."

The Klan claimed credit for Small's re-nomination in April 1924. A publication, *Illinois Fiery Cross,* claimed "Every candidate for state office receiving the support of the Klan's membership was swept to victory," including Len Small at the top of the ticket.

"Even in Cook County, with its strong and well organized Roman Catholic,

Jewish, Negro and alien citizen vote, the victory for patriotic Protestantism was almost as great."

But this caused problems between Klan members who pushed for sympathetic candidates and those who believed the group should be non-political. Charles Palmer, a dragon of the Illinois Klan, was a strong supporter of Governor Len Small. W.H. Evans, the imperial wizard of the entire Klan, wrote from Atlanta that "Palmer is dragging the Klan in Illinois into politics" and was "shoving Governor Len Small down the throats of Klansmen."

Evans blamed the governor's reluctance to send troops to keep the peace in Southern Illinois for the deaths of several Klansmen there.

In Governor Small's Springfield, the Klan found it was welcome. The Klan had a big rally in Springfield on Oct. 11, 1924, with "robing" ceremonies held on state grounds just outside the capitol building.

The Klan held another rally on state property on Oct. 31, using the armory on Broadway in Chicago, where a thousand hooded Klansmen paraded and boosted Small for the upcoming election. Sample ballots were distributed with Small's named marked for governor.

The Klan was allowed to use another state facility for a rally, the University of Illinois armory.

Judge Norman Jones, the governor's Democrat opponent in 1924, referred to the Klan's Springfield rally in a speech a few weeks later. He claimed the Klan was openly working for Small's re-election. Jones said Klan members used rooms in the state capitol building as dressing rooms before parades and rode horses assigned to National Guard cavalry troops in parades. He cited instances when the Klan used the state fairgrounds for night rallies, even though the state legislature banned Klan gatherings on state property.

"The Ku Klux Klan has made itself an issue in this campaign, not only by openly defying the Constitution of the United States but by injecting itself into politics in support of the re-election of its friend and aide, Governor Len Small," Jones said.

"Here in Illinois, the danger of this menace is not imaginary," he continued. "It is real. A day or so ago, the so-called grand dragon of Illinois declared that the Ku Klux Klan now holds the balance of power in the politics of Illinois and ought to get what it wants. There are many indications that the Klan already is getting what it wants from our state government.

"A couple of weeks ago, a state meeting of the Klan was advertised to be held in Springfield. Several thousand Klansmen came to that city. They used the state house and the state arsenal to dress in. They assembled within a few feet of the statue of Abraham Lincoln, the great emancipator, and they marched through the streets of the capital city. We want no Klan-ruled state in Illinois."

Governor Small denied he was friendly to the Klan or that he let them use state property. But in April 1928, a photograph was published in newspapers across the state showing hundreds of robed Klansmen with a burning cross at a ceremony inside the Coliseum on the State Fair grounds. The picture, dated Oct. 14, 1922, was made public by William Harrison, an African-American lawyer and assistant attorney general. He distributed it with his caption, "Len Small, the Klan's Friend."

"I deny being a Kluxer," Small replied.

"Len Small, you know that the Ku Klux Klan despises the people of our race and has despised, whipped, lynched, mutilated and murdered our people during all the years since the broken bodies of our forefathers dripped blood in the wake of the night-riding Klan," Harrison said. "Len Small, now you ask the Negro vote. How dare you do so? Look at the picture and answer us. How dare you ask the citizens of our race to vote for you, the friend and ally of the Ku Klux Klan?"

The Klan connection caught up to Small in the 1928 primary election. The governor's response? Simple -- accuse your opponents of being friendly to the Klan.

In the same breath as denying affiliation with the Klan, Small insinuated that Sen. Otis Glenn, Secretary of State Louis Emmerson and Attorney General Oscar Carlstrom of being allied with the Klan, even though they did not accuse him and even though Small had no evidence that they had the slightest connection.

"The attacks and the contemptible, vicious and veiled insinuations appearing in one of yesterday's newspapers to the effect that I have affiliated with what is known as the Ku Klux Klan are absolutely false and without foundation," Small said on April 5, 1928 while running for nomination for a third term. "I am not now and have never been a member of or affiliated with the Klan. I have never solicited the support of any secret political organization. I have never boasted or paraded my connections with any organizations. I have never made any appointments for any secret organization. In making appointments, I have never asked a person's religion, creed, nationality, race or lodge affiliation.

"I ask Glenn, Emmerson and Carlstrom if they can say the same. I ask them if they have not attended meetings, political and otherwise, and addressed them and have traveled from city to city and been received by secret leaders with open arms.

"This is not the first time that the vicious tools of the grasping, grafting profiteering wealth have attempted to deceive the people by lying about me."

Politics on the local level always had Len Small's hand in it. Albert Goodknecht, a state highway patrolman, was running against Small's candidate for the Republican nomination for sheriff of Kankakee County in 1930. Local party chairman Victor McBroom started a "whispering campaign" among Kankakee's large Catholic community claiming that Goodknecht was a Klansman. Goodknecht obtained a number of affidavits from people who said McBroom told them that Goodknecht's name was on the Klan membership list. Goodknecht sued McBroom. Goodknecht won the primary and was elected sheriff.

It was during this same primary campaign that the Small group tried to ruin the business of Elzie Huot, who owned an oil company and a number of gas stations. Huot was allowed to sell gasoline to the state only after making the required campaign contributions to Len Small's party. When Huot supported Goodknecht in 1930, Small's local political henchmen spread rumors that Huot sold grades of gasoline to the state that were not up to specifications. Huot denied it.

CITY EDITION **KANKAKEE DAILY REPUBLICAN** CITY EDITION

TWICE AS MANY PAID SUBSCRIBERS AS OUR COMPETITOR — WEATHER Showers and much cooler Saturday — MEMBER OF THE AUDIT BUREAU OF CIRCULATIONS

VOLUME XXXV — ASSOCIATED PRESS DAILY SERVICE — KANKAKEE, ILL., FRIDAY, APRIL 20, 1923 — SIXTEEN PAGES — NUMBER 35

KU KLUX KLAN BURNS FIERY CROSS HERE

POLICE HOLD COLORED MAN IN SHOOTING

CLAIMS HE SHOT MAN AFTER HE HAD BROKEN HIS DOOR DOWN

INJURED MAN LEAVES

Taken To Harvey After Shooting; May Be Placed Under Arrest

ASK HENRY FORD TO INSPECT A RAILROAD

SENATE COMMITTEE ON TRANSPORTATION INVITES HIM TO INSPECT C. P. & ST. L. RY.

MANY INJURED IN EXPLOSION AT ARGO, ILL.

EXPLOSION WRECKS STARCH FACTORY OF THE CORN PRODUCTS COMPANY

AT ARGO THIS MORNING

Blast, Due To Dust Combustion, Heard For Many Miles

BURGLAR ROBS HOUSE; JUMPS FOR LIBERTY

ESCAPES WITH NECKLACE AND OTHER ARTICLES VALUED AT OVER $100

SUSPECT ARRESTED

One Man Held Believed To Have Been Implicated In Several Robberies

BIG MANUFACTURERS ARE SENT TO PRISON

BY FEDERAL JUDGE IN NEW JERSEY WHEN CONVICTED OF CONSPIRACY

MULHEIM IN CONTROL OF THE GERMANS

AFTER BEING TERRORIZED THREE DAYS AUTHORITIES AGAIN CONTROL

CASUALTY LIST IS SIX

Burgomaster And City Employes Had Been Besieged For Several Days

RUSH FOOD TO PEOPLE ON ISLAND

AVIATIONS RUSHING NORTH WITH SUPPLIES FOR MEN AND WOMEN

ON FOX ISLAND

Perilous Journey For Occupants Of Planes Flying Over Lake Michigan

WEIRD CEREMONIES ARE HELD TWO SUCCESSIVE NIGHTS IN QUARRY AND WEST KANKAKEE

SOLICITOR FOR MEMBERS ANNOUNCES BIG PARADE TO BE HELD SOON

SHERIFF GETS REPORT

Neighbors See Burning Cross And Notify Rogers—Officer Finds Ashes In Vacant Lot

PRESIDENT HARDING TO TALK TO NEWSPAPER MEN TUESDAY

FUNERAL SERVICES FOR BISHOP TUTTLE TO BE SIMPLE

ARTHUR SUTTON DIES WHILE ENROUTE HOME

FORMER MERCHANT OF ST. ANNE PASSES AWAY IN STATE OF GEORGIA

This April 20, 1923 *Kankakee Daily Republican* edition told of cross burnings at the North Entrance Avenue quarry and on a vacant lot in West Kankakee.

This picture postcard shows a few members of the Joliet Klan in the 1920s.

Small's connection to the Klan resurfaced in his 1932 campaign. Governor Emmerson and Omer Custer, Emmerson's choice in the April primary to replace him, charged that Len Small had made a political deal with the Klan.

A "cowardly and contemptible lie" is how the Small campaign described the accusation, which was printed in pamphlets and circulated in African-American neighborhoods in Chicago. Small threatened to sue but did not.

The Klan endorsed Small for the 1932 primary election, according to an April 8 story in the *Chicago Tribune.* It quoted from a diary of a Klansman who told of a conference in Washington between state Grand Dragon Gail S. Carter "and a high official of the Klan who decided to aid Small."

"I told Carter I was going to devote my time until the primary in the interests of Len Small for governor," a diary entry read. "Carter offered to call Small over the telephone and talk to him for me but he wouldn't give me a letter, saying he and Small never wrote each other letters but always used the telephone."

The Klansman said he and a chief organizer went to several cities around the state on Small's behalf. "He told me that the Klan had submitted a list for appointments to Small when he was elected before. In case of Small's election again, they expected to submit a smaller and more select list for the important positions. He told me there would be a meeting Sunday, April 3, to endorse Small, and he invited me to go with him."

That's exactly what happened. Three hundred Klansmen from more than 100 towns in Illinois met on April 3, 1932 on the eighteenth floor of the Capitol building at State and Randolph streets in Chicago. The Klansmen were not wearing their hoods or robes this time. Illinois Grand Dragon Gail Carter distributed little blue cards on which the delegates were to mark their choice. Booklets had been passed out with the names of the candidates for governor. The booklets had Len Small's name pre-marked.

The KKK delegates that day overwhelmingly endorsed Len Small.

A *Tribune* story also quoted the Klansman as saying that Col. Arthur E. Inglesh, Small's son-in-law, called Carter to talk about campaign organization.

Len Small's angry response contained a veiled insinuation that the *Tribune* was tied to the Klan.

"The *Chicago Tribune,* in it's desperate efforts to defeat the will of the people, is resorting to the same lies that they published four years ago when they charged that I had dealings with the Klan," Small said. "That is absolutely false. I never had any dealings with the Klan or any of the other *Tribune* organizations or with organizations with which their candidate is affiliated."

Several states passed laws against people wearing masks in public, as a means to break up Klan gatherings. Illinois passed such a law and Governor Small signed it.

While Len Small undoubtedly was not a card-carrying member of the Ku Klux Klan, he did accept their endorsement, he did allow them state favors, he never uttered a word of condemnation, and he definitely held the group in higher esteem than he held the *Chicago Tribune* and the rest of his usual gang of suspects.

Governor Small and Mayor Thompson had been praised by Gail Carter at the time when Thompson was giving his anti-British rants and was threatening to host book burnings of British history on the shores of Lake Michigan. Carter sent his approval, and he urged Thompson to also go after the Catholics and the Jews.

The Mine Wars, The Klan Wars, And The Gang Wars In Southern Illinois, And Governor Small's Response

Because of the sensational crimes of Chicago gangsters Al Capone, Bugs Moran, Spike O'Donnell, Dean O'Banion, Frank Nitti and others, the organized gangs in Southern Illinois are largely overlooked by history. But they were there, and two gangs -- Birger and Shelton -- were powerful and often as bloodthirsty as the Chicago gangs.

Southern Illinois is 300 miles from Chicago. It is like being in another world. It has more of a Southern flavor than Northern, and sympathies ran more toward the Confederates than the Union during the Civil War. It has beautiful scenery, equal to almost anywhere else in the nation. But it is rural, sparsely populated and has always been relatively poor.

Southern Illinois, particularly Herrin, went through some very rough and lawless times in the 1920s.

A coal mine strike erupted into the Herrin Massacre in June 1922. Fifty strikebreakers were hired to work the mine, which caused bitter and tense days. An armed mob of striking United Mine Workers (UMW) surrounded the mine. The strikebreakers under siege raised a white flag and said they would surrender if they could come out of the mine unharmed. The union men replied, "Come on out and we'll get you out of the county."

The strikebreakers came out. The union miners started marching them towards Herrin. A group of men waited at a crossing a half mile north of the mine. The strikebreakers were beaten with guns by the UMW men. C.K. McDowell, superintendent of the mine, was beaten and bloodied and unable to walk any further, and was shot to death on the spot. A UMW official drove up and said, "Don't you go killing these fellows on a public highway. There are too many women and children around to do that. Take them over in the woods and give it to them. Kill all you can."

The UMW men marched the others into the woods near a barbed wire fence. The men were told to run, then were gunned down as they started. In the morning, those who were still alive were taken to Herrin Cemetery, where they were slaughtered in front of a crowd. Labor union men took turns beating several captives, then shot them dead. To end the massacre in a final act of grotesque brutality, somebody stepped forward with his pocket knife and slit the throats of those still alive. A total of 20 men were killed.

Local law enforcement had done nothing to stop the massacre. A coroner's jury ruled that the strikebreakers were killed by unknown individuals and it blamed the coal company. Six men eventually were put on trial for murder and were acquitted. A second trial in 1923 also resulted in acquittals.

For this, and for a long violent history prior and subsequent to the Herrin Massacre, Williamson County became infamous as "Bloody Williamson."

This tragedy did not happen overnight. The strike was called April 1, the strikebreakers arrived June 15, and the pot boiled until the massacre on June 22. All the while, National Guard Col. Samuel Hunter was on the scene doing what he could to negotiate a peace. He tried to talk the mine owner into shutting down operations, he tried to talk the union miners into dispersing, he talked to the sheriff and he did what he could to prevent the violence he saw coming. Hunter reported to Governor Small and to Adj. Gen. Carlos Black.

Governor Small was in Waukegan, on trial for embezzlement. At the time, Small was too busy seeing that his jury was "fixed" and selling a pardon to a Capone cop-killer to give any attention to the approaching slaughter in Herrin.

Col. Hunter determined that troops were needed to prevent a war between the miners and the strikebreakers. William Lester, the mine owner, dared the strikers with his arrogance and his unwillingness to cease operations because he believed National Guard troops would be called to save him before the flash point was reached.

Violence started the day before the massacre. There was gunfire and several skirmishes between both armed camps. One man was killed and several were wounded. Hunter called Black. Lester called Black. Lester called Small. The governor asked Black what steps were being taken and Black said three companies were put on alert. Small was satisfied and went back to his business in Waukegan.

On two occasions, as the situation grew worse, Gen. Black told Col. Hunter that troops would not be sent unless the situation was too much for local law enforcement agencies to handle. But that had been established long ago. The sheriff was not going to wage war on union workers, the people whose votes he needed, in defense of illegal strikebreakers. The mine owner and his crew of outsiders had no friends in Williamson County.

Col. Hunter, however, was not the great negotiator he thought he was. He believed he had brokered a truce between both armed camps. Gen. Black had said that he could call up troops on two hours notice, depending on Hunter's assessment on the ground. Hunter reported to Black that a truce had been negotiated. Hunter, Black and Small congratulated themselves on averting a tragedy.

Meanwhile, police on the streets of Herrin were directing heavy traffic -- carloads of armed men on their way to the mine.

After the Herrin Massacre horrified the nation, fingers of blame were pointed all over. An interesting side point came from the Illinois Chamber of Commerce. Its president, John Camlin, solicited each of the state's chambers in all 102 counties, asking for contributions to prosecute the murderers. Camlin said that the only two agencies that could prosecute the matter -- the Williamson County state's attorney and the Illinois attorney general -- did not have the funds to do so. Williamson County was too poor. And as for the state of Illinois, Camlin said Governor Small had cut Attorney General Edward Brundage's budget so deep that Brundage did not have the funds for much more than the routine functions of his office.

Small had claimed that his massive cut in Brundage's budget was a heroic effort on his part to save the taxpayers money. Others claimed it was personal spite against a political enemy, while some claimed it was so that Brundage did not have the resources to prosecute Governor Small or the governor's gangster friends. Now, even the Illinois Chamber of Commerce felt it had to step in to raise money so that the state's top law enforcement official could do his job. Such was the cost of Governor Small's action.

Camlin did receive enough money for the state to prosecute the killers. Brundage's grand jury returned 214 indictments -- 54 for murder, 59 for conspiracy to commit murder, 54 for assault to commit murder and 58 for conspiracy and rioting. It all resulted in no convictions.

The legislature formed a committee in May 1923 to investigate the Herrin massacre. Small was called to testify, concerning the use of troops to prevent the tragedy.

Small said he was away from Springfield from April to June, at his trial in Waukegan. He said Lester called him on June 21 and told him he was worried his miners were going to be killed. The governor said he talked with Col. Hunter and Gen. Black and was told everything there was all right. The next day, the governor got a telephone call about the slaughter.

Still, Small told the committee that neither he nor Hunter nor Black could be held responsible for what happened in Herrin.

The governor did send National Guard troops to Hillsboro in August 1923 on the request of the local sheriff after violence broke out during a strike at the American Zinc, Lead & Smelting Co. mine.

The Klan's emergence as a power in Southern Illinois in the 1920s resulted in local warfare that saw numerous shootouts and a score of deaths. Gang warfare also brought bloodshed and lawlessness that was out of control.

Instead of being decisive and sending in the National Guard to clean up the mess once and for all, the state's response was to send an inadequate number of troops on several occasions. The troops were there only to maintain some sense of order, not to drive out the Klan vigilantes who had virtually replaced the elected law enforcement officers.

Finally, Governor Small told Williamson County that the state had spent enough money sending troops, so they were on their own to keep the peace.

It was not a demonstration of leadership.

The Klan took advantage of the public's desire to clean up the bootlegging, gambling and prostitution that infested Little Egypt at that time. Some citizens, who believed the sheriff was not doing enough, organized their own group in 1923, a group that soon was taken over by Klansmen and became vigilantes who took the law into their own hands.

Williamson County Sheriff George Galligan was opposed to the Ku Klux Klan and he did not like them taking over the county. A very large anti-Klan faction backed him. It was a very serious situation that did erupt into civil war several times between the two sides, both heavily armed.

A committee went to Springfield in 1923 to ask the governor for help in cleaning out the bootleggers. Small dismissed them, saying, "If you want the law enforced, go back and elect someone that will enforce the law."

Getting nothing from Springfield, the committee went to Washington and asked Prohibition officials for help. They were told that the agency's funds were limited, but if they did their own investigating and found proof, the government would send federal agents to make arrests.

It was taken as a blank check to go after bootleggers, with whatever violence and terrorism the Klan deemed necessary.

The committee hired S. Glenn Young, a disgraced former Prohibition agent, and put him in charge of cleaning up vice in Williamson County. Young recruited Klansmen to serve on his rogue police force and he led a number of raids.

Young got permission from Illinois congressmen Richard Yates and E.E. Denison and from Prohibition Commissioner Roy Haynes to deputize hundreds of Klansmen as federal agents to run roughshod over the countryside -- not just at roadhouses but in private homes, in search of liquor. Young and his agents arrested more saloonkeepers and drinkers than the local jails could hold. Young became a larger-than-life hero to the Klan and its sympathizers.

Young's raids were violent and often especially brutal. There was no mistake, these were not lawfully-conducted raids by federal Prohibition agents, they were attacks by vigilante Klansmen who violated every precept of civil rights. A number of people signed complaints for the brutality they received at the hands of the raiders. Even Prohibition officials in Washington told Young's group to cease making raids.

Arrested for severely beating a restaurant owner, Young entered the courtroom on Jan. 8, 1924 with a band of Klansmen, all heavily armed. Two Klansmen even carried a machine gun into the court. Sheriff Galligan, alarmed at the defendant's arsenal in the courtroom, telegraphed Gen. Black and asked for troops. Black, still smarting from his failure to send troops to prevent the Herrin Massacre, sent in the militia.

Troops were called again after another violent incident on Feb. 8. John Layman, deputy police chief, was shot and wounded. As riot conditions brewed, Galligan called Gen. Black and asked for troops. Caesar Cagle, a criminal who became a constable after joining the Klan, was shot dead on the street. Young and his hooded thugs went to the Herrin hospital looking for wounded enemies. The thugs shot up the hospital, terrorizing patients and staff until 3 a.m. when the militia arrived and dispersed them.

Young and his Klan army seized control. Young had Herrin Mayor C.E. Anderson and Sheriff Galligan arrested and jailed for the murder of Cagle. Klansmen patrolled the streets. It was four days before the legally elected officials were released from jail.

How bad was S. Glenn Young? The Klan said he was too brutal and violent even for them. The Ku Klux Klan dismissed Young in February 1924. On Sept. 13, it expelled him from the Klan and later escorted him out of Williamson County.

How bad is someone in order to be too much for that nest of rats!

Young continued his raids and his reign of terror, with sympathetic Klansmen, but without the approval of federal authorities or Klan hierarchy.

On Aug. 30, 1924, a gunfight between Young's thugs and the anti-Klan faction at John Smith's garage in Herrin saw six men shot dead. On Jan. 24, 1925, a shootout in a Herrin cigar store resulted in four men dead, including S. Glenn Young. Another big gunfight followed the election on April 13, 1926, in front of the Herrin

Masonic Temple -- another six men died, three Klansmen and three from the anti-Klan group.

The opportunity provided by Prohibition led gangs to become powerful and vicious in rural Southern Illinois as well as in most large American cities. Wide-open gambling and prostitution also flourished.

Charlie Birger and his gang battled the rival Shelton gang in bootlegging in that part of Illinois. They used tommy guns, shotguns, even bombs fired from home-made "tanks" and dropped from single-engine airplanes.

Among Birger's illegal activities was a car theft operation in which he had the assistance of Illinois State Trooper Lory Price. On Jan. 9, 1927, the Sheltons dynamited the Shady Rest, the roadhouse between Marion and Harrisburg that Birger used as his headquarters and fortress. The roadhouse was destroyed and four people inside were killed. Birger accused Price of helping the Sheltons in the bombing. So, on Jan. 19, Birger's gang kidnapped Price and his wife Ethel. Lory Price was tortured and then shot to death. Ethel Price was murdered and her body was thrown down an abandoned coal mine shaft.

Charlie Birger was an outlaw and a vicious killer but he did hate the Ku Klux Klan with a passion. Birger, a Jewish Russian immigrant, did not like the Klan's anti-immigrant and racist campaign or their promise to fight the gangs and the corrupt officials. In April 1926, Birger's gang joined with the Shelton Brothers gang to attack the Klan in Herrin with high powered weapons. The police did not interfere. The Birger gang's violent war with the KKK was one of the main reasons for the downfall of the Klan in Illinois.

The gang wars in Southern Illinois were piling up bodies and the situation had gotten out of control.

Herrin mayor Marshall McCormack asked for National Guard troops and a state military court to bring order, which local law enforcement agencies were powerless to accomplish. "The gangs have reached such proportions that no sheriff, regardless of his efforts, can relieve the condition," the mayor wrote to the governor on Nov. 12, 1926.

"The prosecution of these outlaws is equally impossible, as no citizen will produce evidence while these gangs are at large, for fear of their own lives being taken, and no prosecuting attorney could live who attempted it," the mayor's letter continued. "I have tried from every angle to work out some hopeful solution and the best minds of Southern Illinois have put their efforts into it, only to find it lost in dismal failure. There is no man in Williamson County who believes civil authorities can ever meet the existing conditions.

"I know that every civil agency has failed, yet realizing the embarrassment it brings to you, to me, and our state, am frank to tell you that the only solution, so far as I can see, is the setting up of a military court so that arrests can be made, that evidence may be submitted without witnesses being intimidated," Mayor McCormack wrote.

In another situation, a concerned governor might send troops and the local mayor might object to outside interference. Here, the opposite was true.

"The people of Southern Illinois cannot expect protection unless they are prepared to help give protection," Governor Small replied.

"We have spent several hundreds of thousands of dollars of the people's money in that section during the last few years trying to maintain the law. The murders that happen there would have happened regardless of whether the state militia was present or not, and would be just the same as having militia in Chicago to stop murders which happen there," Small added.

In what seems illogical, Governor Small continued: "It is up to the people themselves. Ninety-nine per cent of the people down there are law-abiding, and those that make the trouble come from some place else. When troops are there, there is no trouble, because the troublemakers leave."

The *Kankakee Daily Republican* reported all this. Its story added, "Governor Small said it was not the duty of the National Guard to maintain law and order unless the civil agencies had collapsed, and he did not believe this happened. 'This is a government of, and by the people, and if they want to enforce the laws, it is up to them,' the governor concluded."

But local law enforcement *had* collapsed, Mayor McCormack was saying to the governor. He *did* need help, and he was begging for it.

Small said no. That same day, Birger's hoodlums made an attack on West City Mayor Joe Adams, wounding him. A month later, Birger sent two of his gunmen to Adams' home, where they shot the mayor to death in the doorway of his house.

Williamson County State's Attorney Arlie Boswell, who was prosecuting Birger, was shot and seriously wounded in the garage of his Marion home on March 16, 1927.

Bloody Williamson got no more aid from Governor Len Small.

Governor Small was willing to call out the National Guard to keep a sheriff from serving him a summons but was not willing to call out the Guard when chaos broke down all law and order.

Governor Small seemed to be saying a lot in his reply to Mayor McCormack. He was saying that you *can* put a price on human life, and sending the militia into a lawless area would cost too much money. He didn't mind spending tens of millions of dollars to build asphalt roads but he didn't want to spend too much to bring law and order and save lives in areas that were in the death grip of gangsters and Klansmen. We already spent enough money, he said, in sending the militia, even if it was ineffective. If people want law and order and if they want the gangsters stopped, it is up to the people to take the law into their own hands and not look to their elected officials. Sending troops only would make the gangsters leave. That is what Small seemed to be saying.

The West City assassination and the murder of the state trooper and his wife were the final straws. Birger and the assassins were arrested, put on trial and convicted of the murder of Adams. The gunmen went to prison. Charlie Birger went to the gallows outside the Franklin County jail in Benton on April 19, 1928 for the murder of Joe Adams.

(TIME magazine reported on this, with a caution: "(Birger) was to be hanged by the neck on Friday, April 13, unless Governor Len Small, famed pardoner, intervened.")

By the time Birger hanged, Carl, Earl and Bernie Shelton were in Leavenworth penitentiary, serving 25-year sentences for having robbed the U.S. mails in Collinsville on Jan. 27, 1925. When they got out, they joined the dominant gang in Peoria, another wide-open town. Peoria, Galesburg, Rockford, Streator, LaSalle, Ottawa and numerous other towns in Central Illinois had their own home-grown Organized Crime gangs, produced from the gift of Prohibition.

The Sheltons provided the muscle that kept the remnants of Capone's gang from taking over Peoria. But they came to an end befitting their business. In October 1947, Carl was shot dead near his farm. In July 1948, Bernie was shot dead by a sniper outside his Peoria headquarters. Earl was wounded in a shooting at his Fairfield club in May 1949.

Herrin's Mayor McCormack probably thought that if you can't beat 'em, join 'em. He was convicted in February 1929 of having conspired with Charlie Birger in the bootlegging racket. McCormack was sentenced to two years in Leavenworth federal penitentiary. Upon conviction, he resigned as mayor. Convicted along with him were his brother Elmer, a police officer who got one year in prison, and John Stamm, the police chief, who got 18 months.

Governor Len Small did nothing in his power to fight Organized Crime in Chicago, with whom he was allied, and he did nothing to fight Organized Crime in Southern Illinois, even when he was asked and could have shown real leadership.

Chapter 19

Impeach Me, If You Can

Impeachment was talked about from the very first few months of Len Small's administration. It was mentioned constantly throughout both terms.

Even before Small was indicted in July 1921 for embezzling funds from the state treasury, legislators were calling on Small to resign. Calls for his resignation came in June, when Small's emissaries tried to bribe legislators with promises of patronage and higher-paying positions if they would vote for his civil service and tax commission bills. When Small was indicted a month later, calls for resignation changed to calls for impeachment. Impeachment was mentioned frequently as the case proceeded and Small did outrageous things such as running from the sheriff, declaring himself above the law and more.

Critics said the extraordinary work to elect pro-Small candidates and the buying of lawmakers with promises of patronage and pet legislation was done because Small wanted to sew up a legislature that would not impeach him. Small admitted as much, in a backward way, saying the *Tribune* and other foes wanted to elect members who would vote to impeach.

State Rep. Michael Igoe of Chicago, the Democrat minority leader of the House, introduced an impeachment resolution in January 1923 after the governor's involvement in "stealing" a state senate seat in a Chicago election. The resolution was against Governor Small, Lt. Gov. Fred Sterling and State Auditor Andrew Russel, and the resolution added the charges in the indictments alleging theft when each was state treasurer.

Igoe also was an attorney who represented mobster Johnny Torrio at the time. Igoe later became a federal judge in Chicago.

In December 1925, when the Illinois Supreme Court ruled that Governor Small was liable for the interest money, talk of impeachment was renewed. Democrats started impeachment proceedings in 1926 but the Republican majority prevented this from coming to a vote.

Another avenue was tried to oust Small, using a different procedure.

Because of the culpability in the civil suit, it was argued that Small was indebted to the state when he was elected governor, a violation of the state constitution that made him ineligible for office. As such, impeachment was not the proper route. And so, *quo warranto* proceedings were begun to remove him from office.

Legislators cited Article IV, Section 4 of the Illinois State Constitution: "No person who has been, or hereafter shall be convicted of bribery, perjury or other infamous crime, nor any person who has been or may be a collector or holder of public moneys, who shall not have accounted for and paid over, according to law, all such moneys due from him, shall be eligible to the General Assembly, or to any office of profit or trust in this State."

It sounded like the governor's opponents had a good case.

Small's ineligibility was not a new argument in 1926. John Maynard Harlan, an opponent of Small in 1920, first raised the issue during the campaign. Harlan brought it up again in November 1924, just after the master in chancery ruled Small was liable.

James Hamilton Lewis, Democrat candidate for governor in 1920 and a former senator, warned voters in several campaign stops (including Kankakee) that Small was ineligible to become governor for this reason. Lewis repeated his opinion on July 20, 1921, the day Len Small was indicted by the grand jury.

"I pointed out to the people that those funds had not been accounted for," Lewis told *The New York Times* when the indictments were returned. "I told them that the governor could not be a legal candidate until he paid back to the state the amounts of money which he held as treasurer. Now, it is plain that I was right, that Mr. Small was not a candidate nor legally elected governor because the keeping of state funds a secret possession forbade him to hold any office under the state."

The Chicago Tribune editorialized on July 23, 1921 that if Small and Lt. Gov. Sterling were guilty of being indebted to the state, then neither Small nor Sterling constitutionally were eligible for their offices -- and that Frank Lowden still was governor, since he had to remain in office until handing it over to a legitimate successor. Others noted that State Sen. Richard Barr of Joliet, president *pro tem* of the Senate, would become governor if Small and Sterling were removed.

It was an interesting argument, and something that historians should consider today -- perhaps Len Small never was elected governor, either in 1920 or 1924, because he was not eligible since he had not paid the state what he owed.

Governor Small had a trick up his sleeve to fight the *quo warranto* proceedings. He had his Republican majority in the legislature introduce a law in May 1927 giving the governor and other state officials immunity from *quo warranto.*

The bill was sponsored by State Rep. Richard Meents. He was a Republican from Ashkum, a town just south of Kankakee. After the death of State Sen. Edward C. Curtis, Meents had become perhaps the closest local ally of Small.

Small's opponents tried to block the bill. State Rep. J. Bert Miller, a Republican from Kankakee, tried to get the bill amended so that it would not apply to current state officials. State Rep. Arthur Roe of Vandalia suggested an amendment that would exclude members of the General Assembly.

"This is an attempt to throw protection around the thief, the perjurer, the jury briber, the traitor that sits in the governor's chair," Miller told the legislature on May 24. "No one knows him better than I. I have lived in the same town with him for 40 years, and if there is a bigger thief and political crook anywhere, I'd like to see the color of his hair."

Miller continued his statement. "The only reason for this bill is that the present person sitting in the governor's office without right or authority to be there thinks that a *quo warranto* is going to be filed."

J. Bert Miller

"This proposal divides us into two classes, those who want immunity for themselves and those who don't," said Rep. Elmer Schnackenberg of Chicago. "As far as I am concerned, I don't want an immunity bath of any kind."

Rep. Lee O'Neil Browne, the Democrat who was one of the most vocal spokesmen of Small and the Chicago Machine, said, "It is not a question of protecting Len Small but one of protecting the governor of Illinois." Rep. Reed Cutler of Lewistown said he supported the bill because he thought it was unfair for a judge to remove someone who had been elected by the entire state!

The House voted for the *quo warranto* bill 108-29.

The Republican majority passed the law, without any amendments. Governor Small quickly signed it into law.

This meant that if the courts once and for all ruled that Small owed interest money to the state, the constitutional remedy -- to remove him from office because of ineligibility -- was no longer legal. Small's lawyers now could argue that the Constitution was unconstitutional.

Len Small finally had written into law the fact that he was above the law.

There was outrage in the legislature and across the state. Schnackenberg said Small bought votes in the House with promises of hard roads and patronage.

J. Bert Miller was furious at the passage of this bill. He made an impassioned speech before the General Assembly.

He began by saying, "I have no friends in the penitentiary who I desire to have pardoned. I have no friends on the payroll or wanting to get there. Nor am I suffering from that hard roads disease, concreteitis. In January 1917, with uplifted right hand, with perjury on his lips and treason in his heart, Small swore to uphold the Constitution. Within a month, he had his hands up to the shoulders in the state treasury and had removed 10 of the 30 million dollars and loaned it to the packers at 8 per cent." Miller then went into an account of the money laundering scheme and how Small ran from the sheriff to evade arrest. He spoke about the bribing of jurors, and Newmark and Boyle, and how the governor pardoned both men.

Miller then delivered the lines that were quoted in TIME magazine.

"Caesar had his Brutus, Jesus Christ had his Judas Iscariot, the United States had its Benedict Arnold and Jefferson Davis, and Illinois has Len Small. And if the Judas of Illinois had the courage of the Judas of Jesus, he would return the 30 pieces of silver, get a rope and hang himself, and remove the withering blight which will remain upon this state as long as he is governor of Illinois."

Miller's speech inflamed Len Small more than anything else had. Small's newspaper launched an attack in a torrent of ink that could be measured in gallons.

His *Kankakee Daily Republican* did not print Miller's remarks, but the newspaper went on for days with front-page stories condemning Miller, the *Chicago Tribune* and other enemies, in a high-powered frenzy.

The *Kankakee Daily Republican's* front page "news story" on May 26, 1927, which was headlined *GANGSTERS IN LEAGUE WITH THE TRIBUNE,* referred to Miller as "chief loudspeaker for the *Tribune* in its vilification of the governor and chief trafficker in vile epithets hurled at the Kankakee citizen who has done more for the upbuilding of the community than any other living man....Miller for years has been a bad breath in the politics of Kankakee County and who has continuously indulged in language unfit for the gutter when referring to Governor Small...the chief aim of these political bushmen is to poison the minds of the citizens of the state against Governor Small."

Miller's remarks in the General Assembly "is all a part of the plot" by the *Chicago Tribune,* the Kankakee newspaper continued.

And the newspaper included this ironic sentence: "A man such as Miller has proved himself to be not entitled to a single vote, unless at the hands of a jury where all 12 men vote 'Guilty.'"

Small's newspaper continued the attack on Miller's dramatic speech for days on end. It accused him of being the head of an evil cabal that was out to destroy all the great work Governor Small had been doing for the people. It said Miller's Kankakee County organization was the local branch of the *Chicago Tribune's* machine, dedicated to persecuting Len Small. It said Miller would have been sued for slander if not for a law which protects legislators from what they say in session. "That Chicago paper, in its long persecution of the governor, has never before been able to find a man in the state legislature of sufficiently low standards to stoop to the use of terms in which Miller used," the *Daily Republican* wrote.

Irony always seemed to be something that was lost on Len Small. While condemning the use of name-calling, Small's newspaper said that Miller's speech was "the senseless gibberish of a common, cheap, little disappointed office seeker who has never been able to take defeat like a man...and the ravings of a political shyster and permanent lame duck, seeking for a little theatrical puff."

The *Kankakee Daily Republican* started a nasty front-page column using the byline *Jaybirt* (J. Bert).

The governor finally got some political allies to condemn J. Bert Miller's remarks. His newspaper made it look like it was Miller who had been damned. *MILLER IS REBUKED ON FLOOR OF THE HOUSE,* screamed the Kankakee banner headline on June 8.

Rep. Harry McCaskrin of Rock Island introduced a resolution to bar *Chicago Tribune* representatives from the press box, floor and gallery of the House. He was compelled to withdraw his resolution.

Miller made another attempt at *quo warranto* by filing a petition of *mandamus* with the state Supreme Court in September 1927. Miller could not get Sangamon County State's Attorney H.E. Fullenwider to pursue *quo warranto,* so he went to the high court. Fullenwider opposed Miller's request in court.

Miller personally argued his legal appeal against the *quo warranto* bill before finally losing his fight in the Supreme Court on Feb. 24, 1928.

After Small left office, the legislature repealed its amendment to the *quo warranto* law. Governor Henry Horner, who pledged during his campaign to repeal the law, signed the bill.

Chapter 20

Governor Small's Second Term, 1925 - 1929

One might think that Governor Small's second term would not be as lively as his first term -- where he went on trial for embezzlement, faced a grand jury for possible jury tampering, faced impeachment, was accused of ties to the Ku Klux Klan and had numerous scandals both with the legislature and with the pardons he issued.

But one would be wrong.

Governor Small's second term was just as rocky and as controversial as his first. This man could not escape trouble, and that might be because most of his trouble was of his own making.

His major troubles are told in other chapters -- the civil lawsuit to recover the money he embezzled, his ties to the Mob, the Frank L. Smith campaign, the impeachment and *quo warranto* affair and the enlargement of the pardons and paroles scandal.

This chapter looks at a few other highlights of his second term.

Developing a "Lakes to the Gulf" waterways system was a priority for Governor Small. This huge project was undertaken during both his terms in office.

The Division of Waterways was a part of the Department of Public Works and Buildings. Governor Small changed that in 1925, making it a part of the Department of Purchases and Construction. He named his son Leslie the head of that department.

The waterways project was not Governor Small's idea although, like the roads, he acted like it was. A referendum was approved in 1908 to build the waterway but it wasn't until 1919 that the legislature passed the Illinois Waterway Act. It provided for construction of a deep waterway from Chicago's Sanitary and Ship Canal's power plant near Lockport, down the DesPlaines River to the Illinois River near Utica. The Illinois River runs into the Mississippi River and from there goes to the Gulf of Mexico.

Construction of five locks and dams were part of the project. They were at Lockport, Brandon Road at Joliet, Dresden Island between Joliet and Morris, Marseilles and Starved Rock. The first contract was for $1.3 million for the Marseilles lock, awarded in 1920 to Green & Sons. The Lockport contract was given to Green & Sons in 1923 for $1.4 million. The Starved Rock lock contract wasn't awarded until 1926, to Woods Bros. for $1.4 million.

The state decided to build the Dresden and Brandon locks itself after Leslie Small rejected all bids.

This decision brought more trouble for the Smalls. In March 1927, Leslie Small and William Mulvihill, his superintendent of waterways, were accused of trading construction contracts for campaign contributions.

The charge was brought by Chicago contractor Thomas Warner, who was the low bidder on the Brandon Road job. Small rejected Warner's bid along with the others. Small said the state would build it, but he retained Green & Sons as supervisors, with the company's employees transferred to the state payroll and the company equipment leased to the state.

Warner's lawsuit said this was "well devised to be a cover and instrumentality for boodle, graft and corruption."

After a three-day court fight in October 1928 to try to get the charges dismissed, Judge Phillip Sullivan agreed with the attorney general that the state and its departments should be dismissed as defendants, but the judge ordered Small and Mulvihill to stand trial as individuals for their actions.

In holding Small and Mulvihill for trial in October 1928, Judge Sullivan said their actions were "a devious manner of circumventing the law. The defendants have done indirectly what they are forbidden by statute to do directly."

Leslie Small and William Mulvihill also were named in a federal lawsuit in 1928, charged with conspiracy to destroy deep waterway development in part of the south branch of the Chicago River. The suit was filed by the owners of three acres on the river near 31st Street and Ashland Avenue.

The lawsuits went nowhere and did not stop construction.

There was another unpleasant note to this project when Governor Small desecrated Starved Rock for his personal promotion. He had the state put up a huge billboard, right on top of Starved Rock, with the words "Illinois Waterways Commission - LEN SMALL, GOVERNOR."

Starved Rock State Park near Utica is one of the state's most beautiful and most popular parks. The legend (believed now to be untrue) is that the Potawatomi and Fox Indians attacked the village of the Illinois (Illiniwek) Indians by the Great Rock in 1769 to avenge the murder of Chief Pontiac. After a fierce battle, the Illinois tribe retreated to the top of the rock for safety, where they were trapped and starved to death.

The *Chicago Tribune* printed a picture of the billboard on the bluff in its March 24, 1928 edition. It is the least scenic picture of the park you will ever see.

It was re-election season, and at the same time, billboards with Governor Small's picture were plastered in Chicago forest preserves. Board president Tony Cermak took them down, saying people wanted to look at nature, not at Small.

J. Bert Miller decided to run for state representative in 1926. Miller, a prominent Kankakee lawyer and former state's attorney, was one of many local Republicans who started out with Small in the 1890s and later broke with him. Even though Small was governor in 1926, he still kept his hand in local politics, running his hand-picked slates of candidates against the "anti" faction at home.

Small tried a slick trick to thwart J. Bert Miller in the April primary. Small put up his own candidate, Fred W. Miller.

Fred Miller was an assistant janitor at the Kankakee courthouse, in charge of cutting the grass, shoveling coal and washing windows.

Small really was backing State Rep. Clifford B. Sawyer, who was first elected in 1920. However, Small put Fred on the ballot to confuse voters who might want the other Miller.

Fred didn't want to run. But Len Small and Ed Jeffers circulated petitions in his behalf, simply because of his last name. Those circulating the petitions were state hospital workers and other state employees whose jobs depended on pleasing the Jeffers and Small political machine.

However, when the petitions were examined, many signatures were found to be fraudulent. Many signatures were in the same handwriting. Signers included chronic Kankakee bootleggers John Giusto and B.J. Matthews (who also was township supervisor). The petitions were notarized by Victor McBroom, another boss in the local party who ran a Kankakee restaurant and who had a bonus paycheck as a "state dietician."

The ruse did not work. J. Bert Miller beat all the candidates on the ballot and won the nomination. Small's forces could produce just 1,712 votes for Fred.

Small didn't stop there. Small convinced Louis Beckman to run as an independent against Miller. Beckman, a former beer salesman, was cashier in Small's bank and mayor of Kankakee. Beckman was reluctant and did not consent for a while, but ultimately acceded to the wishes of the Boss who made him mayor.

Beckman really didn't elaborate much on his campaign slogan, "More Roads and Governor Small's Policies."

Beckman generally was considered an honest man and a good mayor, aside from his association with Small politics.

Miller's campaign platform was directly opposed to Len Small's policies and included five main points: opposition to the gasoline tax, opposition to assessing state employees for campaign funds, opposition to "indiscriminate" pardoning and paroling of criminals, jailing bootleggers instead of just fining them, and a reduction in taxes.

Small's newspaper attacked Miller daily and it said Miller wanted to get in the legislature just so he could vote to impeach the governor, even if there wasn't good cause.

The governor and his editors never knew that one man is not bigger than the whole party. It wrote that Beckman "is running as a Petition candidate against J. Bert Miller, who was nominated on the Republican ticket and now is an anti-Small candidate."

Governor Small opened the Iroquois County Fair in Watseka on Aug. 31, 1926 with a long speech. He went through his usual self-congratulatory remarks about building hard roads and a waterways system from the Great Lakes to the Gulf and other accomplishments. But he could never make a speech without complaining about the persecution he suffered from his enemies.

Speaking of the crowds who came to his house to cheer him on the night he was first elected governor, and the promise he made to act in the best interests of the people, he said, "Little did I realize that night what that promise meant. What it meant for a public official to stand up and fight for the rights of the people against those great combinations, political and financial, which have been influencing political organizations, parties, yes, even governments, for their own financial gain. Little did I realize what it would cost a governor of the great state of Illinois to get in the way of the *Chicago Tribune,* the traction barons, and the grasping profiteers in an effort to stop the looting of the state treasury and the robbing of the taxpayers."

Chief Swift Bird

Len Small never did get a Mob nickname like "Greasy Thumbs" or "The Enforcer" or "The Embezzler." Even Len "Hard Roads" Small did not stick.

But he did get an Indian name.

His newspaper on June 30, 1927 reported that the governor was made a tribal chief and adopted brother of the Sioux Indian Nation.

He was dubbed "Chief Swift Bird."

This really was no more than a publicity stunt, and even the Kankakee newspaper admitted that it was bestowed by "Indians" from a touring circus as part of the publicity for their Springfield appearance.

Still, the Kankakee newspaper played it as a great honor.

"He is, to them, the reincarnation of a departed chieftain, who once ranked high in their tribunals, according to tradition," the Kankakee newspaper reporter wrote. "This honor was bestowed upon the governor June 27 by a band of Indians under Chief Returned from the Scouts, trouping with the Hagenbach-Wallace Circus. No higher honor can be given by these remnants of a departing race.

"This beautiful tribal custom, fittingly performed at the state capitol engagement of the Hagenbach-Wallace organization, formed a novel opening number for the evening entertainment. Surrounded by his warriors, their squaws and papooses, Chief Returned from the Scouts formally and solemnly initiated Chief Swift Bird. In his native tongue, with his right hand extended upward, the dusky warrior administered an impressive oath or obligation. The initiate, with due solemnity, accepted the honor, probably joining the assembled multitude in mild wonderment, regarding what it was all about.

"At the conclusion of this part of the ceremony, the chieftains thus united, clasped hands. The newly-admitted brother was then presented with a spear, entirely sheathed in ornamental feathers. The feathers render the implement useless as a weapon. It therefore denotes peace, in accordance with the signs and symbols of the Sioux."

A "Calumet Ceremonial," the smoking of a peace pipe, was supposed to be part of this, “but since Governor Small is not addicted to 'the weed,' the sheathed spear was substituted."

News-reel photographers were there to document the ceremony.

"In conclusion of the inauguration, the entire tribe, in full regalia, performed the dance of peace, repeatedly encircling the newly-ordained brother."

The news story, in accordance with the governor's intentions, got to the inevitable. O.D. Odom, the general manager of the circus and a veteran of big-top shows, praised Governor Small for his program of paving roads in Illinois. Good roads meant his wagons could travel more miles to more engagements, and farmers could get to the shows more easily, Odom said.

Governor Small never missed an opportunity to praise his "hard roads" program (or to lament the "persecution" he faced from his enemies). It was a fitting initiation: a solemn ceremony as the opening act of a circus, with fake Indians bestowing an honor upon a chief who spoke with a forked tongue.

Sm'all In The Family

Charges of nepotism are not unusual, particularly in Illinois, where even today there are dozens of little dynasties from the local level to the state level. The same names pop up again and again, and it's not just a case of a politician employing lots of family members in their own office (or employing them outside the office to do nothing). Many of these politicians pass their office on to their children.

Len Small faced his own charges of nepotism. In his case, his critics were alarmed at the extent of the power held by his family and by Kankakee cronies.

Some people argue that nepotism is wrong because it gives someone an unfair advantage and often that person is unqualified. But not always. It is not fair to say that the public is harmed just because a family member is put in a certain public position. Sometimes it is true and sometimes it is not.

Leslie Small

Len Small was a big believer in nepotism. His son Leslie became treasurer of the Kankakee school district in August 1912. The *Kankakee Gazette* wrote in August 1915: "Len Small's first move after he secured control of the board of education was to have his son elected treasurer at twice the salary of the preceding treasurer. Because treasurers were paid two per cent on money handled in former years does not detract from the fact that a former board had reduced this salary to $300 a year and it was immediately raised by Small's orders." Small responded by saying that his son Leslie was the first treasurer to accept a salary in lieu of the one per cent figure, and he said the salary was less than the one per cent figure.

Leslie was named a "confidential aide" to the governor in 1921 at a handsome salary.

Governor Small appointed his son to the Penitentiary Commission in August 1922, which oversaw the building of the massive Stateville penitentiary near Joliet. In 1925, Leslie Small was named director of the newly-created Department of Purchases and Construction, where he was in charge of handling tens of millions of dollars -- all the while he was still full-time editor of the Kankakee newspaper.

His state position put him in charge of the letting of contracts and the supervision of construction of all state projects, except road building. He was instrumental in locating a state mental hospital in Manteno, in Kankakee County, and he oversaw the contracts and construction there. State hospitals also were built at Dixon, Alton and Chicago. Other big projects included the grandstand at the Illinois State Fairgrounds at Springfield, several National Guard armories and more.

Leslie Small wasn't the only family member on the public payroll. The governor's son-in-law, Arthur Inglesh, got on the state payroll in 1921 as an "administrative auditor." Inglesh lived in the executive mansion with the governor. He later got a higher paying state position as administrative assistant in the Department of Finance, where he approved state vouchers. Inglesh also was a director in Small's First Trust bank in Kankakee.

The man who supervised the farm at the Kankakee State Hospital was fired so David McKinstry, the governor's brother-in-law, could have the job, at a raise in pay and an all-expenses-paid house that was needed by the physicians. McKinstry grew up on a farm near Grant Park and eventually managed the family nursery business. He started work as a landscape gardener at the state hospital in 1897, the year he married Mabel Small. In 1921, when Small became governor, McKinstry went on the state payroll as a "garden and dairy consultant" and later was put in charge of the farms operated by the Department of Public Welfare.

Small appointed his sister Mabel McKinstry as assistant superintendent of charities for the state.

Another brother-in-law, William Gray, was a "watchman" for the state.

Werner Schroeder was listed as a "foster son" of the governor. Selma Schroeder, employed as the governor's private secretary, was listed as a "foster daughter." Neither was formally adopted.

Werner Schroeder (1892-1960) was one of 10 children of Rev. Frederick Schroeder, pastor of St. Paul's Lutheran Church in Kankakee. Werner was one of Len Small's protégés and closest friends. Schroeder started as Small's secretary and later became Small's lawyers. In 1921, Schroeder was put on the state payroll. The state also paid Schroeder for his legal fees defending the governor in Waukegan.

Schroeder went on to vie for the position of chairman of the national Republican Party in 1942. TIME magazine described him as "bespectacled and colorless." It was his strong isolationist views that doomed him. *The New York Herald Tribune* said "the suggestion of his name is an insult to sound Republicanism. If the party wished to commit suicide, it could hardly do a quicker or more effective job than by placing a Schroeder in command."

TIME gave this assessment: "Werner William Schroeder's rise in the G.O.P. stems from the turbulent days of the late Len Small, onetime governor of Illinois. Small made him his protégé, gave him his first job at 16 addressing letters. When Small won the governorship in 1920, Schroeder became secretary of the state's Legislative Reference Bureau. When Small was indicted for having withheld state funds while he was treasurer, Schroeder defended him, won a sensational acquittal, which was followed by charges of jury fixing. As the result of a subsequent civil suit, Small coughed up $650,000 to the state treasury. Known as a good organizer and money-raiser, prosperous lawyer Schroeder is close-mouthed and shrewd. When he does make a statement, it is apt to be fence-straddling."

Schroeder later became vice chairman of the Chicago Transit Authority board and was its attorney. He was president of the Chicago Bar Association, a member of the Chicago Bible Society board and a member of the board of the Chicago Chapter of the National Conference of Christians and Jews.

Another family member, who the *Tribune* said may have been on the state payroll at one time, benefited from having friends in high places. William C. Burrell, the father-in-law of Leslie Small, was arrested by federal Prohibition agents on Sept. 14, 1928. Burrell and local bootlegger John Ciochetti operated a roadhouse called the Roamer Inn (yes, that was its name) near Chebanse, south of Kankakee. Agents seized 200 quarts of Canadian whiskey. Burrell was taken to federal court in Danville and bound over to the grand jury.

Governor Small gave a lot of big state jobs to cronies from Kankakee, and they put their own families on the payroll. W.H.H. Miller, named director of Registration and Education, had his daughter and son-in-law working in his office.

Some political appointments were appalling. Chauncey H. Jenkins, director of the Department of Public Welfare, appointed William J. Butler as an "inspector" even though Butler's real job was working in Small's election campaign office. Butler was paid from the department fund that was to provide care for the blind, deaf and insane wards of the state. Isidore Levin, ousted by Small as head of the Civil Service Commission, questioned Butler's qualification, saying Butler was known only as one of the state's biggest promoters of cock fights.

In April 1923, Attorney General Edward Brundage asked the governor why he paid $10,000 to relatives as "inheritance tax investigators" when the state auditor was paid for the same thing.

Several newspapers questioned the large number of Kankakee people on the state payroll in largely do-nothing jobs. The job of "game warden" was one that was handed out liberally.

"It is absolutely astonishing, the tremendous burden placed upon the state in caring for the fish and game of the Kankakee County district," the *Kankakee Daily News* wrote in 1924. "No less than five persons are required to prevent the sucker and carp escaping from the river, and to herd the rabbits away from the highways."

Cornelius R. Miller was another Illinoisan who wanted to be called "colonel." He was from Essex in Kankakee County. He was appointed deputy county clerk in 1894 and he was an assistant cashier at City National Bank in Kankakee. Miller became secretary and treasurer at the Kankakee Asylum in 1897. When Small was elected governor, he named Miller his Director of Public Works and Buildings.

Charles E. Robinson was a director in the First National Bank of Kankakee, a member of the board of trustees at the Kankakee asylum and a part owner of the *Kankakee Daily Republican.* Robinson joined the Kankakee asylum board after Small resigned to become state treasurer.

And people wanted to know why Small drew the pay for his household staff once a year in one lump check. Why did he want that appropriation paid that way? No one before or since had done it that way. Every other governor has paid the workers by individual checks.

This cartoon, from the April 6, 1928 *Kankakee Daily Republican* -- during Small's campaign for a third term, and reprinted locally over the years -- is how Kankakee wants Len Small to be remembered.

Chapter 21

The 1928 Campaign

Len Small announced his candidacy for a third term on Feb. 8, 1928. His announcement came just hours after a midnight conference with Chicago Mayor Thompson. Small said he was using Thompson's "America First" slogan as his own.

"They came from the politically significant conference arm-in-arm and smiling," the Associated Press reported. "Governor Small will seek nomination and election for a third term. Mayor Thompson, in return for political support in Cook County and Chicago, will receive control of state patronage there."

Small made this statement in announcing his candidacy:

"Due to our entire agreement in fundamental principles of public policy, and the friendship of many years that has existed between us, I have determined that in appointments and policies affecting Chicago, I shall seek the advice of Mayor Thompson and shall be guided by his suggestions and counsel, to the end that we may work in harmony in the solution of problems affecting Chicago and the state of Illinois and in the appointment of proper officers on park boards and in other state functions relating to Chicago."

Of course, the campaign began long before the official announcement. After the legislature passed the state budget in June 1927, Governor Small vetoed $100,000 from Secretary of State Louis Emmerson's budget. It was the opening shot in Small's battle with his chief rival.

Republicans in Illinois had fought vigorously to deny re-nomination to Small in 1924. They fought just as hard in 1928. Once again, the regular Republican party fought to dump the incumbent governor of its own party in favor of *anyone else.* They chose Emmerson as their candidate to face Small in the primary.

Emmerson was a good choice. He held a high profile state office and he was a popular individual.

The source of Small's strength in 1928 was a slush fund of two million dollars, assessed from state employees, as well as those 30,000 workers who were paid on state time to campaign for the governor.

Much of Small's rhetoric consisted of touting his accomplishments in building hard roads and his version of fiscal responsibility. It also consisted of negativity, something that Small just could not get out of his system. His statement on April 9, just before the primary election, included these remarks: "Our opposition consists mainly of the greedy, unscrupulous *Chicago Tribune, Chicago Daily News* and their profiteering allies. Their campaign is and has been based on falsehoods and contemptible insinuations and trickery."

To go through the series of campaign appearances and political rhetoric from Small in 1928 would be nothing but a repeat of the previous chapters. Brundage. Cement trusts. Tax dodgers. Profiteers. Hard roads. Lies. Persecution. *Chicago Tribune.* You got it.

What made 1928 so unique was the desperate lengths to which the politicians in Chicago went in order to win this election. Bombings and tommy-guns were not confined to the wars over bootlegging and labor racketeering. The heavy artillery was brought out to convince voters just who was the better man.

The 1928 primary election in Chicago was known as the "Pineapple Primary."

Pineapples were the hand grenades used by gangsters to show that Len Small and the other candidates favored by the Chicago Mob were worthy of the public trust. More than 60 pineapples were used to bomb storefronts and homes in this campaign.

Chicagoans were numb to the bootlegging and the violence on their streets as mobsters shot one another. But the excess of violence in the Pineapple Primary -- violence that went beyond gangland business and went into the electoral system at the very ballot box -- was one of the final nails in the coffin of Big Len and Big Bill's careers. Another turning point was the St. Valentine's Day Massacre ten months later, where Capone's gunmen slaughtered five members of rival Bugs Moran's gang, plus two bystanders, in Moran's garage at 2122 N. Clark St. The carnage horrified America. It was the beginning of the end of Capone and it was the beginning of the end of Capone's mayor, Big Bill Thompson.

Two political figures were murdered during the Pineapple Primary.

One was gangster Giuseppe "Diamond Joe" Esposito, 19th Ward committeeman who made his money from bootlegging, extortion, prostitution and labor racketeering. Esposito was gunned down in front of his wife and daughter.

Esposito worked with U.S. Senator Charles S. Deneen. The day after Esposito's funeral, Deneen's home was bombed. Other homes bombed as part of this "election campaign" were the homes of Judge John Swanson, City Controller Charles Fitzmorris and Public Service Commissioner William Reid.

The other political figure murdered was Octavius C. Granady, a black lawyer who was a candidate for committeeman in the "Bloody 20th Ward." On the day of the primary, Granady was chased in his car, driven off to the curb, then blasted with sawed-off shotguns. The gunmen worked for Granady's opponent, mobster Morris Eller, who also was Republican state central committeeman and sanitary district trustee.

Twenty-three men were indicted for the murder of Granady and for the other election day terrorism. Indicted along with Eller was Harry Hochstein, one of Eller's chief gunmen. Hochstein was known for gangland terror and kidnapping and for his work for Mayor Thompson and Governor Small. Hochstein liked to strap on two guns when he intimidated voters and other people. He was joined by his brother Isidore, who recently got out of Leavenworth penitentiary for dealing in stolen cars. Hochstein was caught in a vote fraud scandal with Fred Lundin in 1926, disenfranchising tens of thousands of voters, particularly in the black neighborhoods.

Along with the gangsters indicted for Granady's murder were Chicago police officers Peter Pacelli, George Hartigan, Marshall Couch and Arthur Swanson; State Sen. James B. Leonardo; and Abe and Martin Klass, cousins of Judge Emanuel Eller and nephews of Morris Eller.

Benny Zion was one of the gangsters indicted for the murder of Granady. The Mob's way of handling his upcoming trial was to put several bullets in Zion in his home on July 31, 1928.

When the defendants went to trial in October 1928, two witnesses testified that Granady had been marked for murder long in advance of election day.

There was testimony about the political meeting Morris Eller held for about 30 of his "campaign workers" on the night before the primary. "Now boys," Eller said, "don't drink any whiskey tonight. Go home early and get to bed because you've got be up at five in the morning. We've got to win this election and it's a big job. The police won't bother you. And any of you boys that don't have guns can get them at Emanuel's house."

This was the testimony of William Sephus to the jury. Sephus was at the meeting.

The *Chicago Tribune* reporter wrote that Eller "told his workers to fear nothing because they had a governor, state's attorney, sheriff, police and a judge, meaning his son, Judge Emanuel Eller, with them, and in which he told those who needed guns they could get them at 'Emanuel's house' was twice repeated to the jury by witnesses who testified they were there and heard it."

The other witness who testified to this was Edward Johnson, an election judge and Eller campaign worker who got a city job from Eller. Both Sephus and Johnson said Judge Eller was at the meeting.

Two boxes of automatic weapons were unloaded from Eller's car that night by Aubrey Reed and Harry Hochstein, who carried them to the third-floor meeting room at 1229 Blue Island Ave.

Sephus and Johnson said that Abe "Humpy" Klass, one of the defendants, told them that "the same thing that happened to Granady will happen to you" after they had testified before the grand jury that returned the indictments against the defendants.

The defendants were represented by four defense attorneys, including Michael Ahern, a Mob lawyer on Al Capone's payroll.

Four policemen and three mobsters went to trial. None were convicted.

TIME magazine on March 5, 1928 sarcastically observed that "Chicago has been peacefully humdrum in recent weeks, except for a few episodes, such as: The bombing of the City Comptroller's home. The bombing of a ward boss's home. The bombing of a judge's home. The bombing of the State's Attorney's secretary's home. The discovery of a bomb large enough to raze a five-story building beside an elevated railway pillar."

The magazine added that 300 policemen were guarding other city officials' homes, and "two families in Thompson's apartment building took good advice and moved out." There also was the holdup of a train by six bandits who bombed open the mail car and took $133,000.

"The bombers' technique appeared to derive from a style of bombing inaugurated last autumn by the Chicago Association of Candy Jobbers, whose methodical representatives found little to deter them from pitching 'pineapples' into independent goody factories," TIME wrote. "Pineapples are convenient, effective and easy to obtain in Chicago, where bomb-making has almost the status of an industry. 'Our people are being terrorized,' said president Frank Joseph Loesch of the Chicago Crime Commission."

Among the bombers was Ben Newmark, who had intimidated jurors into acquitting Governor Small.

TIME magazine's April 2 issue observed that, "Mayor William Hale ('Big Bill') Thompson was frankly borrowing the Coolidge virtues as window-dressing for a campaign in behalf of discredited Governor Len Small."

The Pineapple Primary got a lengthy write-up in TIME's April 9 issue. Here is part of that account:

"In Chicagoese, 'pineapple' is a euphemism for an ugly, black, egg-shaped object known elsewhere as a hand-grenade. Since the first of the year they have been utilized 21 times by racketeers angry for one reason or another with fellow racketeers, politicians, bootleggers, gamblers. Last week, 'pineapples' exploded on the doorstep of U. S. Sen. Charles Deneen and Judge John Swanson. The results were mild for Chicago; no one was killed; only the fronts of two houses were blown to splinters. Then, four days later, a thing too big to be called a 'pineapple' failed to explode in the South Water Street market when wet snow snuffed out its sputtering fuse. It contained 17 sticks of dynamite, enough to wipe out an entire city block.

"Who did the above deeds, and why, remained a mystery, the usual Chicago bombing mystery. Posters were tacked on fences and poles throughout the city, advertising $65,000 in rewards for information concerning the Deneen and Swanson pineapplers. Mayor William Hale 'Big Bill' Thompson, State's Attorney Crowe and others were sponsors of the rewards. Meanwhile, Chief of Police Michael Hughes reported, 'It is almost impossible to trace bombers. There are 50 places in the city where dynamite can be purchased, just as a person buys a package of cigarettes.'

"Bootleg gangsters hold Sen. Deneen responsible for a recent attempt at Prohibition enforcement, in which raids were staged on 11 cabarets that considered themselves immune from such treatment. That may have inspired the bombing as well as the assassination of 'Diamond Joe' Esposito, gangster, Deneen henchman of the 25th ward, flashy hero of Chicago's Little Italy. Fortnight ago, 'Diamond Joe' stood on a corner, five doors from his home, when an automobile drove up to the curb. There was a rat-tat-tat and the automobile drove away, leaving 58 slugs in the body of 'Diamond Joe.' He had a fine funeral. His coffin cost $5,000. Senator Deneen came from Washington to walk in the rain in a procession that stretched for a mile and a half.

"Sen. Deneen is leader of the Republican faction that is fighting to oust the incumbent administration of Mayor Thompson, State's Attorney Crowe, Governor Len Small, plus Frank L. Smith who is again running for the seat in the U. S. Senate in which he was not permitted to sit. The 'better element' and all the Chicago newspapers, except the two Hearst papers, say the Thompson-Crowe-Small-Smith faction is vile, vicious, responsible for Chicago's maladies. But, curiously enough, the maligned fellows have a habit of winning elections. It does not matter that, in 1924,

Mr. Crowe called his present ally, Mayor Thompson, 'the worst political derelict pestering Chicago.' Nor does it matter that Sen. Deneen was the good friend of Mr. Smith when the latter was trying to get into the Senate. Now Sen. Deneen is supporting one Otis F. Glenn, the opponent of Mr. Smith, for the vacant Senate seat. To oust Governor Small, Sen. Deneen is grooming one Louis L. Emmerson. Everything will be settled at the Republican primaries on April 10, if the pineapples permit."

Thompson and Crowe claimed that Deneen and Swanson bombed their own homes to get public sympathy.

TIME continued: "Forget trouble and have a few parades, was Mayor Thompson's solution of the Chicago frenzy. He called together representatives of 50 improvement organizations and business clubs, explained to them his plan of a big improvement parade every other week until Christmas. Said he, 'Holding parades is the only way we can attract the attention of the public to what we are doing. The papers never boost us; they always lie.' Concerning crime, the fat mayor said, as he relaxed in bedroom slippers and short-sleeved, open-necked sport shirt in his hotel suite, 'Sure, we have crime here. We always will have crime. Chicago is just like any other big city. You can get a man's arm broken for so much, a leg for so much or beaten up for so much. Just like New York or any other big city -- excepting we print our crime here and they don't.'"

The Thompson administration, which always hated reformers, decided to make war against the "Untouchables" -- federal agent Eliot Ness and his men who had been sent to Chicago to battle bootleggers. The TIME story added, "Later in the week, Chief of Police Mike Hughes sent out 525 policemen in automobiles with orders to arrest not bombers, but U. S. Prohibition agents. Said he, 'Bring in the whole gang. We'll see whether these roughnecks from the East can shoot up Chicago and get away with it.' The reason for Chief of Police Hughes' sudden activity was that a Prohibition agent had shot and wounded one William Beatty, political worker for Mayor Thompson, in a saloon."

This wasn't a surprise. Thompson opposed the Prohibition law from the beginning. In his 1927 campaign, he spoke against Mayor Dever's crackdown on speakeasies and promised to reopen those that had been raided and closed. Al and Ralph Capone owned one of the area's biggest nightclubs, the Cotton Club in Cicero, one of many Mob-owned places where the Prohibition laws were not enforced. Thompson often was seen there, along with aldermen, judges and police.

Nebraska Senator George W. Norris urged President Calvin Coolidge to pull some American troops out of Nicaragua and send them to Chicago. It was not done, but that was how bad things had gotten in Chicago.

This was the Chicago and the state of Illinois that William Hale Thompson and Len Small handed over to Organized Crime. This is why the Roaring Twenties roared with tommy-guns and corruption.

Later in the year, Frank Loesch went hat-in-hand to see Al Capone at the gangster's Lexington Hotel fortress. Loesch was president of the Chicago Crime Commission. He was afraid that the general election would be a repeat, or possibly worse, than the Pineapple Primary had been. Loesch asked Capone if the Mob boss would allow Cook County to have an honest election in November.

Loesch knew that "Capone ran the city and that his hand reached into every department of the city and county government."

Behind heavily-armed bodyguards, Loesch found Capone sitting at his desk beneath a portrait of Big Bill Thompson. He later related the encounter.

"Now look here, Capone," Loesch said, "will you help me by keeping your damned cutthroats and hoodlums from interfering with the polling booths?"

Capone was arrogant but cooperative. He had Thompson in City Hall and most of the police on his payroll. Capone didn't care who won this election, since Small was out.

"Sure," Capone said. "I'll have the cops send over squad cars the night before the election and jug all the hoodlums and keep 'em in the cooler until the polls close."

It was that simple for a man of Capone's power. He kept his word. Loesch later said it was the cleanest election in 40 years.

Loesch's account is very revealing. It was Capone who sent the police out, it wasn't the chief of police who gave orders. Capone had the police interfere with the election in the spring and he had them keep things clean in the fall. That says a lot about just who was in control in the state of Illinois in the late 1920s.

A Cook County grand jury issued a report in June 1928 about the bloody primary. The *Chicago Tribune* wrote, "The alliance (between politics and crime) is really present, the jurors found. Their report stated that criminals have come to possess powerful public positions; elections have been held to the tune of terrorists' guns; political bosses and gangs of gunmen have seized control of whole wards during election contests; policemen have stood idly by while the hoodlums worked at slugging, shooting and kidnapping."

"Carl R. Latham, recent president of the Chicago Bar Association, declared that leaders of the Small-Thompson-Crowe-Galpin-Eller combination had entered into a desperate effort to forestall defeat by a wholesale theft of votes at the primary," the *Tribune* story continued. "Crime, said Mr. Latham, was the stepchild of crooked politics." (Latham was referring to Homer Galpin, the chairman of Thompson's 1931 campaign and the crooked political boss of the 27th Ward. Galpin also was the owner of eight bootleg breweries. Eller was mobster Morris Eller).

F. Edson White, president of Armour & Co., was foreman of the grand jury that investigated Granady's murder and other events connected with the Pineapple Primary. He said the grand jury "was impressed with the ease with which these crimes may be committed and the criminals go unpunished under the present system under which our elections are conducted." The present system "puts the control of election officials in the hands of the local managing committee and ward leaders of each party." (White died on Jan. 15, 1931, "accidentally" falling from the seventh floor balcony of his Chicago apartment.)

Among the abuses found by the grand jury during the April primary: the abuse of illiterate voters' rights; forcing voters to cast their votes for certain candidates; fictitious names on registration lists and voting in these names by gang members, often repeatedly at different polling places; assaulting voters, even kidnapping them; election judges and clerks aiding such activity and the police turning a blind eye to it; and, of course, the shooting of Granady and others.

"The result of such unlawful and murderous tactics has been the nomination to offices of men who have no right to them and who as criminals may be in influential official positions where they control the destinies of the people of Chicago and Cook County to the scandal and disgrace of the law-abiding citizens of Chicago," the grand jury report read. "The alliance of crime and politics was manifested to us in the testimony produced before us and that alliance is always cemented at the primary election by force, frauds and murder."

"We were also deeply impressed with the total inadequacy of the protection afforded at the polling places in many precincts by the police officers stationed there. Evidence was submitted to us that watchers at the polls in certain precincts were beaten and kidnapped within full view of the police officer stationed there without his turning his hand to prevent such crimes and violence and to protect and aid the citizens so assaulted while performing his lawful civic duty."

In April 1928, Small's chauffeur was driving him to a rally in East St. Louis. Near Girard, Illinois, Small's car passed a car occupied by two country men. Small's chauffeur honked and sped past the other car, and then cut in sharply and sideswiped the other car, sending it into the ditch. The men were cut and bruised in the accident.

Len Small lost his bid for re-nomination in this election to Louis Emmerson by a landslide 63 to 36 percent. He was finished in Illinois politics.

"The disgrace which would accrue to Illinois from a third term of Smallism was blazoned forth from the pages of leading Chicago journals," wrote Carroll H. Woody. "A virulent cartoon campaign was initiated by the *Chicago Tribune* against Smith, Small and Thompson, the 'gold dust triplets' and 'traction trio,' the puppets of Insull. The groundswell of protest rolled up by primary day into an irresistible wave of public feeling, sweeping the offending candidates to well-deserved defeat. Smith-Small-Crowe-Thompson were tossed aside as the 'reform' ticket piled up encouraging majorities for the greater number of its candidates."

But Len Small, the bitter man who always attacked anyone who opposed him, found it impossible to be gracious in defeat. Instead of congratulating his opponent and wishing him well in the general election against the Democrats, Small issued this concession statement on April 11, the day after the election:

"The *Chicago Tribune* and its profiteering allies have won. As I have said many times during the campaign, this was not a contest between Len Small and Louis L. Emmerson. It was a contest between the *Chicago Tribune* and its vicious, profiteering allies on one hand, and the people of Illinois on the other hand.

"They have won. It is a victory of the great wealth of the interests represented by the *Chicago Tribune,* and a victory brought about by the most vicious and unscrupulous lies and falsehoods, circulated through the *Chicago Tribune* and other newspapers. Every Chicago newspaper refused to print my statements, giving my views, even when signed by me. I request that any paper which prints this statement from me be fair enough to print it in full without alteration.

"They prostituted the Masonic organization, which is a fraternal organization, by dragging it into the lowest mire of corrupt politics. They circulated through the state the unfounded and false reports that I was affiliated with the Klan, when the instigators of that story knew that I had never joined the Klan or attended a Klan meeting or was in any way connected with the Klan. They themselves are guilty of all the things of which they have accused me.

"Personally, so far as the results of this election are concerned, I have no regrets. My only concern is for the best interests of the people of our state, and I have endeavored during my official career to protect them from the *Chicago Tribune* and its grasping, grafting, profiteering allies. I will continue during the few remaining months of my administration, as I have in the past, to do the very best I can, the very best I know how, for the welfare of the people of Illinois.

"The confidence shown me by the people who know me best, and especially my home county where I was born and have lived all of my life, and which has always given me an overwhelming majority, means more to me than the holding of any office."

That was his statement, in full, without alteration.

On the front page of that same day's edition of the *Daily Republican* was the news story of the election, with this as its lead paragraph: "For the first time in the memory of many of the oldest citizens of Illinois, the *Chicago Tribune* has succeeded in fooling a majority of the electorate in an important election."

The rest of the story went on in the same vein.

Small spent the remainder of his term fairly low key, giving out ribbons at the Kankakee fair and making a speech at the annual town celebration in nearby Herscher on Aug. 28. In September, Small bought an 81-acre apple orchard in Washington State for $100,000 and a summer home in Michigan City, Ind.

Governor Small later did show one little glimpse of magnanimity in defeat -- he announced he would allow the winner of the general election, Louis Emmerson, to become governor.

Had he been considering calling out National Guard troops to stay in office? Who knows? But he found it necessary to announce that he would not stand in the way of the people's choice. A story from Dec. 7, 1928 (attributed to the Associated Press and printed in the *Kankakee Daily Republican*) began:

"Governor Len Small announced this afternoon that he would not question the eligibility of Louis L. Emmerson to assume the governorship, nor hinder him in any way, nor attempt to support upward of 3,000 state employees on state payrolls in consequence of temporary civil service permits."

That wasn't exactly a generous spirit. Small's more typically blunt flow of bile was evident on Jan. 9, in his final address to the General Assembly, which should have been a dignified event.

"Pointing to the fact that the former Chief Justice of the Supreme Court became a candidate for governor, the message gives credence to common gossip that the Supreme Court had been used against him," the news story in the *Kankakee Daily Republican* (and attributed as an AP story) went.

In reporting on the state of the state, Small got right to the court decision against him in the civil suit.

"Passing years," the governor wrote, "will enable us to look at the decision with candid and unbiased eyes, and we shall all look on that day as a regrettable incident in the history of the judicial department of this state."

The governor called the civil lawsuit "false and malicious" and said that Justice Frank K. Dunn "was writing for the opinion in such a manner as to make it campaign material for himself when he became a candidate for governor."

(Frank K. Dunn was 74 in 1928 and never became a candidate for governor. He served on the Supreme Court from 1907 to 1933. Chauncey Jenkins, Small's crooked paroles chief, ran against Dunn for the Republican nomination for the high court in 1924).

Governor Small continued to give a large part of his speech to defending himself in a case he had already lost.

"The condition under which the civil suit was tried made it impossible for me to obtain a fair and impartial decision," The governor said. "Throughout the pendency of the case, certain newspapers, backed by powerful interests that found it impossible to control my official actions, indulged in a constant assault upon me with the intent of influencing the minds of the judges before whom my case was from time to time pending."

Small continued that he could not have received a fair trial because "terrorism" from certain newspapers was "influencing the minds of the judges."

And, as always, Small made the point that the $650,000 judgment against him stipulated that he did not have to admit guilt. Furthermore, he said, the $650,000 judgment was not "paid back" to the treasury "because it never was in the state treasury and it never belonged to the state. None of it had ever been received by me as interest on public funds."

It was a good thing that Len Small was not standing before a judge's bench when he made the accusation that the court decision was made on a personal political basis, or that a judge was brainwashed by what he read in a newspaper.

Small also used the occasion to defend his record on pardons and paroles. It was the same speech he made time and time again, that Illinois had the best record of any state in the nation in regard to parolees keeping on the straight and narrow path. He did not mention Al Capone or the selling of pardons.

A few days later, Small decided to put on a more relaxed and reflective image. In an interview in the Jan. 11, 1929 *Kankakee Daily Republican,* Small said he was "satisfied with his work and ready to take a rest."

"They tell me that I'm to learn golf," Small said. "Maybe I may learn golf, but I doubt it. I think I'll not stay in one place long enough to learn to play anything."

His life had been all work and no play. "I have never been an entertainer. I cannot play cards, and public speaking is a hardship.

"I leave a poorer, much poorer man, if you mean financially. But money counts for little. I have always had enough to live. There is another loss that pains. I go away without the wife I brought here."

Small revealed a lot about himself in this little interview.

"There are some things I never can forget. Disappointments in some who have turned away from me have been keen but I find joy in the thought that in Illinois today I have more friends of the kind that count than I had when I became governor. I have learned with some sadness that there are many who are friends only while favors are to be had, while the governor, for instance, still dispenses pardons and appointments."

Reflection turned to boasting, as it always did. "I know what it is to bring cheer to cheerless hearts, of thoughts of Illinois' unfortunates. That I have been the means of greater happiness to many, that I have served fully and have withheld nothing is a continuing reward. The building of hard roads where hard roads have never gone before has been one of my chief pleasures."

Candidate Louis Emmerson spoke at a big political rally at the Kankakee armory on Oct. 17, 1928. With him were Congressman (and former governor) Richard Yates and Lt. Gov. Fred Sterling.

Governor Small did not attend.

After his loss in 1928, Len Small continued to seek the nomination for governor for the rest of his life.

Kankakee Daily Republican, March 31, 1928

Chapter 22

The Governor's Last Campaigns

Len Small never gave up his political ambitions and he really never stopped running for office or trying to control other elections. Even local elections saw the former governor fighting as he always had.

And Small continued to find ways to remain in the news while out of office -- beginning on the day he left the governor's mansion.

Governor Louis Emmerson was surprised when he entered the executive mansion on Jan. 14, 1929.

He may have thought burglars had cleaned out furnishings and other valuables belonging to the state. He was right.

When Len Small moved out, he took more than just suitcases of clothes. Three truckloads of furnishings, including tables, wall hangings, rugs, linens, dishes, valuable silverware and more were packed up and taken to Kankakee.

Emmerson had wondered why he hadn't been allowed to inspect the mansion before moving in. Now he knew why.

The new governor and his wife were embarrassed at an informal reception in the executive mansion the night of his inauguration, and their guests were shocked.

The furnishing and kitchenware in the mansion were far below the standards one would have expected. The fine glassware was gone, replaced by "dime store" glasses. Dishes and silverware also were cheap replacements, and there wasn't enough dinnerware for a dozen guests. Drawer after drawer where towels and linens should have been found, now were bare. Even the flour bin was empty.

The lamps were old and rusty. A maid told a guest that she had gotten them down from the attic where Lowden had stored them. Small had taken the good stuff home.

The legislature in 1917 had appropriated $25,000 to Lowden to furnish the house when he became governor. The very wealthy Lowden donated $25,000 in china, crystal and silverware to the executive mansion from his own pocket.

Governor Small spent a huge amount of state money on furnishings and equipment during his eight years there. The figure totaled $91,000 in just the last two years of Small's administration. But where was it?

The Emmersons had to equip the mansion with their own possessions and from their own pocket until the legislature appropriated funds for new furnishings to replace those taken by Len Small.

"Yes, State Mansion Is Still There -- But Little Else Of Value Found When Gov. Emmerson Moves In" was the headline in the *Kankakee Daily News.* The *Chicago Tribune* said the "mansion" was now a "shack."

The story was circulated once more in 1932 when Small ran again. A Sept. 21 article in the *Chicago Times* was headlined *Claim Silver Vanished With Small, Democrats Say Nominee Stripped State Mansion,* and it repeated the story that Emmerson was not allowed to inspect the mansion until after Small had left, and that Emmerson found "an empty shell. Small apparently had devoted the last few days of his regime to clearing the mansion." The *Times* said that the theft included $25,000 in silverware that had been presented to the mansion by his predecessor, Frank O. Lowden, and another $25,000 in silverware and furnishings that was bought with taxpayer money.

It said that Small left office "with his pockets full" and he sent three truck-loads of furnishings from the governor's mansion to his home in Kankakee.

The story was expanded in the *Chicago Tribune.* "Rugs, linens, draperies, dishes were said too have been carried through the back door of the mansion at night and loaded on trucks that carried them to Kankakee. These charges were printed at the time, almost four years ago, and not until a few weeks ago was there an attempt at a public denial. This belated move was considered an attempt to stop circulation of the facts during the campaign."

Small found this story was embarrassing to his 1932 campaign, so he sued the *Chicago Times.* He dropped the lawsuit a year later.

But it's funny how some things stick. In June 2008, I asked 94-year-old Bill O'Connor of Irwin if he remembered Governor Len Small. "He stole all the silver from the governor's mansion when he left office!" was the first thing he said.

Small's campaign to regain the governor's mansion began in earnest in 1931. A story in his newspaper on July 10 told of a "boom" to restore him to power. It quoted *Chicago's American* newspaper, a *Tribune* competitor friendly to Small.

The *American* story said Mayor Thompson and Small formed a "political alliance" and a rally was planned at Kankakee to kick off the 1932 campaign. Thompson promised to be there.

"I regard Len Small as the best governor Illinois has had in my time," Thompson said. "He is an American. As governor, he has carried through more improvements, did more for the Illinois waterway and kept more men at work than any governor ever did. He is conscientious and painstaking."

He said Small would sign a law repealing Prohibition and "provide the lead-ership to bring Illinois out of the Depression and back to prosperity."

(Small could not repeal Prohibition. It was an amendment to the Constitution and could only be repealed by another amendment, which it was in 1933.)

The *Quincy Whig,* another pro-Small newspaper often quoted by the Kankakee newspaper, went even further in its praise. It suggested naming an impor-tant new bridge over the Mississippi River for the former governor, even though it already was named for another man.

Len Small really began running for the 1932 nomination in April 1931. The campaign informally was launched by former Mayor Thompson with a boat ride on the *Cape Girardeau* down the Mississippi River. Thompson enjoyed these boating trips. He sailed from Chicago on a publicity tour after leaving office in 1923. Former Governor Small joined Thompson at Beardstown for the 1931 trip. A whole lot of other politicians, lawyers and union bosses joined the cruise. They rode all the way to Cairo, making speeches at towns along the way.

The kickoff rally was at the Kankakee Armory on Sept. 19, 1931. At the rally were Mayor Thompson, Frank L. Smith, William Lorimer and a number of state politicians and union bosses. Among the union bosses was Thomas J. Murray, business manager of the Electrical Workers Union and vice president of the Chicago Building Trades Council -- at the time, known for its use of thugs to intimidate non-union workers and contractors through bombings and beatings. Several labor unions with ties to the Chicago Mob supported Small in 1932.

Small said the economy was prosperous during his terms in the 1920s and said Governor Emmerson was partly to blame for the Depression. Among his campaign issues, Small said, would be to repeal the state search and seizure law, protect bank deposits from dishonest bankers, provide more state construction jobs, oppose the League of Nations and promise to stay out of foreign entanglements and -- his campaign slogan -- bring the state "Back to Prosperity."

Frank L. Smith suggested another slogan to the crowd: "We Want Len, Lou Won't Do." The crowd repeated the chant on command.

Big Bill made the keynote speech and his was the last speech at the rally. That was because he was a show-stopper who could not be followed. He was "dynamic and almost violent in his spectacular showmanship...accompanied by flailing gestures and punctuated by crashing blows with his fist to the table before him," the Kankakee reporter wrote.

"Coining apt phrases rapidly and extemporaneously, coatless and drenched with perspiration, his declamation that of an old fashioned spellbinder was received with wild cheering and applause by his audience. When he had finished, hundreds pressed forward to shake his hand." It was everything that Big Bill lived for, and a reason why it always was hard to tell whether a rally was for him or for Small.

The *Kankakee Daily Republican* used its usual modest journalistic behavior in promoting the event. A huge headline in its Sept. 17 edition read *"WHOLE STATE RALLIES FOR SMALL -- REPORTS SHOW HOPES REST ON KANKAKEE MAN."*

The headline on Sept. 19 was even larger: *"OVATION FOR SMALL TREMENDOUS EVENT -- Kankakee Man Agrees to Become GOP Candidate for Governor -- CROWD CHEERS WILDLY AT WORD OF ACCEPTANCE -- SMALL IS LAST HOPE OF PARTY TO SAVE STATE."*

Edward Brundage announced his candidacy for the Republican nomination for governor in February 1932. He promised to work for repeal of Prohibition. He said it was a failure, unenforceable and had given rise to a murderous criminal element. It was an economic and social issue, not a moral issue, he said.

Brundage came out swinging on April 1, attacking what had long been a source of corruption, the West Side Park Board. He said it was a "playground for gangsters, political pay-rollers and Republican party racketeers." Brundage said the parks had 1,700 employees and only 1,000 did any work. The rest were "lagoon watchers" on patronage payrolls. Two of these people were relatives of a west side alderman allied with Al Capone.

"I am told that the plague of political locusts is responsible for the fact that 24 playgrounds and recreation centers were closed on Feb. 1 for lack of funds to maintain them," Brundage said. He could have made that speech a dozen years earlier when Mayor Thompson was in control of the system.

Len Small won the Republican nomination for governor in 1932.

He won by quite a large margin, beating Omer Custer, Oscar Carlstrom, Edward Brundage and William H. Malone. Small's victory was credited to a large effort by the still-powerful Machine.

TIME magazine printed this campaign story in its April 25, 1932 issue: "Last September, three notorious Republicans of Illinois journeyed to flat, sun-baked Kankakee, site of the State Insane Asylum, on high political business. One was William Hale 'Big Bill' Thompson, whom Chicago had booted out as its profligate mayor the spring before. Another was William Lorimer, expelled in 1912 from the U. S. Senate for employing 'corrupt methods and practices in his election.' The third was Frank Leslie Smith, barred in 1928 from the U. S. Senate for excessive campaign expenditures.

"In Kankakee, this trio, with many a rowdy follower, called on buck-toothed old Lennington Small, twice governor of Illinois. Banker Small, whose political record was no better than those of his callers, accepted their invitation to run again for the Republican nomination for governor. His battle cry: 'America first! Back to prosperity with Len Small!'

"Last week, news-hawks flocked about the Small home in Kankakee. Len Small had won his nomination. Though he got only 36 percent of the GOP primary vote, he managed to nose out four other candidates. As a Wet, he handily defeated a weasler, one Omer N. Custer, whom repeal-vetoing Governor Louis Emmerson had selected as his successor. Nominee Small declaimed: 'I accept the responsibility of leading the people in their battle against the forces of wealth, greed and privilege back to prosperity!'

"While Big Bill Thompson exulted loudly over having nominated 'his man' and rolled his eyes in anticipation of long happy days at Springfield, the righteous Republican *Chicago Daily News* grieved aloud at the primary result in a front-page editorial entitled *Dead on the Field of Dishonor and Beginning: Here Lies Dodo, Ironically Called The Republican Party Of Illinois, It Died From Lack Of Brains And Honesty."*

The Democrat nominee for governor in 1932 was Judge Henry Horner. As such, Horner was supported by Chicago's Democrat mayor, Anton Cermak. TIME magazine quoted Cermak as saying, "The two greatest spendthrifts Illinois suffered in public office were Thompson and Small. To think that those Gold Dust Twins are talking about economy is laughable. They have brought Chicago and Illinois nothing but disgrace and contempt."

Said Cermak to TIME, "God help the people of Illinois if Len Small should be elected governor and do to Illinois what his friend, Big Bill Thompson did to Chicago."

However, readers of the *Kankakee Republican-News* would have thought that Len Small's Democrat opponent was Cermak. Small did not campaign against Horner, he campaigned against Cermak.

Small hardly mentioned Horner's name at all. Almost every speech and editorial was against Cermak. A chart in the Kankakee newspaper, "Compare the Records," compared the accomplishments of Len Small not with Henry Horner but with Anton Cermak.

"Horner will be Cermak's man," was Small's theme. "Cermak will be Horner's boss," he repeated often.

Imagine that. The governor of Illinois would be a puppet of the mayor of Chicago. That hadn't happened before, had it?

"Boss Cermak Controls Chicago Newspapers," Small's newspaper wrote.

While Small campaigned against Cermak, Thompson took on Horner. And Big Bill enjoyed taking the campaign into the gutter.

One of the campaign swings by Small and Thompson became notorious for its wild antics and bigoted rhetoric. It was another wild boat tour of 20 cities along the Illinois River and the Mississippi River on the steamboat *Cape Girardeau.* A barge followed their boat with a dance band to further entertain their crowds.

Small drove from Kankakee to Peru to join the cruise on Sept. 10.

At each stop, a brass band would play and Thompson would appear. TIME magazine covered this spectacle: "And the voice of a choking giant began to croak through amplifiers, 'Good roads...used to peddle milk in Kankakee...in his own ward he got 700 votes against but 25 for his distinguished opponents...your support for the Republican ticket...cross in the circle at the top ...don't change doctors in the midst of an illness!"

The TIME magazine account continued: "In Illinois, such an exhibition could mean but one thing. William Hale 'Big Bill' Thompson was on the loose again. Kicked out of Chicago's mayoralty last year, Big Bill the Builder, brassiest showman out of show business, had taken the stump once more. No candidate himself, he was urging the re-election of two-time Governor Lennington Small, the character who was indicted, tried and made to disgorge withheld interest on state funds in 1925."

A few other Republican candidates joined part of this campaign. The cruise ended on Sept. 20 at Shawneetown, when the boat went from the Mississippi River to the Ohio River.

There was some controversy about a government boat being used for political purposes. Congressman William Hull of Peoria sent the federal government $200 to pay for the use of the barge.

Thompson's disgraceful campaign rhetoric against Horner must have made Len Small and the Ku Klux Klan proud. Horner's birth name was Levy, but his mother gave him her maiden name of Horner after her divorce. TIME described the campaign speech thus: "On behalf of his snaggle-toothed partisan Small, Big Bill proceeded to give Judge Horner a forensic log-ride. Downstate rural clodhoppers gawped, snickered and nodded approvingly when he shouted, 'My friends, I don't have to tell you that Levys don't eat hogs. If Horner is elected, hog prices are bound to drop. Furthermore, Jews run pawnshops, and the first thing Horner will do if he gets to Springfield is open a pawnshop. He was put up by Tony Cermak to get the Jewish vote, and he's trying to get the Catholic vote, too, by sending his children to a Catholic parochial school!"

TIME added, "In the primary, one-time Mayor Thompson had employed 'stooges' in rabbinical dress to ridicule Judge Horner's racial origin."

Small's campaign managed to find some Jewish lawyers and publishers in Chicago who told their fellow Jews that it was wrong to support Horner on the basis of religion. Samuel Golan was featured in the Kankakee newspaper as saying, "Every Jew ought to refuse to vote for a candidate only because he is a Jew," and said support for Horner in the *Chicago Jewish Chronicle* was "misguided."

"There is no such party as the Jewish Party in American politics," Golan said.

The tactics of the Republicans were so bad that Horner said, "They seem to be champions at spreading poison." To friend and editor Dick Finnegan, Horner wrote that the things being said by Thompson and Small "are the filthiest things I have ever heard from human lips. Thompson and Small are using the methods used in the Al Smith campaign, but much more viciously."

Horner was referring to Al Smith's 1928 presidential campaign, when vicious anti-Catholic rhetoric was used against the nominee.

Small's dirty politics continued. A "news story" in the Oct. 10 Kankakee newspaper was headlined *King Tony Is On Throne -- Health Restored by European Sausage, Dumplings and Beer -- Rosenberg Is In.* The lead paragraph was, "We are advised that the political campaign can now start officially -- Tony Cermak is back from his personally-conducted tour of Europe, where he went in search of health in the beer gardens, sausage kitchens and cabarets of the continent, posed as Anton the First Emperor of Cook County, sat in the thrones of 15th century kings, engaged in medieval pageantry and investigated nudist movements."

It continued: "After testing his gastric machinery on Bohemian sausage and dumplings, and learning how the other busted governments increase taxes without starting new revolutions, Tony says his sick stomach is better, in fact, he is feeling like a king.

"Well, that's not a new feeling for Tony. He's felt and acted like a king ever since he took over the forest preserves, the county institutions, Sanitary District, South Parks and City of Chicago as his personal domain. All he wants now is the state of Illinois.

"Tony hesitated for months before he decided to let someone else run for governor, but he finally hand-picked a docile candidate who would obey orders and selected Moe Rosenberg to be prime minister at Springfield, so if the Cermak state acquisition plans go through, King Anton would feel perfectly secure in his state-wide empire. His dynasty would be firmly established.

The article went on, but we have read enough already. You get the point.

Henry Horner had his fun with his opponent's boat tour, calling it a "vote catching expedition" reminiscent to Caligula's saturnalia in ancient Rome. "This comic opera reminds me of the gladiatorial contests, the bull fights, the feasts and the spectacles staged by the decadent emperors of antiquity to keep the attention of their people from the affairs of government," Horner told a crowd at Belleville on Sept. 23.

In August, two teenage paperboys who had delivered the *Kankakee Republican-News* for five years were fired because their mother worked for Horner's campaign. Gene and Edward LaRocque were told by Arthur Deslauriers, business manager of the newspaper, "Your mother is working for Horner and this newspaper is for Small. The two don't go together and we'll have to get someone else in your place."

And one more bizarre side story came out of the 1932 campaign. The only source comes from the *Kankakee Republican-News,* in one front page story, three days before the election. The story told of Vernon Cordes, a Kankakee boy, who was "kidnapped by local members of the Horner-Cermak gang, and through trickery and third degree methods, frightened into signing a statement intended to be injurious to the candidacy of Len Small."

Three "local hoodlum members" of the Horner "gang" allegedly went to the boy's home six weeks earlier and forced him into a car. They took him first to the law office of J. Bert Miller, then to the political headquarters (cigar store) of Ben Alpiner, where the boy was intimidated into signing an affidavit stating that workers on the Small family farm were paid inadequate wages. This statement was intended to hurt Small with the labor union vote. In the *Republican-News* newspaper story, Cordes said the Small family had always paid him fairly, "and if I was old enough to vote, I would most certainly vote for Len Small because I think he is one of the best men I ever knew."

There was no follow-up story, no criminal charges filed, no further mention.

Small continued his 1932 campaign against the "trust press" that marked his past campaigns. And, of course, his opponent was a tool of the Chicago press.

"Cermak's crowd is composed of the toughest and worst element in Chicago, which will stop at nothing to accomplish their ends," Small said on Nov. 5.

True to form, Small's *Kankakee Republican-News* constantly printed stories on how popular Len Small was across the state and how he would win big. It reprinted editorials from favorable small-town newspapers. It also printed its own fuzzy indicators as fact. For example, a Nov. 4 story trumpeted a local traveling jewelry salesman who went through five downstate counties and said that 179 of his customers preferred Small and only 19 wanted Horner.

Another Kankakee editorial on Oct. 29 criticized Horner for making "personal attacks" against Small. The editorial and accompanying news story never did say what this was, except that Horner spoke in Kankakee and "belittled" the war record of A.E. Inglesh, Small's son-in-law. The *Republican-News* countered by saying that Horner was 36, unmarried and without dependents when the war started, and did not serve in the conflict. The editorial claimed that Horner said the women who went on Small's and Thompson's notorious cruise were "coochie-coochie" dancers, "as slanderous a remark as was ever made against the womanhood of Illinois."

In an Oct. 17 rally in Waukegan, Horner had said, "Small and his principal backer, the former mayor of Chicago, have desecrated the memory of Illinois pioneers by taking a boatload of hula dancers down the Illinois River. The former mayor is sticking by Small because he hopes that he will be able to clean out the state treasury as he cleaned out all Chicago's treasuries."

As to the charge that Cermak would be his boss, Horner said, "I have never had any boss but my conscience."

Mayor Cermak came out fighting for Horner. He told a rally in Carlinville, "The two most discredited men who ever served in public life are trying to recapture the public treasury of Illinois. All the troubles and misfortunes of Chicago, not only in a financial way but in its gangdom and racketeering, I inherited from the previous mayor." Cermak said state government's costs went from $37 million in Lowden's last year to $123 million in Small's last year.

"These two men, a spendthrift and a clown, have brought Illinois and Chicago nothing but disgrace and contempt," Cermak said. "They hope to capture the state government in the belief that there are more imbeciles in Illinois than there are responsible men and women. We are asked to choose between this gigantic public figure and the two pygmies who have been dancing on showboats while shooting poison gas into the eyes of citizens of Illinois."

Horner claimed he would carry Kankakee County. This was answered by Victor McBroom, Republican county chairman, who said Horner's assertion "proves conclusively that he is utterly unreliable in everything he says," and that Horner "would have to visit the violent wards in the insane asylum to find anyone in Kankakee to agree with him."

Then the Kankakee newspaper went on: "So far as the farmers and laboring men are concerned, they know that Len Small was the only governor in their lifetime who was truly a 'people's' governor and who carried into the governor's chair a complete understanding and sympathy for the common man. They know whatever legal persecution was carried on against Len Small was maintained by agents representing privileged wealth, and was instigated, moreover, in a vain attempt to 'smear' Len Small in the minds of the voters. The common people of the state know that this persecution was carried on by privileged wealth against Len Small because of the fight Len Small has made throughout his public career on behalf of the common man against privileged trusts working to gouge the taxpayers and wage earners. The common people of the state know that their enemies are Len Small's enemies, and that Len Small's enemies are their enemies."

One of the issues raised by Henry Horner was the passage of the law exempting Len Small from *quo warranto* proceedings in 1927. Horner promised to repeal the "insidious" legislation and be accountable for his own actions.

He also assailed Small's career of shaking down state employees for campaign contributions.

Horner hit Governor Small's padding of state payrolls with patronage workers. In 1920, Horner said, there were 7,371 state workers. That figure was 11,232 in 1928. The state tax rate rose 30 per cent during Small's two terms as governor, Horner said.

In Crystal Lake, Horner took on Small over another tax issue -- the "rich tax dodgers," a favorite canard of Small for years. Small claimed that Horner did not pay taxes on a $60,000 mansion. Horner said it was true, because "I don't own a $60,000 mansion. My home is an apartment, which I rent."

But since Len Small brought up the subject, Horner said, he would look at the tax situation of Small's 700 acre farm of which he liked to brag.

"One campaign story tells of 80 head of Holstein cows he owns, and points out that the herd gives 200 gallons of milk daily," Horner said. "But what does my opponent tell the tax collector? The herd of 80 cows suddenly and magically becomes a herd of only 30, and the fine Holsteins which give 200 gallons per day mysteriously falls in value to $30 per head. And my opponent's fine farm is valued, for the tax collector, at just a little more than $1,600! We can probably deduce from that, that my opponent is really in favor of low taxes after all. For himself."

Edward Dunne, who was governor from 1913 to 1917, campaigned for Horner on the tax theme, saying state spending was four and a half times higher in Small's administration that it had been in his administration.

Henry Horner got a very vigorous endorsement in the campaign from former Judge Claire Edwards, now in private practice. Judge Edwards, a Republican, knew Len Small well enough to support Henry Horner.

Horner attracted large crowds wherever he went. In Aurora on Oct. 19, he drew four times more people than Small did a short time earlier. There were 2,500 people in the Paramount Theatre, with 1,500 more listening from loudspeakers. More than 2,000 people packed the Chamber of Commerce auditorium in Joliet two days later. Horner spoke to 4,000 in Kankakee the day after that, and in the evening 1,400 people heard Horner speak in the Dwight Township High School gym.

Horner did not go easy in the governor's hometown. He cited Small's scandal with the Grant Park Bank, the state jobs for jurors in his trial and the infamous pardons.

"You know the shameful story of the pardon for Harry Guzik and his wife Alma, convicted as panderers and white slavers, and freed by Small because of the political influences wielded by Al Capone and his chief lieutenant, Jack Guzik," Horner told the crowd in Kankakee. "You know the story of other criminals pardoned by Small, not by scores but by hundreds."

And Horner added, "You even know that when Small left the executive mansion, the $25,000 silver set that had been donated by former Governor Lowden was not found by Governor Emmerson, and you know that it has not been returned."

"There are two kinds of state executives. One sticks to his desk, is accessible to the public, creates plans and sees they are executed, rules for the people and is devoted to their interests. The other carries out the orders of a boss indifferent to public welfare and forgetful of those who made him possible."

That was from a Nov. 7, 1932, editorial in the *Kankakee Republican-News.* But it said Len Small was the first executive and Henry Horner was the latter. It was one of the few times that Small's campaign acknowledged that Horner was the opponent, not Cermak.

It is ironic that most of the accusations Small made against Horner applied to himself, in double and triple terms. Consider this Oct. 25 Kankakee newspaper story, which called Horner the "Cermak-picked nominee."

"With amazing stupidity, Horner has indulged in falsehoods and personal tirades against the integrity of his opponent while addressing well-informed downstate voters. Such tactics have only resulted in arousing the outraged indignation of his hearers and of others who might have been favorably inclined towards his candidacy.

"Horner's campaign of falsehood and trickery is considered by them to be an insult to their intelligence. The shameful guttersnipe campaign being waged by him and in his behalf has stamped him in the eyes of the people as unworthy of the high office he seeks. These despicable tactics being employed against Len Small have been used before, but never in such a manner as is the case today.

"Horner has lowered his methods to those of the demagogue and trickster, instead of attempting to discuss the issues uppermost in the minds of the voters.

"The Chicago press has made much of Horner's so-called 'get acquainted' tour. All in all, it has served the people well, affording to them an opportunity of discovering the insincerity of his true character and utter lack of a comprehensive understanding of the problems that confront Illinois and her citizens today."

Henry Horner

It would have been more accurate to substitute Small's name for Horner's name in the description above.

And the newspaper never did say just what falsehoods Horner told.

Henry Horner and Len Small were supposed to debate twice in Evanston on Oct. 28, at the City Club and at Northwestern University. Horner, who had urged Small to debate him, welcomed the opportunity. Horner was there and so was Socialist candidate Rev. Roy Burt. Len Small didn't show up.

Len Small was not known as a skilled orator. He read most of his speeches, and sometimes clumsily so. His talent in politics was as an organizer and an enforcer. Small did send a letter to the City Club, in which he wrote that he wasn't running for governor "on my appearance or my ability as an orator."

A number of Republican newspapers across the state endorsed Henry Horner. One was the *Bloomington Pantagraph.* Another was the *Rock Island Argus* -- a newspaper the Small Newspapers Group would buy in 1986.

Anton Cermak

During the 1932 campaign, Len Small and Big Bill Thompson tried one more dirty trick. W.W. O'Brien, a Mobbed-up criminal attorney from Chicago, was to run for governor as an independent to take some votes away from Horner.

O'Brien was the same dirty lawyer whose courtroom trickery in 1919 won an acquittal for hit-man Walter Stevens for the murder of an Aurora policeman. O'Brien represented Courtney and Kaufman, the gangsters who bribed the jurors at Small's trial, and he was at the side of his pal Earl "Hymie" Weiss when the mobster was "whacked" by Capone's gunmen.

"I'll campaign like hell, but in the last week I'll withdraw and throw my support to Len Small. I'll be giving the Democrats hell in the meantime," is what O'Brien told Thompson. Big Bill asked him what he wanted in return.

"We want 100 pardons, $50,000 in cash, and payment for radio time," O'Brien replied.

"No cash. You get money for the radio time, and I promise you, you'll get the pardons," Thompson said.

O'Brien was the "Independent Party" candidate. O'Brien made headlines by asking Cook County State's Attorney John Swanson to start *quo warranto* proceedings to remove Mayor Cermak from office on the grounds that Cermak owned stock in public utility companies. O'Brien claimed this was a conflict of interest for the mayor.

True to his dirty bargain, O'Brien campaigned and then withdrew. The Oct. 22, 1932 *Kankakee Republican-News* bannered the headline, *O'BRIEN QUITS RACE TO BACK SMALL.*

"After being in the race for governor for several months and making numerous investigations on my own behalf and at my own expense, I feel that it is my duty to see that Mayor Cermak is given no further control in the state of Illinois than he already has," O'Brien told the Kankakee newspaper. "I have decided to align myself with Len Small, who in my opinion would make a much better governor than the Democratic nominee for the reason that the Democratic nominee would be controlled and dominated by Cermak and his clique. And from the experience that the city of Chicago has gone through since Cermak has been mayor, would certainly not recommend either him or his clique for any greater power in the state of Illinois.

"I shall now devote considerable of my time from now on campaigning for Len Small, and believe that voters, when they weigh all the facts and circumstances connected with the candidacy of Len Small and the Democratic nominee for governor, will come to the same conclusion that I have, and that is that Len Small should be elected the next governor of this state. Instead of asking my friends to give me a large complimentary vote, thereby wasting their votes, I ask them to give their votes to Len Small."

It was too late to remove O'Brien's name from the ballot. He did not get any kind of complimentary vote -- his 1,182 votes, or 0.04 percent, was miles behind even the Socialist, Socialist Labor and Communist party candidates.

Fortunately for the state of Illinois, Small lost the 1932 election. O'Brien did not get the pardons for his clients in the penitentiary.

Illinois voters finally were so repulsed by Len Small and his crowd that

Horner won the governorship by a plurality of 566,287 votes, 57 to 40 per cent. Horner's 1.9 million vote total was 117,000 more votes than Franklin Roosevelt received at the top of the ticket in the state. Even Herbert Hoover was more popular than Len Small in 1932.

Len Small blamed his defeat entirely on Herbert Hoover, saying the backlash against the incumbent president and the Republican party because of the Great Depression was the cause of his defeat. Small's bitterness against Hoover was a stark contrast to the previous weekend, when a grinning Small campaigned with Hoover in Springfield.

The *Kankakee Republican-News* on the day after the election focused more on the plurality Small received in his home precincts than on his statewide defeat.

Small won his home county, but not by a tremendous margin -- 14,893 for Small, 9,383 for Horner.

In a concession statement, Small said, "My greatest concern is for the poor people and the people of moderate means in our state who, I fear, may suffer. The result of this election is due to economic conditions, which are worldwide, and a desire of the people for a change. Let us hope for the best."

The same election saw the defeat of State Sen. Richard Meents, an Ashkum banker and a long-time friend and political ally of Small. He had been in the legislature for 24 years, and he lost by 12 votes.

In an eerie situation similar to his pal Small, Meents was indicted in 1936 for embezzling funds from the Ashkum school district and the drainage district as treasurer. Meents owned banks in Ashkum, Clifton and Cullom that failed during the Great Depression. Meents claimed that his "political enemies" in Iroquois County vowed that his banks would not re-open, and only the Cullom bank re-opened because it was in another county. Meents said his political enemies promised they would ruin him at all costs, and his indictment was a "political persecution" made possible only after one of his enemies became a grand juror.

Meents died in 1945 at the age of 69.

TIME wrote that Small lost "because of his unsavory record at Springfield. Small was ditched by most decent GOP partisans at the polls."

The Nation magazine editorialized on Oct. 19, 1932, "Getting rid of Small (in 1928) was a good job, and the state of Abraham Lincoln heaved a sigh of relief. No one ever dreamt that four years later, Len would attempt a comeback. The scandals which had blighted his years as governor seemed sufficient to send any man into retirement for the rest of his life."

Governor Horner died in office in 1940. History has judged Henry Horner as a capable and competent governor who had honesty and integrity and who fought the intrusion of his own Democrat political machine in Chicago.

Len Small continued to remain in the public eye while out of office, and not all the publicity was favorable.

A big fire burned three large barns on the Small farm on March 17, 1930, killing 11 valuable thoroughbred horses. It was reported as a normal fire in one column of the Kankakee newspaper. But this was local primary election season. In another column in the same issue, the former governor was claiming the fire could have been started by "political enemies." He said he got threatening letters saying "harm might come" and that Small "might be sorry." The "whispering campaign" of his political troops hinted that candidates on the opposition ticket, Albert Goodknecht, Walter Richert, A.J. Huot and Stache Deslauriers were behind the fire. Small said he would hire investigators to get to the bottom of it, but it never was mentioned again.

Col. William Henry Harrison Miller (another Illinois colonel with no explanation for the title) was director of the state Department of Registration and Education when Small was governor. He was indicted in April 1922 for selling state medical licenses and selling answers to state exams. Miller and others sold more than a thousand fake medical, dental and pharmaceutical diplomas for $1,000 each to people who couldn't pass the medical school exam. Miller was convicted in 1923 and was fined. Miller left office but took a stack of licenses and the official seal, and he continued his sale. Miller was indicted on additional charges and was able to delay court proceedings, but he finally was convicted on Dec.10, 1929.

W.H.H. Miller was sentenced to seven months in the county jail and was fined $2,000 but he managed to delay reporting to jail while the case was being appealed. The state realized in September 1931 that Miller had not renewed his bond, and when it went looking for him, he could not be found. Miller jumped bail and wasn't apprehended until early 1932. His served his jail sentence and was to have been released in September, but he was kept in jail because he did not pay the fine. Miller asked the judge for mercy, claiming he was penniless -- not mentioning the fact that he deeded his expensive Champaign home to his wife in March. The judge turned him down. Miller finally paid his fine and was released in April 1933.

Cornelius R. Miller

Another Col. Miller -- Cornelius R. Miller -- was one of Small's most trusted aides. He was with Small since the 1890s, at the state hospital, at the bank and as his director of Public Works. After leaving the Small administration, Miller became president of the City State Bank of Chicago. The state auditor closed the bank on Nov. 4, 1929 after a bank examination. Miller died in Kankakee on Dec. 1, 1930.

William H. Malone was chairman of the Illinois Tax Commission in the Small and Emmerson administrations, from 1921 to 1931. The Park Ridge man was indicted in October 1933 of defrauding the government of $59,574 in income taxes and shaking down corporations for $330,000 in graft. Malone fled the country and was arrested when he returned in December 1936. His trial finally started in May 1937. His lawyer was Albert Fink, the same lawyer for Len Small and Al Capone. In July, Malone was convicted and sentenced to two years in Leavenworth federal penitentiary.

Col. Charles Kraft, a commander in the Illinois National Guard, was indicted in 1930 for embezzling $200,000 from the government. Kraft was in charge of the Broadway armory, which he rented for private entertainment. He used a double contract method, in which he got an extra check equal to what the government was paid. He also submitted false contracts. The scheme had been going on for years. Kraft served under Maj. Gen. Roy Keehn, a Small appointee.

Kraft also worked as a state construction engineer, a job he got for his political work on behalf of Governor Small. The armory practically was a campaign headquarters for Small.

The investigation uncovered another questionable link to Small. Capt. Roy Davis, a supply officer of the Illinois National Guard, had his pay suspended in 1928 while he was being investigated for the mishandling of confiscated liquor in a government warehouse. Davis wrote a $500 check to the Len Small campaign fund. He was cleared and his pay was restored. It was Col. Kraft who suggested the contribution to Small.

Col. Otis Duncan, who commanded an infantry of African-American Guardsmen, was given another state job as a reward for delivering the black vote in Chicago for Small. Duncan served four months in prison for his thefts.

Dr. James Parker was kidnapped from his Peoria home by gangsters on March 14, 1932 and held for ransom for two weeks before being released. The kidnappers were caught and convicted. The leader of the kidnappers was James Betson, the manager of Len Small's Peoria campaign headquarters and a former Ku Klux Klan official in the state.

Arthur Steuben worked in the secretary of state's office until he was fired in 1926. He and John Little were charged with taking payoffs from corporations in exchange for reducing their franchise taxes. One of the companies involved was Major Engineering Co.

Small's crony, Clifford B. Sawyer, was indicted in June 1936 on charges of fraud and conspiracy. Sawyer, a Kankakee Park District board member, along with his son Thomas Sawyer, a lawyer and secretary of the park board, owned property on North Hobbie Avenue. The Sawyers conspired with Louis Ray, a realtor and president of the park board, to have the park district pay significantly more for the property than it was worth.

In 1936, Len Small was back, running to regain the office he craved his entire life.

Small's candidacy in 1936 was endorsed by the anti-Semitic radio priest, Father Charles Coughlin, and the Kankakee newspaper proudly embraced this endorsement in its April 9 edition. Small had been smart enough to distance himself from the Klan's endorsement a dozen years earlier, but it may have been from a sense of desperation that he now gladly stood with Coughlin.

At that time, Coughlin was very popular in a large part of America. He had a radio show that reached 30 million people. He was more political than spiritual. He was anti-Semitic, and was sympathetic to Hitler and Mussolini in those years before America decided they were enemies. Father Coughlin's National Union for Social Justice tapped into America's isolationists who wanted to keep us out of war with Nazi Germany, and it appealed to the masses of poor people during the Depression. Coughlin was a socialist who hated both capitalism and communism, and he blamed the hard economic times on the "international conspiracy of Jewish bankers." He blamed a lot of things on the Jews. Coughlin's teachings were not the teachings of the Catholic Church. Even the Pope told Father Coughlin to shut up.

Just why Coughlin endorsed Len Small, it is not clear. Why Small accepted his support, well, that's politics.

The Kankakee Republican-News gave the 1936 primary campaign a strong, constant boosting of Small's candidacy. The newspaper started in October 1935 with stories of a "boom" for Small's candidacy being voiced in the state, urging him to run, while Small claimed that he hadn't made up his mind. In January, Small knew he didn't have a chance in going before party leaders to get their endorsement, so he made an announcement that he was "refusing to submit his candidacy to party leaders" and that he would go directly to the people as a candidate on the primary ballot.

By this time, the primary election to nominate candidates already had bypassed slatemaking by party leaders. Small would have sought their endorsement if he thought he could have gotten it, but he still would have had to win the primary to get the nomination.

Despite his age, the 73-year-old Small campaigned to regain the office he so desperately wanted. He attacked his opponents, both on the issues and with petty personal sniping, as was his style. His main issue was his record as governor, when he presided over the building of about 7,000 miles of hard roads. His "Return to Prosperity" theme promised to transform the Depression years of the 1930s back to the prosperous years of the 1920s.

About this campaign, TIME magazine's April 27, 1936, issue said, that "a vote for Len Small was a vote for malodorous machine politics."

Leading up to the April primary, daily stories in his Kankakee newspaper told of Len Small's great qualifications, his popularity, how politicians and newspapers across the state were behind him, how enthusiastic this group and that group were, and how he was sure to win. The headline on April 7 was *SMALL WILL CARRY EVERY COUNTY.* And a banner headline on April 11 read *SMALL TO GET RECORD VOTE.* On April 13, the day before the election, the front page banner headline was *LEN SMALL TO WIN BY 150,000.*

In an election eve statement, in addition to its usual campaign promises and rhetoric, Small said, "I was never so confident of winning." The statement bragged that he had the "best organization" and would "carry downstate by 75,000 to 100,000 and Cook County by as much or more."

In reading those old newspapers today, the rhetoric was still there but not to the extent to which it had been in previous campaigns. And a lot of the fire was gone. There seems to be an authenticity missing. In the last weeks of this final campaign, it seems the newspaper was going through the motions, in what it had to believe was an impossible effort.

C. Wayland Brooks won the Republican primary handily, getting 596,445 votes to Small's 268,903 votes. Small got just 25 per cent of the vote but he still finished ahead of Oscar Carlstrom and four other candidates.

As was his style, Len Small was not gracious in defeat. He was bitter, saying he never really wanted to win. He made a statement on April 15, 1936.

"The people have trusted and honored me by twice electing me to the highest office in the state, and while I had no particular desire to again exercise the power of governor, I felt it my duty to offer my services in the interest of good government, which I did by filing my name as a candidate and submitting a platform of principles for which I stand. As far as I am personally concerned, it is a relief to me that the people of our state have selected another as the Republican candidate. My only regret is the disappointment of many people who had hoped for relief from the heavy load of taxes and other oppressive laws.

"I was born in Kankakee nearly 74 years ago and have lived here all of my life. The wonderful vote cast for me in this county was a tribute probably never given to any other living candidate for high office. While my opportunity to be of real service to my many friends in the state will not be very great, I appreciate their confidence and evidence of friendship more than I can express."

The main reason for his defeat, he added, was a bitter contest among Democrats that led thousands of Republicans to take Democrat ballots. That usually is considered a dirty trick, and one that Small should have understood since he played that game many times himself.

The news story in the *Kankakee Republican-News* said the large vote for C. Wayland Brooks in Cook County was "aroused by the fact Chicago newspapers have been opposed to Small as governor because they could not control him." Rather than focus on the overwhelming statewide vote against Small, his newspaper gave a lot of ink to the large majority he received in the precincts of Kankakee County.

In that election in April 1936, local lawyer Samuel H. Shapiro was elected state's attorney of Kankakee County. Shapiro was a Democrat and he was J. Bert Miller's law partner. The *Kankakee Republican-News* often denigrated Shapiro -- in one headline it called him, "J. Bert Miller's Office Boy, Little Sammy Shapiro." Even a typhoid epidemic in 1939 that killed 63 people at Manteno State Hospital was blamed on Shapiro and Governor Horner by the newspaper.

Shapiro served just one term as state's attorney. The Kankakee newspaper was vehemently against him and he lost by just 293 votes in 1940. But the *Republican-News* wasn't up to its usual self in its attacks on Shapiro. Its criticisms of his first term were very minor. And some of its criticisms were just plain silly: "He has four telephones listed in the directory under his name. He frequents expensive Chicago nightclubs which the average person could not afford. He resides in a luxurious apartment in the Hotel Kankakee. He is using expensive billboards, neon signs and all kinds of extravagant and sensational methods to campaign. Recent family connections have improved his financial condition."

One charge was, "Three members of the Shapiro family are holding political jobs." This, despite the long list of lucrative state jobs several Small family members, not to mention that publisher Leslie Small had just been appointed to an important state position in the tax department by the governor (a year later, Leslie Small's son, Len H. Small, would be appointed as the youngest assistant attorney general for the state, even though he was just 26 and fresh out of law school.)

In a twist of fate, prosecutor Shapiro often faced young public defender Len H. Small in the late 1930s. The two adversaries became friends years later, when Shapiro was a legislator and Small was publisher of the family newspaper.

Big Bill Thompson was not with Len Small in his final campaign in 1936. Thompson eventually broke with everyone he had once trusted. He turned against Fred Lundin, Robert Crowe and even Len Small. Sometimes, these people would be brought back into the fold. It was all very personal and very capricious.

Crowe was one of many figures in and out of Thompson's good graces. He was with Thompson in 1920, an enemy for several years, then with Thompson and Small in 1927 when Capone backed them all. Crowe's finest hour was as chief investigator and prosecutor in the "trial of the century" of Nathan Leopold and Richard Loeb in 1924 for the "thrill killing" of Bobby Franks, in which Crowe won convictions against defense lawyer Clarence Darrow. Crowe was accused of being both aggressive and lax in prosecuting gangsters, and both accusations were right. But although Crowe did convict a lot of criminals, he did not win a single conviction for a gangland murder. During Crowe's two terms in the 1920s, there were hundreds of gangland bombings and murders but not one conviction. In that time, convictions for major crimes fell by half while the number of murders doubled.

With Thompson out of office in 1924, Small did not support Thompson's schemes as before. Worse, Small was taking advice from Lundin, who Thompson had turned against. Thompson declared he would not support Small in 1928, and Small responded by firing many of Thompson's political appointees. Small and Thompson later made up, in time for Thompson to endorse Small in 1928. In exchange, Small agreed to give Thompson control of all Park Board jobs.

Thompson was with Small's campaign in 1932. But when Small ran again in 1936, Thompson and Small became bitter enemies.

Big Bill's choice for attorney general in 1936 was Tommy Sullivan, his new fair-haired boy. Thompson believed Small had promised to support Sullivan; when Small didn't, a furious Thompson branded Small a traitor. Thompson then believed he had a deal with C. Wayland Brooks, that Thompson would refuse to support Small in the primary in exchange for Brooks supporting Sullivan. There was no such deal. An angry Big Bill ran for governor against Brooks, on the Union ticket.

Len Small's death after the primary did not stem the fervor of Big Bill's bile.

Big Bill campaigned in Kankakee, speaking at the Armory on Oct. 13, 1936 with the ticket's presidential candidate, William Lemke, a populist North Dakota congressman. As usual, Thompson's appearance overshadowed that of the main attraction. Instead of addressing the issues, Thompson went on a personal rant against the Republican party, the *Kankakee Republican-News* and editor Leslie Small. Thompson said that if Len Small was still alive, he'd support the Union ticket over the Republicans.

Leslie Small answered the "vicious, personal" remarks of Thompson in the next day's edition. He said his father endorsed Brooks after losing to him in the primary and always endorsed the Republican ticket. He said Thompson's whole campaign was based on spite.

The vote totals in November were 1,955,378 for Governor Henry Horner, 1,577,352 for C. Wayland Brooks and just 107,562 for William Hale Thompson.

Big Bill Thompson died of pneumonia in 1944 in his suite in the Blackstone Hotel. His Anglophobia never ceased, and as World War II approached, Thompson spoke in sympathy for fascist forces in Europe.

Len Small died on May 17, 1936, in St. Mary's Hospital in Kankakee. The cause was an embolism after having undergone surgery for bladder and prostrate trouble. His family did not blame the *Chicago Tribune.*

More than 5,000 people attended his funeral. Among the mourners were former governors Emmerson and Deneen, who both defeated Small; Governor Henry Horner, who beat Small in 1932; and Wayland Brooks, who recently beat Small in the primary.

Governor Small was buried next to his wife in Mound Grove Cemetery. As governor, he had been commander of the Illinois National Guard, and so he was accorded full military rites at the cemetery. Three National Guard companies escorted the casket from the home to the cemetery. As the casket was lowered into the ground, taps were sounded, a 21-gun salute was fired and three National Guard airplanes flew overhead.

On June 28, 1945, the state legislature approved a resolution that appropriated $25,000 and set up a commission to establish a memorial to Governor Small. The resolution was introduced in the Senate by Sen. Louis Beckman of Kankakee, and in the House by representatives Victor McBroom, Harry L. Topping and Ben Alpiner, all of Kankakee. The resolution led to the creation of Governor Small Memorial Park, which is on the site of the former Small family home on Kankakee's south side.

Governor Small Memorial Park opened Oct. 17, 1948. The site contains the restored Small family house, the Civic Auditorium and the Kankakee County Museum. The legislature gave another $200,000 in 1989 to expand the museum.

The Dr. Abram L. Small House and Kankakee County Museum in Governor Small Memorial Park, Kankakee, Illinois. Photo by Jim Ridings

Chapter 23

Good Roads and Hard Roads

Len Small was the "Good Roads Governor" who "pulled Illinois out of the mud" by building 7,700 miles of highway during his eight years.

For lack of a better name ("The Embezzler" is not preferred) and for lack of any other real accomplishment, the "Good Roads Governor" is how his image is presented today. The Kankakee keepers of the flame don't say much about him and they don't have much they could say about him, except this. This is his official image and legacy.

But Small is given too much credit for road building.

The program was well under way before he became governor. The Illinois legislature in 1917 approved a $60 million bond issue to build 4,800 miles of road. It was subject to voter approval, and Samuel E. Bradt, superintendent of highways, said the effort to convince the voters was "the most strenuous campaign ever carried on in the state on a public utility question." Half of the bonds and interest were supposed to be paid from vehicle fees and the other half were supposed to be paid from general taxes. But Governor Frank O. Lowden decided that it would be better if the entire cost was paid from vehicle fees. The voters approved the program overwhelmingly on Nov. 6, 1918.

While the program was promoted by most business and civic organizations across the state, including most newspapers, Bradt gave Governor Lowden the most credit for making this happen.

The state already had received $3.3 million from the federal government for roads in 1916. It gave the state another $8.7 million in 1919. The state appropriated $15.8 million from 1917 to 1919 for roads. This gave Illinois $27.8 million for roads before money from the bond issue started coming in.

Even the locations where the major roads would be built were laid out before Small took office in 1921.

Governor Lowden had state crews begin the road building program in May 1919. A good many miles were built before Small became governor. It was Small's good luck to come into office at a time when this program really was getting under way. It was something he could push and cling to, in the face of the criticism he received on just about every other front.

Bradt, in the 1919 *Illinois Blue Book,* said that the state expected to build 1,000 miles of road each year. That prediction certainly should have increased in the ensuing years. But the 7,700 miles that Small bragged about fell short of even the 1919 projection. (For the record, Len Small did not build 7,700 miles of road, as is most frequently cited today. By the governor's own total, cited in his closing report in January 1929, it was 6,801 miles of road built during his terms. Maybe. He used two sets of figures. The first showed 6,801 miles built, the second showed 5,579 miles built with the state bond issue).

When Small took office, he didn't need Bradt, and so Bradt went back to banking in DeKalb. But Bradt gave his assessment of Governor Small's eight years of road building in a 1928 interview.

"To further his political fortunes, he calls himself 'The Master Builder' and 'Hard Roads Governor.' As a matter of fact, he has done about as badly with the facilities placed in his hands as any man could. He has directed the expenditures and construction work with a view to gain personal political advantage and perpetuation in office."

Bradt continued, "Ordering construction of small pieces of road here and there, as preferential gestures for political purposes, which has characterized the Small administration, has become tiresome, costly and irritating to motorists in general, and useless to the development of the road system as a whole.

"Juggling road projects for political purposes has led to the construction in large amounts in one year and small amounts in another. In 1924, Small's last campaign year, 1,230 miles of road was contracted. In 1926, an off year, 464 miles was contracted. The variation of volume was so great that contractors were and are unable to exercise the economies of construction that would be possible if a more definite and certain amount of work were decided upon for each season.

"The manner in which the development of the state road system has been carried on by the present administration has all the earmarks of extravagance. Everyone who has the ability to think and reason knows that Small has misrepresented the costs of highway construction in his verbal reports to the people."

Bradt, one of the architects of the state road building program, questioned Governor Small's claim about building roads for $30,000 a mile. That figure is the contractor's cost, he said, and didn't include $7,200 a mile for cement or the high cost of grading.

He was right. And he was not alone in exposing Small's continuous claim that he built roads for less than $30,000 a mile despite the "cement trust's" effort to rob the taxpayers by demanding $40,000 a mile. S.S. Tanner, a member of the Republican State Central Committee, already had said in 1923 that the real figure was closer to $40,000 if grading and bridging was included.

Governor Small was claiming in 1924 that he was building roads for $26,360 to $28,550 per mile. But a federal report in 1924 showed the cost in Illinois was $35,467 per mile just for the pavement, with an additional cost of $24,950 for grading and drainage -- although the grading and drainage was done in advance of the paving and included miles yet to be paved. The report showed the actual cost expended was closer to $40,000 per mile.

Small's dubious and changing figures were examined in February 1924 by State Rep. L.S. Holderman of Morris. He said Small was not telling the truth when he said the roads would be paid from bonds, license fees and federal funds, without any direct taxes to Illinoisans. Holderman cited Small's own biennial message that 3,700 miles of roads cost $139,444,035 to that date. Holderman figured this meant the cost per mile was $37,686.

Something else that Bradt touched on was the politicization of road building by Governor Small. That also was true. The governor did not use this program as a public benefit as much as he used it as a political tool.

Governor Small used his hard roads program as a weapon, rewarding friends and punishing enemies. Roads were built in areas where he got political support and campaign funds. Those who did not pay and who did not give support stayed in the mud.

Lowden said in 1923 that "Governor Small's plea appears to be 'Support my ticket and you will get good roads. Vote against me and you will get none.'"

State Sen. Thurlow Essington, who was running against Small for the nomination in 1924, did not mince his words -- he said Small was using the hard roads program as "bribery."

"For the first time in the history of this or any other state, we find the governor of a great American commonwealth out brazenly and boldly offering to trade roads, paid for out of public money, in return for votes," he said in Watseka in February 1924.

Essington said the governor came into his own district "and he made that proposition, absolutely and frankly and boldly." All the issues at a legislative session "were influenced by promises on the one hand, or threats on the other, of hard road construction," he added.

The *Ziegler News* in Southern Illinois endorsed Small in 1924, saying the towns of Ziegler, Royalton and Benton were in the state's plans should Small be re-elected. "In order to secure these roads, it will be necessary to pile up as large a majority as possible for the governor to overcome other parts, which are more favorable to Brundage and Essington."

The path of the Egyptian Trail south from Kankakee was chosen to keep the route on Washington Avenue as a favor to Jeffers and McBroom (it passed their automobile dealership) and it continued in a route that passed the property of a relative. The Corn Belt route took a longer and more complicated path so it would pass property owned by the Meents family. Other routes were chosen in similar manners.

The Legislative Voters League, which monitored the voting records and the conduct of state lawmakers, published a report in February 1924 that was severely critical of Governor Small's methods.

"The passage of the big road bond bill was the result of one of the most elaborate and tireless propaganda campaigns the state has ever seen," the report read. "As soon as the session opened, delegations from the various counties began to arrive in Springfield demanding that their localities be awarded certain desired roads. If a legislator who was inclined to be politically opposed to the governor hesitated to cooperate in this way with the delegation from his district, he was soon made to feel that he was the only stumbling block in the way of getting the routes which his constituents were asking. Hesitating members were bombarded with telegrams and appealing letters from their districts, and those who could not be influenced by local pressure or by promise of favor from the state administration were threatened with the veto of their pending bills."

The report noted that the state highway department organized these delegations with the help of road contractors. And, it added, Small consistently told downstaters that the bill would be paid by people up north.

"The campaign of propaganda was worked so skillfully and persistently that the downstate opponents of the bond issue were fairly overwhelmed by the eager demand from almost every downstate county for the construction of promised roads at the expense of the state.

"The road bond issue bill was framed and put through the legislature with enormous labor on the theory that it would enable Governor Small to capitalize the good roads sentiment of the state as a means of securing re-election."

The league was one of many voices that questioned the need for the additional $100 million bond issue at that time. It said only half the 4,800 miles of road authorized in 1917 had been completed and enough funds were on and hand, and coming in from fees, for the next three years.

There was opposition to the way Small proposed and planned his road program, not to the road program itself. Many people thought the $100 million bond proposal sought by Small in 1924 was excessive. Most of the money from the 1918 bond issue was unspent. A lot of people thought taking on a hundred million dollar debt was just too much. State Sen. Clarence Buck of Monmouth introduced a bill seeking to reduce the bond proposal to $30,000,000.

State Sen. Harold Kessinger of Aurora broke with Small on the $100 million bond issue in May 1923. Small's campaign claimed that the bond issue would not cost one penny of direct taxes and that it will be paid from ever-increasing automobile license fees. Kessinger didn't buy that argument. He said the roads would be falling apart while the state was still paying the 30-year bonds. Kessinger noted there were no bonds ten years earlier. Now, there was a $20 million waterways bond from Governor Dunne, a $60 million road bond from Governor Lowden and a $55 million soldiers bond from Governor Small.

The "hard roads" issue in 1924 was one that brought out former Governor Frank O. Lowden on behalf of Thurlow Essington.

Lowden said Small's record was one of using roads as a method of extortion -- vote for my candidates or you won't get roads in your district, an "insidious" proposition that has "debauched the electorate."

"But I want to remind you," Lowden told voters in Rockford on April 2, "that the moment you get something from the state to which you are not entitled, that thing will in the end prove of no value to you. You are either entitled to this particular road or not. If you are, you should demand it as a matter of right and not receive it as a bribe for somebody for re-nomination. And if you buy that road by selling your votes, you may have the road but you won't have the kind of conscience in your breast which will comfort you in riding on that road after you have gotten it."

When he was governor, Lowden said, no road building decision was based on politics.

The *Kankakee Daily News* was famous for hard-hitting editorial that exposed the core of the real Len Small. The *Daily News* editors knew him better than anyone else. A Feb. 5, 1924 editorial asked if Small's roads promise was the real issue. It asked a number of questions: "Small is accused of stealing millions of taxpayers' money from the state. Do a few miles of highway condone this alleged theft?" It asked several more questions: his belated final interest payment, his pardons of vicious criminals, his association with gangsters, his causing of so much strife, and each question ended by asking if a few miles of roads was worth putting up with Small.

"Road building is his one argument," a March 22 editorial added. "He uses this to the exclusion of everything else. From his campaign literature and his speeches, it might be assumed the governor was actually constructing the highways for the state at his own expense. He would create the impression that no other man would or could construct highways in Illinois. But Small is actuated by some self interest in road building. He never became an enthusiast for anything unless there was personal profit or political advancement to be gained.

"To charges of graft, he answers roads. To charges of alliance with vicious criminals, he answers roads. To violations of the civil service laws, he answers roads. To charges that he owes the state about two million dollars grafted as treasurer from interest payments, he answers roads. To any and all charges of corruption in his administration, the answer is roads. Highways are to Small only a campaign issue and something through which he can hope to prevent too close scrutiny of his official acts as governor."

The road building program accelerated during election years. In 1927, only 600 miles of pavement was laid even though there was $80 million in the fund. In 1928, as Small sought a third term, he promised 1,400 miles. Emmerson noticed it. "Last year was not a campaign year and Governor Small did not need to influence voters," Emmerson told a rally in Lincoln on March 3, 1928.

As far as "the master builder" was concerned, Emmerson told a crowd at Princeton two weeks later that the plan and the financing were done under Governor Lowden. "Governor Small did what any other governor would have done. He accepted the system established for him and spent the money provided."

"It would be preposterous, to say the least, for the contractor who builds your house with the money you have provided and according to the plans drawn by your architect to tell you that you owe your house entirely to him and should let him occupy it and use it for his own purposes simply because he supervised the construction," Emmerson said. "These roads are your roads, built with your money and at a cost of $40,000 a mile -- not $27,000 as you have so often been told. Moreover, you now should have enough additional pavement to extend twice the length of this state if Governor Small had built roads as rapidly as funds would permit."

And despite all of Small's bragging, Emmerson noted, in 1928 only five percent of the state's roads were paved. The other 95 per cent were dirt roads.

A *Chicago Tribune* editorial on Nov. 1, 1932 -- when Small was seeking a comeback based on his roads program -- noted that the program was all planned and funded under Governor Lowden. "In 1924, when Small was about to run for re-election, the department speeded up and 1,018 miles of modernized roads were built, not according to any logical plan of development for maximum need and use, but where they would return the maximum political profit to Len Small." It added that in 1924, Small got another $100 million bond issue approved even though two-thirds of the original $60 million bond issue had not been spent.

Small successfully pushed through his $100 million bond issue in 1924. Newspapers pointed out that by that time, only 1,650 miles had been built of the 4,800 miles authorized in 1918. And there was enough bond money and federal funds left for pay for two more years' work. His plan was "politics, not business," the *Orange Judd Farmer* commented.

There was a lot of opposition to the road bond issue proposed by Small and it wasn't political opposition. When the $100 million bond issue was being debated in the legislature in May 1923, Republican State Sen. Rodney Swift of Lake Forest said that road contracts were being awarded in areas where Small was getting votes. Others wondered why Small was pushing this program so hard and so fast. State Sen. Henry Dunlap of Savoy said the state could save millions of dollars in bond interest payments if the roads were built as the money was collected.

Essington said the motorist, who paid for the roads in taxes and fees, was being given "one dollar's worth of roads for every two you pay us, because we are going to give the other dollar to someone for interest."

"Politics doesn't mix with cement and gravel to make good roads," Essington told a Kankakee campaign rally in February 1924.

State Sen. Richard Barr of Joliet, one of Small's most loyal lieutenants in the legislature, used a "good roads" meeting in Wheaton in March 1922 as a campaign promotion. In the middle of his speech, Barr pulled a check for $72,542 from his pocket and presented it to county officials. The customary manner was to have the money sent to the county treasurer. Barr told the gathering how difficult it was to obtain this money for them, emphasizing that he and the governor were fighting for them.

When Small was running for the Republican nomination in 1932, rival Omer Custer accused Small of being "up to his old tricks again" by promising people in the 37th legislative district that they would "be accorded a number of routes in various sections of certain counties" in exchange for political support.

"That is typical of him," Custer said. "For eight years, he has used the road money paid into the state treasury by the people of Illinois to further his own interests. Now he informs the voters he intends to continue this policy."

The idea that Governor Small used his "good roads" program as a weapon --promising that roads would be built where voters elected men who supported him in the legislature -- was not just a charge his opponents used. It was something that Governor Small himself used as a promise or a threat. A few examples were at "good roads" meetings in Paris, Dixon, Freeport and LaSalle in March 1922, where Small said, "If you send to the legislature men who approve my program and stand with the governor, I will see to it that roads are built in your county and in your districts."

Small wanted to have control of the legislature not just to pass the laws he wanted but also to avoid impeachment. In effect, the governor was again "fixing" a jury, the legislative jury that could impeach and remove him. This had worked, as seen in the failure of the impeachment measures and the passing of the *quo warranto* law.

Even before taking office, Small announced that there would be no road contracts awarded because the price of material was too high. After a conference at the Great Northern Hotel in Chicago on Nov. 29, 1920, Small announced, "Cheaper materials or no contracts."

Some people thought this was a veiled reference to his preference to giving contracts to connected companies. Several mobsters had their tentacles into many of the road construction unions and companies, and it is said that Organized Crime ended up with a lot of that "hard roads" money.

Governor Small had spent his first months in office delaying road building, as he claimed he was fighting the "cement trusts" over prices, but really he was taking his time in lining up jobs for connected contractors. Cornelius R. Miller, the governor's political and banking partner from the earliest days of his career, was director of Public Works. He controlled the road building contracts.

And some of that money came back to Len Small in the form of kickbacks from contractors as the price of getting the contracts. Judge Norman Jones exposed that issue in his 1924 campaign against Small. Members of the Illinois Contractors Association admitted to it.

The governor claimed his delays were caused by his battles with the "cement trust" to lower the cost per mile. But this simply was not true.

The *Chicago Tribune* editorialized in 1922, "A conspiracy of cement firms would hold up the taxpayers by making them pay more for their roads, but Small would keep an independent district from getting any roads at all."

A report in August 1921 from Ohio engineers studying Illinois' road program found that delays caused by Small resulted in just 10 miles of roads built in the first eight months, even though the state had $80 million for roads and thousands of idle men.

Governor Small had the audacity to claim that there would be no roads program without him. Part of a campaign letter mailed by Small in March 1924 stated, "Frankly, I believe that if I am defeated, hard road construction in Illinois will practically cease."

Small told a campaign rally on March 18, 1924, "I wish you would tell me how in the world I'm going to build you these roads unless I am re-elected."

Nonsense, replied his primary election opponent, Thurlow Essington, who said "When I'm elected, I'll build more hard roads, put them where they belong and will do it cheaper because I'll build hard roads and not political roads."

Judge Norman Jones, Small's opponent in the fall, said basically the same thing to a gathering on Aug. 6 in Farmersville. "No man has a proprietary right on road building. The people want them and will have them, and they shall be built for miles, not for votes."

Speaking at the LaSalle County Fair in Ottawa on Sept. 1, Jones said the governor's road building program was nothing to be proud of. Delays due to political consideration caused the program to lag. And, he said, not one mile of road in the previous four years was built with money appropriated during Small's term.

State Sen. Otis Glenn of Murphysboro slammed Governor Small's road building claims in his successful 1928 campaign for U.S. senator. Glenn was a Republican, and the Illinois Republicans ran against the record of their own governor that year. Glenn reiterated the position he took several years earlier in the state legislature. "This is nobody's fund but the people's fund. I want to know whether the next $30 million is to be devoted to road building, instead of using it as a club over the members of this body. I protest against the people's money being used to hammer men into submission."

And, "Governor Small is attempting to bribe you men and women of Illinois with your own money. Down in Egypt, we are content to travel over the old mud trails that the pioneers trod until we get an honest and on-the-square governor. Down our way, we are looking at no hard roads during the next two years."

Len Small always claimed that the *Chicago Tribune* was against the hard roads program and was trying to defeat it in the legislature. That was a lie. The *Tribune* never had any such position. The *Tribune* only criticized the governor's handling of the program.

"The *Tribune* is for good roads in every part of Illinois, put there as rapidly as possibly and honestly put there. Small cannot do anything honestly," is what a Dec. 23, 1923 editorial said. "We agree that the bulk of the money will be raised in Cook County and must be spent in other counties, and should be and will be. But there'll be rotten deals all over the state if Illinois trusts its road building to a political scamp."

The highly touted road building program was brought into other areas of Small's administration whenever possible. He used it to boast when he could, but the publicity wasn't always favorable.

Marshal Ferdinand Foch, the French war leader, came to Chicago on Nov. 5, 1921 and spoke to a huge crowd at the Auditorium. As usual, City Hall henchmen tried to hijack the event to turn it into a political rally for Thompson and Small. A good part of the crowd was made up of military leaders and political workers who whooped and hollered for Thompson and Small. Even General Milton Foreman, recently appointed head of the Illinois National Guard by the governor, shilled for his boss. He started with a glowing introduction of Foch and his accomplishments and then went into an introduction of the governor. "And now I am going to introduce to you a man who made these great highways possible, the man responsible for the great roads that traverse this state from on end to the other," the politically-connected General Foreman said. "I am going to present to you Illinois' greatest governor, Governor Len Small."

A.R. Hirst, Wisconsin's state engineer, angered Governor Small in May 1921 when he questioned Small's figures about cost per mile. Small responded with an attack on Hirst and Wisconsin Governor J.J. Blaine. Small claimed that Hirst dined with company officials of the "cement trust" who had been indicted, saying that dining with people under indictment was not proper for a state official. It was high irony the following November when Hirst and Blaine similarly snubbed Small (then under indictment) by refusing to attend a banquet in Rockford to celebrate the completion of a road from Rockford to Beloit.

In declining the invitation, Hirst wrote to the committee, "Under other circumstances than those named in your letter, I would be very glad to accept the invitation. I note, however, that Governor Len Small is listed as one of the speakers. I could not be present at any function with the governor of Illinois and maintain my self-respect."

Snubbing the unsavory Len Small became a habit. At a "good roads" meeting in Gilman on Nov. 21, 1923, Mayor R.A. Buckner and other town officials boycotted the dinner at the Gilman Commercial Club because of their distaste for Small. "The city officials refused to attend the dinner out of respect to the decent citizens of Gilman, as well as the soldiers of the world's war, and because of their own self respect, they could not sit down at a dinner table with a man of the caliber of Governor Small, a man every man, woman and child knows was disloyal during the war, a man who to this day has refused to deny under oath that he now possesses $2 million of interest which belongs to the state of Illinois." Buckner was an opponent of State. Sen. Richard Meents in that district.

(Small came back to Gilman two weeks later for another "good roads program." However, his hour-long talk got off the road several times. He talked about his Waukegan trial, and one reporter counted 57 denunciations of the *Chicago Tribune.* The farmers there were not friendly, since the Corn Belt Route bypassed their town in favor of another route along property owned by the Meents family. When Small said Ed Brundage should be prosecuted, one heckler shouted, 'Don't pardon him, governor.' Small frowned, appeared flustered and cut his speech short.)

And on Dec. 23, 1923, Metropolis Mayor A.N. Starkes avoided a Rotary Club luncheon for the same reason. "Metropolis is not a large place and the office is not a great one, but I did not want to disgrace it by sitting at a table with a man like Governor Small…the man who has dragged the mantle of the governor through such mire as has Len Small."

Len Small's political machine and family was adept at putting a spin on events and this continued after Small's death. It continues today. Werner Schroeder, Small's protégé and lawyer, wrote a few lengthy articles for the *Kankakee Daily Journal* in October 1948, upon the dedication of Governor Small Memorial Park.

Schroeder touted the time-worn story of how the governor stood up to the "cement trusts" who wanted to build roads for $40,000 per mile. Schroeder said, "The state engineers advised the governor that it would be hopeless to try to live up to his campaign promises…and was advised to accept the bids and build what roads could be constructed within the money available from the bond issue. Then followed a long week of study and consultation during which pressure was brought to bear on the governor from every side to go ahead with the program as bid." Schroeder said "threats, intimidations and promises" were made to the governor.

"Finally, the governor called in his engineers and advisers, and in a memorable scene, announced that he was instructing the Divisions of Highways to reject all bids" and that no work would be done if it exceeded $30,000 per mile. Schroeder wrote that this brought "a storm of criticism" from those who "demanded that the road construction proceed regardless of cost."

"The governor and his friends always insisted thereafter that the bitterness engendered as a result of this action and the hostility of various selfish interests which preferred the letting of bids at all costs, was the foundation for the famous interests suits in Waukegan, during which the governor was tried for embezzlement and acquitted by a Lake County jury," Schroeder wrote.

His same article said the civil suit resulted "in a compromise settlement" where the state supreme court's minority decision "stands as a classical masterpiece of sound legal reason, dissecting the majority report with a coldly logical analysis." He added, "Beyond question, Len Small was one of the greatest governors of Illinois. No administration in the history of our state accomplished more or brought about greater progress."

Despite advice that he would never get roads built, Schroeder wrote, the determined governor found a way to do it for $30,000 a mile "in the face of almost insurmountable difficulties."

This is the story that has been told regarding Small's road building program over the years. It basically is accepted as the authoritative history.

Len Small did not invent concrete and he did not come up with the idea that roads should be paved. It was a totally fortunate accident of good timing that Small became governor when automobiles were becoming common and people wanted roads to have the freedom to go where they wanted. It was an idea whose time had come. Roads were being built in all the other states across America.

Len Small's "hard roads" program was something that already was being done in Illinois and it was something that would have continued no matter who was governor.

However, even before taking office, Small saw the "hard roads" issue as one he could use for all it was worth. And Small started taking credit for building Illinois' entire system of hard roads before he had built one mile.

"Every mile of hard surfaced road contracted during the administration of Governor Len Small was laid out by former Governor Lowden and paid for out of moneys provided under Lowden's administration. When Len Small took office, he found the system of roads laid out, the engineering department created and functioning and actually building roads," State Sen. Thurlow Essington said in 1924. "Sixty million dollars worth of unissued bonds, authorized by the people of this state under Governor Lowden, were in the state treasury. There was another $8 million each year from automobile licenses and $5 million more in federal funds.

"No mention of the road matter was made in the platform of Len Small as a candidate for governor four years ago," he continued. "It was taken for granted that any governor would continue the work begun under Governor Lowden. Yet, in spite of all these facts, we find Len Small styling himself the father of good roads in Illinois. And we find further that, instead of pressing the button and permitting the efficient highway department to continue to build roads, Len Small has prostituted this great proposition of great roads into a great political bludgeon."

But even though Small has to be given credit for his part in road building in Illinois, his use of the program to extort votes and political favors, the awarding of contracts to Mob-controlled contractors and unions, and all the other factors mentioned here, must be remembered.

It also should be remembered that Governor Len Small built two-lane roads between Kankakee and Dwight. It was President Dwight D. Eisenhower who built the interstate highway system that opened up America.

Chapter 24

Power of the Press

"The Chicago Tribune championed a cause against the Governor which impressed upon the Small family the importance of their hometown newspaper."
--- Small Newspapers Group website today

Governor Len Small was trying to do his best for the people of Illinois but was persecuted his entire life by the *Chicago Tribune.*

That is what the keepers of the flame in Kankakee would like you to believe.

In reality, the *Chicago Tribune* told the truth about Len Small, and Small could not stand it. Small's crooked ways and his ties with the Mob and the Machine in Chicago made him a particular target of the *Tribune.* He already had been pegged as a crook by the Kankakee newspapers (*Kankakee Gazette* and *The Evening Democrat*) from his earliest days in politics in the 1890s.

Small's reaction was to buy his own newspaper.

It is the very reason why the Small Newspapers Group empire exists today.

Small Newspaper Group today is a respectable corporation publishing highly-regarded newspapers. It earned that reputation only after the governor's grandsons took control.

But the reason Len Small got into the newspaper business was totally self-serving and political.

Len Small bought the *Kankakee Times* in 1903 (a newspaper which had been friendly to Small's political machine) and changed its name to the *Kankakee Republican.* Among the other investors were men who would be part of Small's business and political circle for more than 30 years, all the way through his administration in Springfield -- Edward C. Curtis, Cornelius R. Miller, Edward Jeffers and Charles Robinson.

The two anti-Small publications, the *Gazette* and *The Evening Democrat*, merged in 1919 to become the *Kankakee Daily News.* It continued to be anti-Small.

The Great Depression helped Small eliminate his competition, when he finally was able to buy the *Daily News* in 1931 and put it out of business.

Incidentally, this trail of ownership allows the Small Newspaper Group today to claim a heritage to the beginning of the first newspaper in Kankakee in 1854, the *Gazette.* It does not publicize the foul words its ancestor newspapers had to say about their ancestor Len Small.

Both the *Chicago Tribune* and the *Kankakee Gazette* were Republican newspapers and they did not like Small's brand of Republicanism. Len Small decided there should be another newspaper to tell his side of the story.

The *Tribune* didn't take much note of Len Small before 1899, when Small was mentioned as being linked to the unpopular governor Tanner. But Small seemed to harbor a grudge against the *Tribune* as early as 1896. In a *Tribune* story published Jan. 1, 1897, a number of Kankakee County politicians were asked who they were supporting for U.S. senator. Of the 15 respondents, nine said William Mason. Len Small said Martin Madden. "I am in favor of him for one reason," Small said. "On account of the opposition of certain Chicago papers which have been most abusive without grounds." That is a revealing comment at such an early age.

Examples of the *Chicago Tribune's* coverage and of Len Small's reactions are shown throughout this book.

When Len Small was defeated for re-nomination as governor in 1928, the *Chicago Tribune* took the opportunity to crow about it and to toot its own horn. "Chicago can again walk proudly among the cities. Illinois has purged herself of her shame." The *Tribune* even took out a full-page ad in the *New York Times.* And it claimed that Bill Thompson and Len Small gave more credence to *Tribune* influence as enemies than any friend could.

An entire book could be written of all the accusations against Len Small printed in Kankakee's *Daily Gazette, The Evening Democrat* and *Kankakee Daily News.* They attacked him for more than 30 years. Another book could be written from the newspaper accounts in the *Kankakee Daily Republican,* telling what a great man Len Small was, and how his evil enemies were out to get him.

Len Small's newspaper saw things differently than did other newspapers. When Thompson won the Republican nomination for mayor in 1931, against the efforts of regular Republicans who wanted to be rid of this pariah, the *Kankakee Daily Republican* ran the huge headline *THOMPSON DEFEATS THE TRIBUNE.* And when the City Hall crowd won a reversal of their "expert fees" conviction on appeal, the *Kankakee Daily Republican* reported the story in a huge headline *THOMPSON AGAIN DEFEATS TRIBUNE.*

When Small's lawyers were pleading that the governor was immune from arrest, *The New York Times* reported that the judge "told Small's counsel that he had been 'delighted and enlightened' by their statements" but "was apparently unmoved by the pleas." Then the judge went on to shoot down their arguments. *The Kankakee Daily Republican* reported the same scene in a different way. Its headline read *Jurist Enlightened By Argument And Thanks Lawyers.*

The *Kankakee Daily News* wrote things differently than the *Daily Republican.* The July 14, 1921, *Kankakee Daily News* story of the grand jury investigation began, "The fascinating fairy tale of the Grant Park Bank, creature of the Small-Curtis crowd for fattening off the interest earnings of the state funds controlled by Governor Small when he was state treasurer, is becoming more entertaining and ludicrous as it is being unfolded." The grand jury was "surprised to learn how a practically extinct bank, one that existed only in name and which Senator Curtis usually carried around in his hat, something like Abe Lincoln did his post office years ago, could handle $10,000,000 of the state's money."

There was no distinction in those days between editorial opinion and news writing. Consider this from a *Kankakee Daily Republican* news story about the possible indictment of Small, Sterling and Vernon Curtis: "The attorney general, unable to enter the grave of the late Sen. Edward C. Curtis with his indictment of hate, may seek to gratify his desire for vengeance against the honored name of Curtis by indicting Vernon Curtis because he chances to be a brother of the late senator and a close friend of the governor."

Although much mud was thrown at Small by the opposing newspapers, an equal amount was thrown by Small's *Kankakee Daily Republican.* His newspaper just didn't endorse his candidates, it savaged the opposition. Benjamin Alpiner, a Jewish cigar store owner and the son of pioneer Kankakee merchant Solomon Alpiner, got a taste of yellow journalism when he ran against Small's candidate for mayor of Kankakee in 1911. The *Daily Republican* called Alpiner a "Shylock who got his pound of flesh from the misery of others." The anti-Semitic literary reference (in a huge page-one headline) was not lost on anyone.

Alpiner and his entire ticket trounced Small's ticket. Alpiner served with distinction as Kankakee mayor and later as a state representative. A park in Kankakee is named for the Alpiner family.

The anti-Semitic slur appeared in the *Kankakee Daily Republican* again 16 years later. Frank J. Stransky, yet another lawyer who found steady employment getting the boss out of legal predicaments, was making an argument in court in 1927 as to why Small should not have to pay the state in the civil suit. "The people of Illinois do not want Shylock methods used to persecute Small, nor do they demand a pound of flesh."

Stransky later became chairman of the Pardons and Paroles Board.

Ed Otis had a lengthy criminal career in Kankakee, although you might not know his first name from reading the Kankakee newspaper. From 1909 to 1918, the *Kankakee Daily Republican* regularly referred to him (in headlines as well as in the stories) as "Nigger Otis." The words "nigger" and "coon" were liberally used in news stories and headlines in all the Kankakee newspapers from the 1890s into the 1920s. Until the death of publisher Leslie Small in 1957, the newspaper referred to a man as a Negro if he was African-American. If he was white, he was just a man. The newspaper somehow felt the need to let the readers know that the subject of a story was a Negro, a Negress or Colored.

When a black man wanted for robbery was shot to death by Kankakee police in May 1918, the *Kankakee Daily Republican* story's lead paragraph began: "One bad negro was sent to the jungles of everlasting peace yesterday afternoon about 4:45, following an exciting chase in a cornfield, a mile south of Jeffrey Street."

As late as 1941, it was not unusual for such language to be standard in the Small's newspaper. A story on the front page of the Jan. 14 edition, headlined *Negro Breaks Store Window, Steals 3 Guns,* had this lead paragraph: "Caldwell 'Chicken Fry' Sheppard, 40, colored, of 959 North Evergreen Avenue, may not know how close he came to being a 'dead nigger' at 1:43 o'clock this morning, when he committed burglary and larceny at the Jack Brown sport shop, 326 South Schuyler Avenue."

In 1919, *The Daily Republican* attacked Alderman Henry Reuter when he ran for mayor of Kankakee against Small's candidate because Reuter (an immigrant) could speak German. Reuter, who won the election despite Small's opposition, also was attacked for approving $3,000 in legitimate fees for street paving.

"Think of a man who will absolutely close his eyes, hold his nose and put through a plain $3,000 grab of your money; then come to you and ask you to vote for him as mayor of your city," the story read

This was at the exact same time that State Treasurer Len Small was continuing his embezzlement of two million dollars!

Small's newspaper championed the horribly corrupt William Hale Thompson and William Lorimer, in spite of all evidence against them.

When Lorimer was kicked out of the U.S. Senate for bribing legislators, the headline in the July 13, 1912, *Kankakee Daily Republican* read *LORIMER IS DEPRIVED OF HIS SEAT IN UNITED STATES SENATE BY A CONSPIRACY.* It named the state's attorney, the *Chicago Tribune* and Governor Deneen as those who conspired against Lorimer.

Rival editors regularly threatened each other...in print. But in August 1907, after a series of exchanges between the newspapers, followed by a challenge over the telephone to a duel, *Gazette* editor Herman Schmidt went to *Republican* editor Arthur Sweeney's office looking for a fight. Sweeney hid behind a counter, his pistol nearby. Sweeney had Schmidt arrested.

Sweeney was beaten up by Perry LaBounty, a *Gazette* pressman, on a Kankakee street in 1908.

William Surprenant, a local prizefighter, did not like the story *Daily Republican* reporter Bruce Brown wrote about his bout in Momence on Jan. 31, 1931. Surprenant met Brown on East Oak Street as the reporter was walking to work two days later. He beat up Brown, blackening both his eyes. The trouble was, Brown wasn't the writer of the story. Surprenant was arrested and fined $100.

Herman Schmidt became editor of the *Kankakee Daily News.* He went to Springfield in 1921 to cover the grand jury hearings on Small's corruption charges, which the *Kankakee Daily Republican* said was "for the purpose of besmirching the name of Governor Small in connection with the grand jury frame-up." Small's page one headline was, *Schmidt (hic) Is Home (hic) Again.* It was not subtle in calling Schmidt a drunk, "all of which accounts for the items that have been appearing in the *Daily News.*"

A front page editorial in the Feb. 6, 1924, *Kankakee Daily Republican* began, "The booze-soaked editor of the *Kankakee Daily News* gets considerably agitated over the fact that the *Daily Republican* recently published a letter from a Kankakee merchant in which the merchant said he had withdrawn his advertising from the *News.*" It went on for months with more references to its "booze-soaked (hic) editor."

"No matter whether it is a wedding, a funeral or a dog fight, the *Kankakee*

Daily News always finds some excuse to throw mud at the governor," a Feb. 25, 1925 news story in the *Kankakee Daily Republican* noted.

As many times as the *Daily Republican* and Len Small talked about the "lies, hatefulness, spite" and more from the *Chicago Tribune*, the *Tribune* never used the name-calling, the hatred or any similar type of journalism that was typical of Small's newspaper.

It was common to see front page stories using words like double-cross, dictator, bunk, liar and worse. After J. Bert Miller's condemnation of Governor Small in the state legislature in 1927, the *Daily Republican* ran a regular derogatory, sarcastic column in the *Republican* bylined by *Jaybirt.*

A.J. Huot, in a campaign speech in March 1930, said, "Mr. Miller calls Small's sheet *The Daily Calamity*. I would give it a more fitting name if there was not so many ladies present. In my estimation, it ranks zero among the other newspapers but you can't expect much where there are no brains. When it is possible to publish more dirt in one paper, the Small outfit will have the honor if doing it."

A story from May 7, 1931 was headlined *More Slander By Schmidt's Yellow Sheet.* It was a news story, not an editorial. It started, "A full column of misrepresentation and slander, probably concocted in an alcoholic haze, broke out like measles in Hermie Schmidt's junk newspaper last evening."

A May 12 *Daily Republican* story responded to a *Daily News* story critical of appropriating $1,000 for an official painting of Governor Small. The *Daily Republican* story included, "Last evening, Herman Schmidt's scandal sheet, a political organ which reflects in every line the booze-soaked mentality of its editor, pounced with characteristic spitefulness upon some senseless bunk which fermented in the editorial room of the *Milford Herald,* an Iroquois County affliction controlled by the same type of mentality and morals as its step-brother in Kankakee, and republished it. The policies of the *Milford Herald* are dictated by C.W. Raymond, called the J. Bert Miller of Iroquois County, a radical hated by the self-respecting citizens of our neighboring county with the same just indignation and distrust as Miller is hated in Kankakee County, and for the same reasons. Raymond is the poor excuse of a man who conspired with Miller to trick and fool the people of Iroquois County to vote for the present governor. Now, unable to make plausible excuses any longer for the failure of the Emmerson administration, like Miller he is trying to throw up a smoke screen by maligning the administration of Governor Len Small. So warped and biased have their minds become from the momentary power in their control that they believe their prejudices to be greater than custom and precedent in the history of Illinois. According to their argument, the picture of Len Small -- the man who lifted Illinois out of the mud and made the greatest record as a road builder of any man or administration in the world, and under whose administration Illinois enjoyed the most prosperous eight years of its history -- should be omitted from the walls of the state house."

That was the lead to a news story, not an editorial, and it was typical of the *Daily Republican* when it came to covering opponents of Small.

In June 1931, a month after these stories, the *Kankakee Daily Republican* acquired the *Kankakee Daily News* and the slurs against the "drunken" *Daily News* managing editor Herman Schmidt came to an end. It was called a merger but the officers of the corporation were Len Small, Leslie Small, Ed Jeffers, H.M. Stone and Shirley E. Moisant.

Part of the deal included bringing Schmidt on board as city editor. When Schmidt died on Jan. 24, 1936, the newspaper gave him a big front-page tribute that hailed him as "unfailingly generous, tolerant and cooperative" and "possessing the priceless gifts to a newspaperman." He was "highly regarded in Kankakee business and professional circles" and "an exceptionally able man in any phase of the business." Pallbearers included Leslie Small and J. Bert Miller. The newspaper closed its offices for the afternoon so the entire staff could attend the funeral and the burial in Mound Grove Cemetery.

And when J. Bert Miller died on Sept. 2, 1937, the *Kankakee Republican-News* also gave him a nice tribute in a front page story. It noted his many offices and accomplishments and said that he "took an active interest in political affairs" and "was recognized as an able attorney, especially as a trial lawyer."

After Len Small died in 1936, the Kankakee newspaper ceased indulging in the vicious personal attacks and name-calling that was common in its pages during the entire Len Small era.

The feud with the *Chicago Tribune* was brought up again when another scandal rocked the Kankakee State Hospital in 1954. A theft ring that had stolen millions of dollars was uncovered. The *Chicago Tribune* editorialized against the Kankakee County grand jury that returned no indictments, not even against employees who were caught with tons of stolen goods and confessed. The *Tribune* took a swipe at Kankakee as the home of crooked Len Small. *The Daily Journal* exploded with its own editorial against the *Tribune*. One more time, the *Tribune* and the Small newspaper locked horns. The *Tribune* was just spewing "its venom against the dead," the *Daily Journal* editorial read. "The *Tribune* opposed him at every turn when it found it could not control him. The Chicago newspaper has never forgotten or forgiven its defeats at the hands of the Kankakee man."

There were the occasional lawsuits. Kankakee lawyer W.R. Hunter sued the *Kankakee Daily Republican* for libel in July 1906. The newspaper published a series of nasty articles alleging Hunter was unethical in handling a divorce case. The sensational trial in January 1908 ended when the judge dismissed the jury after it could not reach a decision following 22 hours of deliberation.

Kankakee County Sheriff L.J. Cyrier sued the newspaper in October 1906. George Mullaney sued the *Daily Republican* in March 1911. He was a township assessor who the newspaper said was guilty of "brazen and unjust trickery" for increasing taxes, a charge printed just before the primary election. Colton Chapman, acquitted twice for burglary in 1924, sued the *Daily Republican* and Leslie Small in 1926. Chapman's brothers-in-law had been tried and convicted. Chapman blamed the newspaper for linking him to the crime. Leslie Small was arrested on a charge of criminal libel on June 8, 1933 for publishing a story questioning the morality of Joseph Adams, publisher of the *Kankakee Bulletin*. Small was taken into custody by Sheriff Albert Goodknecht and released in $1,000 bond. A month later, a Kankakee justice of the peace dismissed the case.

Publisher Len H. Small, the governor's grandson, was killed in a car crash in March 1980. Illinois United Press International set up a Len H. Small Memorial

Award for Community Service Journalism that year. Small's widow presented the first award to Lee Strobel -- a writer for the *Chicago Tribune.*

A different kind of newspaper controversy came from the Small family not long after they bought the Ottawa *Republican-Times* for $750,000 in 1955.

The Ottawa newspaper was enjoying a prestigious reputation in the state at that time, thanks to managing editor Herbert E. Hames Jr.

Ottawa, LaSalle, Streator and other towns in LaSalle County had underworld connections and vice of all kinds for decades, some associated with Chicago mobsters and some with home-grown gangsters. LaSalle County was famous for wide-open gambling joints, bootlegging, prostitution and even bank robbery and murder. Chicago Mob boss Paul "The Waiter" Ricca had a country hideaway near Norway in LaSalle County. Ottawa's City Council issued an official "thanks" to Ricca, after the brutal Mob boss sent some of his hoodlums to help in a community wood-chopping effort during a coal strike. LaSalle gambling boss Thomas Cawley was a subject of the Kefauver Crime Commission hearings in the 1950s. John Looney (whose real life gangster activity was fictionalized in *The Road To Perdition* film) was from Ottawa, although his reign of terror was in Rock Island. The honor roll of gangsters and hoodlums is lengthy. LaSalle County still is a wild place.

Herb Hames joined the Ottawa newspaper in 1951. His crusading journalism helped close some of Ottawa's gambling dens, exposed poor enforcement of liquor laws and crooked La Salle County tax assessments, and revealed local political connections to gangsters. Other newspaper stories pushing local improvements won for the Ottawa newspaper the Inland Daily Press Association's award for coverage of local government for the three straight years after Hames became editor.

Things changed after publisher Fred Sapp died in 1955 and the Smalls bought the newspaper. The controversy even made the national news.

A story in the Feb. 10, 1958 issue of TIME magazine said "the new publishers frowned on controversial stories and insisted that all editorials on local topics be cleared with the business office." This is against the beliefs of journalists but very much the rule of the accountants who run the newspapers. Hames was muzzled.

However, in late 1957 Hames wrote an editorial about scandals at the mismanaged Ryburn-King Hospital in Ottawa, including trouble between the hospital board and the city council. Hames printed it without front-office approval because the wife of *Republican-Times* general manager Edward Kelly was a member of the hospital board. The controversy led to the resignation of the entire hospital board under pressure from the city council. Hames was fired.

A committee of 61 business, professional and religious leaders called for Hames' reinstatement. TIME quoted one committee member, "If Herb Hames is fired, freedom of the press is dead in Ottawa." Hames stayed fired.

Chapter 25

Rule or Ruin

Len Small's political philosophy can be summed up in the phrase, "Rule or Ruin."

From the 1890s, when Len Small became the political boss of Kankakee County, until the day he died in 1936, the city -- and later the state -- was torn apart by the factional fighting and vicious attacks that were caused personally by Len Small.

Small's political method of operation was best expressed in this quote from a July 21, 1921 editorial in the *Kankakee Daily News:*

"His leadership constantly kept the party embroiled in factional strife. A 'rule or ruin' policy was his favorite method, and his tactics drove the better element of the party from his leadership until he was able to hold in line only those who profited personally in acknowledging his kingship."

This theme was expanded in an editorial in the same newspaper three weeks later. It said that Small's indictment and arrest on corruption charges was a bigger shock to the rest of the state than it was to the people of Kankakee, who knew him best. "In a city and county where the only political, social and business issue has been based either upon allegiance or opposition to Small, nothing less can be expected. Small forced that issue and his enemies were never passive. The governor has a peculiar faculty of dealing brutally with those who do not bow to his political leadership, and men have become estranged in a spirit of bitterness which has grown with the years.

"Probably no man ever attempting to rule a community created the same turmoil as has Len Small. Where he could not rule he threatened ruin, and the history of Kankakee for 20 years past is written in large letters of one word which spell 'Strife.' His neighborhood activities have been confined to those where his selfish interests were best served, and he drew his friends and following from those who had something to gain in a material sense by accepting his leadership.

"His life may be best summed up in the statement that while as a politician he has achieved some measure of success, as a citizen he was a total failure."

This philosophy was not something that happened in 1921, springing from "persecution" by the attorney general. It started at the beginning of Small's career.

The Kankakee County Republicans held their convention in March 1898. It was when Len Small was just consolidating his power as Boss of local politics. It is interesting to note the language of the convention's resolutions, which had Len Small's stamp on it. One resolution praised Governor John Tanner "for the brave, magnificent stand he has taken against the perverted Chicago newspaper trust that has sought to rule or ruin in matters of state legislation."

All in one sentence, Small hit the Chicago press (which already was on to him) while hypocritically accused his opposition of "rule or ruin."

It was Small who tried to destroy those who he could not control, the very charge he leveled at the Chicago newspapers.

As early as Oct. 24, 1898, the *Chicago Tribune* had this incredibly insightful assessment: "Len Small is bold and aggressive. He is a good organizer and he is a fighter. The average political boss evens up his score and lets it go at that. Not so with Small. He never forgives and he never forgets. He will kill off a political opponent and then scalp him. Pity is not in his vocabulary. It is fight all the time, from start to finish. So, soon as Small got command of the politics of Kankakee, he began to antagonize a lot of men who had for years and years been the bone and sinew of the Republican party. Any man who didn't do exactly as Small said was visited with the boss' wrath.

"Curtis, of course, is the beneficiary of Small's political power and prestige. Curtis and Small are distinct individuals but a unit in politics. One is equally hated as the other. Small never conciliates; he applies the knout."

The story added that the *Kankakee Times* (which Small bought five years later and renamed the *Kankakee Daily Republican*) was controlled by Small. "Any Republican who dares resent anything Small says, or fails to do whatever Small commands, or expresses an opinion or determination contrary to that of Small, is made the victim of Small's wrath through the columns of Mr. Dunlap's newspaper."

There are more tales in this book. Chapter 4 tells of Small's attempt to ruin Sen. William Mason, and bribe and then ruin candidate James Dawson in 1902, how Small almost ruined the local party by trying to force his brother John on the ballot in 1905, and how Small tried to ruin political foe William R. Hunter in 1905.

One thing to remember is that most of Len Small's political enemies were fellow Republicans. There were few Democrats in Kankakee at the time, and the state and the nation were Republican-dominated. Most of Small's Republican enemies started as friends or allies.

One of those friends was J. Bert Miller, who became one of Small's most bitter enemies. A story in the March 27, 1907 *Kankakee Evening Democrat* about a political meeting describes Miller as "one of Len's hired hands." Miller was named one of Small's ward committeemen that day, as was Arthur W. Deselm. A lot of prominent local names, such as Dyer, Grinnell, Bratton, Koon, Legris, Alpiner, Granger, Harney, Huot, Goodknecht, Lanoue, Hunter and more eventually became enemies to be attacked.

Big Bill Thompson, William Lorimer, Fred Lundin and a number of other Republicans in the state also eventually became Small's enemies. The criteria was simple: you are either on Len Small's side, to be used, or else you are an enemy to be destroyed.

Daniel H. Paddock, one of the most prominent men in Kankakee history, was a Small friend (and his lawyer) in the 1890s. But when Paddock wouldn't agree with his slate-making in 1899, he said Small called him a liar, spread false stories about him and threatened him. Paddock's statement was: "Mr. Small came to my office and in substance said to me that if I did not withhold my support of the policy of nominating a ticket upon which Mr. Byrns should be a candidate as against Mr. Jeffers, that he would, from now and to all time, in every way that he could by direction and indirection, do all things to injure my business and my professional standing, and the business and interest of those who were my friends; that he would use every means within his power to deprive me and my friends of business; and that this would last through my entire life."

Small denied all of this. "I told him that I was aware of the underhand and trickery that he was practicing toward me and of some of the falsehoods that were being circulated, calculated to injure me, and I told him I would resent his dishonorable methods by every honorable means within my power," Small wrote in a letter published in the *Gazette.* Small concluded by writing, "I did not threaten him...as stated in the *Gazette*."

And Republican W.R. Hunter criticized Len Small and political partner Edward C. Curtis in a Dec. 12, 1899 *Gazette* story. "Just before the election of 1898, I denounced Mr. Curtis, and I denounce any man who will attempt to use the power given him by the people to destroy the private business of a private citizen, as Mr. Curtis threatened to destroy mine. I am still of the opinion that to place power in the hands of a man of that disposition is a dangerous thing to the rights of the people."

Len Small always bragged about being a loyal Republican. But Len Small was a Republican only when it suited him. He supported his own rogue candidates or he supported Democrats when it suited his ends or his grudges.

The *Gazette* observed in 1899 that Small punished Republicans in county board assignments if those Republicans were anti-Small, while he rewarded Democrats who worked in their precincts for him.

"When the Republicans of the town of Kankakee resented your bossism at the primaries, in pursuance of your favorite motto 'rule or ruin,' you turned your organized forces against the Republican ticket and defeated it," W.R. Hunter wrote in a lengthy open letter to Len Small in the Dec. 8, 1899 *Gazette.* "I repeat that you are entitled to another office but consistency would require that you run for it not on the Republican but on the Democratic ticket."

Hunter was one of the local men who started the Kankakee County Republican Club in 1899 to counter Len Small's dictatorial control. He referred to Small as a "political boss," to which Small replied in the Dec. 15, 1899 *Gazette,* "I had rather be a political boss than a political anarchist." That's right. A loyal Republican who questioned the Boss' rule in Kankakee County made one an anarchist, a pretty strong term in that era.

Hunter shot back in the next issue of the newspaper. "I am inclined to think that by the use of that term, you mean to imply that I have revolted against your methods and opposed your political trickery."

Len Small's publicity machine tried to portray him as a kindly ruler trying to do his best for the people of Illinois. In reality, Small and his cohorts were bullies who sought to destroy anyone who crossed them. Len Small didn't believe in compromising with the opposition, he believed in rubbing them out. Anyone who was not with him was against him and they needed to be destroyed. Friendly opposition was an incomprehensible concept to Len Small, and agreeing to disagree was a joke. He really did have a "rule or ruin" policy as his local critics charged, and it resulted in two Republican parties, the "regulars" and the "antis," and the party struggle lasted all through Small's career. This was true statewide and was particularly so in Kankakee County. A year after Small left the governorship, Victor McBroom became chairman of the Kankakee County Republican Central Committee and brought together the "anti" and the "regular" Republican factions of the party into one big, powerful and dominant political machine.

Forcing John Small on the Republicans in 1905 tore the local Republican party apart but that did not matter to Len Small. That was part of his strategy, divide and conquer, as was shown again and again in Len Small's career.

Commenting on Len Small's brand of politics during John Small's campaign for circuit court judge, a June 17, 1905 editorial in the *Kankakee Daily Gazette* summarized the state of politics in Kankakee and in Illinois: "A large majority of the common people have lost faith in the legislative bodies in this county and feel the rights of the people have become a matter of barter and sale among the members of such bodies."

"Is Ex-Judge John Small free from political influence when his brother Len is the political boss of the county and the only man who really wanted his brother to make the race?" asked the *Gazette.* "With plenty of good judicial timber at hand, why was brother John so essential? If John Small must be taken care of, why not get him an appointment or make him assistant state treasurer, so long as the people must contribute to the demands of the Small family?"

And, "In order to add another office to the already lengthy role held by John and Lennington Small, they are willing to plunge the party into another factional fight, when an able and acceptable candidate could have been secured who would have still further cemented the factions which were fast becoming reconciled. This is either political recklessness or gigantic selfishness."

It added that Small's political efforts kept the Republican party "in an uproar, when scandal has been rife, when politics has been caused to be looked upon in this community as something to be shunned by honest men, when the power of office, instead of being used for the public good is made the vehicle of personal ambition and get-rich-quick schemes."

The fact that Len Small portrayed himself as a loyal Republican while helping Democrats and others to defeat Republicans cannot be disputed. When Len Small could not defeat Republican rivals in the primaries, he worked for their Democrat opponents in the fall.

Small backed Richard Yates for the Republican nomination for governor in 1908 against incumbent Governor Charles Deneen. When Deneen won, Small sent out sample ballots marked for Deneen's opponent, Democrat Adlai E. Stevenson.

When Small first ran for the gubernatorial nomination against Governor Deneen in 1912 and lost, his organization sent out sample ballots marked for Democrat Edward Dunne, and Small's organization worked for Dunne's election.

As chairman of the Republican party's central committee in 1915, Small sent out sample ballots marked against Medill McCormick, the Republican nominee for congressman. In 1918, Small worked for James Hamilton Lewis, the Democrat candidate for U.S. senator against McCormick.

State Sen. John A. Wheeler of Springfield, the man behind the bill to wreck civil service in Illinois in 1921, was overwhelmingly defeated for re-nomination in April 1922. In November, Governor Small backed Wheeler as an independent candidate against the Republican nominee. Wheeler lost.

Small worked against Republican State Sen. Thurlow Essington of Streator in 1922, and this was two years before Essington challenged Small for the nomination. Other unfriendly Republican who Small worked against in 1922 were State Sen. Patrick J. Sullivan of Chicago, State Sen. Lowell Mason of Oak Park, State Sen. James MacMurray of Chicago, State Rep. William Cruden of Chicago and State Rep. L.S. Holderman of Morris.

Len Small pulled every trick he could to defeat J. Bert Miller for state representative in the April 1926 primary. Small put courthouse janitor Fred W. Miller's name on the ballot, in the hope that voters would be confused between the two Millers so his real candidate Clifford B. Sawyer would win. J. Bert beat both Fred and Sawyer. Small then ran a reluctant Louis Beckman as an independent party candidate. Louis Beckman was a Republican but he was not the Republican nominee. Miller was the rightful nominee of the Republican party.

Small worked against Republican candidates in Kankakee County for decades.

"Party means nothing more to him than a means to secure everything possible in the way of pelf and personal advancement," wrote the *Kankakee Daily News.* "The party regularity, of which he has boasted for so many years, means nothing when he finds an opportunity to secure personal preferment."

Len Small was out for himself. While the 1920 primary votes were in dispute, and it appeared Small might not win the Republican nomination for governor, Small took petitions to have himself listed on the ballot as an independent candidate. But he didn't have to run as an independent because enough votes were "found" to give him the nomination.

Small's revenge wasn't confined to working against candidates. He also punished opponents after they won. When Small became governor and the legislature organized into committees, Governor Small chose to carry on a long-standing local political feud by blocking State Rep. Ben Alpiner (a Republican) from the Appropriations Committee. Small cited Alpiner's political opposition in years past, as well as Alpiner's ownership of stock in the *Kankakee Daily News.*

Chief Justice Clyde Stone was one of the Supreme Court justices who ruled against the governor in the civil case in 1925. Len Small decided to put all his political power into the effort to defeat Justice Stone for re-election in 1927.

The governor convened a council of state department heads in January, including Cornelius R. Miller, Frank Sheets, H.U. Bailey, William Scanlon and William Perrin.

In Peoria, Stone's judicial district, Small started giving state jobs to precinct committeemen. The governor also used the hammer of granting new roads to areas in the district where he could squeeze support. Small was determined to use his muscle to deny Stone re-nomination at the party convention in March.

One job that caused a stir was when Small put J. Shirley West, the former police chief of Peoria, on the state payroll. West had been forced to resign as police chief the previous August when it was found he was operating a stolen car ring.

The governor announced in February that the state would buy $2 million in supplies for state institutions in Peoria. Leslie Small, director of the Department of Purchases and Construction, and his state purchasing agent, Lawrence Becherer (another crony from the Kankakee bank), called on wholesale suppliers in the Peoria area and told them what they needed to do in the judicial campaign if they wanted the state's business.

Justice Clyde Stone

Never before in Illinois had there been such an effort in a judicial campaign, especially against a judge whose name was not tainted by scandal. It was driven by pure spite.

The governor convinced House Speaker Robert Scholes of Peoria to be his candidate against Stone.

On Feb. 13, the Illinois Bar Association endorsed Justice Stone and called for a grand jury investigation into the governor's actions in trying to destroy a Supreme Court justice, a genuine separation of powers issue.

Judge Arthur Deselm

Delegates from the Peoria area were selected at the Feb. 16 county convention, and despite the governor sending in a large number of his state pay-rollers to stampede the convention, the delegates chosen for the state convention were Stone delegates.

Stone was re-nominated in March by the state convention.

But Len Small did not let it lie there. Secretary of State Louis Emmerson certified Stone's nomination. Small filed a writ of *mandamus* with the state Supreme Court to have the certification overturned. With Stone recusing himself, the other justices threw Small's petition out of court.

And once again, loyal Republican Len Small bolted his party to work for the Democrat. It didn't matter. Justice Stone won the election by a large margin.

Clyde Stone served as a Supreme Court justice from 1918 to 1948.

Len Small tried to ruin several judges, from the local circuit court to the state Supreme Court. At the very same time Small was trying to ruin Justice Stone, he also was trying to ruin Kankakee County Circuit Court Judge Arthur Deselm.

Deselm had served on the bench for a quarter century. He was from a pioneer family. A village in Kankakee County bears the family name. But in April 1927, Small used his power at the caucus to deny Deselm re-nomination in favor of John Mayhew, a Kankakee lawyer loyal to the Small machine.

The *Kankakee Daily Republican* and its editor Leslie Small had been sued for libel. Judge Deselm denied a motion to dismiss the case when it came to court. This was one strike against him. Judge Deselm also refused to contribute to the Governor Small Defense Fund. Strike two.

State Rep. J. Bert Miller of Kankakee revealed a third reason why Small was after Deselm. Miller said that when the governor anticipated a *quo warranto* would be filed to remove him from office, Small approached Deselm with a proposition that it be filed in Kankakee County, where a "friendlier judge would do nothing about it." Judge Deselm rejected the idea, and Small worked against him ever since.

Deselm's distinguished career had earned him the respect of the public. He decided to run as an independent candidate to let the voters, and not the Small delegates, decide. He was endorsed by the Kankakee County Bar Association over Mayhew.

Governor Small's forces fought Deselm desperately. The governor sent letters on embossed stationary to every voter in the district. Small threw a free luncheon in the Kankakee Armory for anyone who wanted to come.

On June 6, the same day Justice Stone won his election, Judge Deselm was re-elected as an independent candidate, by an even larger margin. Mayhew lost every county in the judicial district, including Kankakee.

Small & Co. also tried to defeat Judge Kickham Scanlan when he ran for re-election in 1921, a vendetta from the Chicago school ruling. Scanlan won.

Judge James T. Burns not only was a distinguished jurist, he was a real war hero. He also was targeted for defeat by Small in 1922. Why? Because Judge Burns refused the organization's request to drop charges against two bootleggers who had influence with Small. Burns maintained his integrity even after being warned that to buck the organization would be detrimental to his career. Judge Burns was defeated that fall.

Small wielded the hammer against others. He used his road building program as a "rule or ruin" weapon. Areas that supported him politically got roads; those that didn't support him politically did not. And he wasn't shy about making that threat before an election.

Governor Small even used his pardoning power as a weapon against those who crossed him. Chicago's black pastors lined up in April 1924 to oppose Small's re-election. They cited Governor Small's ties to the Ku Klux Klan and his refusal to pardon 14 black men who were in prison for their part in the 1917 race riots in East St. Louis. Small did not forget this opposition. On the day after the 1924 election, Governor Small pardoned 11 white men who were convicted of murder during the riots. The black men who were convicted for defending themselves during those riots remained behind bars.

Kankakee grocer George Granger was arrested in 1910 by federal agents for defrauding the government by evading the tax on oleomargarine. He paid a $10,000 fine. Criminal charges were filed but later dismissed through the influence of Len Small and Ed Curtis. In 1928, when Claude Granger was a Democrat candidate for state's attorney, the *Kankakee Daily Republican* threatened to bring up the story of his uncle unless he stopped criticizing Small's candidates.

Governor Small's "rule or ruin" policy extended even to ruining the state of Illinois, if necessary, to serve his purpose. This was seen when he threatened to call out the National Guard against the sheriff to prevent his arrest on the embezzlement charges. Can you imagine National Guard troops exchanging gunfire with sheriff's deputies, Illinois boys shooting Illinois boys, just to protect a thief and embezzler from coming to justice? And yet this might have happened if Small could have gotten away with it. Small thought the National Guard was under his orders. In fact, the law says when National Guard troops are sent into an area, they are under the jurisdiction of the local authorities. It was only this realization that led Small to back down from his threat, avoiding a bloodbath that would have been one of the most outrageous acts in American history.

Small said the indictment was brought in Sangamon County because it was the home of the most vile and murderous gang in the state. In fact, Sangamon County was the only county where charges could be brought since Springfield was there, and that is where Small committed his crimes. And it says a lot about Len Small that he considered political rival Dick Sullivan's "gang" to be worse than the Chicago gangs of Al Capone, Spike O'Donnell, Dean O'Banion, Bugs Moran, Hymie Weiss and others.

The governor ignored what was happening in Herrin because he was too busy bribing a jury. The pot boiled for weeks in Herrin before the massacre that took 20 lives.

Len Small hated his rival newspaper, the *Kankakee Daily News.* He could not rule it so he decided to try to ruin it. In early 1924, Small's people put pressure on local merchants to not advertise in the *Daily News.* The *Daily News* editors, in a front page editorial on Feb. 5, acknowledged that a boycott was a serious thing, especially when pushed by someone with so much power.

The editor wrote that his newspaper opposed Small "because it knows he is an evil influence in this community and in the state. Small has gained political eminence through the most corrupt methods ever witnessed in this country."

The editor added his opinion as to Small's ruinous and vindictive ways. "Small has been, all his life, a liability to the community in which he lives, opposed to every movement he did not control. Where factions have grown and clashed among business interests, in social life, in religious life, in fraternal life, Small has been the root of the trouble. Can a few miles of highways wipe out the bitterness he has engendered here for 30 years among erstwhile neighbors and friends? Yes, on second thought, Kankakee and its businessmen might inaugurate a boycott, one greatly to their advantage, a political boycott that would drive the nemesis of good government out of public life. And the city and state would be better off for it."

Unfortunately, the small city of Kankakee could not support two daily newspapers once the Great Depression took hold. Small was able to buy the rival newspaper and kill it in 1931.

Chapter 26

Poor Len

There seems to have been a persecution complex and paranoia in Len Small's personality. It is something that Small referred to again and again, and it is something that started at the very beginning of his career.

And it wasn't always a result of "persecution," justified or not. Even when he wasn't being "persecuted" by any definition of the word, he claimed it. Was he paranoid or was it calculated so he could assume the sympathetic mantle of a martyr?

When accused of bribing another candidate to withdraw in 1902, Small claimed that it wasn't bribery on his part, it was extortion by the other man -- with the threat (according to Small) that if Small didn't pay, a United States senator would tell lies in the Chicago newspapers, and those newspapers would not print Small's denials because "they are all against you" (the *Chicago Tribune* did print Small's denials.)

An insight into his early days is seen in a sarcastic article in the Sept. 30, 1907 Kankakee's *The Evening Democrat,* which took a shot at a *Kankakee Daily Republican* story that praised Len Small. The *Daily Republican* was "making a mighty effort to attach wings to Len Small's shoulders, put a crown upon his head and suspend a halo above him," *The Evening Democrat* wrote, "on the supposition that the people really didn't know Len, and it was his (the *Daily Republican* editor) mission in life to tell folks what a great man the Boss really is."

It continued, "The people do know Len and that's what's the trouble. Len was born and raised here. Old settlers remember him in his youth. His initial appearance in politics in a scrap centering around a school election in Limestone, his fight with the late Mike Butz, Len's withdrawal from the contest, in fact Len's entire career is well known, with a few exceptions. The Bump (the *Republican* editor) might begin at the milk route, carry Small's career through the nursery business and tell interesting facts about how Len has accumulated a large fortune while trustee at the hospital on no set salary...and go into details, giving Len all the praise on the hospital contracts."

Most prophetically for 1907, it included, "There are really many interesting things about Len that the public has never known nor the grand juries ever discovered."

The front page of the *Kankakee Daily Republican* on Aug. 15, 1916 carried a "character sketch" of state treasurer candidate Small. It was written by Small's secretary Werner Schroeder. After listing all of Small's great qualities -- energy, sane judgment, the human touch, hard work, attention to detail, loyalty, good character -- the story inevitably sinks into addressing the criticism Small has attracted, particularly from newspapers as the *Kankakee Gazette* and the *Chicago Tribune.*

"Like every other public man who has risen from the bottom upward, Len Small has been subjected to much public criticism," Schroeder wrote. "Criticism, which at times has been unjust, untruthful and vicious. The average man not only would have quailed beneath the storm of this injustice but his attitude toward life would have been changed and his disposition soured. But the personality of Len Small was greater than these vicious attacks. He is today as pleasant, genial and good-natured as he could have been in his youth."

In other words, unjust criticism made him a better man...a pleasant man without spite, hate or a thirst for vengeance.

Continuing in this vein, Schroeder adds: "He has spent comparatively little money on his candidacies. Whatever political force he has gained has come through personal friendships which he has formed throughout the state. It has not been through chicanery, nor shrewd manipulation, nor purchase of power by great wealth, but it has been the simple virtue of being true to friendship, accommodating to all people, and faithful to one's trust. That has given him the standing and the reputation which he enjoys."

As mentioned previously, one characteristic of Small's campaigns was that he had to have an enemy to vilify. It took the spotlight off his own record and put it on the opposition. It rallied his troops against a villain, rather than rallying them in support of him.

Small's lifelong enemy, the main culprit he blamed for his continued persecution, was the *Chicago Tribune,* a Republican newspaper that was strongly opposed to the Small-Thompson-Lorimer political machine. As he was about to go on trial for corruption in 1922, a shrill editorial in the April 5 *Kankakee Daily Republican* compared Len Small (again) to Abraham Lincoln. This time, it claimed that the *Chicago Tribune* had attacked Abraham Lincoln, U.S. Grant, John A. Logan, and now Len Small.

A box on the front page of his March 8, 1924 newspaper listed "Len Small's Record" in support of his re-election. Among the usual things any candidate would list are these three bizarre "accomplishments" -- "He is the people's Governor and cannot be controlled by the *Chicago Tribune* or sinister interests who rob the people." -- "He cannot be bought, bossed or bluffed; therefore, he is the most maligned Governor in the United States." -- and, "His re-election means vindication and the cleansing of the fair name of our great commonwealth which has been besmirched by conspiring cowards and dishonest editors who are controlled by un-American international bankers."

Len Small's indictment for embezzlement was never depicted as a legitimate charge. In his newspaper at the time -- as well as in local histories since then -- it has been portrayed as nothing but a vendetta by Attorney General Edward J. Brundage and the *Chicago Tribune* and not the result of any of Small's actions.

At the time, Small's newspaper characterized the indictment this way: "Attorney General Edward J. Brundage (was) nursing the pet political peeve of the century because Governor Small refused to permit him to take $1,500,000 out of the pockets of Illinois taxpayers to build up his personal Political Machine."

It added that Brundage was a political boss in Sangamon County who even controlled the grand jury. Brundage lived in Lake County, 230 miles to the north.

Sometimes, Small's shifting of the blame was unbelievable. When he pardoned gangster and cop-killer Ignatz Potz, he said he was doing it because it was his dead wife's last request. When a coal strike became a bloody massacre in downstate Herrin, he blamed the situation on Attorney General Edward Brundage, because Brundage had the governor on trial in Waukegan instead of on the job in Springfield, where he could have monitored the riot and kept it under control.

And yet, when Herrin Mayor Marshall McCormack asked the governor for help in keeping order in November 1926, the governor said no.

Whenever Len Small's *Kankakee Daily Republican* wrote about Small's critics, they were always vilified. It wasn't the state or the attorney general who prosecuted Small, it was the "vicious enemies of the governor" who were persecuting him. In most cases, the name-calling was pretty intense.

Len Small listed quite a number of enemies -- the *Chicago Tribune*, the *Chicago Daily News*, Attorney General Edward Brundage, State's Attorney Robert Crowe, the "cement trusts" and a whole raft of other businesses and politicians. He never once named the Ku Klux Klan or Al Capone or any other Chicago mobster as an enemy.

Small was obsessed with playing the victim and he seemed to enjoy the accompanying opportunity to defend himself. This began in the 1890s when he was just starting in small town politics and it continued all his life. The day after his trial ended, when doctors told him there was no hope for his wife to live, he said, "Thank God she lived to see me vindicated." Even as his wife lay dying, it was always about Len Small. In his 1924 campaign, he used his acquittal and his wife's death for all the sympathy and pity it was worth.

Small did have plenty of critics, right from the beginning. But how many of them were simply honest critics and how many were lying political enemies? There hardly was a move in his entire political career that didn't draw suspicion. Was this persecution, from everyone he ever faced, or was it legitimate suspicion from what Small was doing? Was Len Small right and the rest of the world wrong? He and his newspaper would have the public believe so.

And his newspaper never was subtle about it. When State Rep. J. Bert Miller was arguing before the Illinois Supreme Court in December 1927 in favor of *quo warranto* proceedings to remove Small from office, the "objective news story" in the *Kankakee Daily Republican* called it a "tirade of abuse and spite...indecent and repulsive invectives...a discredit to the legal profession" and more. The reporter added this comment:

"Many people in Springfield today could hardly believe that one man from Kankakee, where Governor Small is admired and adored by everybody, would get up before the Supreme Court of Illinois and use such language as Miller did. 'We know that Governor Small has done a great deal for Kankakee and Kankakee County,' said a man conversant with state affairs today. 'And I can't understand how any man can get up and say the things Miller said today. He is a disgrace to his community.'"

The Supreme Court justices, who tolerate no nonsense before their bench, did not find fault with Miller's delivery or language.

In Kankakee, Small is portrayed as a great man who built 7,700 miles of the state's hard roads, managed the Kankakee Inter-State Fair, and whose only trouble came from persecution by his enemies. In the 1968 book, *Of The People, A Popular History of Kankakee County,* Small is practically portrayed as a saint.

Of the People was published by the Kankakee County Board of Supervisors and the authors were writers for the *Kankakee Daily Journal.* The chapter on Small was more of a love letter than a biography.

Let us quote a few good things about Len Small from *Of The People.*

Len Small was a farmer, talented in horticulture and livestock breeding. The chapter on him is titled *A Big Man.* "Len Small surely was a big man, not only in political circles where his name had been mentioned as possible presidential material, but in times of crisis. He was soft-spoken, kind and friendly, but he was strong. His attention to government responsibilities and his successful development and improvement programs during his term of office, despite the continuing legal harassment, seemed to prove his strength."

The authors quote the *Manteno Independent* in the election of 1920: "Twenty-five years of hard work has carried Len Small's name to all parts of the commonwealth and by reason of his honesty and straightforwardness of his dealings he is known with favor. Len Small stands high with the plain people, probably because he is one of them and is not ashamed. He is not a rich man. If he is well to do, he has gathered in through his own hard work and business ability, two characteristics most certainly to be desired in a governor." And it quotes the *Herrin News* in reference to the road-building program: "For generations to come, the tens of thousands of travelers as they move swiftly and smoothly along the splendid highways of Illinois will thank God that Len Small lived."

The book continues: "He was known for his kind manner and soft spoken ways. And it was often said that he was never too busy to help people in need, to discuss grain prices or dairy cows with another farmer or to participate in county events."

When Len Small died, his *Kankakee Republican-News* had columns of tributes and praise, including this one: "Governor Len Small was outstanding for his executive ability, his gift of leadership, of acquiring and deserving confidence, the integrity of his pledges, his tactfulness and his force of character. He sought, with all the power of a keen mind and a sturdy physique, to do the best he could at all times for his state."

The only mention of Governor Small on the website of today's Small Newspaper Group ignores any trouble the governor had. This is all it has to say: "Leslie was Managing Editor of the *Kankakee Daily Republican,* while his father was Governor of Illinois from 1921 to 1929. The *Chicago Tribune* championed a cause against the Governor which impressed upon the Small family the importance of their hometown newspaper. The Governor is best known for the 7,000 miles of hard roads he built in Illinois and for his support of the State Fair."

Even the favorable account in *Of The People* does not credit Small with much more than his road building and his earlier management of the Kankakee Inter-State Fair. If Governor Small is best known for roads and fairs, it is because the rest of the story is not known in Kankakee. The big shots do not want it known.

Len Small dominated Kankakee politics in the early 1900s. That included his newspaper and its present-day successor. That is a big part of why his legacy is that of a saintly statesman. Those who have written Kankakee history are Small newspaper reporters or civic boosters -- they want to put a positive image on everything local, they rarely mention anything negative, and they strive to grasp for anything that brings fame to Kankakee. Len Small has been modified to fit the bill.

Carroll Woody had this observation about Len Small in his 1931 book: "The career of Len Small illustrates, with peculiar effectiveness, the tactics which have enabled their practitioners to remain for a long period dominant factors in state political activities. Such careers are not based upon adherence to any particular set of political principles."

For example, Small was friendly to corporations early in his career but that changed under the influence of Fred Lundin. And to counter the criticism from newspapers, reformers and civic interest groups, Small developed political friendships and a "machine based on patronage and spoils."

"His removal from the gubernatorial chair was widely regarded as marking the turning point in Illinois politics from spoils administration to newer and improved standards of governmental efficiency. That he could have maintained himself so long in influence and power is, however, a unique commentary upon the standards of political activity in the state of Illinois during the third of a century just passed," Wooddy wrote.

Poor Len. He was always the victim, the martyr, the man everyone was out to "get." It was a broken record that played for more than three decades. Column after column told endlessly about Brundage, the *Tribune,* the *Daily News,* the cement trust, the traction barons, the tax dodgers and everyone else who was against him. Hundreds and hundreds of news stories over those decades tell the same tales of these same enemies and the "lies" that were constantly being told against him. It never ended.

Let's look at some of the issues, the enemies, the defense Len Small gave, and just what was the truth of it all.

State Treasurer: Small always proudly claimed (and it is one of the bedrock tenets of Small's legacy in his hometown today) that he turned in to the state treasury more interest than any other state treasurer in the history of Illinois. There are a few problems with this claim, beyond those mentioned in chapter 9 of this book. First, some state treasurers before Small also kept the interest on state deposits as spoils of the office. Second, Small's record $450,010 was more than doubled by his successor, Fred Sterling, who deposited $996,121 in his two-year term. After Sterling, Edward Miller deposited $1.6 million in interest and Oscar Nelson deposited a similar figure.

Len Small maintained he never kept a penny of deposit money of the state but ignored the interest. His foes always pointed to the fact that Small never took the witness stand at his trial as proof that he would not swear to it.

Small would have had a legitimate bragging claim about interest if he had turned in the other two million dollars in interest that he and Ed Curtis kept.

Interestingly, Small used a similar argument in December 1899, in an open letter to the *Kankakee Gazette.* "During the three years of my term, the circuit clerk's office, after paying all salaries and other expenses of the office, has earned and collected for the county of Kankakee more than double the amount turned over to the county in 12 years by the president of your Anti-Republican Club while holding the same office." He was referring to J. Frank Leonard, who was clerk from 1880 to 1892. This time, however, Small was called on his deceitful boast by W.R. Hunter, in an open letter in the Dec. 18, 1899 *Gazette*. "In respect to the earnings, you have done exactly what Leonard and Durfee did. You have turned over to the county what was left of the earnings of the office after payment of salaries and expenses; you have done nothing more. You are not the cause of the increase of a few hundred, not thousands as you put it, of dollars. This increase was not due to your abilities but is attributable to several causes." Hunter cited the end of litigation costs, different payments when lawsuits were filed, and increased business.

Hard Roads: Governor Small took full credit for building the state's roads (another bedrock tenet of Small's legacy), even though it was well under way before he became governor and even though it would have been done no matter who was governor. His administration built only a tiny portion of the roads found in Illinois today. Successors who built more miles of road did not similarly brag; perhaps it was because they had other achievements or because they did not need to use it to hide dubious acts. His road building legacy does not mention how he used road contracts as a weapon against political enemies or as a means for shaking down contractors.

Len Small spent more time building his image as a road builder than he spent building the roads.

Chicago Tribune: Len Small always maintained that the *Tribune* opposed him because it could not control him. But the *Tribune* started reporting on Len Small's crooked path beginning in 1896, when Small was just a small town political boss who showed no promise of achieving statewide office. The *Tribune* had no thought of "controlling" this self-proclaimed "farmer candidate" from downstate Illinois at that time.

Vote Totals: Another tenet of his legacy is the brag that Small got a higher total in 1920 than previous governors had received. But that was because there were more voters (women were allowed on the voting rolls for the first time) and because Big Bill and Co. stole votes in Chicago. Still, Small ran behind the other candidates on the ticket in this heavily Republican year. He always ran behind the ticket. And every governor after Small got higher totals, as the population increased.

In 1905, the *Kankakee Daily Gazette* noted that Len Small "squeezed through on general elections when national tickets were in the field. It is true Mr. Small ran behind his ticket badly, but the majorities always carried him through."

Tax Dodgers: Small continuously went after the "tax dodgers" who didn't pay their share of taxes and he pledged many times over the years to make them pay. But Small never kept that pledge. And Small himself was a big tax dodger. It became an issue several times over the years, when documents showed that Small under-reported the value of his farm holdings, his home, his personal property. And don't forget the million dollars he embezzled on which he paid no income taxes.

The Kankakee Daily News on July 26, 1921 saw hypocrisy in Small's attacks on "big interests." One of his lawyers was John Drennan, chief counsel for the Illinois Central Railroad. Another Small attorney, George Gillespie, was a lawyer for the Big Four Railroad. And the Chicago meat packers who took loans from the Grant Park Bank were among the big corporations who Small called "tax dodgers."

Justice: Small claimed immunity from arrest, citing the unconstitutionality of the judicial branch interfering with the executive branch. He didn't mind the executive infringing on the judiciary by granting questionable pardons and paroles on a massive scale to criminals who were legally imprisoned by the judiciary.

A *Chicago Tribune* editorial on Dec. 21, 1923 said that in the upcoming election, the "sole issue is the elimination of the unsavory remains of the Lundin-Thompson-Small regime. The issue is not merely political. It is moral.

"The governor has a powerful and widespread army of henchmen and beneficiaries. He is trying desperately to turn the minds of the voters from the only relevant issue, himself. He has inherited the buncombe and dust throwing tactics of the old City Hall crowd. He says he is a victim of persecution, but he has no answer for the charges of his alleged persecutors. He says the trial for keeping state money in his pocket was persecution, but he has not told the people where that money is nor offered to return it. No victim of persecution ever had a better chance to blow his persecutors out of the water than Small had at the Waukegan trial. No victim of false charges ever had a better chance to answer them and confound his enemies. That was the time for Small to show his innocence and prove persecution. Did he do so? He did not. He has not since. He does not now."

The reader may be wondering, how did Len Small ever get elected if he was this bad? There is only one explanation.

Illinois is different.

The outrageous acts of Len Small were not secret deals that later were uncovered and led to his undoing. His acts were on public display and were criticized and condemned as they happened. He was prosecuted and pursued for them as they happened. They were known to the public before he was elected and re-elected as governor.

The public knew about Small keeping the interest on state deposits before he was elected governor. They knew about his ties to the Klan and to Chicago gangsters before he was re-elected. They voted for him anyway. The public knew about Frank L. Smith and his illegal campaign contributions from the utilities magnates he was regulating. Smith won the election anyway.

In 1998, everyone knew that Secretary of State George Ryan sold driver's licenses for bribes and they knew about the Willis children being victims of this scheme. They knew about Ryan's shakedowns and the investigations into his activities. The voters elected him governor anyway. In 2006, everyone knew that Governor Rod Blagojevich was a crook and was under investigation and probably would follow Ryan to the penitentiary. The voters re-elected him anyway.

Public awareness of all this should have been enough to end any candidate's career. But Illinois is different.

Small's luck is explained in a Jan. 22, 1924 *Chicago Tribune* editorial.

"Maybe his bad record is a help to him. Sometimes we think it is a vote-getter for him. It is so bad it is unbelievable. When the truth is told, people say it cannot be so, and that there must be a vicious reason behind the telling of it.

"Some of the women are just discovering that he pardoned out of the penitentiary a man and woman sent there for pandering. Small will say that he was protecting them from injustice and some people will believe that, because they cannot believe he would let a pair of convicted panders out. Small's explanations of his pardons, including the pardon of his silent friends and protectors, Newmark and Boyle, puts the courts of the state in a conspiracy to do injustice, nothing less. He is forever undoing the work of judge and jury.

"His explanation of having the packers' notes, of the nonexistent Grant Park Bank, and the disappearance of the interest the packers paid is ridiculous. People may believe him, reasoning to themselves that the truth cannot be true, it is so bad."

Was Len Small as bad as all the information presented here? His biggest critics were not Democrats but the fellow Republicans who he could not control. Outside of the local museum, and the newspapers and politician controlled by Small, it is tough to find any good word about Governor Len Small.

The *Chicago Journal of Commerce* noted in a 1924 editorial that it usually confined its comments to business, not politics. But it had to make an observation about the governor in his re-election campaign. It wanted to know if Len Small was really as bad as some people were saying. After looking at the evidence, it wrote:

"Len Small actually is as black as he is painted. We know that politicians are a selfish lot. But it seems to us that Len Small is extraordinarily selfish. We know that every man has two sides, and yet, as far as public activities are concerned, we are simply unable to find any other side of Len Small."

The *Journal* cited three "outrageous" things about Small: "First, he has granted pardons by the wholesale to some of the vilest criminals in the state, including a pair of panders who were so unquestionably guilty that they dared not take the stand in their own defense. Second, he incurred passage of an utterly unnecessary $100,000,000 road bond bill in order to be re-elected. He did not hesitate to tell various districts bluntly that they would get no roads under this bill unless they sent men to the legislature who would obey his orders. Pressure from these districts compelled the legislators to vote for the bill. In effect, Len Small is seeking to win re-election with $100,000,000 of the state's money. Third, he retained $10,000,000 of state money for two years after leaving the state treasurership. Fred Sterling succeeded him in 1919 but Small retained the state money. What arrangement he had with Sterling is unknown -- by the people. Of the 12 jurors who acquitted Small, eight were later given political positions.

"No matter where an Illinoisan travels elsewhere in the country, if politics is mentioned, he is asked about Small. Small is one of the state's two burning disgraces of recent years. The other is the Herrin massacre."

The *Chicago Tribune* published this editorial on April 5, 1923.

"Len Small was made governor by Thompson and Lundin when their control over Chicago was tightest. Chicago has cleaned house. Thompson quit. Lundin is under indictment. The city is making a fresh start.

"Small is even worse than either Thompson or Lundin. He has always been bad. Twenty-five and thirty years ago, his connection with the corruption of public institutions such as the Kankakee insane asylum was notorious. He always has been notorious.

"Temperamentally, he is timid, but he is so unscrupulous that his lack of principle gives him the appearance of audacity. When he was shaking in his boots for fear a Lake County jury would send him to the penitentiary, he was amazing some of the stoutest rascals in the state by his boldness in offering voters the bribe of good roads in exchange for legislators who would protect him.

"He is not guided by courage, shrewdness or strength, but by his lack of principles. He is stupid, and his stupidity plus his indifference to public decency allows him to do the outrageous things for which any governor ought to be impeached.

"He was a public nuisance when he was a little grubbing downstate politician, picking up offices which would allow him to control coal contracts for an institution, levy an assessment on poorly paid institution employees, and gather in nickels and dimes where he could find them. He was more than a nuisance when he could get an office which permitted him to hold public money and handle the interest on it. Then Chicago's misfortune became the state's misfortune, and the small time politician took over the control of Illinois as governor.

"To make himself entirely insufferable, he took up tricks which he had learned from Lundin and Thompson. He had been a small minded, realistic gangster, but aping Thompson, he tried to be a flannel-mouth and to spout phrases regarding the people and the profiteers.

"His whole political life has been one of profiteering at the expense of people who pay taxes, and even now he is trying to dodge a civil accounting for $2,000,000 of interest on public money which disappeared while it was in his hands. There may be more heard of the matter in which he was acquitted of the criminal charge in this connection. There are indictments in Lake County now which may result in disclosure. Whether or not we ever learn more of that verdict, we are entitled to learn more of where the $2,000,000 went.

"Until Mr. Small remembers where it went, and tells this part of the world, we are entitled to believe that a careless janitor burning up bank records did Mr. Small a great favor and made it greater by conveniently dying.

"Wherever Small puts his hand, he leaves a black spot, and by this time the black spot begins to take the shape of the state of Illinois. Herrin was not a crime of passion. It was a crime of misgovernment. The men at Herrin were drunk and insanely mad, but there was something worse than drink and insanity at Springfield, which prevented the intervention of the state in time to prevent massacre.

"This unprincipled governor in his stupidity which appears as audacity, is now bulldozing the state. He is scaring citizens and making weaklings of them. He is making legislators confess their lack of self respect. It seems to be easy if an unscrupulous man tells a county it must stay in the mud and cannot have good roads unless its politicians protect him. The citizens do not want to stay in the mud, and they do themselves the atrocious disservice of whining at the door of decent legislators. Misrule is piled on misrule, and the cause of it is a weakling whose political career is done.

"A self-respecting legislature could handle him in a minute. If the assembly has not the moral will and courage to impeach him for misdeeds which demand it, the members of it might have enough regard for themselves to say that they were independent and intended to remain so.

"They appropriate for Small's establishment and could tell him to go around to the back door for a handout. If he uttered another threat against the decency of the state and the independency of the legislature, he would not get one thin dime for the upkeep of the executive office and residence. Then roads would go where roads are needed. Small would be quiet and the air in Illinois would be cleaner."

Governor Len Small's legacy in Kankakee is brief but set in stone: the good roads governor who pulled Illinois out of the mud, the state treasurer who returned more money than anyone else. The story that Governor Len Small went to trial on phony charges, was found innocent and was vindicated, is the biggest lie ever told in Kankakee history.

Len Small thought everyone was out to get him. He lied about everything and then claimed that everyone else was lying about him. He thought there was a disconnect between his words and his actions. After all his lies, he never understood why people didn't believe him.

Len Small never believed that where there was smoke, there was fire, and he never could see that he, Big Bill, the Poor Swede and the Blond Boss were the political arsonists. It seems Small doth protested too much. Small's continued defense, often against possible rather than real accusations, says more than his detractors could.

Chapter 27

Who Was the Real Len Small?

Who was the real Len Small? Through the haze and the smoke of biased journalism of the era, both pro and anti Small, getting to the truth can be hard. Court documents also do not tell the whole story, as lawyers argue (often untruthfully) pro and con, and decisions are sometimes flawed or even bought.

History still asks several questions that may or may not be a matter of fact or opinion. For instance, Len Small was accused of being a crook, but didn't a jury find him "not guilty"? Could this have been the biggest witch hunt in political history? Here are a few questions, in summing up, and the author's answers after a lot of research.

Was Len Small guilty of stealing more than a million dollars in state funds?

Of course he was. It is unbelievable that he could funnel so much state money into a phony bank in a tiny farm village -- a "bank" owned by a close friend and partner -- and then have that money juggled in questionable loans without knowing about it and without personally profiting from it. It is too much to accept that a slick operator like Len Small did not know exactly what was going on, at all times.

It was a classic money laundering scheme, a conspiracy between Small and Curtis, with Treasurer Small providing the money and Banker Curtis making the loans.

Len Small and Edward Curtis were partners in politics. They were partners at the *Kankakee Daily Republican.* They were partners in owning and directing banks in Kankakee, Springfield and elsewhere downstate. Are we to believe they were not partners in the "Grant Park Bank?" A partnership in the "Grant Park Bank" (which was proven to not exist) and the intention to use it to launder money would be the only logical reason for Small to have state funds deposited there.

Remember, when Edward Miller became treasurer in 1921, he collected an additional seven per cent interest on loans from the meat packers. That interest was never claimed by Curtis or by the "Grant Park Bank." If it was a legitimate loan from the bank, instead of a money laundering scheme by Small and Curtis, it should have gone to the bank, right? Why didn't the bank, or Curtis, claim it?

Some of the arguments made at Small's trial inadvertently admitted his guilt. Charles LeForgee argued that Small did not steal interest money from the state because the money did not belong to the state; since Small did not deposit the interest money into the state treasury, it was not state property. So he did have it.

As far as being acquitted, there is ample evidence that Small tampered with the jury to buy his acquittal. And if you read the narrative laid out by the grand jury and the prosecutor (chapter 9), you will realize there is no way Len Small could have been acquitted without bribing the jury. His guilt *was proven* in court; a "fixed" jury let him go.

Len Small had the records in his possession which would have proved his innocence if he was telling the truth. He didn't turn them over, not even when subpoenaed. He never produced them because they would have proved his guilt.

Ultimately, the Illinois Supreme Court ruled that Small *was guilty,* when it affirmed a lower court decision, ordering him to pay $650,000 of the money he stole.

Len Small always claimed that he did not personally profit from the loans the Grant Park Bank made to Swift, Armour and the other packers. He was never convicted in a court of law of personally profiting from these loans. Doesn't that let him off the hook?

Then who profited? It was proven that the money laundering scheme of Len Small and Edward Curtis netted the "Grant Park Bank" perhaps two million dollars in profit. When Edward Curtis died in 1920, his list of assets included stock in a number of banks and other companies. These included part ownership in Len Small's First Trust & Savings Bank of Kankakee, and in Grant Park Trust & Savings Bank. Curtis' estate did not show any stock or other ownership in a "Grant Park Bank." And his estate was valued at $175,000. There was no trace of the two million dollars profit from interest payments by the packers.

So where did that interest money go? The only other person involved in the scheme was Len Small. At his trial, the vice president of Small's bank testified there was no record of an account in the bank in Len Small's name prior to November 1921. There were no records anywhere of Banker Small having an account that could be examined.

In a concession as part of the plea bargain settlement of the civil suit, Small got the state to stipulate that "the evidence fails to establish" that Small got any of the interest money. He blamed his dead friend Curtis. But does it seem logical that Curtis got all that money and Small got none of it? If it wasn't in Curtis' estate when he died, where else could it have been?

What was wrong with a bank taking state deposits with the promise to pay two per cent interest, and then loaning it out at eight per cent interest? Isn't that just business, pure capitalism, a bank making a decent profit for itself?

It can be argued so, until you figure that the man making the deposits and making the profit is the state treasurer, the one who is supposed to be trusted with the state's money. If it was above board, why was the money deposited in a "bank" that did not exist? And is it right or wrong to keep interest that is earned on money that does not belong to you?

No one but Small and Curtis handled the transactions between the treasurer's office and the "Grant Park Bank" and no one else in his office was allowed to see these records. When Len Small ended his term as treasurer, he took all books and records from the office. These could not be found, even after being subpoenaed for his trial. And after ending his term, he continued as the examiner of collaterals, continuing to approve the "collateral" of this phony bank.

Could Len Small have been right, that his indictment was just a political persecution, revenge for cutting the budget of Attorney General Edward Brundage?

The investigation into Len Small really didn't originate with Brundage. It started when Edward Miller took office as state treasurer and found a corrupt mess than needed to be reported. Attorney General Brundage, as chief law enforcement officer, could do nothing but investigate the matter and go where the evidence took him. When you look at all the facts outlined in this book, it is obvious that the cutting of Brundage's budget had absolutely nothing to do with bringing charges against Small.

The budget was cut ***after*** Brundage began an investigation. The investigation was not a result of the cut. Just the opposite. The cut was the result of the investigation that was underway. It wasn't Brundage's revenge against Small, it was Small's revenge against Brundage for conducting the investigation, and it was intended to cut off funds for that investigation. It was Small who had the sequence backwards for his own "persecution" cry.

The investigation and lengthy indictment did not happen in one week. It took months to put together. Only Len Small could think he could get away with this accusation.

And it should have come as no surprise. The fact that Len Small did not pay the state what he owned as treasurer was known before the 1920 election. It was mentioned in the newspapers as a legitimate reason why Small did not qualify as a candidate. It was not something dreamed by the attorney general in July 1921.

The Legislative Voters League, an independent watchdog group, in its biennial report in 1924 called Small's veto of Brundage's budget "clearly prompted by personal reasons...unjustified, unwarranted and open to suspicion."

Small claimed his indictment was revenge by Brundage. Small also claimed it was engineered by the *Chicago Tribune* because the newspaper could not control him. Which was it?

Was Len Small really connected to Al Capone?

Yes. Len Small was connected to Big Bill Thompson, and Big Bill was connected to Big Al. And the connections were close ones, politically and financially. Len Small sold pardons and paroles to Capone's men and to other underworld figures in the 1920s.

Len Small never did a thing to fight the Chicago Mob; he preferred to fight the *Chicago Tribune.*

Was Len Small really legally elected governor of Illinois?

This is a legitimate question. It was mentioned before and after he took office. The state constitution makes a person ineligible to be elected governor if he owes the state money. Small did owe the state money in 1920 when he was elected governor -- the state Supreme Court ruled so in 1926 when it held Small responsible for interest from his money laundering scheme as state treasurer and forced him to repay some of the stolen money.

Even without a court judgment, Small *admitted* he owed the state money before he became governor -- he held onto $10 million in state deposits for two years after he left the state treasurer's office and didn't give it up until *after* he became governor.

Article IV, Section 4 of the Illinois State Constitution of 1870, which was in effect in 1920, states: "No person who has been, or hereafter shall be convicted of bribery, perjury or other infamous crime, nor any person who has been or may be a collector or holder of public moneys, who shall not have accounted for and paid over, according to law, all such moneys due from him, shall be eligible to the General Assembly, or to any office of profit or trust in this State."

It is something that historians and constitutional scholars should debate. Len Small served as governor of Illinois for eight years. But was he legally the governor? Did he legitimately hold the office? Should there be an asterisk next to his name?

Of course, this doesn't include the argument that his 1920 election was stolen in Chicago. That's another matter.

Was Len Small living in the real world?

Was he crazy? Was he in a lifelong state of denial? To paraphrase an old joke, was he paranoid because everyone was out to get him? Or was everyone out to get him because he was a crook? Was there really a conspiracy of "big interests" against him because he was the champion of the honest man? Did he really believe everything he said? Was he a colossal liar, deluded, or both?

The headlines, the stories, the accusations of some of the things printed in Small's newspaper, documented in this book, may be considered by the reader to judge how grounded in reality the governor was.

His explanations for the Potz and the Guzik pardons are just plain crazy. Len Small would have been better off just to take the bribe money, grant the pardons and issue no explanation.

This book has presented stories from Small's own newspaper about "hit men" from Denver plotting to rub him out, of Len Small crawling from a automobile wreck to lift the car like Superman to rescue others, of Indians making him a tribal chief because he was the reincarnation of a departed chieftain, a fire on his farm in 1930 which he imagined was started by local political enemies. These are passing stories, never mentioned again. But they always seemed to come at a time when Small needed something else to divert attention from a hot scandal. Is this clever or is this someone not living in the real world?

Was Len Small really viciously and unfairly attacked?

Viciously, yes. Unfairly, not for the most part.

TIME magazine called him "buck-toothed old Lennington Small" and "a snaggle-toothed partisan," a "crook pardoner" and "a cold-blooded crook." (TIME reported on Small's infamous exploits dozens of times over the years and could not refer to the governor without adding crooked, discredited, malodorous or some similar epithet to his name.) State Rep. J. Bert Miller compared him, unfavorably, to

Judas. Al Capone compared Small, unfavorably, to himself. Noted historian and author Richard Norton Smith described Small as "a ferret-faced Kankakee banker." Author Edward Behr called Small "an unprincipled political hack...who granted pardons not only to Thompson appointees but to gangland members." Historian Charles Masters called Small "Thompson's creaky marionette-like candidate." John Kobler, a biographer of Al Capone, called Len Small "an embezzler and a protector of felons." Capone biographer Robert J. Schoenberg called Governor Small a "recruitment and personnel officer" for Torrio and Capone.

The rival *Kankakee Daily News* called him the "master of trickery and spoils politician" and "a manikin full of platitudes." It said he was "a member of the most disreputable gang of highbinders ever organized to raid a citizenship in this or any state."

One of Small's recurring themes was that the *Chicago Tribune* was opposed to him because be could not be controlled by the big newspaper. Really? With Small's unstoppable ambition and his willingness to do anything to advance his political career, wouldn't it have been better for him to submit to the "control" of the *Tribune*? He didn't mind being controlled by Big Bill Thompson. He didn't mind being controlled by Fred Lundin. He didn't mind being controlled by Al Capone.

Small's 1924 campaign borrowed a slogan from Big Bill: "He cannot be bossed, bluffed or bought." The *Onarga Leader & Review* noted, "Boss Small cannot be bossed unless it's a greater boss than Mr. Small. For twenty-five years, Mr. Small has bossed Kankakee County. The world is full of people who can't be bossed or bluffed or bought, though they seem to be somewhat rare in Kankakee."

Small's opposition newspapers in Kankakee were unusually rough and often unfair. There were a lot of nasty names and accusations against him, some cruel, some fair, but no more cruel than what Small dished out. No matter how nasty the accusations got, Len Small was no less mean or petty than his opposition.

While many of the criticisms and attacks were unfair, to the extent of which they were taken, they basically were right from a factual standpoint. The journalism of the day was harsh and often lacked objectivity in news stories. But politics always has been a rough business, and more overtly so in those days.

Did the Chicago Tribune do a fair job of reporting or did it attack Governor Small in a biased and unfair and even vicious manner?

Newspaper reporting in those days was tough, and bias was not confined to the editorial page. This was true of practically every newspaper in America. The *Chicago Tribune's* reporting had its occasional bias but it basically was fair. If you want to read biased news writing, to an extreme degree, read Small's *Kankakee Daily Republican* any time it wrote about a political enemy (see chapter 24). Did the *Tribune* have a bias against the governor, did it go on a crusade against Governor Small and Mayor Thompson? Yes, it went on a crusade against Small, but it was fair in the news writing and rough in the editorial columns. Small argued the *Tribune* was unfair; others might call it crusading journalism to uncover corruption. After reading more than a thousand *Tribune* stories in this research, I agree with the latter.

On only a few occasions, the *Tribune* wrote a really blistering editorial on Len Small. The one published Jan 22, 1924 explained its motivation and said it was time to stop "pussyfooting" and tell the cold, hard truth about Len Small in order to rid the state of him.

"The *Tribune* is doing most of it and at times is almost alone in doing it. People will soon get the idea that it is a contest between Small and the *Tribune.* It does not matter to the *Tribune,* as a commercial institution, whether Small remains as governor or not. As a newspaper, with the public welfare at heart, it does matter, and it is a question of conscience to expose and oppose such a man. No self-respecting person, knowing Small, would cease to denounce him so long as he is in public life. It is a fight in which there are no quits or quarter. It would be difficult for Democrats to nominate a dog so yellow as not to get the votes of decent citizens of ordinary common sense if the Republican alternative were Small. That intemperate language is all that can do justice to the situation which is an open threat to the well being of the state. Men who speak softly about it are increasing the danger which is further increased by the incredulity and apathy of the citizens.

"This is not a controversy between a newspaper and a politician. The lies which screen Small should be smashed by the kind of blows which will smash them. His acts and his purposes should be made so apparent that a vote for him will be the conscious endorsement of just such a record and such a character. Pussyfooting will not do this and pussyfooting will not win."

The *Chicago Tribune* never liked Len Small, but it liked Big Bill Thompson even less. Col. Robert R. McCormick's Republican newspaper could not abide the corruption, the thievery or the stench that Big Bill Thompson and Len Small brought to his Republican party.

What are a few more points that were not directly made about this whole Grant Park Bank scheme?

First, if Len Small wanted to help his friend Ed Curtis by putting state deposits in his bank, he could have put the money in the legitimate, established Grant Park Trust & Savings Bank. Small and Curtis invented the "Grant Park Bank" for the expressed purpose of laundering money by hiding the loans and the excess $2 million in interest that they kept for themselves.

It also was done to avoid paying income taxes on that $2 million. Neither Small nor Curtis declared this money on their income tax forms. Al Capone went to prison for this a decade later.

When the banking laws changed at the beginning of 1921, which barred state deposits in private banks, the "Grant Park Bank" officially went out if existence. If it existed, it still could have received deposits from individuals. How could a bank with $10,000,000 in deposits a year earlier be liquidated with just $2,000 in assets (which was in an account in the other, legitimate bank in Grant Park)?

What about the "disappearance" of all the records of the "Grant Park Bank." How would a janitor have access to vital bank records? How could he mistake ledgers and record books as "waste paper?" How could a bank do business if its records were gone? How could it make annual reports to the state? How could it be audited by state bank examiners without its records? And wasn't it convenient that the janitor died just before he would have had to testify about this?

Both Armour and Swift testified they took loans from Curtis as an individual. They were not taking loans from a bank. They never heard of the "Grant Park Bank" and they did not know the money was coming from the state of Illinois. Yet Small and Vernon Curtis said the loans were made by a legitimate "Grant Park Bank." Didn't this prove a fraudulent scheme?

And let's look at something defense lawyer Charles LeForgee said in his opening remarks at Small's trial that has never been examined. LeForgee said that even though Curtis was a very wealthy man who owned banks, factories, businesses and property, he occasionally borrowed money from Len Small. In fact, LeForgee said Curtis owed Small a great deal of money. As early as 1907, Curtis was turning over a large amount of collateral to Small in consideration for this debt. Curtis continued borrowing money from Small. A new arrangement was agreed upon in 1909, with Curtis making bigger payments and taking out more loans from Small.

A year before Curtis died, LeForgee said, Curtis gave notes for the amount he owed to Small. One of the notes was for $75,000. (This note was used in evidence by the state to prove that Small was profiting from interest in state deposits.)

LeForgee said the certificates for the 500 shares in the Ridgely bank in Springfield was collateral used as security for the payment of that note. (Prosecutor Wilkerson didn't believe this, and said he had records showing Small and Curtis got Ridgely stock with the profits from the packer loans.)

This raises a number of questions. Why was a very wealthy man like Edward Curtis borrowing huge sums of money from Len Small for nearly 20 years? How did Curtis get so indebted to Len Small? What did Curtis need this money for? Where was the collateral Curtis had given Small and what happened to this great debt when Curtis died? Why did LeForgee introduce this at Small's trial? Couldn't this indicate that Small funneled state deposits into Curtis' bank to help reduce this debt? Was this just a lie to put the blame on a dead man?

Was Len Small a member of the Ku Klux Klan?

No. Not as far as is known. But the Klan endorsed him and he did not reject their endorsement. He never uttered a word in condemnation of the resurgent Klan and its brutal acts. He never commented on a single cross burning, not even cross burnings in Kankakee. He didn't even comment when the Klan opened a chapter in Kankakee. As governor, he did nothing to stop them; on the contrary, he allowed them use of state facilities. Small had a long list of enemies who he hated. But the Klan was not on that list. Neither was Al Capone or any other Chicago mobster.

A Few Comments About Len Small

"Len Small's gubernatorial pardons had made him, in effect, Johnny Torrio's recruitment and personnel officer." Robert J. Schoenberg, *Mr. Capone: The Real & Complete Story of Al Capone.*

"Illinois Governor Len Small signed pardons for mobsters as fast as they were convicted." Jack Kelly, *American Heritage,* April 1995.

"Perhaps the worst handicap this office confronts is Len Small's pardon and parole system. He lets them out as fast as we put them in." Cook County State's Attorney Robert Crowe.

"Guzik bribed the governor to obtain his freedom. The pimp knew every man had his vice and every politician his price." Laurence Bergreen, *Capone, The Man and the Era.*

"The city was run by roguish mayor Big Bill Thompson, while the state was controlled by the equally thuggish Les (Len) Small, a former farmer from tiny Kankakee, Illinois. Both men were tightly linked with mobster Al Capone." Brock Yates, *Umbrella Mike.*

"(Len Small is a) Governor whom decent thousands regard as a cold-blooded crook." TIME magazine, July 12, 1926.

"There's one thing worse than a crook, and that's a crooked man in a big political job. A man who pretends he's enforcing the law and is really making dough out of somebody breaking it. There are worse fellows in the world than me." Al Capone, 1927.

"Governor Small, I have three warrants for your arrest. In the name of the people of the state of Illinois, I arrest you." Sangamon County Sheriff Henry Mester, Aug. 9, 1921.

"Some men go into politics with the idea of leaving footprints on the sands of time. And others are lucky if they get out without having their thumbprints taken." *Kankakee Daily News,* July 16, 1921.

"By all means, give Small another term, but we may disagree as to where he should serve it." U.S. Senator Otis Glenn, Republican from Illinois, April 1928.

"Len Small's candidacy has impaired the true Republican principles of the state. By doing so, it has injected an element into the state election which stains the state Republican ticket." *New York Times,* Oct. 15, 1920.

"His leadership constantly kept the party embroiled in factional strife. A 'rule or ruin' policy was his favorite method, and his tactics drove the better element of the party from his leadership until he was able to hold in line only those who profited personally in acknowledging his kingship." *Kankakee Daily News,* July 21, 1921.

"Len Small, now you ask the Negro vote. How dare you do so? Look at the picture and answer us. How dare you ask the citizens of our race to vote for you, the friend and ally of the Ku Klux Klan?" William Harrison, an African-American lawyer and assistant attorney general, April 1928.

"Caesar had his Brutus, Jesus Christ had his Judas Iscariot, the United States had its Benedict Arnold and Jefferson Davis, and Illinois has Len Small. And if the Judas of Illinois had the courage of the Judas of Jesus, he would return the 30 pieces of silver, get a rope and hang himself, and remove the withering blight which will remain upon this state as long as he is governor of Illinois." State Rep. J. Bert Miller, to the General Assembly of Illinois, May 1927.

"Twenty years he has spent in public office, and during all that time has been of benefit only to himself. He has never engaged in a constructive work, and the meaning of statesmanship is unknown to him. A single object from which he has never deviated is that of lining his pockets with gold. His rapacity and greed have always marked his work as a politician. He has never denied taking interest money which belonged to the state." *Kankakee Daily News,* Sept. 2, 1920.

"Now followed an administration which for waste, mismanagement, inefficiency, intrigue, manipulation and downright disregard of the public interest has few parallels in the history of the United States." Carroll H. Wooddy, *The Case Of Frank L. Smith: A Study In Representative Government,* 1931, University of Chicago Press.

"Under Small, taxes and expenditures have gone up until there isn't a worse administered state in the Union." U.S. Vice President Charles G. Dawes, Republican from Evanston, Oct. 14, 1922.

"The unholy alliance of Small and the Republican mayor has brought about shame and disgrace upon Illinois and Chicago." Illinois Attorney General Oscar Carlstrom, Republican from Aledo, April 1, 1928.

"He is the worst governor the state ever had. We believe he is the worst governor any state ever had. He has contaminated everything with which he has come in contact in politics." *Chicago Tribune* editorial, Jan, 22, 1924.

“It is obvious that Small was one of the most corrupt, if not the most corrupt, governor in American history.” Mark Grossman, *Political Corruption In America.*

"This witness, ex-Treasurer Small, has testified. His testimony is in the form of a general denial. He has had under his control all of the evidence of the entire transaction. I wish I could believe that testimony. I have tried to. I cannot." Judge Frank Burton, 1924.

"There are really many interesting things about Len that the public has never known nor the grand juries ever discovered. The Bump has acted on the supposition that the people really don't know Len and that it was his mission in life to tell folks just what a great man the Boss really is. The people do know Len, and that's the trouble." *Kankakee Evening Democrat,* Sept. 30, 1907.

"Small evidently thought he had 'put it over' and the remainder of the audience, most of them residents of Kankakee who know Small for what he is, were not deceived in the least by the hypocritical cant, but instead enjoyed the monumental gall of Abraham Lennington for trying to get away with such bunk in his own home town, where everybody knows him." *Kankakee Daily News,* March 19, 1924.

Chapter 28

George H. Ryan: The Other Corrupt Illinois Governor from Kankakee

While Len Small may have been the most crooked governor Illinois has ever seen, there was another man from Kankakee who became governor who also was corrupt.

George H. Ryan was not a pin-striped gangster with a tommy-gun, in the mold of the Roaring Twenties -- although Hollywood casting agents might agree that he *looked* like one.

But he was convicted on multiple counts of racketeering and fraud.

Like Len Small, George Ryan was prosecuted while he was governor for corruption he committed in a prior state office. However, he wasn't as lucky or as crafty or as cut-throat as Len Small, and he couldn't manipulate the system or bribe juries as Len Small did. And so, George Ryan went to prison.

The scope of his corrupt brand of politics for more than 30 years is astounding. George Ryan surrounded himself with crooks and thieves, and it seemed the Ryan organization's main job was to see what crooked deal could they pull next. As investigators got close, the lying, cover-up and overt obstruction of justice rivaled Watergate. And it went all the way to the top.

This governor *was* a gangster.

In April 2006, George Ryan was convicted on all 22 counts of racketeering and fraud and other crimes. As secretary of state, his office sold driver's licenses for bribes, gave multi-million dollar contracts based on payoffs, shook down state workers for campaign contributions, used state workers to run his campaigns, and quashed investigations into all the corruption.

And he went to jail wondering what he did wrong.

George Homer Ryan was born in Maquoketa, Iowa in 1934 and was raised in Kankakee, attending local schools. He became a pharmacist in Kankakee (his family owned three stores) before getting involved in politics. In 1956, he married high school sweetheart Lura Lynn Lowe, the sister of Miss Kankakee 1949.

Ryan never lost an election. He was appointed an assistant township supervisor on the Kankakee County Board in 1966 and was elected in 1967. He was elected a state representative in 1972 and became Speaker of the House in 1981. Ryan was elected lieutenant governor in 1982, secretary of state in 1990 and governor in 1998.

The man who the press dubbed "Governor Grumpy" got to the top by being a rough and ruthless campaigner. His 1982 Democrat opponent for lieutenant governor, Mary Grace Stern, was quoted in the Sept. 25, 1982 *Chicago Tribune* as calling Ryan "an abrasive, sexist state legislator who has risen to the top like scum on cocoa."

Ryan's primary opponent was State Rep. Susan Catania. Two female janitors at the Capitol, Mary Lawson and Edna Stalets, sued Ryan when they were fired after attending a Catania fundraiser.

While campaigning for governor, Ryan promised the voters that he would not raise taxes. He broke that promise. He promised to eliminate tolls. He broke that promise. He campaigned against expanding O'Hare airport. He broke that promise. He campaigned as a fiscal conservative yet state taxes and budgets exploded under his direction as governor. He campaigned in opposition to expanding gambling, then pushed for new casinos with Mob connections. He campaigned as a pro-life candidate and then vetoed abortion restrictions. He campaigned as a supporter of the death penalty and then freed murderers from Death Row.

In October 1999, Governor Ryan went to Cuba on a five-day tour and became friends with the murderous tyrant Fidel Castro. He went back in 2002 to see his friend in Havana. Ryan described this as a "humanitarian mission," bringing medicine and other needs. Ryan never did explain why the hardworking people of Illinois needed to send their money to this Communist Paradise. Part of George Ryan's exhibit in the Kankakee Museum is a large photograph showing Ryan and Castro embracing. Plans are being made in Cuba to build a statue of George Ryan, now a hero in that communist dictatorship.

Kankakee was born from corruption. The Illinois Central Railroad was building a line through that prairie area in 1853 and it needed a spot for a station. Kankakee County was formed in 1853 only after railroad workers in the Limestone area voted fraudulently and frequently. Another vote was taken to set a county seat, and again the Illinois Central rigged an election to choose a place on their rail line. The choice was a mud hole that commonly was known as Kankakee Depot, rather than the established Bourbonnais or Momence. The first county board of supervisors meeting was held on July 18, 1853 in Momence -- because there were no buildings in the primitive railroad settlement called Kankakee Depot.

The village of North Kankakee got the huge David Bradley Implement factory to relocate from Chicago in 1895 only after a deal that included changing the name of the town to Bradley. Just west of Kankakee, the village of Verkler got a railroad station located there in 1882 only after being shaken down by Thomas Bonfield, a slick Kankakee lawyer and attorney for the railroad who demanded the cash payoffs. Bonfield promptly renamed the village for himself.

Many scandals dot Kankakee's history. In 1961, Kankakee County Sheriff Carl McNutt was indicted on 13 charges, including conspiracy with six others to operate houses of prostitution, making false bills against the county and letting prisoners escape. McNutt had been elected three years earlier by a very narrow margin, his only apparent qualification was that he was the sergeant of the Kankakee American Legion's national championship color guard. The investigation started when a big bag of money was found in the basement of the jail. State's Attorney Edward Drolet asked the state police superintendent to send troopers to take over law enforcement in Kankakee County, and the superintendent granted the unprecedented request. On March 7, 1962, McNutt pleaded guilty to official misconduct, was removed from office and fined. He then was given a state job.

Jack Samlin, the first president of Kankakee Community College, pleaded guilty in 1978 to felony charges of taking $14,500 in illegal bonuses in 1975 and 1976 and of altering board minutes to hide it from trustees.

Kankakee once was a thriving small city. It had huge factories like David Bradley Implements, Roper Corp., A.O. Smith, American Marietta, Simoniz, Texize, Florence Stove, Armour Pharmaceutical, Gould National Batteries, General Mills, General Foods, Armstrong Cork, Fibre Drum, Amberg File, Bear Brand Hosiery Co., Kankakee Container Corp., Pepsi-Cola Bottlers, Henkel, Bunge, Turk Furniture Manufacturing, Kroehler Manufacturing, Chicago Bridge & Iron and more. *The Daily Journal* ran full-page ads in 1953 claiming that *Sales Management Magazine* ranked Kankakee as number ten among cities with a population above 25,000 in "quality of market rating." Beverly Hills, Calif. was number one. Just what this meant, or how it was determined, was never explained.

But by 1999, Kankakee was designated in *Places Rated Almanac* as the worst place to live among 354 metropolitan areas in the United States and Canada. It had dramatically declined into an area of blight during the rule of Tom and George Ryan, as the factory town saw factory after factory leave. *Crain's Chicago Business* reported that Kankakee had 10,400 factory jobs in 1977 and just 6,400 in 1983. And that wasn't rock bottom yet. Its 22 per cent unemployment rate in the 1980s was one of the highest in the nation and equaled Great Depression figures.

As a side note, comedian David Letterman made Kankakee's "worst place" rating the butt of his jokes at the time. He even made Kankakee the subject of his Top 10 List, with devastating digs as "You'll come for our pay phone, you'll stay because your car's been stolen," and "Ask about our staggering unemployment rate." Letterman kept up the running gag by donating two prefabricated gazebos to the city to give it a new identity as "The Home of the Twin Gazebos." The clueless city leaders, eager for any notoriety, took the mockery as a great honor. It still does.

Kankakee also boasts that it is the home of Dairy Queen. It is not. The first Dairy Queen opened in Joliet in 1940. It didn't open in Kankakee until 1947. But Sherb Noble, a man who helped start the company, had an ice cream shop in Kankakee ("Sherb's Ice Cream Shoppe"), so that is close enough.

Going back to the 1890s, Edward Jeffers, a Kankakee businessman and political leader, became chairman of the Kankakee County Republican Central Committee and held the job for 30 years. Jeffers also took over the patronage at the Kankakee State Hospital after Len Small left the board. Jeffers grew rich from his own state contracts.

Victor McBroom got into the inner political circle by marrying the Boss' daughter, Leona Jeffers, in 1912. He started in politics that year by working on Len Small's campaign for governor. McBroom owned a restaurant in Kankakee with his brothers, where business and political deals were made. McBroom was appointed head dietician at the Kankakee State Hospital by Governor Small. The appointment came after the governor wrecked the state civil service system and this merit job became a political plum. McBroom spent most of his time at the Jeffers & McBroom automobile dealership.

Jeffers and McBroom worked with Len Small at the state hospital and on the boards of Small's newspaper, bank and InterState Fair.

Jeffers relinquished his position as Republican county chairman in 1930. Victor McBroom took over and held it the rest of his life.

Victor McBroom was appointed state representative in 1940 and held that until being elected state senator in 1946. He held the county chairmanship and the state senator jobs until his death on Feb. 21, 1959. The state legislature closed for his funeral. There were 46 honorary pallbearers at his funeral, including Governor William Stratton, most of the state officers and a long list of other elected officials.

His son, Edward McBroom, followed him as county chairman in 1959. He was state representative from 1962 to 1966, from 1976 to 1982, and state senator from 1968 to 1974. He died in 1990 at age 65.

Patronage jobs were given to applicants who bought a new car from the McBroom dealership, and they kept their jobs by buying a new car when it was time. People given regular jobs had their prescriptions filled at Ryan's Pharmacy.

George Ryan became Edward McBroom's campaign manager in 1962. McBroom picked George's brother, Tom Ryan, to become mayor of Kankakee in 1965. McBroom picked George Ryan for the Kankakee County Board in 1966.

Edward McBroom helped George Ryan in his election to the Illinois House in 1972. McBroom was a valuable mentor who taught the Ryans the fine art of politics, in giving contracts and favors to those who paid. When Ed McBroom was defeated for re-election as state senator in 1974, George Ryan became the boss.

George Ryan had his own battle with "regular" and "anti" Republicans. In 1985, some Republicans formed a Lincoln Club to separate themselves from the boss politics of Ryan and McBroom. Ryan spoke to the group in 1987 with "face flushed, knees bent and left arm stabbing downward at times," according to *The Daily Journal.* He called them a "rump group" and "renegades" who ran candidates against incumbent Republicans. But that is what George Ryan did in 1988 in the state's attorney race. Ryan's candidate lost.

Secretary of State Ryan handed out low-number license plates to campaign donors (an important prize in Illinois, for some reason) and put friends on his payroll briefly to let them enhance their state pension benefits (including former legislators Roger Stanley and Ted Lechowicz.) Former state representative Robert Brinkmeier got a $35,500 job to promote the secretary of state's speaker's bureau. After heading Ryan's 1998 campaign, Scott Fawell was given the $195,000 job of managing McCormick Place and Navy Pier.

Like Len Small, Ryan had at least a dozen family members in state jobs, and many of these (such as jobs for his daughters) were do-nothing jobs.

"Ryan embodied the archetypal cigar-chomping politician ready to do business in a backroom," wrote Dave McKinney in the November 2002 *Illinois Issues.* "The Kankakee Republican organization from which he and his older brother Tom emerged revolved around helping friends and family first, and maintaining an iron grip on power. Political fundraising tickets were distributed among public employees with the expectation they would sell them or cover the price themselves."

George Ryan's first public scandal preceded his conviction by more than 20 years. Ryan and McBroom were accused of trying to bribe Bourbonnais Police Chief Larry Hildebrand in 1973 to not run against Sheriff Thomas Maass. Hildebrand said McBroom and Ryan offered him his choice, assistant police chief or chief of detectives in the Kankakee Police Department, if he declined to run. Kankakee Police Chief Dean Bauer was supposed to be in on the deal. Michael Berz, a Kankakee lawyer and Hildebrand's campaign manager, confirmed the story to the local newspaper. McBroom, Ryan and Bauer denied that an offer was made. Ryan threatened to have the state legislature investigate Berz -- Ryan said Berz's position as chairman of the Illinois Liquor Commission and as a political campaign manager was a conflict of interest. In November 1974, Hildebrand beat Maass.

Bauer was appointed Kankakee chief of police by Mayor Tom Ryan in 1970. His main qualification was that he was a friend of the Ryans. Bauer created his own scandals, and morale on the police department sank so low that it was an issue in Mayor Ryan's campaign in 1977. Bauer ran the police department strictly on a political basis. Important people in Kankakee or those who supported the party had traffic tickets torn up or charges dropped. A Kankakee police officer who was arrested for shoplifting at Shopper's Fair in May 1974 had his case "fixed" and all charges dropped. Bauer explained that Gerritt Osenga was the security guard who made the arrest, and that Osenga had cleared the officer; then it was disclosed that Osenga had died in August 1972. Another cop got into trouble for taking two shotguns that belonged to a suspect. And in October 1975, it was revealed that Bauer used his police force as chauffeurs for local officials and connected businessmen, taking them to and from O'Hare airport and other Chicago destinations.

Bauer was a campaign issue again in 1985. Russell Johnson said one of his first acts if elected would be to fire Dean Bauer. Johnson defeated Tom Ryan 60 to 40 per cent.

Two months after losing the election, Tom Ryan got a $34,000 "job" as a "public relations technical advisor" with the state Department of Transportation while keeping his full-time job at his pharmacy. In 1988, Tom Ryan and other "connected" politicians and businessmen (including Duke Edwards, the brother of Danny Edwards, see page 325) started Comguard, which manufactured ankle bracelets to monitor convicts on house arrest. Comguard promptly got a $180,000 state contract. Even with this, the company had financial problems and it took a questionable $150,000 loan from Kankakee County in 1993. Two years later, it defaulted on the loan. In 1997, it made a deal with the county, paying $93,633 to settle the debt in full. The Kankakee *Daily Journal* called the arrangement a "bizarre scheme." In the midst of this, Comguard's president was indicted for mail fraud with another company. The whole affair was another big scandal in Kankakee, but so what?

George Ryan got into a fight with State Rep. William Walsh of LaGrange Park for the House minority leader position in December 1976. Walsh said "political payoffs" were made in "an awful and blatant attempt to buy the election" for Ryan. Walsh said Ryan promised State Rep. Gilbert Deavers of Normal the spot as assistant minority leader if he would just drop out of the race and bring his support to

Ryan. Walsh also said that Deavers used $10,000 raised at a cocktail party to buy legislator's votes for Ryan.

"I have done nothing to be ashamed of," Ryan told reporters.

Walsh was an assistant minority leader. The outgoing leader, James "Bud" Washburne of Morris, favored Ryan. Walsh said Washburne had 43 people on his payroll in do-nothing jobs. Several of these people were Kankakee pals of Ryan.

Ryan told reporters he knew nothing of this, but "I won't have any part of any political cronies...they're either going to earn their keep or get off the payroll."

It was a bitter fight but George Ryan won.

Ryan led the fight that defeated a bill in 1976 to require pharmacists to inform the public about less expensive generic drugs. Between 1980 and 1982, Ryan's pharmacy sold medical equipment to Manteno Mental Health Center and to the University of Illinois, in violation of the Illinois Purchasing Act that prohibited state officials from doing business directly with state agencies.

Ryan drew up a reapportionment map in 1981 that even fellow Republicans called "gerrymandering ...that treats black suburbanites in a manner that is uncouth and unconstitutional." The fight over the map was decided by Democrats. Ryan put up a long fight, which ended with him losing and the state presenting him with a $75,000 bill since the battle was a political one. Ryan solicited contributions to pay the bill.

In 1980, Ryan and McBroom made news by admitting they had legislative aides cast votes for them in the House. They were too busy to attend sessions.

McBroom owned the Cadillac dealership and Transeas Travel Agency. In July 1982, McBroom had to pay the state for travel agency commissions his firm got from the state, a violation of state law. And in September 1986, McBroom tried to have the director of Shapiro Developmental Center fired because he resisted McBroom's efforts to get certain people hired.

Westview Terrace nursing home at 1050 W. Jeffrey St. in Kankakee gave Ryan's Pharmacy more than $60,000 in Medicaid scrips each year but switched its business to another pharmacy after it was purchased by Morris Esformes. In 1981, the Illinois Department of Public Health investigated neglect and abuse of elderly residents at a few of Esformes' other nursing homes. One patient died of infected bedsores. Ryan arranged a meeting between Esformes and William Kempiners, the director of the IDPH and a political crony of George Ryan. Kempiners then dropped the charges against Esformes, over the objections of the two other members of the IDPH board, Dr. George Mosley and Alan Litweiler. Ryan's pharmacy got back its annual $60,000 in business with Westview Terrace.

"I haven't done anything wrong," Ryan said after the *Chicago Sun-Times* and the Better Government Association exposed the deal. Ryan threatened to sue the "little squirt" Terrence Bruner, BGA's executive director, for his "lies and innuendoes." Ryan did not sue.

Westview Terrace was cited with 20 violations of federal standards in 1982, including inadequate care, poor sanitation and rodent infestation. Maggots were found in a plastic catheter tube on 87-year-old patient James Dowdell when the bandage was changed.

In October 1986, NBC-Channel 5 in Chicago exposed Ryan's misuse of state airplanes over the previous two years as lieutenant governor. Ryan and his family used state airplanes hundreds of times at a cost of hundreds of thousands of dollars to fly to golf outings, to the theatre, to dental appointments and more. Ryan's response was to rip Channel 5. He paid the state $19,000 for the flights in 1987.

George Ryan's 1990 campaign for secretary of state was called the "nastiest" of all state races by the Associated Press. His televised debate with his opponent, State Treasurer Jerry Cosentino, was a study in mud slinging. It would have been more amusing to the viewers if they knew that these two dirty campaigners both would be convicted jailbirds in a few years.

They both accused one another of improprieties in private and public dealings, and accused each other of using their public office for personal gain.

"All you've ever done is put your own interests ahead of the state," Ryan said. Cosentino responded, "You've hired every family member in Kankakee, all of your friends, and now it's alleged you have a system whereby you're passing out money through the trade center to Joe Hannon (former Chicago schools superintendent) and others that run a business out of their apartment and have lucrative contracts with the World Trade Center while they are on that payroll."

These charges came from an NBC-5 report that a state World Trade Center Association under Ryan's control had two Ryan aides who also owned a part of three companies that got no-bid contracts with the association. Ryan said the association benefited state businesses, but it also benefited Ryan and his cronies.

Cosentino aide Rick Davis said Ryan spent $16,622 in two years at a Springfield bar owned by Chicago politician Sam Panayotovich. Davis said the bar overcharged Ryan and he pocketed the difference, which amounted to money laundering. Davis said Ryan had "established a pattern whereby he does funky stuff with money. Jerry Cosentino borrows money and George steals it."

The *Chicago Sun-Times* reported that Ryan's biggest contribution was $10,000 from a Kankakee company convicted of bid-rigging. Azzarelli Construction and its vice president, John Azzarelli, both were convicted in October 1978 on 13 counts of bid-rigging and mail fraud. The company was fined $212,000 and barred from bidding on road projects involving federal funds for three years.

The *Springfield State Journal-Register* reported that Ryan tried to get Lambert Kane hired by the state Department of Children and Family Services. Kane had been convicted a decade earlier of delivery of LSD and possession of amphetamines and he spent seven months in jail. Ryan explained that Kane had "cleaned up his act." But Kane was convicted a third time, for selling cocaine, after Ryan wrote his letters in support of Kane.

NBC-Channel 5 reported that Tom Ryan was working full time at his pharmacy and spent no time at his $40,000 do-nothing job with the state. Aware that ghost pay-rolling was a felony, Ryan resigned his position, which had paid him a total of $235,000. Channel 5 also said George Ryan had 11 relatives in state jobs at a total of nearly $2 million a year.

George Ryan was accused of paying consultant Paul Lis $54,000 a year for three years, at taxpayer expense, to work on his political campaign. State Sen. Denny Jacobs made the charge in September 1993. Rich Miller, editor of Capitol Facts, said Paul Lis was promising *Chicago Tribune* endorsements to candidates in exchange for cash.

A November 1993 report by Channel 5 and the BGA said Ryan turned his "statutory responsibility to police the automobile business into a political profit center." The report said Ryan got $237,000 in campaign contributions from automobile dealers. Ryan's inspectors "who hold life and death power over these small businesses...routinely solicited (money), sometimes in the middle of an inspection." Michael Lyons, BGA deputy director, said, "Clearly fear and intimidation are an overwhelming element. Small business owners in Illinois ought to be able to do business free from harassment by government inspectors."

A Copley News Service report in February 1994 revealed that Secretary of State George Ryan's housing allowance in Springfield was the biggest of all state officeholders. Ryan was paid $22,260 a year for his house. State Treasurer Pat Quinn's home cost the state $8,179 a year and Comptroller Dawn Clark Netsch billed the state $5,700 a year.

For the first time since Governor Small gave the Ku Klux Klan the run of state facilities, the KKK was granted a permit to hold a rally on the Capitol steps. It was on Martin Luther King's birthday in 1994. And it was Secretary of State George Ryan who granted the permit. The rally brought minimal violence. "Everybody had their right to free speech and to express themselves," Ryan said after the rally. Ryan claimed he had no choice but to grant the permit. But he did have a choice. Another Secretary of State, Jesse White, held to the courage of his convictions in refusing to certify Governor Blagojevich's dubious choice for senator in 2008, even after others made deals and dropped their objections. It's called integrity.

State Treasurer Pat Quinn was Ryan's opponent for the secretary of state job in 1994. Quinn hit Ryan's practice of using state inspectors to shake down businesses for campaign contributions. "For three years, Secretary of State George Ryan has used an army of taxpayer-financed inspectors as front-line collectors of

The front entrance to Kankakee Community College in 2009. Photo by Jim Ridings

campaign cash. We need a tough state law to end this kind of high-pressured political strong-arming," Quinn said.

A bill to bar state inspectors from soliciting campaign funds from businesses they regulate failed in the House in April 1994. The debate turned into an attack on George Ryan's ethics. Oak Lawn auto body shop owner Larry Clarida told the House committee he was frequently bothered by inspectors after he refused to cough up a donation to Ryan.

Ryan was caught giving a $15,000 no-bid contract to a company run by Don Adams, a former state Republican party chairman. Quinn called it "political cronyism." Ryan responded in his usual fashion -- accusing Quinn of his own conflicts of interest.

As the 1994 race heated up, Ryan suddenly decided that his office's organ donation program needed more publicity. He spent $1.2 million in tax dollars saturating TV airwaves with commercials -- with himself as the on-screen pitchman. In one ad, Ryan sits with a small child, used for sympathy. Rep. Jan Schakowsky said she thought it was a campaign ad. Several Democrats called the ads a "misuse of public funds for political purposes."

Pat Quinn (who became governor in January 2009 when Rod Blagojevich was thrown out) criticized Ryan's political junkets to Australia, Mexico, Scotland, Denmark, England, Germany, Sweden, Canada, Belgium, Hawaii, Arizona, Las Vegas and Florida. Quinn also questioned Ryan's need for eight bodyguards as lieutenant governor and secretary of state. "State troopers should be fighting crime here in Illinois, not carrying George Ryan's golf clubs in Scotland," Quinn said.

George Ryan defeated Pat Quinn on Nov. 8, 1994 in that secretary of state race, by a margin of 61 to 38 per cent. "The voters have entrusted me with the position and it is a trust I value," Ryan said on election night.

There had been allegations of selling driver's licenses for awhile. Ryan acknowledged a "culture of corruption" that he said had been going on in the office for decades, even as he paradoxically claimed he knew nothing about it. Investigators raided the Libertyville driver's license station on March 9, 1993. Dean Bauer illegally removed a briefcase full of cash and campaign fundraising receipts during that raid.

But it was a horrible accident on Nov. 8, 1994 that really got the investigation moving. A part fell off a truck near Milwaukee. Following behind the truck was a van driven by Rev. Scott Willis. The van hit the part and the gas tank on the van exploded. It was a scene of horror, as the six children of Scott and Janet Willis burned to death in the van.

Nov. 8 was election day. The accident happened just hours after Scott and Janet Willis had voted for George Ryan for re-election as secretary of state.

The driver of the truck, Ricardo Guzman, did not speak English and did not understand the warnings on the CB-radio about the part dangling from his truck. Guzman was an unqualified driver who paid a bribe to get his license at the Melrose Park facility.

While some people blamed George Ryan for the deaths of those six young children, Ryan denied any involvement in the "licenses for bribes" scandal.

Ryan first was elected secretary of state in 1990. He had been offered the appointment by Governor Jim Thompson in 1980 when Secretary of State Alan Dixon was elected U.S. senator but he declined, preferring to become Speaker. Jim Edgar got the job and was elected governor in 1990.

When Governor Jim Edgar chose not to seek a third term, Ryan was the party's choice. George Ryan was elected governor of Illinois on Nov. 3, 1998.

It wasn't long before Ryan's past deeds caught up with him. On Nov. 23, 1998, two former employees at the Melrose Park driver's license facility pleaded guilty to charges of racketeering conspiracy for using some of the money to buy fundraising tickets for Ryan's campaign. An investigation showed the corruption was widespread. On Sept. 27, 1999, a former trucking company official admitted he paid to fix the license test of Ricardo Guzman.

Ryan made an apology on Jan. 27, 2000 *for the corruption of others* in the secretary of state's office, but he took no responsibility.

The investigation into Ryan's conduct expanded beyond "licenses for bribes." Ryan was accused of giving illegal contracts to campaign contributors like Larry Warner, and accepting illegal gifts such as staying at a campaign donor's Jamaica vacation home and putting several family members, including all five of his daughters, on a campaign "ghost payroll" to be paid without working.

On Feb. 1, 2000, Dean Bauer was indicted on federal charges of obstructing investigations and hiding evidence. Bauer's job was to find corruption in the off-

Governor George H. Ryan provided the spoken word at a concert by the Kankakee Valley Symphony Orchestra at Olivet Nazarene University in Bourbonnais on March 13, 1999. Photo by Jim Ridings ice, but instead he worked full time to cover it up, particularly the Guzman license. Bauer pleaded guilty to obstructing justice on Jan. 17, 2001.

"Citizens For Ryan" and aides Scott Fawell and Richard Juliano were indicted in 2002 on charges of racketeering, mail fraud and using state resources to benefit Ryan's campaign. Juliano pleaded guilty to mail fraud. Fawell and "Citizens for Ryan" were convicted on all counts. Fawell was sentenced to six-and-a-half years. Fawell was charged in 2004 for his part in an $11.5 million bid-rigging scheme at the Metropolitan Pier and Exposition Authority. Fawell pleaded guilty, agreeing to cooperate for a reduced sentence.

On May 22, 2002, Ryan cronies Larry Warner and Donald Udstuen were indicted for steering government contracts to businesses that paid kickbacks. Udstuen pleaded guilty to tax fraud. Warner was convicted along with Ryan. Two cases showed how George Ryan did business. Honeywell had a contract to provide computers to the Secretary of State. After Ryan took office, Warner, Udstuen and Ron Swanson tried to shake down the company for a $750,000 bribe in order for it to keep the contract. Honeywell balked. IBM agreed to a $991,000 bribe to Warner. IBM got the contract. The second case involved American Decal Manufacturing, which made license plate renewal decals. Warner asked ADM for $2,000 a month as a bribe or else 3M would get the contract. They paid. Warner then asked for a $67,000 bribe, for which he would take the contract to put security strips on vehicle titles from 3M and give it to ADM. They paid again and got the contract.

Ryan approved sweetheart deals for people who helped developer Harry Klein. Ryan stayed at Klein's vacation homes in Jamaica and California. In order to make it look proper for ethics and tax purposes, Ryan wrote a check to Klein for $1,000 each time he stayed there; Klein, in turn, gave the money back to Ryan in cash. Ryan continued to do this as governor...even after federal agents asked him about it and he lied to them.

It was business as usual. In 1999, after Dean Bauer resigned in disgrace, Governor Ryan gave Bauer a $71,580 Department of Transportation job. The position, now with a big raise in pay, had been vacant for nine years -- ever since Tom Ryan resigned this do-nothing job. Bauer stayed only long enough to boost his state pension benefits.

Al Capone was gone from Chicago but his spirit lived on when Governor Ryan and his henchmen made a deal to grant a casino license to the Mobbed-up Chicago suburb of Rosemont in 1999. That deal ended when Organized Crime figures were revealed to be part of the casino operation. Even the governor's own Illinois Gaming Board would not approve the license in the face of this, even as Ryan replaced board members in order to force the deal to happen.

What had started with an investigation into "bribes for licenses" after the Willis tragedy turned into an unraveling of a career of corruption.

As a pharmacist, Ryan could read a doctor's handwriting on a scrip. As a politician, he could read the writing on the wall. And so, on Aug. 8, 2001, he announced that he would not seek a second term as governor.

Ryan was indicted on Dec. 17, 2003 on charges of taking payoffs, gifts and vacations in return for government contracts and leases while he was secretary of state -- one count of racketeering conspiracy, nine counts of mail fraud, three counts of lying to FBI agents, one count of tax fraud and four counts of filing false income tax returns.

Federal prosecutor Patrick Fitzgerald said, "Mr. Ryan steered contracts worth millions of dollars to friends and took payments and vacations in return. When he was a sitting governor, he lied to the FBI about this conduct and then he went out and did it again." He said that Ryan, rather than end "licenses for bribes" instead tried to end the investigation that uncovered it. Fitzgerald called this "a low-water mark for public service."

"What we're alleging in the indictment basically is that the state of Illinois was for sale, for friends and family at times. It was cronyism where contracts were awarded to people, people were given inside information, they were acting upon it, and at times George Ryan was stepping into the process to make sure those interests were taken care of."

Fitzgerald said Ryan looked out for his friends, covering up his crimes and continuing to commit them even after FBI agents interrogated him.

The state's charges includes accusations that the governor's friends invested $6,000 in a cigar store owned by Ryan's son, George Homer Ryan Jr., made loans to Tom Ryan's Comguard and paid for a trip to Disney World for Ryan's family.

When Ryan was indicted, Joe Power, the attorney for Scott and Janice Willis, said, "It's a sad day for Illinois to know that the people of Illinois elected to the secretary of state's office, as well as the governor's office, a serial criminal."

Gov. Jim Thompson, 1978
Photo by Jim Ridings

Ryan's response to the Willis tragedy was to rip into Joe Power, saying Power's motive was to profit from the tragedy.

George Ryan was represented by one of Chicago's top law firms, with former Governor James Thompson as his lawyer. And the legal services (estimated as being worth $20 million) were provided at no charge to George Ryan.

George Ryan's trial began on Sept. 28, 2005 and lasted more than five months.

Eighty-three witnesses testified at the joint trial of George Ryan and Larry Warner. During closing arguments on March 6, 2006, prosecutors said that George Ryan "might as well have put up a 'For Sale' sign over his office."

On April 17, the jury found George Ryan and Larry Warner guilty on all charges, including racketeering, mail fraud, extortion, money laundering, filing false tax returns, tax fraud, lying to the FBI and obstruction of justice. They were found guilty of steering state contracts to cronies, rigging phony leases, shaking down companies for bribes to get state contracts, using state money to run campaigns, killing an investigation of driver's license bribery during his terms as governor and secretary of state, and a lot more.

Ryan said he did nothing wrong and he had a clear conscience.

George Ryan was sentenced on Sept. 6, 2006 to six-and-a-half years in prison. Warner was sentenced to three-and-a-half years. Ryan was ordered to report to prison on Jan. 4, 2007 but legal maneuvering kept him out of jail for ten months.

The jury that convicted Ryan felt like his lawyers tried to make them look like villains. Juror Leslie Losacco told the *Chicago Tribune* that the jury was "dragged through the mud, face-down, so a powerful law firm could help a governor." Her own seven-year-old son came home from the playground "and asked me why I sent this nice governor to jail. People talk. And now we're the brunt of it. He's apparently the victim now."

After his conviction, Ryan asked to remain free while he appealed his convictions. Prosecutors said this was something that almost never is granted, and the judge refused the request. But an appellate court did grant an appeal bond and Ryan remained free.

On Aug. 21, 2007, the Seventh Circuit federal appeals court upheld Ryan's conviction. On Oct. 25, a federal appeals court refused a new hearing. On Nov. 6, the U.S. Supreme Court denied the request to remain free on bail while his appeal was pending.

George Ryan finally entered a federal prison in Oxford, Wisc. on Nov. 7, 2007. It was almost 19 months after he was convicted and nearly 14 years after the Willis children died in the fiery accident that sent George Ryan on his path to prison.

The man who presided over multi-billion-dollar state budgets was doing menial prison work for 12 cents an hour. He was no longer governor; he was inmate 16627-424.

Ryan was transferred to a federal prison at Terre Haute, Ind., on Feb. 28, 2008, because Oxford stopped housing prisoners over age 70.

The U.S. Supreme Court rejected Ryan's final appeal on May 27, 2008.

A state board stripped Ryan of his $197,000 annual pension in 2007. Ryan sued to keep the portion of his state pension he earned before the proven crimes but a judge ruled to deny Ryan's entire state pension. That later was reversed.

Just before Thanksgiving 2008, after only a year behind bars, an intense publicity campaign by some very influential people sought a presidential pardon for Ryan, as President George W. Bush was about to leave office. These included Sen. Dick Durbin, Governor Rod Blagojevich, Jim Thompson and Jim Edgar

But Kevin Rein, a juror at Ryan's trial, wrote a letter to Durbin in the *Chicago Sun-Times* on Dec. 1: "Should you and Mr. Bush decide to release Mr. Ryan early, it will take away a little more of the faith that the average American has in this country."

When a criminal asks for mercy, he usually apologizes for his crime and shows remorse. George Ryan did neither. John Kass cut to the heart of the matter in a Dec. 3 *Chicago Tribune* column. He said the six Willis children were just an "abstraction" in Durbin's pathetic plea, but when Ryan killed the investigation into the licenses for bribes "the children weren't abstractions to him then. They were threats....(and) the kids weren't an abstraction in 1998 as Ryan campaigned for governor...those kids were in the way, they were inconvenient, and so they were stepped over by the powerful in this state. And now, Durbin and Thompson and Ryan want Bush to help them step over those kids again."

Even when seeking a presidential commutation, George Ryan could not admit guilt or real remorse for his actions. In a statement on Nov. 27, 2008 released through Jim Thompson, Ryan said his "failings" brought "humiliation" on his family and on his reputation. "My heart is heavy, knowing that I have hurt the public, my family and my friends in failing to keep their trust. I failed them, and for that I have profound remorse... there is deep shame for me in serving this 78-month sentence."

This was an apology? This was remorse? Just what did he think was his failing? For what exactly did he feel remorse? He didn't say. Ryan didn't apologize, he just said his heart was "heavy" for "failing to keep their trust." A year sitting in stir to think about it all, and Ryan still could not tell the difference between a crime and a failing, a major racketeering operation and a minor flaw in his personality.

His plea was poorly-timed. Governor Blagojevich's arrest on corruption charges made it a bad season for Illinois governors. So on Dec. 12, Jim Thompson read an "apology" issued by George Ryan -- it was brief, vague and was not believed.

Mrs. Ryan also showed a tough and defiant arrogance, even as she pleaded for mercy for her husband. She gave an interview to Natasha Korecki of the *Chicago Sun-Times,* published on Nov. 26, 2008. Amazingly, when Korecki asked Mrs. Ryan "if there was anything George Ryan would change, Lura Lynn Ryan said neither she nor her husband has any regrets."

"His conscience is as clear as his mind," Mrs. Ryan said. "If he had it to do over, and I've heard him say this, he would govern the same way as he did before."

Governor Ryan was credited with successes. "Illinois First" provided $12 billion for programs around the state. But it came from huge tax hikes and the heaviest borrowing in state history. Ryan tried to spin it as a great public works program but it really was a great public pork program. The program was good only for those who got a piece of the pie, and was particularly good for connected contractors.

A big amount of that money went to Kankakee. There is the George H. Ryan Activities Center, gymnasium and Workforce Center at Kankakee Community College. Across the road is the eight-million-dollar Splash Valley water park, officially called The George H. and Lura Lynn Ryan Aquatics Center. Tens of millions for a new county jail, sheriff's office, new bridges and more for Kankakee County were paid from this program.

Ryan was named the Kankakee *Daily Journal's* "Citizen of the Year" for 2002, not for being a governor from Kankakee but for the large amount of pork he brought back to Kankakee.

Private solicitations were made for a bronze bench and a plaque dedicated to George and Lura Lynn Ryan on the courthouse lawn. Kankakee was grateful for the money George Ryan brought home, even though there was no money for Kankakee's poor neighborhoods. Political enemies did not get public works projects in their districts. Not everyone who shelled out their tax dollars got pork in return.

In all, 79 former state officials, lobbyists, truck drivers and others were charged in the "Operation Safe Roads" investigation, and 76 were convicted.

For his part, George Ryan faced the overwhelming evidence against him with the defiance and arrogance he had shown all his life. He maintained his innocence and had no apologies, not even to the Willis family. He kept repeating that he did nothing wrong and had a "clear conscience." Prosecutor Patrick Fitzgerald said Ryan still "didn't get it."

But perhaps he did. Perhaps he thought that what he did was standard operating procedure in corrupt Illinois politics and was not wrong.

George Ryan's corruption practically destroyed the Republican party in Illinois. His successor should have been Illinois Attorney General Jim Ryan (no relation) but he lost to Rod Blagojevich in 2002, ending 25 years of Republican governors. State Treasurer Judy Baar Topinka was left as the only Republican state officeholder. When she ran against Blagojevich in 2006, George Ryan's image was the scary "Boogey Man" used negatively by *both* campaigns. Even though Blagojevich was known as corrupt, incompetent and one of the most unpopular state politicians ever, Topinka lost the election. George Ryan's legacy was a complete Democrat sweep of all state offices in 2006.

"I keep coming back to those six dead Willis children," wrote Rich Miller, publisher of Capitol Fax. "The children died in a fiery car crash after their father ran over a chunk of metal that fell off a semi truck driven by someone who had paid a bribe to get his license.

"Ryan didn't invent the licenses-for-bribes scheme," Miller added. "It goes back decades...but Ryan not only didn't clean up the office when he was first elected in 1990; he actually made the situation much worse in his second term, immediately after those kids were killed in '94. Instead of wiping the slate clean, Ryan installed the vigorously corrupt Scott Fawell as his chief of staff, ramped up the license-for-bribes program beyond anything seen before, harassed whistle-blowers, and shut down all investigations that attempted to root out the corruption and get to the truth about why those Willis children died. And for that, he should rot."

Ramsin Canon wrote on GapersBlock website in 2003, "George Ryan did not pursue his office because he wanted to improve Illinois. George Ryan devised ingenious ways to coordinate bribes, kickbacks and favors. It was not just a conspiracy to defraud; it was a cruel, cynical prairie sensibility, the type that abandons all notions of civilization. Ryan and Warner did not just take cash in an envelope or misuse campaign funds. What Ryan did was engage in a calculated pattern of corruption. He knowingly dealt with shadow and dummy companies, accepted loans, kickbacks, and handed out business to companies that subsequently provided loans or cash payments to companies controlled by his friends and family. Ryan had his thumb on most of the state business from 1990 to 2002, and meticulously controlled that business to benefit himself and his friends. That makes him a racketeer."

As for Scott and Janice Willis, who were horribly burned in the accident that took the lives of six of their children, they first came face to face with George Ryan at a prayer breakfast during Ryan's 1998 campaign for governor. Instead of giving condolences, Ryan started ripping into their attorney, Joe Power. Scott Willis was shocked at Ryan's outburst.

The next time Scott and Janet Willis saw Ryan was when they went to court to observe Ryan's trial. Ryan saw them but pretended he did not.

Scott and Janice Willis sent a letter to Judge Rebecca Pallmeyer before she sentenced Ryan. In the letter, they told of the toll of the tragedy. They expressed sadness that George Ryan had shown no responsibility or sorrow: "Six children were innocent victims resulting from a political scheme to raise campaign money."

The Chicago Tribune estimated that George Ryan's office sold between 1,000 and 2,000 licenses for bribes, and at least nine innocent people were killed in crashes caused by drivers with fraudulent licenses.

The only people in Illinois who were safe from these drivers were the fiends on Death Row. The six Willis children died because of George Ryan's corruption, but the murderers in the Illinois penitentiaries will not.

As George Ryan was about to leave office under a cloud of scandal and the possibility of going to prison, he decided to make a bold move by emptying Death Row.

As a state representative, George Ryan was one of the legislators who voted to reinstate the death penalty in Illinois in 1977. It was a popular issue that he used as long as it was beneficial to him. As he ended his term as governor, he saw it as politically beneficial to take a different view.

George Ryan had shown a sympathetic view for a few murderers before, but his conscience wasn't always as saintly and benevolent as he portrayed it in 2003. His favorable treatment came from politics, not conscience, as seen in two local cases. J. B. Hairston Sr. of Kankakee was convicted in 1974 of killing his girlfriend, Willie Mae Robertson, shooting her as she tried to hide in a restaurant bathroom. In prison, Hairston wrote to his state representative, George Ryan. Ryan intervened with state officials in Hairston's behalf, explaining that Hairston was a customer of his pharmacy and was "hard-working and conscientious." This conflict

ed with Ryan's tough public position on favoring a life sentence for anyone who shoots somebody during the commission of a crime. Hairston got out of prison in 1982. In another case, Eric Lee was convicting of murdering Kankakee Patrolman Anthony Samfey in 1996 during a routine traffic stop. Lee shot Samfey with a .357 Magnum revolver. After Samfey fell to the pavement, Lee fired four more shots into the policeman's body, then calmly walked back to his car and drove away. Lee's father, an old high school classmate and political backer of George Ryan, approached Ryan on his son's behalf. Eric Lee was one of the men freed from Death Row by Governor Ryan.

Opening the doors on Death Row became Ryan's last act as governor. On Jan. 11, 2003, just three days before leaving office, Ryan commuted the sentences of all 167 convicts on Death Row to "life" terms and he pardoned four inmates. It was seen by many as an attempt to pander to those who held his fate in their hands. Ryan wanted to be seen as a humanitarian. He even was suggested for a Nobel Peace Prize by a misguided university professor. How could the feds prosecute a Nobel winner? It did not work.

Ryan at first had publicly promised to review every case of the inmates on Death Row before deciding on individual cases. In a cruel farce, Ryan held public hearings for nine days. The families of the victims, and the prosecutors, were furious that the governor would reopen old wounds and disregard the workings of the judicial system.

Then Ryan issued his blanket commutations.

George Ryan didn't outlaw the death penalty in Illinois; he just commuted the sentences of those who were on Death Row at that time. As Len Small had shown, commutation is the first step toward parole. What are the chances that some of these killers will be paroled and what are the chances that some will kill again? George Ryan does not care.

In a sick irony, one of the lives spared by Ryan's edict was that of Danny Edwards, the man who murdered Stephen B. Small in Kankakee in 1987. Edwards, a local failure, kidnapped Small for ransom. Small died because he was buried alive in a box with insufficient air holes. Stephen Small, a wealthy Kankakee businessman, was a great-grandson of Governor Len Small. As a child, Stephen was a neighbor who mowed the lawn and shoveled snow at George Ryan's house, and he babysat the Ryan children.

Nancy Small, Stephen's widow, told the *Washington Post* in 2003 that George Ryan betrayed her family for political gain. As he cleared Death Row, Ryan's twisted logic used Stephen's killing to make the point that he understood the families' suffering. Nancy received no advance notice. "I can't believe that our family friend and neighbor from years ago, who saw our grief first-hand, could do this," Nancy told the *Post*. "I really feel he has used our family."

Nancy told the *New York Times* she "felt a particular sense of betrayal," calling Ryan's speech "a real slap in the face." She added, "He used our family. I would like George to personally hand-write a letter to each of my three boys telling them why he decided to have their father's murderer taken off Death Row."

Ramsey Small, one of Stephen Small's three children, was 14 when his father was murdered. He told the *New York Times,* "This was such a blow. It was like going through it all over again." He also said, "I believe in the death penalty and I think it should be executed. Why didn't he just keep those sentences as is? It's really just very confusing and frustrating."

As for Danny Edwards, he told the *New York Times* he didn't particularly want his sentence commuted. Those on Death Row share a bond "like one big family," he said. His guards knew about his heart condition and saw that he exercised daily. Edwards wanted a new trial and was afraid of losing his free lawyer if he were no longer on Death Row. Plus, he had his own cell on Death Row and did not want a cell mate. "I'm not looking forward to group showers," Edwards told the *Times.*

Another monster who benefited from George Ryan's conscience was Timothy Buss, also from Kankakee County. Buss sexually assaulted and murdered five-year-old Tara Sue Huffman of Bradley in 1981. Buss was sentenced to 25 years in prison but was released in April 1993. Just two years later, Buss murdered nine-year-old Christopher Meyer in Aroma Park. The boy had been fishing when Buss kidnapped him, sexually mutilated and stabbed him more than 50 times. Then Buss buried the boy in a shallow grave. For this, Buss was convicted and sentenced to death. But George Ryan decided that Buss, and the other condemned murderers, should live.

"How can you in good conscience just wave this wand and take all these people off Death Row? It is beyond belief," said Cook County State's Attorney Dick Devine, who called the decision "stunningly disrespectful to the hundreds of families who lost their loved ones to these Death Row murderers."

DuPage County State's Attorney Joe Birkett said Ryan showed no respect for prosecutors or survivors. "He hasn't heard the cries of these families," Birkett said. "And there's nothing I can do or anyone can say to undo the pain that he has inflicted on these families." Peoria County State's Attorney Kevin Lyons said it was "offensive for Ryan to compare himself to Lincoln and say 'I am a friend to these men on Death Row.' My reply is, yes, Your Excellency, you certainly are. Now go home before you make any more friends who are murdering the good people of Illinois."

Among those who gained new life through Ryan were Jacqueline Williams and Fedell Caffey, sent to Death Row for the murder of Debra Evans, her young daughter and son in 1995. They wanted Evans' unborn baby, and they cut it from her womb.

"George Ryan broke the system when he commuted the sentences of all convicted murders," said Sam Evans, father and grandfather of the victims. "I have nothing to say to Governor Ryan. I have nothing but contempt and disgust for a man who abused the powers that the state of Illinois granted him."

"He spit in our faces," Katy Salhani, the sister of Debra Evans, said to the *Daily Herald* newspaper. "This should be a criminal act," said Dawn Pueschel, sister of murder victim Dean Pueschel. "This is a crime, to do what the governor has done."

Stacey Caulk Warcup told the *Springfield Journal-Register* that she had nightmares when Ryan made his announcement. Her ex-boyfriend murdered her mother and brother in front of her in her home. She dreamed that murderer John

Cole "was coming after me. The fear never goes away until he pays, or we'll never have closure."

"I wish that George Ryan would have cared as much about the lives of innocent children as he has claimed to care for convicted criminals," said Amy Moody, one of the surviving children of Scott and Janet Willis.

Bridget Drobney, age 16, was driving to a wedding reception in 1985 when Robert Turner and two other men used a flashing red light resembling a police light to pull her car to the side of the road. They stabbed her to death in a Macoupin County cornfield.

Bridget's father, George Drobney of Downers Grove, said of Governor Ryan, "I think he is not thinking of the victims. He is thinking only of himself. I think the governor is only concerned about getting the Nobel Peace Prize. I, for one, hope he burns in hell."

George Ryan never did get that Nobel Prize.

"Hell, I know some of those people are guilty," Ryan said when he made his announcement. "But you can't pick and choose. That's what drove us to mass commutations."

George Ryan -- the man with a conscience, the compassionate man who could not send another man to his death -- showed no compassion for the mothers, fathers and children of those slaughtered by the monsters on Death Row.

George Ryan said he had only one regret during his term as governor. It wasn't the bribes and illegal gifts he took, or the shakedown of state employees for contributions, or the Organized Crime manner of doing state business, or the insensitivity to innocent victims, or the deaths of the six Willis children. It wasn't even the typical crook's regret that he got caught. No, he said his sole regret was that he allowed Andrew Kokoraleis to be executed in 1999. Who was Kokoraleis? He was a skinhead who, as part of a satanic cult, kidnapped, tortured and murdered at least 18 women, and committed foul acts such as mutilating corpses and eating breasts. Kokoraleis was the only man executed while Ryan was governor. Allowing this execution troubled Ryan's conscience as nothing else did, he said.

That was Governor Ryan -- a man who cared more about the murderers, cop-killers, rapists and other fiends than he cared about the innocent victims of these monsters. It seems George Ryan's compassion was limited to humane treatment of the inhuman creatures who were proven guilty of their heinous acts.

In his mind, that's the definition of a humanitarian.

George Ryan's Legacy

It appears that George Ryan's legacy will be that of a crooked politician going to prison on fraud and racketeering convictions. "Licenses for bribes" and other corrupt practices during his years in office will be how people remember him.

But there is more to his legacy than that. If you want to measure George Ryan's legacy in human terms, you have to look at what he did in his last-minute commutation of 167 Death Row sentences.

The death penalty is not something that is considered lightly. A person has to commit heinous acts to get this sentence. Liberals have hailed George Ryan as a hero for emptying Death Row. But what about the other side of the coin? What about the cries of the families of the victims of these criminals when Ryan made his decision? The accounts from newspaper and court files could fill a whole book, but we will give just a passing glance to this sorry chapter in Illinois history.

Here is a look at a few people whose lives were saved by George Ryan.

Henry Brisbon was the "I-57 killer" who stopped, robbed and killed motorists. Betty Lou Harmon was on her way home after leaving her dog at her mother's house in Manteno on June 3, 1973. Betty and her husband Jerry were planning to leave for a vacation. Betty's car was stopped by Brisbon. She was forced to undress at gunpoint and killed with a shotgun blast. Dorothy Cerny and James Schmidt were engaged to be married. They were returning from a family gathering on June 3 when they were stopped and robbed by Brisbon, who told the couple to "kiss your last kiss" before firing shotgun blasts into their backs as they lay on the side of the road.

John Childress broke into a woman's Chicago home in 1989, raped and stabbed her to death in front of her six-year-old son. When a neighbor woman walked in as Childress was raping and stabbing his victim, Childress looked at the neighbor woman and smiled. Reginald and Jerry Mahaffey were convicted of the 1983 murders, rape and robbery of a woman and her husband in front of their son. Mimi Covert was a Good Samaritan who picked up stranded motorist Dewayne Britz near Springfield in 1985. Britz repaid the kindness by raping and strangling Covert. Arthur Hickey shot and killed a man outside his home near Ritchie, northwest of Kankakee in 1991, then forced the man's wife into the house where he raped her before shooting her in the face. Leonard Kidd fatally stabbed two women, a man, and a 10-year-old boy in Chicago in 1984. Kidd also confessed to setting a fire in 1980 to a Chicago apartment building in which *ten children,* ages 7 months to 17 years, died. Gabriel Solache stabbed a Chicago couple 60 times in 1998 so he could steal their infant. Keith Shum was the first Illinois man convicted under a 1981 law that made it a crime to kill a fetus. He broke into the Chicago home of a 21-year-old woman who was nine-months pregnant and raped and killed her. Sanantone Moss sexually assaulted a 10-year-old Chicago girl in 1990. While awaiting trial, Moss murdered the girl and her mother. Anthony Enis raped and murdered a Waukegan nurse in 1977 to prevent her from testifying about a previous rape.

Jonathan Haynes was a self-styled Nazi who believed in killing inferior people. In 1993, he murdered Dr. Mark Sullivan in his Wilmette office. Haynes didn't like the plastic surgeon altering the looks of "inferior" people to disguise their non-Aryan heritage. He also killed a San Francisco hair colorist for the same reason.

Eight cop-killers were freed from Death Row. One was Kenneth Allen, who shot Chicago police officers William Bosak and Roger Van Schaik in 1979. Edgar Hope murdered Chicago police officer James Doyle in 1982 as Doyle and his partner tried to arrest Hope on suspicion of burglary. Police found a gun in Hope`s apartment used in the 1982 slaying of a guard at a Chicago McDonald`s. Eric Lee murdered Kankakee Policeman Anthony Samfey in 1996. Elton Williams shot and killed Crest Hill Police Officer Timothy Simeson in 1994. Tyrone Strickland shot Wheeling Police Officer Kenneth Dawson to death in 1985. Ronald Alvine hit and killed Police Officer Michael Browning while stealing a car in 1996. Daniel Raines, in Vermilion County court in 2001, grabbed the gun of Deputy Myron Deckard and shot him to death. Chris Davis killed off-duty Chicago policeman Gregory Young in 1979. James

Munson robbed and killed Chicago firefighter Marvin Cheeks in 1991.

In 1991, Latasha Pulliam and her boyfriend lured a six-year-old girl to Pulliam's Chicago apartment, where the child was tortured, sexually assaulted and murdered. In 1985, Drew Terrell sexually assaulted and beat to death his girlfriend's 15-month-old daughter when the baby would not stop crying. Tony Dameron dropped his 3-month-old daughter to her death in 1995. Dameron hid the body and reported her missing. The jury believed forensic testimony that the fatal injuries were intentional. Lenard Johnson raped two girls, ages 11 and 13, sexually assaulted a 7-year-old girl and murdered an 11-year-old boy in 1990. Delbert Heard broke into the Chicago apartment of his pregnant ex-girlfriend in 1992 and killed her and her boyfriend and her cousin, all witnessed by the woman's 10-year-old daughter. Andrew Urdiales killed at least eight women before being caught in 1997. Jeffrey Rissley kidnapped and murdered a 6-year-old girl. Jesse Raymond Burgess fatally beat a 3-year-old boy in 1994. Dale Lash lured a Springfield realtor to an empty house in 1998, then raped and murdered her. Robert Clotier raped and strangled two Chicago women in 1990. Patrick Wright broke into a Mattoon apartment in 1983 and slashed a woman to death. Demetrius Henderson raped and murdered a 15-year-old girl in Chicago in 1986, stabbing her 37 times and running over her three times with a car. A number of men were on Death Row for street gang and drug-related murders: Edward Graham, Samuel Karim, Mario Flores, James Ashford, Dedrick Coleman, Terrence Brooks, Willie Thompkins, Marlon Watford, Raul Ceja, Luis Ruiz, Juan Caballero, John Szabo. Joseph R. Miller murdered two women in the 1970s and disposed of their bodies by the side of a road. Five months after he was released from prison in 1993, Miller killed three more women and disposed of their bodies in drainage ditches in Peoria County. Reginald Chapman murdered his former girlfriend and their five-month-old son in 1994, then weighed down their bodies and threw them in the Cal-Sag Channel. Howard Wiley murdered a former girlfriend, her daughter and her sister in 1985. Milton Johnson stabbed four women to death in a ceramics shop near Joliet in 1983. When Johnson was caught, he already was on Death Row for an earlier murder of a man. Mark Johnson murdered a man in 1985 during a sexual assault on the man's niece; Johnson also confessed to the 1984 stabbing and mutilation of a Chicago woman. Jerry Ward killed a man and his girlfriend during a 1986 robbery in Chicago. William Riley broke into a Chicago apartment in 1997 and beat a Loyola University student to death with a crowbar. Geno Macri murdered a woman with a crowbar in 1993 in an Addison apartment, then raped her after she was dead. Donald Armstrong clubbed an 86-year-old Chicago woman to death with her own cane. Robin Owens used a hammer to kill a woman in 1980 during a home invasion and robbery in Kankakee. In 1993, while attempting his third armed carjacking in less than a week, David Harris shot and killed a 71-year-old Chicago man. Richard Morris was convicted in 1998 of aggravated kidnapping, carjacking and murder in Cook County. Thomas Umphrey stopped his pickup truck near Springfield to help a woman fix a flat tire. Umphrey kidnapped her and shot her in the back of the head. While making a getaway after trying to rob a man in 1992, Oasby Gilliam kidnapped a 79-year-old woman, forced her into the trunk of her car, drove to a field and beat her to death with a tire iron. Ronald Kitchen strangled two women and their three young children in 1988 and then set fire to their Chicago home. Paris Sims raped and murdered a Belleville woman in 1994 as her husband watched. In an eight-month period in the 1990s, Ralph Harris committed nine armed robberies, shot 11 men (killing six) and sexually assaulted six women at gunpoint. James Harris shot Chicago tavern owner Jesse James in the head in 1983, then shot waitress Theresa Woods while she lay on the ground pleading for her life. Woods, the mother of four children, was pregnant with her fifth child. Harris told her he cared nothing about her children and cursed her as he fired. Woods survived but James died. Julius Kuntu poured gasoline in a wooden stairwell of a crowded Chicago apartment building on March 20, 1994 and set it on fire, killing four children and three adults. Kuntu laughed as he told a friend he was going to burn the place down to get back at his landlord. Charles McLaurin broke into a Sauk Village home in 1992, tied a 17-year-old boy to a chair, doused him with gasoline and set him on fire, burning down the house and killing the boy. Darrin Shatner went to a man's home in 1986, beat and robbed him, and set the place on fire, killing the man. Neils Neilsen shot his ex-wife and her 13-year-old daughter to death in 1995 in Wayne City, then burned their bodies on a trash pile, stuffed their remains in a gym bag and tossed them in a pond on his mother's farm. In 1993, Remon Williams, Michael Coleman and Sherrell Towns shot five people to death. James Westray murdered a woman in 1998 in a bar in Johnston City. Juan Cortez killed two men in Chicago in 1991. Derrick King killed a clerk in 1979 in Chicago. William Jones stabbed an elderly widow during a 1982 burglary. Johnny Neal Jr. used a pipe to fatally beat a Waukegan widow in 1982. Ulece Montgomery raped and strangled his landlord and her sister in 1981 in Robbins. Lorenzo Fayne sexually assaulted and murdered five females ages 6 to 17 in 1993. Evan Griffth killed a man in 1985, then killed another inmate in 1990. Mark Ballard killed a person in Hanover Park in 1999. Ronald Burt killed two men in Stephenson County in 1992. Bobby Sims killed two men during a robbery in Chicago in 1988; Sims previously was convicted of the murder of Rev. James Williams. Anthony Brown raped and murdered a woman and her boyfriend in 1994. Another murderer with a similar name, Anton Brown, killed a woman and her two children in 1990. Robert Casillas robbed and killed the owners of Key Jewelers in Chicago in 1989. Eric Daniels robbed, sexual assaulted and murdered a woman in Champaign County. Grayland Johnson shot Douglas Coleman to death in Chicago in 1988. Tyrone Fuller pleaded guilty in Cook County to armed robbery and murder. Bobby O. Williams murdered a Convenient Food Mart clerk in Belleville during a robbery in 1994. Luther Casteel walked into an Elgin bar in 2001 and started shooting, killing two people and wounding 16 others. Floyd Richardson shot a Chicago grocer to death in 1980. Johnnie Evans raped and murdered a 16-year-old girl in 1983 in an elevator in a Chicago tenement. Darryl Simms raped and murdered a neighbor woman in Addison in 1985. Thomas Odle stabbed his father, mother, two brothers and a sister to death in 1985 in Mt. Vernon because he was tired of his parents "comin` down on my case" about alcohol and drug abuse. Edward Spreitzer kidnapped, murdered and mutilated Linda Sutton of Chicago in 1981. Sutton was one of 17 women abducted, killed and mutilated in 1981 and 1982 by a gang of young men that included Spreitzer. Ronald Barrow shot an 86-year-old man to death during a 1984 robbery in La Salle County. James Foster of Aurora beat his girlfriend to death with a baseball bat in 1985. Walter Thomas stabbed a woman to death in 1986 in Aurora during a burglary. John Pecoraro shot Jimmy Ray Christian to death in 1982 in Chicago because he had fallen in love with Christian`s wife. Jimmy Pitsonbarger shot a man and his wife to death in 1987 in their home near Peoria. Harry Gosier murdered his estranged wife's mother and sister in 1988 in Champaign. David Smith raped and murdered a teenage girl as she was babysitting in Chicago in 1987. Tuhran Lear murdered a gas station attendant in 1988 during a robbery in Farmersville. Hector Sanchez kidnapped a woman in 1984 outside a Gurnee bar, then raped and strangled her. James Tenner murdered two people in 1987 in Chicago Heights. In 1989, Anthony Mitchell murdered a teenage brother and sister near Belleville. William Peeples stabbed a female neighbor to death in her Schaumburg apartment in 1988. Robert Simpson killed a woman in 1992 while robbing a grocery store in Glenwood. Patrick Page stabbed a man to death in 1985 and buried him in a hole he had dug in advance in Park Forest. Robert Todd strangled and stabbed a woman to death in 1989 while trying to rape her. Charles Silagy choked, stabbed and stomped his girlfriend and her sister to death in 1980 near Danville. Dennis Emerson stabbed two people in a Chicago lounge during a 1979 robbery and then set fire to the building, killing one of the victims. Cortez Brown was convicted of two 1990 murders. Robert Evans stabbed an acquaintance to death in a dispute over a stereo in Decatur. Jojulien Hicks murdered a pawnshop owner in Mt. Vernon during an armed robbery. Maurice King was convicted in 2000 of murdering a Carpentersville woman and her four-year-old daughter. Sean Reynolds was sentenced to death for a 1996 murder during a home invasion robbery. Aldwin McNeal killed two people while robbing a pizza place in Waukegan in 1994. Ernest Jamison murdered a woman during an armed robbery at a convenience store in McLean in 1995. Glenn Wilson murdered a man in 1988 while robbing a Bloomington liquor store. Samuel Morgan shot and killed two people in 1982 in Chicago. Frank Williams shot his ex-girlfriend and her boyfriend in cold blood in 1991 outside their Berwyn home. Lawrence Jackson stabbed four people to death to eliminate witnesses to a 1986 Chicago burglary. William Bradley Kirchner stabbed and killed a man, his wife and daughter in their rural Douglas County home in 1997. William Bracey, Roger Collins and Murray Hooper killed three men in a South Side viaduct in Chicago in 1980. Tafford Holman fatally shot a 17-year-old boy during a 1980 home invasion in Joliet. Gregory Madej raped and killed a woman in 1982 after meeting her in a Chicago bar. Paul Erickson raped and fatally stabbed a 15-year-old girl in Arlington Heights in 1982. Robert K. Jones was sentenced to death for killing two neighbors in Jo Daviess County. Maurice McDonald was convicted of armed robbery and the murder of two people in Cook County. Bernina Mata picked up a man in a Belvidere bar in 1998, took him back to her apartment and stabbed him to death. Dorothy Williams strangled a 97-year-old woman in 1989 and killed two other elderly people she robbed. Felipe Hall shot two women to death in 1994. Ron Janes killed his adoptive parents and his grandmother in 1990. William Keene and Paul Taylor committed murders while in the course of other felonies. Douglas Oaks murdered a child in a heinous manner. Robert St. Pierre killed a man and his wife with a hammer in 1982 in their Skokie home. Larry Scott raped and strangled a Moody Bible Institute student in 1984. Andrew Johnson murdered a man in a 1985 home invasion. William Franklin killed a man in Chicago Heights in 1980. Andre Jones killed a cleaning store owner and a mail carrier in 1979. Renaldo Hudson, posing as a repairman, tortured and stabbed to death a man in his Chicago home in 1983. Maynard McCallister murdered three people in 1995. Henry Watson shot his wife in the head in 1999 as their son watched. Hector Nieves murdered four homeless people. Robert Fair murdered a woman and her 11-year-old son. Martin Woolley robbed and murdered two people in Kewanee in 1995. Corey Moore killled a man while robbing a Chicago Baskin-Robbins store in 1996. Moore was worried that his girlfriend was talking to the police, so he shot her in the back with both barrels of a shotgun.

Ronald Kliner shot a woman five times in the face as she got out of her car in front of her home in 1988, in a murder-for-hire deal with her husband. Court records show Kliner "laughed as he looked at the terrified expression on her face as he shot her." Peter Burton shot and killed a man and his wife after robbing them in their Calumet City home in 1992 in a murder-for-hire by the son of the victims. Henry Griffin carried out the contract murder of a Chicago man in 1984. Harold Bean, disguised as a priest, entered the home of an 81-year-old Chicago widow in 1981 and killed her in a murder-for-hire deal.

Randy Banks deliberately deprived his 16-month-old step-daughter of food and warmth in 1986. Banks snatched food away from the starving child because she ate too noisily. He kept her in a room with no heat, no blanket or cover, clothed only in a thin shirt, often with the window opened in subfreezing temperatures.

John Hester admitted in a court document in 1998 to this treatment of his 22-year-old disabled and retarded step-daughter: “He beat the defenseless victim several times a week with his hands, belts and electrical cords. Occasionally, he would duct-tape her to the toilet. As a result of the torture inflicted upon her, she was beaten blind in both eyes and was unable to walk. Unable to call for help or leave her place of captivity, she endured this torture for more than five years before her emaciated, broken and scar-riddled body ceased to function."

Anthony Guest, a Missouri prison escapee serving a life sentence for murder, killed a store employee while shoplifting a toothbrush and toothpaste in Chicago in 1982. Anthony Hall, in Pontiac prison for robbery, stabbed prison cook Frieda King to death in 1983. Ike Easley and Roosevelt Lucas, inmates at Pontiac, murdered prison superintendent Robert Taylor in 1987. Victor Ganus, while serving a life term for murder, killed fellow Menard Prison inmate Lucas Gonzales in 1988.

Chicago street gang member Michael Williams savagely beat and raped 19-year-old Estelle Jones in 1994, then shoved her into the trunk of her own car and drove to a vacant lot in Cook County. As Estelle lay on her back in the snow, Williams fired his sawed-off shotgun into her face at close range and left her to die.

Edward Moore, who had been hired to paint the Zeman house near Morris in Grundy County, sexually assaulted Judy Zeman at her home on July 7, 1991. Moore beat and tortured the woman, tied her hands, doused her with gasoline and burned the young lady alive on a wood pile. She was barely alive when deputies arrived, but she was able to identify Moore before she died.

These are some of the criminals whose lives George Ryan thought were worth saving.

Chapter 29

Illinois Politics

Illinois -- the Prairie State, the Land of Lincoln, the land of tall corn and abundant soybeans, hog butcher to the world, Home of the Twin Gazebos -- has had the reputation for a long time as one of the most corrupt states in the union.

New Jersey and Louisiana, eat your hearts out.

Former Governor James Thompson, in a March 11, 2007 interview in the *Chicago Sun-Times,* was asked if Illinois was the most corrupt state in the union. Not exactly the most corrupt, Thompson said. "Look, we've had instances of corruption in Illinois for my lifetime and more. You could just name them. We've had governors indicted for selling pardons, or at least accused of selling pardons. Is Illinois more corrupt than Minnesota or Wisconsin? Probably."

As a senator from Illinois in 2006, Barack Obama traveled to Kenya and spoke against the political corruption in that country. Obama told the Kenyans, "My own city of Chicago, Illinois, is the home of some of the most corrupt local politics in American history over the years, from patronage machines to questionable elections."

"If Illinois is not the most corrupt state in the nation, it is one hell of a competitor," said FBI agent Robert Grant in a press conference following the arrest of Governor Rod Blagojevich in 2008.

And sometimes, the truest things are said in jest. A *Saturday Night Live* skit had a senator saying to Blagojevich, "Governor, you are a disgrace to the state of Illinois. Well, maybe not to Illinois. But if you were governor of *any* other state, you would be a disgrace to that state."

The chapter on "Illinois Politics" can go hand-in-hand with the chapter on "The Chicago Mob." Gangsters and politicians have always been linked in Illinois.

The marriage of politics and crime in Chicago began in the city's earliest days and was fine-tuned in the 1890s with the infamous First Ward aldermen Michael "Hinky Dink" Kenna and "Bath House John" Coughlin.

At his death, Hinky Dink's relatives proved they really were members of his family. Hinky Dink left his heirs more than a million dollars, with $33,000 designated for a mausoleum. The heirs kept the money and bought him an $85 tombstone.

Legendary Chicago newspaper columnist Mike Royko was one of many writers who made a career of chronicling the shady dealings of political characters, from Mayor Richard J. Daley to Mayor Richard M. Daley.

"Land of the Free, Home of the Fix," where the motto is *"Ubi Est Mea"* ("Where's Mine?") is how Royko described his city through the eras of both Mayor Daleys. Chicago, "The City That Works," where the dead regularly get up and vote, has provided a steady stream of crooks for local writers. Today, *Chicago Tribune* columnist John Kass is as good as any newspaper writer ever in carrying on the tradition of exposing the crooks in Chicago.

What regularly is called the Chicago "Machine" now is called the "Combine," which is defined by Kass as the "iron triangle" of the Democrat Machine, Republican Insiders and the Chicago Outfit.

That's Chicago politics!

A book of brief biographies of Illinois governors, *Mostly Good And Competent Men: Illinois Governors 1818 to 1988,* was written by Robert P. Howard, a former *Chicago Tribune* Springfield correspondent and past president of the Illinois State Historical Society. The word "mostly" is the operative word, in what could be (or should be) a sarcastic or ironic title.

Howard lists those he considers Illinois' best governors. And he lists the four he considers the worst governors: Otto Kerner and Daniel Walker, who went to prison, and Joel Matteson and Len Small, who should have gone to prison.

Joel Matteson

"The Small-Thompson-Lundin era was a low point in the state's history," he wrote. "During (Small's) eight scandalous years, machine politics triumphed over the cause of good government."

Otto Kerner Jr. was the Democrat governor of Illinois from 1961 to 1968, until resigning to become a federal judge. In 1969, Marge Everett, manager of Arlington Park and Washington Park race tracks, admitted having bribed Kerner and his finance director Theodore Isaacs to get choice racing dates and two expressway exits for Arlington.

Gov. Otto Kerner (right), on the platform outside the Joliet courthouse, campaigning for re-election in 1964
Photograph taken by Jim Ridings

Incredibly, the scandal was revealed because Everett deducted the bribe on her federal income tax returns, believing that bribery was a normal business expense in Illinois! Kerner was convicted in 1973 on 17 counts of bribery, conspiracy, perjury and more. He was sentenced to three years in federal prison and was fined $50,000.

Kerner also said he had a "clear conscience" about what he did. He was convicted in February 1973 and went on collecting his full judicial salary for a year and a half. He finally resigned on July 24, 1974, just five days before he was to report to the slammer, as he faced impeachment from the U.S. House, which did not want him to continue to be paid as he sat in a federal pen.

Daniel Walker, Democrat governor from 1973 to 1977, gained fame by heading the commission that blamed the Chicago police for the riots at the 1968 Democrat convention and for walking 1,197 miles across Illinois in 1971 while campaigning for governor. For some reason, Walker decided to feud with Chicago Mayor Richard J. Daley, the Democrat party machine and anyone else he could find. This cost him re-nomination in 1976.

In 1987, Walker was convicted of improprieties with First American Savings & Loan Association of Oak Brook. The judge said Walker used First American, which was declared insolvent with a deficit of $23 million, as his "personal piggy bank." He served 18 months of a seven-year sentence.

Joel Matteson, Democrat governor from 1853 to 1857, was a Joliet businessman and one of the contractors who dug the Illinois & Michigan Canal. When he became governor, he found a trunk and a shoebox filled with more than $338,000 in old Canal scrip that already had been cashed. Because of slipshod bookkeeping, the scrip had not been cancelled or recorded. Matteson was able to cash it in again. He also cashed in unissued scrip. Through legal maneuvering and by repaying some of the money he claimed he had not stolen, Matteson avoided prosecution.

At the time Howard's book was written, George Ryan and Rod Blagojevich had not yet served as governor. Those two definitely belong with Len Small as the absolute worst of all time.

As this book is being written, Blagojevich is being prosecuted on a number of criminal charges including trying to sell the U.S. Senate seat vacated when Barack Obama was elected president and withholding $8 million in money due to Children's Memorial Hospital while trying to extort $50,000 from its chief. FBI agents arrested Blagojevich at his Chicago home on Dec. 9, 2008 and carted him away in handcuffs. Federal Prosecutor Patrick Fitzgerald said Blagojevich was in the middle of a "political corruption crime spree."

This was another governor who was a gangster!

Blagojevich rose through the Democrat political Machine by marrying the daughter of a Chicago alderman. Blagojevich followed George Ryan as governor. Before that, he was a congressman who succeeded Dan Rostenkowski, another crook who went to prison.

It would take a whole book to detail the many crimes of Rod Blagojevich. Since he is not the focus of this book, the reader is referred to search elsewhere to find more about this continuing story of corruption in the state of Illinois.

Len Small had the good fortune to be in control of a Republican legislature and a political machine that gave him plenty of protection and support. The machine today is Democrat, but Democrat Blagojevich never had any friends in his own party and never built any political capital to draw upon. Like Dan Walker, Blagojevich preferred to alienate and feud with everyone else. He won as a fluke, a reaction against George Ryan.

Len Small was slippery enough to escape impeachment and removal. Blagojevich did not. We will see if the oily Blagojevich can stay out of jail.

William G. Stratton (son of a Small appointee) was the Republican governor of Illinois from 1953 to 1961. He went on trial in 1965 for income tax evasion, centering on his use of campaign funds. He was acquitted.

Orville Hodge, state auditor in the 1950s, pleaded guilty to embezzling more than $1.5 million in state funds. He spent the money for two airplanes, four automobiles and homes in Illinois and Florida. Hodge went to prison.

And who in Illinois can forget Democrat Secretary of State Paul Powell and his famous shoeboxes? Powell represented downstate Illinois from 1935 to 1965, then was secretary of state until his death in 1970. Powell never earned more than $30,000 a year but left an estate of $4.6 million, including $750,000 in shoeboxes found in his home after his death.

William J. Scott, the popular attorney general from 1969 to 1980, won legal victories against industrial polluters and for consumers. But in 1980, Scott was convicted on tax charges for misusing campaign funds and was sentenced to one year.

Jerry Cosentino, state treasurer from 1979 to 1983 and from 1987 to 1991, was the Democrat candidate for secretary of state in 1990, losing to George Ryan. State Treasurer Cosentino deposited $10 million in a bank and in turn, the bank loaned Cosentino's trucking company $250,000. Cosentino was accused of a number of crooked deals but he pleaded guilty in April 1992 only to bank fraud.

Dan Rostenkowski, Democrat congressman from Chicago from 1958 to 1995, was charged with corruption in 1994, pleading guilty only to mail fraud. He was sentenced to 17 months in jail and was pardoned in 2000 by President Clinton.

And in 2002, Betty Loren-Maltese, mayor of the "Mob Town" of Cicero (and widow of convicted mobster Frank Maltese) was convicted with nine other officials on federal charges of wire, mail, and bank fraud and racketeering. She was involved in an insurance scam that skimmed $4 million from employee policies. Loren-Maltese and others who were involved in this went to prison.

Political corruption and the connections between politicians and mobsters goes far beyond governors and other top officials in Illinois. Police, lawyers, judges, aldermen and political workers on all levels have been involved.

Fred Roti was one of Chicago's most powerful aldermen. In 1993, a federal jury convicted Roti on 11 counts of racketeering, racketeering conspiracy, bribery and extortion. It found him guilty of taking $10,000 for influencing a civil court case and $7,500 to fix a zoning change but cleared him of sharing in $72,500 for fixing a Chinatown murder trial. He went to prison for four years. Fred was born in 1920, and his father was "Bruno the Bomber" Roti, a member of the Capone Mob who was arrested twice in murder investigations. A 1999 Justice Department report flatly stated that Fred Roti, "convicted of RICO [Racketeer Influenced and Corrupt Organizations Act] conspiracy, bribery and extortion charges, fixed criminal cases in the Circuit Court of Cook County, including murder cases involving organized crime members or associates." Pat Marcy (born Pasqualino Marchone), who ran the First Ward with Roti, was indicted in 1991 on RICO conspiracy, bribery and extortion counts. Marcy arranged for the bribery of Judge Frank Wilson to fix the trial of Mob hit man Harry Aleman. Marcy died during his trial in March 1993.

Richard Cain was a Chicago police officer and a ranking member of the Chicago Outfit. He was chief investigator for the Cook County Sheriff (and future governor) Richard Ogilvie. Cain, fired in 1967 for staging drug raids and stealing narcotics from the evidence locker, was convicted and went to prison for four years. Cain, a close associate of Sam Giancana, was gunned down by the Mob in 1973.

William Hanhardt got his job as chief of detectives for the Chicago Police Department through the influence of Roti and other Mob bosses. After retiring from the police department in 1986, Hanhardt ran a nationwide jewel theft ring for the Chicago Outfit. He was charged in 2000, convicted and sent to prison.

Chicago Police Officer Joseph Miedzianowski and 14 others were charged with running a drug distribution ring on Chicago's northwest side. Prosecutors called him the most corrupt cop in Chicago's history. Prosecutors said he "hid a wanted killer from police, shook down drug dealers for cash and narcotics, provided warring gangs with semi-automatic handguns, misused confidential informants, fixed state drug cases and may have placed undercover officers' lives in jeopardy by revealing their identities." Miedzianowski was convicted in federal court in April 2001 of racketeering, narcotics conspiracy and firearms violations and was given a life sentence.

Even some Illinois judges are corrupt.

Roy Solfisburg Jr. and Ray Klingbiel both served as Chief Justice of the Illinois Supreme Court -- Solfisburg from 1962 to 1963 and 1967 to 1969, and Klingbiel from 1956 to 1957 and 1964 to 1967. Both had to resign from the high court in 1969 after revelations that both justices took stock from the Civic Center Bank & Trust Company of Chicago at the same time that litigation involving the bank was before the Illinois Supreme Court. Klingbiel lied when he said he purchased the stock after the court's decision; he really received the stock as a gift before the decision. He then claimed the stock was a campaign contribution; he really got it after the election. And it came out that Klingbiel was assigned the case even though it wasn't his turn in the court's rotation. It was revealed that Solfisburg suggested to bank officials to "do something nice" for Klingbiel. Ironically, a year after the justices resigned, the high court ruled again on the same case and came to the same decision in the bank's favor.

David J. Shields, chief judge of the Chancery Division of the Circuit Court of Cook County, was convicted in 1992 of taking $5,000 from a lawyer to fix a case. Shields was convicted on seven counts, including conspiracy to engage in extortion, attempted extortion and lying to the FBI. Shields was sentenced to 37 months.

Other Illinois judges actually took bribes to fix murder trials. Thomas Maloney and Frank Wilson are two who got caught.

From 1977 to 1990, Cook County Circuit Court Judge Thomas J. Maloney took bribes from Chicago street gangs to convict members of other gangs for murder or manslaughter. Maloney fixed at least three, possibly six, murder trials. He was convicted in 1993 for taking $10,000 to fix the double murder trial of two former El Rukn street gang leaders, receiving a cut of a $100,000 bribe to acquit three New York street gang members and $4,000 for a favorable verdict in a voluntary manslaughter case. Maloney was sentenced to 15 years and 9 months in prison.

Cook County Circuit Court Judge Frank J. Wilson took a $10,000 bribe to acquit Mob hit man Harry Aleman of the murder of a union boss in 1977. Marcy, Roti and their First Ward Mob associates were involved in this bribery. The evidence against Aleman was overwhelming, but Wilson acquitted him. As the investigation into Wilson got closer, the retired judge blew his brains out.

Corruption in Illinois and in Chicago is not a matter of a few bad apples or the occasional public official going astray. It is endemic to the political system.

Bribery of politicians, bureaucrats and judges is one of Illinois' biggest industries, just behind corn and soybeans.

The experts know that these few examples are not the beginning and the end. The ranks of state and city officials, police, judges and other officials are loaded with crooked people who will never be caught.

Former Chicago Alderman Dick Simpson, a professor at University of Illinois-Chicago (UIC), had this statement about Chicago and Illinois politicians:

"Since 1973, the U.S. attorney has indicted 30 aldermen and convicted 27. The Public Corruption and Accountability Project at UIC calculates that there have been more than 1,000 local and state governmental officials convicted since the 1970s. The 'corruption tax,' or cost of government corruption for Cook County residents, is now more than $300 million a year, greater than the local government tax increases this year. We can't really afford more local 'Hired Truck' schemes, patronage hiring or the state pension and driver license scandals of recent years."

Corruption in Illinois is so ingrained that the FBI consistently over the years has conducted undercover investigations. Among the government stings:

Operation Gambat ("Gambling Attorney"): Robert Cooley, a "connected" attorney, worked with federal prosecutors from 1986 to 1989 to expose the ties of the judicial system in Chicago to the First Ward and the Mob. One case was the bribing of Judge Wilson in the Aleman trial. Another case involved Marcy and Roti taking $75,000 for fixing the trial of three men in a 1981 murder in the Chinatown neighborhood.

Operation Greylord: In the 1980s, nearly 100 people, including 13 judges and 51 attorneys, were convicted in a probe of judicial ties to Organized Crime and corrupt lawyers. Maloney and Wilson were two of the judges trapped.

Operation Haunted Hall: A ghost payroller investigation that netted several aldermen, including "reformers."

Operation Phocus: Federal sting in 1985 to net public officials regarding zoning variances and licensing.

Operation Lantern: An investigation into how contracts were handed out and vendors chosen for city business in Mayor Harold Washington's administration.

Operation Safebet: This 1984 FBI Chicago investigation targeted Organized Crime control of prostitution throughout the Chicago area, resulting in the indictment and conviction of more than 30 individuals.

Operation Incubator: A 1986 bribery investigation, where "moles" were used to get city contracts in exchange for bribes. The operation netted a dozen convictions or guilty pleas, including five members of the City Council.

Operation Silver Shovel: In the 1990s, six aldermen and 12 others were taken down in a massive sting operation. John Christopher, a waste hauler with ties to Organized Crime, decided to work with the Feds to avoid his own prosecution. He wore a wire and caught contractors paying bribes to politicians to allow the illegal dumping of industrial waste in poor neighborhoods. It "uncovered everything from labor union corruption to drug trafficking and Organized Crime activity."

Operation Safe Roads: The investigation into the selling of driver's licenses for bribes and other corruption, the scandal that brought down George Ryan.

Operation Crooked Code: In May 2008, 15 people, including developers, contractors and city inspectors, were arrested on bribery charges. U.S. Attorney Patrick J. Fitzgerald claims that these individuals took cash and other benefits in exchange for Chicago zoning permits and other city services. The *Chicago Tribune* said, "City inspectors ignored problems, fabricated reports and sped up paperwork in exchange for envelopes of cash, work on their homes and tickets to skyboxes for Bulls games, the federal charges allege. One inspector took $10,000 to approve two illegal basement units in a building, while another allegedly took $7,000 to 'inspect' plumbing that was already covered by concrete, investigators said. City Inspector General David Hoffman said 'we're talking about systemic corruption,' which Mayor Daley denied, trotting out the few-bad-apples model."

And perhaps the biggest Mob trial since the Capone era was held in Chicago in 2007, "Operation Family Secrets." It included 18 Mob murders over a period of decades. A federal jury found mobsters James "Little Jimmy" Marcello, Joey "the Clown" Lombardo, hitman Frank Calabrese Sr., Paul "the Indian" Schiro and retired Chicago police officer Anthony "Twan" Doyle guilty on nine counts of racketeering, conspiracy, running an illegal video gambling business, obstruction of justice, extortion, sports bookmaking, tax evasion and obstructing and impeding an official proceeding. Doyle was not accused of any murders. At the trial, prosecutors presented 18 people whose families had been the victims of Mob "hits." The victims had been strangled, shot-gunned or had their throats slit. Calebrese Sr. committed 13 of the 18 murders. His son, Calabrese Jr., secretly recorded his father in prison, describing the murders. Someday, books will be written and movies will be made about this. This trial could fill a whole season of *The Untouchables.* Another defendant, Frank "the German" Schweihs, died while awaiting trial. Schweihs may have committed dozens of contract murders. Fellow defendants nicknamed him "Hitler."

In 2009, Arenda Troutman was the 27th alderman to be convicted since 1972. Troutman shook down bribes from developers in exchange for contracts, and once blocked a low-income housing development because the developer wouldn't pay a bribe. She also used gang members as campaign workers to get out the vote.

Public officials are indicted by the score. And Mayor Richard M. Daley, the Boss of Bosses, claims he doesn't know a thing about any of it.

That's just a brief overview. We don't need a book to detail all of this, we need an encyclopedia. And we don't need to stray too much farther afield. But it helps to understand the ingrained culture of Illinois politics that Len Small and George Ryan were a part of, and that continues to this day.

There are a lot of ironies in life -- such as Al Capone's older brother Jimmy being a lawman and a Prohibition agent, and Prohibition agent Eliot Ness becoming an alcoholic who died at age 54 from that condition (both true).

There also are a lot of ironies in Illinois politics.

One was when George Ryan brought Dean Bauer to Springfield as inspector general to investigate corruption in the secretary of state's office.

Another was when Ryan first ran for secretary of state and said his top priority would be "highway safety." And when Ryan said opponent Jerry Cosentino "might put us back into the Paul Powell days." And when Rod Blagojevich ran as a "reformer" after George Ryan's term.

James R. Thompson (no relation to Big Bill), governor of Illinois from 1977 to 1991, was the lawyer who defended George Ryan on corruption charges and he was the lawyer who led the appeals and the request for a Presidential pardon or commutation. Ironic, since Thompson made his reputation as a federal prosecutor, and who a few decades earlier would have been the lawyer prosecuting someone like Ryan and arguing to keep him behind bars. Thompson's high-profile conviction of Otto Kerner Jr., and of several corrupt politicians connected to Chicago Mayor Richard J. Daley, helped propel Thompson into the governor's office.

Kerner (who in 1934 married fellow Bohemian Helena Cermak, daughter of the Mobbed-up Chicago mayor) also gained fame as a prosecutor. His high-profile case was prosecuting automobile executive Preston Tucker for alleged stock fraud. The jury acquitted Tucker and the other executives. Ironically, when Kerner became the first federal appellate judge in history to be jailed, stock fraud was among the charges.

Kerner became a judge on the United States Court of Appeals for the Seventh Circuit after serving as governor from 1961 to 1968. His father, Otto Kerner Sr., also was a judge on the United States Court of Appeals for the Seventh Circuit, from 1939 until his death in 1952, after having served as Illinois attorney general from 1933 to 1938 (where he asked the court to have the civil judgment against Governor Small overturned so he could sue Small for more money.)

Otto Kerner Jr. was elected governor in 1960, defeating incumbent William G. Stratton, who went on trial for income tax evasion five years later.

When Supreme Court justices Solfisburg and Klingbiel were forced to resign in 1969 after taking bank stock as bribes, who was the bank attorney who made the bribes? It was Theodore Isaacs, the same Theodore Isaacs involved in Otto Kerner's bribery.

And when hitman Harry "The Hook" Aleman was going on trial before Judge Frank Wilson, who was Aleman's lawyer at the beginning of the case? It was Thomas J. Maloney, just before he himself became a corrupt judge.

There are a lot of books with exciting stories of Al Capone and other Chicago gangsters, crooked Chicago politicians and judges and other tales. The truth is, there are as many or more crooked Chicago politicians today in Cook County than there were in the Capone-Thompson-Small era, and the street gangs today are far more murderous and pose a far greater public danger than the gangs of the Capone era.

The Chicago Mob used to be seen as a group of Italian gangsters. Now, the Chicago Mob is a Combine of gangsters, elected officeholders, judges, politicians and political workers -- and the crime family winds all the way from Chicago, through Kankakee and other points, to Springfield.

This is just a brief account of governors and gangsters in Illinois.

Postscript:

Kankakee's Heroes

Governors Len Small and George Ryan. Governor Hard Roads and Governor Safe Roads. The governor who sold pardons to murderers and the governor who commuted the death sentences of murderers. Pardons for bribes and licenses for bribes. Kankakee has given Illinois two of the most corrupt politicians in a state known as one of the most corrupt in the union.

And yet, Kankakee is proud of both men. You see the huge "George H. Ryan Activities Center" sign as you drive onto the Kankakee Community College campus. The Kankakee County Museum is in Governor Small Memorial Park and features positive displays of both Small and Ryan.

Of course, Len Small's family owns the daily newspaper and the radio station in Kankakee. The Kankakee Museum sits on the Small family property. There isn't a negative word about Small or Ryan in any of the local history books in Kankakee.

But the most ironic tribute of all is a bench on the Kankakee County courthouse lawn, dedicated to George and Lura Lynn Ryan. It includes bronze figures of two children on the bench. More than one person has wondered if these might represent two of the Willis children.

Bench dedicated to George Ryan on the Kankakee County courthouse lawn.
Photo by Jim Ridings

Postscript 2:

Governor Sam

Governor Samuel H. Shapiro campaigning on Schuyler Avenue, just north of Court Street, in downtown Kankakee in 1968, in a previously unpublished picture. His campaign slogan was "Luv the Guv."

Kankakee does brag about the men from its town who became governor. Len Small and George Ryan have become infamous. But there was one other man from Kankakee who became governor of Illinois.

The second man from Kankakee to become governor was Samuel H. Shapiro.

Shapiro never was elected governor. He was elected lieutenant governor twice, and became governor when Otto Kerner resigned in 1968. Shapiro lost the 1968 election, a bad year for Democrats because of the Vietnam War and civil unrest.

Shapiro was born in Estonia in 1907. His family came to Kankakee the following year. His father Joseph was a shoemaker with a shop at 289 S. Schuyler. The family lived in the back of the shop for four years before moving to a house on South Rosewood Avenue. Sam earned his way through St. Viator's College and the University of Illinois as a violinist with Vic Sandstrom's dance band. Shapiro became a lawyer (a partner of J. Bert Miller) in 1929. Shapiro was city attorney, state's attorney and served with gallantry as a lieutenant in the U.S. Navy during World War II.

He was elected a state representative in 1946 and sponsored much progressive mental health legislation over the years, and was honored by many organizations for his efforts. His work for mental health was real leadership, not just for show. That is why the state hospital at Kankakee was renamed for Shapiro in 1977.

Sam and Gertrude (Adelman) Shapiro married in 1939 and lived at 1300 Cobb Blvd. in Kankakee. Gertrude Shapiro died in 1983. Sam Shapiro died in 1987.

Governor Sam was a very unusual Illinois politician -- he really was a decent and competent man.

Select Bibleography

A large number of sources were used in the research for this book. They are listed here, along with other sources and references for further reading. Look into these books and sites for more information on subjects that were only briefly touched in this book. Big Bill Thompson, Al Capone, William Lorimer, Fred Lundin, Frank L. Smith, Col. McCormick, George Ryan, Charlie Birger, Huey P. Long, the Kennedys, the Herrin Massacre, the Klan in the 1920s, gang warfare in Chicago in the 1920s, the never-ending story of corruption in Illinois -- all are fascinating subjects, and much more information can be found to supplement the story told here by looking into these sources. You will not be disappointed.

Newspapers

The archives of three newspapers were relied upon heavily in this research:
the ***Chicago Tribune*** (all articles available on-line for a fee); and the
Kankakee Daily Republican and the ***Kankakee Daily News.***

Also researched were issues of the *Kankakee Republican-News, Kankakee Evening Democrat, Kankakee Daily Gazette* and *Kankakee Daily Journal,* all available on microfilm at the library. Also, some issues of the *Chicago Daily News* and the *New York Times.*

Books

The Case of Frank L. Smith: A Study In Representative Government,
by Carroll H. Wooddy, University of Chicago Press, (1931);
Big Bill of Chicago, by Lloyd Wendt and Herman Kogen (1953);
The Dry And Lawless Years, by Judge John H. Lyle (1960);
Mr. Capone: The Real & Complete Story of Al Capone, by Robert J. Schoenberg (1992);
Capone, The Man and the Era, by Laurence Bergreen (1994);
Capone: The Life and World of Al Capone, by John Kobler (1971);
Al Capone: A Biography, by Luciano Iorizzo (1993);
The Gangs of Chicago: An Informal History of the Chicago Underworld,
by Herbert Asbury (2002);
Al Capone: The Biography of a Self-Made Man, by Fred Pasley (1930, 2004);
Prohibition: The 13 Years That Changed America, by Edward Behr (1997);
A Study In Boss Politics: William Lorimer of Chicago, by Joel Arthur Tarr (1971);
A History of Kankakee County, by William Kenaga & George Letourneau (1906);
Of The People: A Popular History of Kankakee County,
by Mary Jean Houde and John Klasey (1968);
Constructive Work By Governor Len Small, 130 pages (1928);
Illinois Progress, 1921-1928, Len Small, Governor, 382 pages, (1928);
Kankakee County Atlas, 1900 and 1915;
Illinois Blue Book, 1919-1936;
World Encyclopedia of Organized Crime, by Jay Robert Nash (1989);
*Political Corruption in America: An Encyclopedia of Scandals, Power,
and Greed,* by Mark Grossman (2003);
The New Encyclopedia Of American Scandal, by George Childs Kohn (1989);

Illinois: A History Of the Prairie State, by Robert P. Howard (1972);
Mostly Good And Competent Men, by Robert P. Howard (1988);
The Man Who Got Away: The Bugs Moran Story, by Rose Keefe (2005);
Guns And Roses: The Untold Story of Dean O'Banion, Chicago's Big Shot Before Al Capone, by Rose Keefe (2003);
The Colonel: The Life and Legend of Robert R. McCormick, by Richard Norton Smith (1997);
The Colonel Of Chicago, by Joseph Gies (1979);
Henry Horner And His Burden Of Tragedy, by Thomas Littlewood (2007);
Governor Henry Horner, Chicago Politics, And The Great Depression, by Charles Masters (2005);
The Man Who Emptied Death Row: Governor George Ryan And The Politics Of Crime, by James L. Merriner (2008);
Umbrella Mike, by Brock Yates (2006);
Illinois Justice: The Scandal of 1969 and the Rise of John Paul Stevens, by Kenneth A. Manaster, University of Chicago Press, (2001);
Murder City: The Bloody History of Chicago in the Twenties, by Michael Lesy (2007);
The Wicked City: Chicago From Kenna To Capone, by Curt Johnson and R. Craig Sutter (1998);
When Corruption was King: How I Helped the Mob Rule Chicago, Then Brought the Outfit Down, by Robert Cooley (2006);
When Capone's Mob Murdered Touhy: The Strange Case of Touhy, Jake The Barber and the Kidnapping That Never Happened, by John William Tuohy (2001);
Syndicate City: The Chicago Crime Cartel And What To Do About It, by Alson J. Smith;
The Racketeer's Progress: Chicago and the Struggle For The Modern American Economy, 1900-1940, by Andrew Wender Cohen (2004);
Hooded Americanism, by David Chalmers (1965);
Bloody Williamson, by Paul M. Angle (1952);
A Knight of Another Sort: Prohibition Days and Charlie Birger, by Gary DeNeal (1998);
Huey Long. by T. Harry Williams (1981).

Recommended reading about the Kennedys: *Death at Chappaquiddick*, by Thomas L. Tedrow; *The Kennedy Men: Three Generations of Sex, Scandal and Secrets,* by Nellie Bly; *The Sins of the Father*, by Ronald Kessler; *Goddess: The Secret Lives of Marilyn Monroe,* by Anthony Summers.

Magazines Various issues of ***TIME*** magazine, 1922 to 1978.
American Heritage magazine, April 1995. These can be seen on-line.

Internet sites *The Lawless Decade,* Paul Sann; CapitalFax.com; AmericanMafia.com; MyAlCaponeMuseum.com; CrimeMagazine.com; CrimeLibrary.com; MisterCapone.com; River Cities Reader; Wikipedia.

Other Sources Kankakee Community College, Learning Resource Center (much thanks to the great facilities and the great people at KCC).
Kankakee Public Library.
Kankakee County Museum.

Select Index